READINGS
IN
MANAGEMENT

Philip B. DuBose, editor

James Madison University

PRENTICE-HALL, INC.
Englewood Cliffs, NJ   07632

Library of Congress Cataloging-in-Publication Data

Readings in management.

Designed to be used in conjunction with
Management, principles, and practices by
David H. Holt.
Includes bibliographies.
1. Management. 2. Industrial management.
I. DuBose, Philip B. (date)   . II. Holt,
David H.   Management, principles, and practices.
HD31.R4175 1988   658.4   87-2301
ISBN   0-13-755166-5

**This book is dedicated to my wife, Pam,
and our sons, Matt and Jake.**

Editorial/production supervision: Maureen Wilson
Cover design: Lundgren Graphics, Ltd.
Manufacturing buyer: Barbara Kittle

© 1988 by Prentice-Hall, Inc.
A Division of Simon & Schuster
Englewood Cliffs, New Jersey 07632

Printed in the United States of America

10 9 8 7 6 5 4 3 2 1

ISBN 0-13-755166-5   01

PRENTICE-HALL INTERNATIONAL (UK) LIMITED, *London*
PRENTICE-HALL OF AUSTRALIA PTY. LIMITED, *Sydney*
PRENTICE-HALL CANADA INC., *Toronto*
PRENTICE-HALL HISPANOAMERICANA, S.A., *Mexico*
PRENTICE-HALL OF INDIA PRIVATE LIMITED, *New Delhi*
PRENTICE-HALL OF JAPAN, INC., *Tokyo*
PRENTICE-HALL OF SOUTHEAST ASIA PTE. LTD., *Singapore*
EDITORA PRENTICE-HALL DO BRASIL, LTDA., *Rio de Janeiro*

CONTENTS

PART FOUR: LEADING: MANAGING HUMAN RESOURCES

PART FIVE: CONTROLLING: MANAGING FOR RESULTS

PART SIX: EMERGING CONCEPTS AND GLOBAL MANAGEMENT

CROSS-REFERENCE MATRIX

The following matrix is provided to facilitate using this readings book with a number of popular management textbooks.

Name of Reading	Aldag & Stearns, South-Western, 1987	Bedeian, Dryden, 1986	Boone & Kurtz 3/E, Random House, 1987	Certo 3/E, W.C. Brown, 1986	Donnelly, Gibson & Ivancevich 6/E, BPI, 1987	Griffin 2/E, Houghton Mifflin, 1987	Hellriegel & Slocum 4/E, Addison-Wesley, 1986	Holt, Prentice-Hall, 1987	Kreitner 3/E, Houghton Mifflin, 1986	Mondy, Sharplin, Holmes, Flippo 3/E, Allyn & Bacon, 1986	Newman, Warren & McGill 6/E, Prentice-Hall, 1987	Robbins 2/E, Prentice-Hall, 1987	Schermerhorn 2/E, Wiley, 1986	Stoner & Wankel 3/E, Prentice-Hall, 1986
1. Managerial Work: Analysis From Observation	1	1	1	2	1	1	1	1	1	1	1	1	1	1
2. Quality and Productivity: Challenges for Management	3	8	18	17	3	18	19	1	1	1	1	19	1	8
3. The Ideas of Frederick W. Taylor: An Evaluation	2	2	2	2	1	2	2	2	2	1	2	2	2	2
4. Minds and Managers: On the Dual Nature of Human Information Processing and Management	16	7	6	5	16	7	6	3	6	5	8	4	3	6
5. A Look at Planning and Its Components	7	4	4	4	4	6	8	4	4	3	6	5	4	4
6. Business Planning Is People Planning	7	5	10	6	5	6	8	6	9	9	6	7	4	4
7. The Ethics of MBO	12	5	5	3	20	4	9	6 S-1	4	3	5	5	14	4
8. Socio-Political Forecasting: A New Dimension to Strategic Planning	4	6	4	7	4	8	9	6 S-2	5	4	3	3	4	7
9. Trends in Organizational Design	9	10	8	9	6	9	10	7	8	6	9	8	6	10
10. Structure Is Not Organization	8	11	9	8	6	9	11	7	7	7	9	8	6	9
11. Evolution to a Matrix Organization	8	11	9	8	7	11	10	9	8	6	11	9	6	9

PREFACE

Introductory management courses are typically a survey of the field and, as such, expose the student to a wide array of topics, none of which is examined in great depth. *Readings in Management,* therefore, is intended to provide a supplemental examination of many of the topics surveyed in those courses. A conscientious effort was made to include articles that are applications-oriented, interesting, readable, and integrative.

Although many of the articles are data-based, they have been selected with the practitioner, rather than the researcher, in mind. The selections are a nice "blend" of classical works and very recent writings. Contributors are several of the most prestigious scholars in academia as well as some of today's most highly successful business people. All share an interest in management and how it can be accomplished more effectively.

This reader was designed primarily to be used in conjunction with *Management: Principles and Practices* by David H. Holt. The organizational arrangement parallels that of the textbook and consists of six parts. After an introductory segment, Part One, the next four parts are devoted to the managerial functions of planning, organizing, leading, and controlling, respectively. The concluding segment examines emerging perspectives and global management.

It should be pointed out that, while the organizational scheme of the reader parallels that of the Holt textbook, the universal nature of the reading selections makes them suitable for use with the leading Principles of Management books on the market. To facilitate using the reader, a matrix cross-referencing the readings with the appropriate chapters of selected management texts is included. Finally, the reader has a "stand-alone" capability. As such, it serves as an excellent reading list for both current and aspiring managers, who have a desire to grasp the wealth of ideas associated with the study of management.

I would like to take this opportunity to acknowledge the authors and publishers of these articles, who have given their permission for them to be reproduced. Special recognition should be given to David H. Holt, since he is the person who wrote the main textbook and involved me in this project. My appreciation is extended to the Prentice-Hall staff, particularly Alison Reeves, Editor, her assistant, Liana Rojas, and the individual(s) charged with typing this manuscript. Most of all, I would like to thank my wife, Pam, who helped me with virtually every facet of this book. Her support and encouragement sustained me throughout this project.

ABOUT THE EDITOR

Dr. Philip B. DuBose served as an administrative officer and squadron commander in the United States Air Force. He received his Master of Science degree in Industrial Management from Clemson University and went on to work as a planning and scheduling engineer for a national arthitectural-engineering firm. He earned his Ph.D. degree in Business Administration at the University of North Carolina at Chapel Hill.

Dr. DuBose is presently an Assistant Professor of Management at James Madison University in Harrisonburg, Virginia, where he teaches undergraduate and graduate courses in the areas of management and organizational behavior.

MANAGERIAL WORK: ANALYSIS FROM OBSERVATION*

Henry Mintzberg+
McGill University

The progress of management science is dependent on our understanding of the manager's working processes. A review of the literature indicates that this understanding is superficial at best. Empirical study of the work of five managers (supported by those research findings that are available) led to the following description: Managers perform ten basic roles which fall into three groupings. The interpersonal roles describe the manager as figurehead, external liaison, and leader; the information processing roles describe the manager as the nerve center of his organization's information system; and the decision-making roles suggest that the manager is at the heart of the system by which organizational resource allocation, improvement, and disturbance decisions are made. Because of the huge burden of responsibility for the operation of these systems, the manager is called upon to perform his work at an unrelenting pace, work that is characterized by variety, discontinuity and brevity. Managers come to prefer issues that are current, specific, and ad hoc, and that are presented in verbal form. As a result, there is virtually no science in managerial work. The management scientist has done little to change this. He has been unable to understand work which has never been adequately described, and he has poor access to the manager's information, most of which is never documented. We must describe managerial work more precisely, and we must model the manager as a programmed system. Only then shall we be able to make a science of management.

What do managers do? Ask this question and you will likely be told that managers plan, organize, coordinate and control. Since Henri Fayol [9] first proposed these words in 1916, they have dominated the vocabulary of management. (See, for example, [8], [12], [17].) How valuable are they in describing managerial work? Consider one morning's work of the president of a large organization.

As he enters his office at 8:23, the manager's secretary motions for him to pick up the telephone. "Jerry, there was a bad fire in the plant last night, about $30,000 damage. We should be back in operation by Wednesday. thought you should know."

At 8:45, a Mr. Jamison is ushered into the manager's office. They discuss Mr. Jamison's retirement plans and his cottage in New Hampshire. Then the manager presents a plaque to him

*   Received January 1970; revised October 1970, January 1971.
+ This report is based on the author's doctoral dissertation, carried out at the Sloan School of Management, M.I.T. The author wishes to thank for their help the three thesis committee members, Donald Carroll, Jim Hekimian, and Charles Myers, and Bill Litwack as well.
   Reprinted from Management Science, October 1970, Vol. 18, No. 2, B97-B110, by permission of the publisher and author.

1

commemorating his thirty-two years with the organization.

Mail processing follows: An innocent-looking letter, signed by a Detroit lawyer, reads: "A group of us in Detroit has decided not to buy any of your products because you used that anti-flag, anti-American pinko, Bill Lindell, upon your Thursday night TV show." The manager dictates a restrained reply.

The 10:00 meeting is scheduled by a professional staffer. He claims that his superior, a high-ranking vice-president of the organization, mistreats his staff, and that if the man is not fired, they will all walk out. As soon as the meeting ends, the manager rearranges his schedule to investigate the claim and to react to this crisis.

Which of these activities may be called planning, and which may be called organizing, coordinating, and controlling? Indeed, what do words such as "coordinating" and "planning" mean in the context of real activity? In fact, these four words do not describe the actual work of managers at all; they describe certain vague objectives of managerial work. ". . . they are just ways of indicating what we need to explain." [1, p. 537]

Other approaches to the study of managerial work have developed, one dealing with managerial decision-making and policy-making processes, another with the manager's interpersonal activities. (See, for example, [2] and [10].) And some empirical researchers, using the "diary" method, have studied, what might be called, managerial "media"--by what means, with whom, how long, and where managers spend their time.[1] But in no part of this literature is the actual content of managerial work systematically and meaningfully described.[2] Thus, the question posed at the start--what do managers do?--remains essentially unanswered in the literature of management.

This is indeed an odd situation. We claim to teach management in schools of both business and public administration; we undertake major research programs in management; we find a growing segment of the management science community concerned with the problems of senior management. Most of these people--the planners, information and control theorists, systems analysts, etc.--are attempting to analyze and change working habits that they themselves do not understand. Thus, at a conference called at M.I.T. to assess the impact of the computer on the manager, and attended by a number of America's foremost management scientists, a participant found it necessary to comment after lengthy discussion [20, p. 198]:

I'd like to return to an earlier point. It seems to me that until we get into the question of what the top manager does or what the functions are that define the top management job, we're not going to get out of the kind of difficulty that keeps cropping up. What I'm really doing is leading up to my earlier question which no one really answered. And that is: Is it possible to arrive at a specification of what constitutes the job of a top manager?

His question was not answered.

Research Study on Managerial Work

In late 1966, I began research on this question, seeking to replace Fayol's words by a set that would more accurately describe what managers do. In essence, I sought to develop by the process of induction a statement of managerial work that would have empirical validity. Using a method called "structured observation," I observed for one-week periods the chief executives of five medium to large organizations (a consulting firm, a school system, a technology firm, a consumer goods manufacturer, and a hospital).

Structured as well as unstructured (i.e., anecdotal) data were collected in three "records." In the *chronology record*, activity patterns throughout the working day were recorded. In the *mail record*, for each 890 pieces of mail processed during the five weeks, were recorded its purpose, format and sender, the attention it received and the action it elicited. And, recorded in the *contact record*, for each of 368 verbal interactions, were the purpose, the medium (telephone call, scheduled or unscheduled meeting, tour), the participants, the form of initiation, and the location. It should be noted that all categorizing was done during and after observation so as to ensure that the categories reflected only the work under observation, [19] contains a fuller description of this methodology and a tabulation of the results of the study.

Two sets of conclusions are presented below. The first deals with certain characteristics of managerial work, as they appeared from analysis of the numerical data (e.g., How much time is spent with peers? What is the average duration of meetings? What proportion of contacts are initiated by the manager himself?). The second describes the basic content of managerial work in terms of ten roles. This description derives from an analysis of the data on the recorded *purpose* of each contact and piece of mail.

The liberty is taken of referring to these findings as descriptive of managerial, as opposed to chief executive, work. This is done because many of the findings are supported by studies of other types of managers. Specifically, most of the conclusions on work characteristics are to be found in the combined results of a group of studies of foremen [11], [16], middle managers [4], [5], [15], [25], and chief executives [6]. and although there is little useful material on managerial roles, three studies do provide some evidence of the applicability of the role set. Most important, Sayles' empirical study of production managers [24] suggests that at least five of the ten roles are performed at the lower end of the managerial hierarchy. And some further evidence is provided by comments in Whyte's study of leadership in a street gang [26] and Neustadt's study of three U.S. presidents [21]. (Reference is made to these findings where appropriate.) Thus, although most of the illustrations are drawn from my study of chief executives, there is some justification in asking the reader to consider when he sees the terms "manager" and his "organization" not only "presidents" and their "companies," but also "foremen" and their "shops," "directors" and their "branches," "vice-presidents" and their "divisions." The term *manager* shall be used with reference to all those people in charge of formal organizations or their subunits.

Some Characteristics of Managerial Work

Six sets of characteristics of managerial work derive from analysis of this study. Each has a significant bearing on the manager's ability to administer a complex organization.

Characteristic 1. The Manager Performs a Great Quantity of Work at an Unrelenting Pace

Despite a semblance of normal working hours, in truth managerial work appears to be very taxing. The five men in this study processed an average of thirty-six pieces of mail each day, participated in eight meetings (half of which were scheduled), engaged in five telephone calls, and took one tour. In his study of foremen, Guest [11] found that the number of activities per day averaged 583, with no real break in the pace.

Free time appears to be very rare. If by chance a manager has caught up with the mail, satisfied the callers, dealt with all the disturbances, and avoided scheduled meetings, a subordinate will likely show up to usurp the available time. It seems that the manager cannot expect to have much time for leisurely reflection during office hours. During "off" hours, our chief executives spent much time on work-related reading. High-level managers appear to be able to escape neither from an environment which recognizes the power and status of their positions nor from their own minds which have been trained to search continually for new information.

Characteristic 2. Managerial Activity is Characterized by Variety, Fragmentation, and Brevity

There seems to be no pattern to managerial activity. Rather, variety and fragmentation appear to be characteristic, as successive activities deal with issues that differ greatly both in type and in content. In effect the manager must be prepared to shift moods quickly and frequently.

A typical chief executive day may begin with a telephone call from a director who asks a favor (a "status request"); then a subordinate calls to tell of a strike at one of the facilities (fast movement of information, termed "instant communication"); this is followed by a relaxed scheduled event at which the manager speaks to a group of visiting dignitaries (ceremony); the manager returns to find a message from a major customer who is demanding the renegotiation of a contract (pressure); and so on. Throughout the day, the managers of our study encountered this great variety of activity. Most surprisingly, the significant activities were interspersed with the trivial in no particular pattern.

Furthermore, these managerial activities were characterized by their brevity. Half of all the activities studied lasted less than nine minutes and only ten percent exceeded one hour's duration. Guest's foremen averaged 48 seconds per activity, and Carlson [6] stressed that his chief executives were unable to work without frequent interruption.

In my own study of chief executives, I felt that the managers demonstrated a preference for tasks of short duration and encouraged interruption. Perhaps the manager becomes accustomed to variety, or perhaps the flow of "instant communication" cannot be delayed. A more plausible explanation might be that the manager becomes conditioned by his workload. He develops a sensitive appreciation for the opportunity cost of his own time. Also, he is aware of the ever present assortment of obligations associated with his job--accumulations of mail that cannot be delayed, the callers that must be attended to, the meetings that require his participation. In other words, no matter what he is doing, the manager is plagued by what he must do and what he might do. Thus, the manager is forced to treat issues in an abrupt and superficial way.

Characteristic 3. Manager Prefer Issues That Are Current, Specific, and Ad Hoc

Ad hoc operating reports received more attention than did routine ones; current, uncertain information--gossip, speculation, hearsay--which flows quickly was preferred to historical, certain information; "instant communication" received first consideration; few contacts were held on a routine or "clocked" basis; almost all contacts concerned well-defined issues. The managerial environment is clearly one of stimulus-response. It breeds, not reflective planners, but adaptable information manipulators who prefer the live, concrete situation, men who demonstrate a marked action-orientation.

Characteristic 4. The Manager Sits Between His Organization and a Network of Contacts

In virtually every empirical study of managerial time allocation, it was reported that managers spent a surprisingly large amount of time in horizontal or lateral (nonline) communication. It is clear from this study and from that of Sayles [24] that the manager is surrounded by a diverse and complex web of contacts which serves as his self-designed external information system. Included in this web can be clients, associates and suppliers, outside staff experts, peers (managers of related or similar organizations), trade organizations, government officials, independents (those with no relevant organizational affiliation), and directors or superiors. (Among these, directors in this study and superiors in other studies did *not* stand out as particularly active individuals.)

The managers in this study received far more information than they emitted, much of it coming from contacts, and more from subordinates who acted as filters. Figuratively, the manager appears as the neck of an hourglass, sifting information into his own organization from its environment.

Characteristic 5. The Manager Demonstrates a Strong Preference for the Verbal Media

The manager has five media at his command--mail (documented), telephone (purely verbal), unscheduled meeting (informal face-to-face), scheduled meeting (formal face-to-face), and tour (observation). Along with all the other empirical studies of work characteristics, I found a strong predominance of verbal forms of communication. *Mail.* By all indications, managers dislike the documented form of communication. In this study, they gave cursory attention to such items as operating reports and periodicals. It was estimated that only thirteen percent of the input mail was of specific and immediate use to the managers. Much of the rest dealt with formalities and provided general reference data. The managers studied initiated very little mail, only twenty-five pieces in the five weeks. The rest of the outgoing mail was sent in reaction to mail received--a reply to a request, an acknowledgment, some information forwarded to a part of the organization. The managers appeared to dislike this form of communication, perhaps because the mail is a relatively slow and tedious medium to use. *Telephone and Unscheduled Meetings.* The less formal means of verbal communication--the telephone, a purely verbal form, and the unscheduled meeting, a face-to-face form--were used frequently (two-thirds of the contacts in the study) but for brief encounters (average duration of six and twelve minutes respectively). They were used primarily to deliver requests and to transmit pressing information to those outsiders and subordinates who had informal relationships with the manager. *Scheduled Meetings.* These tended to be of long duration, averaging sixty-eight minutes in this study, and absorbing over half the managers' time. Such meetings provided the managers with their main opportunities to interact with large groups and to leave the confines of their own offices. Scheduled meetings were used when the participants were unfamiliar to the manager (e.g., students who request that he speak at a university), when a large quantity of information had to be transmitted (e.g., presentation of a report), when ceremony had to take place, and when complex strategy-making or negotiation had to be undertaken. An important feature of the scheduled meetings was the incidental, but by no means irrelevant, information that flowed at the start and end of such meetings. *Tours.* Although the walking tour would appear to be a powerful tool for gaining information in an informal way, in this study tours accounted for only three percent of the managers' time.

In general, it can be concluded that the manager uses each medium for particular purposes. Nevertheless, where possible, he appears to gravitate to verbal media since these provide greater flexibility, require less effort, and bring faster response. It should be noted here that the manager does not leave the telephone or the meeting to get back to work. Rather, communication is his work, and these media are his tools. The operating work of the organization--producing a product, doing research, purchasing a part--appears to be undertaken infrequently by the senior manager. The manager's productive output must be measured in terms of information, a great part of which is transmitted verbally.

Characteristic 6. Despite the Preponderance of Obligations, the Manager Appears to Be Able to Control His Own Affairs

Carlson suggested in his study of Swedish chief executives that these men were puppets with little control over their own affairs. A cursory examination of our data indicates that this is true. Our managers were responsible for the initiation of only thirty-two percent of their verbal contacts and a smaller proportion of their mail. Activities were also classified as to the nature of the managers' participation, and the active ones were outnumbered by the passive ones (e.g., making requests vs. receiving requests). On the surface, the manager is indeed a puppet, answering requests in the mail, returning telephone calls, attending meetings initiated by others, yielding to subordinates' requests for time, reacting to crises.

However, such a view is misleading. There is evidence that the senior manager can exert control over his own affairs in two significant ways: (1) It is

6

he who defines many of his own long-term commitments, by developing appropriate information channels which later feed him information, by initiating projects which later demand his time, by joining committees or outside boards which provide contacts in return for his services, and so on. (2) The manager can exploit situations that appear as obligations. He can lobby at ceremonial speeches; he can impose his values on his organization when his authorization is requested; he can motivate his subordinates whenever he interacts with them; he can use the crisis situation as an opportunity to innovate.

Perhaps these are two points that help distinguish successful and unsuccessful managers. All managers appear to be puppets. Some decide who will pull the strings and how, and they then take advantage of each move that they are forced to make. Others, unable to exploit this high-tension environment, are swallowed up by this most demanding job.

The Manager's Work Roles

In describing the essential content of managerial work, one should aim to model managerial activity, that is, to describe it as a set of programs. But an undertaking as complex as this must be preceded by the development of a useful typological description of managerial work. In other words, we must first understand the distinct components of managerial work. At the present time we do not.

In this study, 890 pieces of mail and 368 verbal contacts were categorized as to purpose. The incoming mail was found to carry acknowledgements, requests and solicitations of various kinds, reference data, news, analytical reports, reports on events and on operations, advice on various situations, and statements of problems, pressures, and ideas. In reacting to mail, the managers acknowledged some, replied to the requests (e.g., by sending information), and forwarded much to subordinates (usually for their information). Verbal contacts involved a variety of purposes. In 15% of them activities were scheduled, in 6% ceremonial events took place, and a few involved external board work. About 34% involved requests of various kinds, some insignificant, some for information, some for authorization of proposed actions. Another 36% essentially involved the flow of information to and from the manager, while the remainder dealt specifically with issues of strategy and with negotiations. (For details, see [19].)

In this study, each piece of mail and verbal contact categorized in this way was subjected to one question: Why did the manager do this? The answers were collected and grouped and regrouped in various ways (over the course of three years) until a typology emerged that was felt to be satisfactory. While an example, presented below, will partially explain this process to the reader, it must be remembered that (in the words of Bronowski [3, p. 62]: "Every induction is a speculation and it guesses at a unity which the facts present but do not strictly imply."

Consider the following sequence of two episodes: A chief executive attends a meeting of an external board on which he sits. Upon his return to his organization, he immediately goes to the office of a subordinate, tells of a conversation he had with a fellow board member, and concludes with the statement: "It looks like we shall get the contract."

The purposes of these two contacts are clear--to attend an external board meeting, and to give current information (instant communication) to a subordinate. But why did the manager attend the meeting? Indeed, why does he belong to the board? And why did he give this particular information to his subordinate?

Basing analysis on this incident, one can argue as follows: The manager belongs to the board in part so that he can be exposed to special information which is of use to his organization. The subordinate needs the information but has not the status which would give him access to it. The chief executive does. Board memberships bring chief executives in contact with one another for the purpose of trading information.

Two aspects of managerial work emerge from this brief analysis. The manager serves in a "liaison" capacity because of the status of his office, and what he learns here enables him to act as "disseminator" of information into his organization. We refer to these as *roles*--organized sets of behaviors belonging to identifiable offices or positions [23]. Ten roles were chosen to capture all the activities observed during this study.

All activities were found to involve one or more of three basic behaviors-- interpersonal contact, the processing of information, and the making of decisions. As a result, our ten roles are divided into three corresponding groups. Three roles-- labelled *figurehead, liaison*, and *leader*--deal with behavior that is essentially interpersonal in nature. Three others--*nerve center, disseminator*, and *spokesman*-- deal with information-processing activities performed by the manager. And the remaining four--*entrepreneur, disturbance handler, resource allocator*, and *negotiator*-- cover the decision-making activities of the manager. We describe each of these roles in turn, asking the reader to note that they form a *gestalt*, a unified whole whose parts cannot be considered in isolation.

The Interpersonal Roles

Three roles relate to the manager's behavior that focuses on interpersonal contact. These roles derive directly from the authority and status associated with holding managerial office.

Figurehead. As legal authority in his organization, the manager is a symbol, obliged to perform a number of duties. He must preside at ceremonial events, sign legal documents, receive visitors, make himself available to many of those who feel, in the words of one of the men studied, "that the only way to get something done is to get to the top." There is evidence that this role applies at other levels as well. Davis [7, pp. 43-44] cites the case of the field sales manager who must deal with those customers who believe that their accounts deserve his attention.

Leader. Leadership is the most widely recognized of managerial roles. It describes the manager's relationship with his subordinates--his attempts to motivate them and his development of the milieu in which they work. Leadership actions pervade all activity--in contrast to most roles, it is possible to designate only a few activities as dealing exclusively with leadership (these mostly related to staffing duties). Each time a manager encourages a subordinate, or meddles in his affairs, or replies to one of his requests, he is playing the *leader* role. Subordinates seek out and react to these leadership clues, and, as a result, they impart significant power to the manager.

8

Liaison. As noted earlier, the empirical studies have emphasized the importance of lateral or horizontal communication in the work of managers at all levels. It is clear from our study that this is explained in terms of the *liaison* role. The manager establishes his network of contacts essentially to bring information and favors to his organization. As Sayles notes in his study of production supervisors [24, p. 258], "The one enduring objective [of the manager] is the effort to build and maintain a predictable, reciprocating system of relationships. . . ."

Making use of his status, the manager interacts with a variety of peers and other people outside his organization. He provides time, information, and favors in return for the same from others. Foremen deal with staff groups and other foremen; chief executives join boards of directors, and maintain extensive networks of individual relationships. Neustadt notes this behavior in analyzing the work of President Roosevelt [21, p. 150]:

> His personal sources were the product of a sociability and curiosity that reached back to the other Roosevelt's time. He had an enormous acquaintance in various phases of national life and at various levels of government; he also had his wife and her variety of contacts. He extended his acquaintanceships abroad; in the war years Winston Churchill, among others, became a "personal source." Roosevelt quite deliberately exploited these relationships and mixed them up to widen his own range of information. He changed his sources as his interests changed, but no one who had ever interested him was quite forgotten or immune to sudden use.

The Information Roles

A second set of managerial activities relate primarily to the processing of information. Together they suggest three significant managerial roles, one describing the manager as a focal point for a certain kind of organizational information, the other two describing relatively simple transmission of this information.

Nerve Center. There is indication, both from this study and from those by Neustadt and Whyte, that the manager serves as the focal point in his organization for the movement of nonroutine information. Homans, who analyzed Whyte's study, draws the following conclusions [26, p. 187]:

> Some interaction flowed toward [the leaders], they were better informed about the problems and desires of group members than were any of the followers and therefore better able to decide on an appropriate course of action. Since they were in close touch with other gang leaders, they were also better informed than their followers about conditions in Cornerville at large. Moreover, in their positions at the focus of the chains of interaction, they were better able than any follower to pass on to the group decisions that had been reached.

The term *nerve center* is chosen to encompass those many activities in which the manager receives information.

9

Within his own organization, the manager has legal authority that formally connects him--and only him--to *every* member. Hence, the manager emerges as *nerve center* of internal information. He may now know as much about any one function as the subordinate who specializes in it, but he comes to know more about his total organization than any other member. He is the information generalist. Furthermore, because of the manager's status and its manifestation in the liaison role, the manager gains unique access to a variety of knowledgeable outsiders including peers who are themselves *nerve centers* of their own organizations. Hence, the manager emerges as his organization's *nerve center* of external information as well.

As noted earlier, the manager's nerve center information is of a special kind. He appears to find it most important to get his information quickly and informally. As a result, he will not hesitate to bypass formal information channels to get it, and he is prepared to deal with a large amount of gossip, hearsay, and opinion which has not yet become substantiated fact.

Disseminator. Much of the manager's information must be transmitted to subordinates. Some of this is of a *factual* nature, received from outside the organization or from other subordinates. And some is of a *value* nature. Here, the manager acts as the mechanism by which organizational influencers (owners, governments, employee groups, the general public, etc., or simply the "boss") make their preferences known to the organization. It is the manager's duty to integrate these value positions, and to express general organizational preferences as a guide to decisions made by subordinates. One of the men studied commented: "One of the principal functions of this position is to integrate the hospital interests with the public interests." Papandreou describes this duty in a paper published in 1952, referring to management as the "peak coordinator" [22].

Spokesman. In his *spokesman* role, the manager is obliged to transmit his information to outsiders. He informs influencers and other interested parties about his organization's performance, its policies, and its plans. Furthermore, he is expected to serve outside his organization as an expert in its industry. Hospital administrators are expected to spend some time serving outside as pubic experts on health, and corporation presidents, perhaps as chamber of commerce executives.

The Decisional Roles

The manager's legal authority requires that he assume responsibility for all of this organization's important actions. The *nerve center* role suggests that only he can fully understand complex decisions, particularly those involving difficult value tradeoffs. As a result, the manager emerges as the key figure in the making and interrelating of all significant decisions in his organization, a process that can be referred to as *strategy-making*. Four roles describe the manager's control over the strategy-making system in his organization.

Entrepreneur. The *entrepreneur* role describes the manager as initiator and designer of much of the controlled change in his organization. The manager looks for opportunities and potential problems which may cause him to initiate action. Action takes the form of *improvement projects*--the marketing of a new product, the strengthening of a weak department, the purchasing of new equipment, the reorganization of formal structure, and so on.

The manager can involve himself in each improvement project in one of three ways: (1) He may *delegate* all responsibility for its design and approval, implicitly retaining the right to replace that subordinate who takes charge of it. (2) He may delegate the design work to a subordinate, but retain the right to *approve* it before implementation. (3) He may actively *supervise* the design work himself.

Improvement projects exhibit a number of interesting characteristics. They appear to involve a number of subdecisions, consciously sequenced over long periods of time and separated by delays of various kinds. Furthermore, the manager appears to supervise a great many of these at any one time--perhaps fifty to one hundred in the case of chief executives. In fact, in his handling of improvement projects, the manager may be likened to a juggler. At any one point, he maintains a number of balls in the air. Periodically, one comes down, receives a short burst of energy, and goes up again. Meanwhile, an inventory of new balls waits on the sidelines and, at random intervals, old balls are discarded and new ones added. Both Lindblom [2] and Marples [18] touch on these aspects of strategy-making, the former stressing the disjointed and incremental nature of the decisions, and the latter depicting the sequential episodes in terms of a stranded rope made up of fibres of different lengths each of which surfaces periodically.

Disturbance Handler. While the *entrepreneur* role focuses on voluntary change, the *disturbance handler* role deals with corrections which the manager is forced to make. We may describe this role as follows: The organization consists basically of specialist operating programs. From time to time, it experiences a stimulus that cannot be handled routinely, either because an operating program has broken down or because the stimulus is new and it is not clear which operating program should handle it. These situations constitute disturbances. As generalist, the manager is obliged to assume responsibility for dealing with the stimulus. Thus, the handling of disturbances is an essential duty of the manager.

There is clear evidence for this role both in our study of chief executives and in Sayles' study of production supervisors [24, p. 162]:

> The achievement of this ability, which is the manager's objective, is a never-to-be-attained ideal. He is like a symphony orchestra conductor, endeavoring to maintain a melodious performance in which contributions of the various instruments are coordinated and sequenced, patterned and paced, while the orchestra members are having various personal difficulties, stage hands are moving music stands, alternating excessive heat and cold are creating audience and instrument problems, and the sponsor of the concert is insisting on irrational changes in the program.

Sayles goes further to point out the very important balance that the manager must maintain between change and stability. To Sayles, the manager seeks "a dynamic type of stability" (p. 162). Most disturbances elicit short-term adjustments which bring back equilibrium; persistent ones require the introduction of long-term structural change.

Resource Allocator. The manager maintains ultimate authority over his organization's strategy-making system by controlling the allocation of its resources.

By deciding who will get what (and who will do what), the manager directs the course of his organization. He does this in three ways:

(1) *In scheduling his own time*, the manager allocates his most precious resource and thereby determines organizational priorities. Issues that receive low priority do not reach the *nerve center* of the organization and are blocked for want of resources.

(2) In designing the organizational structure and in carrying out many improvement projects, the manager *programs the work of his subordinates*. In other words, he allocates their time by deciding what will be done and who will do it.

(3) Most significantly, the manager maintains control over resource allocation by the requirement that he *authorize all significant decisions* before they are implemented. By retaining this power, the manager ensures that different decisions are interrelated--that conflicts are avoided, that resource constraints are respected, and that decisions complement one another.

Decisions appear to be authorized in one of two ways. Where the costs and benefits of a proposal can be quantified, where it is competing for specified resources with other known proposals, and where it can wait for a certain time of year, approval for a proposal is sought in the context of a formal *budgeting* procedure. But these conditions are most often not met--timing may be crucial, nonmonetary costs may predominate, and so on. In these cases, approval is sought in terms of an *ad hoc request for authorization*. Subordinate and manager meet (perhaps informally) to discuss one proposal alone.

Authorization choices are enormously complex ones for the manager. A myriad of factors must be considered (resource constraints, influencer preferences, consistency with other decisions, feasibility, payoff, timing, subordinate feelings, etc.). But the fact that the manager is authorizing the decision rather than supervising its design suggests that he has little time to give to it. To alleviate this difficulty, it appears that managers use special kinds of *models* and *plans* in their decision making. These exist only in their minds and are loose, but they serve to guide behavior. Models may answer questions such as, "Does this proposal make sense in terms of the trends that I see in tariff legislation?" or "Will the EDP department be able to get along with marketing on this?" Plans exist in the sense that, on questioning, managers reveal images (in terms of proposed improvement projects) of where they would like their organizations to go: "Well, once I get these foreign operations fully developed, I would like to begin to look into a reorganization," said one subject of this study.

Negotiator. The final role describes the manager as participant in negotiation activity. To some students of the management process [8, p. 343], this is not truly part of the job of managing. But such distinctions are arbitrary. Negotiation is an integral part of managerial work, as this study notes for chief executives and as that of Sayles made very clear for production supervisors [24, p. 131]: "Sophisticated managers place great stress on negotiations as a way of life. They negotiate with groups who are setting standards for their work, who are performing support activity for them, and to whom they wish to 'sell' their services."

The manager must participate in important negotiation sessions because he is his organization's legal authority, its *spokesman* and its *resource allocator*. Negotiation is resource trading in real time. If the resource commitments are to be large, the legal authority must be present.

These ten roles suggest that the manager of an organization bears a great burden of responsibility. He must oversee his organization's status system; he must serve as a crucial information link between it and its environment; he must interpret and reflect its basic values; he must maintain the stability of its operations; and he must adapt it in a controlled and balanced way to a changing environment.

Management as a Profession and as a Science

Is management a profession? To the extent that different managers perform one set of basic roles, management satisfies one criterion for becoming a profession. But a profession must require, in the words of Random House Dictionary, "knowledge of some department of learning or science." Which of the ten roles now requires specialized learning? Indeed, what school of business or public administration teaches its students how to disseminate information, allocate resources, perform as figurehead, make contacts, or handle disturbances? We simply know very little about teaching these things. The reason is that we have never tried to document and describe in a meaningful way the procedures (or programs) that managers use.

The evidence of this research suggests that there is as yet no science in managerial work--that managers do not work according to procedures that have been prescribed by scientific analysis. Indeed, except for his use of the telephone, the airplane, and the dictating machine, it would appear that the manager of today is indistinguishable from his predecessors. He may seek different information, but he gets much of it in the same way--from word-of-mouth. He may make decisions dealing with modern technology but he uses the same intuitive (that is, nonexplicit) procedures in making them. Even the computer, which has had such a great impact on other kinds of organizational work, has apparently done little to alter the working methods of the general manager.

How do we develop a scientific base to understand the work of the manager? The description of roles is a first and necessary step. But tighter forms of research are necessary. Specifically, we must attempt to model managerial work--to describe it as a system of programs. First, it will be necessary to decide what programs managers actually use. Among a great number of programs in the manager's repertoire, we might expect to find a time scheduling program, an information disseminating program, and a disturbance-handling program. Then, researchers will have to devote a considerable amount of effort to studying and accurately describing the content of each of these programs--the information and heuristics used. Finally, it will be necessary to describe the interrelationships among all of these programs so that they may be combined into an integrated descriptive model of managerial work.

When the management scientist begins to understand the programs that managers use, he can begin to design meaningful systems and provide help for the manager. He may ask: Which managerial activities can be fully reprogrammed (i.e., automated)? Which cannot be reprogrammed because they require human responses? Which can be partially reprogrammed to operate in a man-machine system? Perhaps scheduling, information collecting, and resource allocating activities lend themselves to varying degrees of reprogramming. Management will emerge as a science to the extent that such efforts are successful.

Improving the Manager's Effectiveness

Fayol's fifty year old description of managerial work is no longer of use to us. And we shall not disentangle the complexity of managerial work if we insist on viewing the manager simply as a decision-maker or simply as a motivator of subordinates. In fact, we are unlikely to overestimate the complexity of the manager's work, and we shall make little headway if we take overly simple or narrow points of view in our research.

A major problem faces today's manager. Despite the growing size of modern organizations and the growing complexity of their problems (particularly those in the public sector), the manager can expect little help. He must design his own information system, and he must take full charge of his organization's strategy-making system. Furthermore, the manager faces what might be called the *dilemma of delegation*. He has unique access to much important information but he lacks a formal means of disseminating it. As much of it is verbal, he cannot spread it around in an efficient manner. How can he delegate a task with confidence when he has neither the time nor the means to send the necessary information along with it?

Thus, the manager is usually forced to carry a great burden of responsibility in his organization. As organizations become increasingly large and complex, this burden increases. Unfortunately, the man cannot significantly increase his available time or significantly improve his abilities to manage. Hence, in the large, complex bureaucracy, the top manager's time assumes an enormous opportunity cost and he faces the real danger of becoming a major obstruction in the flow of decisions and information.

Because of this, as we have seen, managerial work assumes a number of distinctive characteristics. The quantity of work is great; the pace is unrelenting; there is great variety, fragmentation, and brevity in the work activities; the manager must concentrate on issues that are current, specific, and ad hoc, and to do so, he finds that he must rely on verbal forms of communication. Yet it is on this man that the burden lies for designing and operating strategy-making and information processing systems that are to solve his organization's (and society's) problems.

The manager can do something to alleviate these problems. He can learn more about his own roles in his organization, and he can use this information to schedule his time in a more efficient manner. He can recognize that only he has much of the information needed by his organization. Then, he can seek to find better means of disseminating it into the organization. Finally, he can turn to the skills of his management scientists to help reduce his workload and to improve his ability to make decisions.

The management scientist can learn to help the manager to the extent he can develop an understanding of the manager's work and the manager's information. To date, strategic planners, operations researchers, and information system designers have provided little help for the senior manager. They simply have had no framework available by which to understand the work of the men who employed them, and they have had poor access to the information which has never been documented. It is folly to believe that a man with poor access to the organization's true *nerve center* can design a formal management information system. Similarly, how can the long-range planner, a man usually uninformed

14

about many of the *current* events that take place in and around his organization, design meaningful strategic plans? For good reason, the literature documents many manager complaints of naive planning and many planner complaints of disinterested managers. In my view, our lack of understanding of managerial work has been the greatest block to the progress of management science.

The ultimate solution to the problem--to the overburdened manager seeking meaningful help--must derive from research. We must observe, describe, and understand the real work of managing; then and only then shall we significantly improve it.

References

1. Braybrooke, David, "The Mystery of Executive Success Re-examined," <u>Administrative Science Quarterly</u>, Vol. 8 (1964), pp. 533-560.

2. _____ and Lindblom, Charles E., <u>A Strategy of Decision</u>, Free Press, New York, 1963.

3. Bronowski, J., "The Creative Process," <u>Scientific American</u>, Vol. 199 (September 1958), pp. 59-65.

4. Burns, Tom, "The Directions of Activity and Communications in a Departmental Executive Group," <u>Human Relations</u>, Vol. 7 (1954), pp. 73-97.

5. _____, "Management in Action," <u>Operational Research Quarterly</u>, Vol. 8 (1957), pp. 45-60.

6. Carlson, Sune, <u>Executive Behavior</u>, Stromberts, Stockholm, 1951.

7. Davis, Robert T., <u>Performance and Development of Field Sales Managers</u>, Division of Research, Graduate School of Business Administration, Harvard University, Boston, 1957.

8. Drucker, Peter F., <u>The Practice of Management</u>, Harper and Row, New York, 1954.

9. Fayol, Henri, <u>Administration industrielle et generale</u>, Dunods, Paris, 1950 (first published 1916).

10. Gibb, Cecil A., "Leadership," Chapter 31 in Gardner Lindzey and Elliot A. Aronson (editors), <u>The Handbook of Social Psychology</u>, Vol. 4, Second edition, Addison-Wesley, Reading, Mass., 1969.

11. Guest, Robert H., "Of Time and the Foreman," <u>Personnel</u>, Vol. 32 (1955-56) pp. 478-486.

12. Gulick, Luther H., "Notes on the Theory of Organization," in Luther Gulick and Lyndall Urwick (editors), <u>Papers on the Science of Administration</u>, Columbia University Press, New York, 1937.

13. Hemphill, John K., <u>Dimensions of Executive Positions</u>, Bureau of Business Research Monograph Number 98, The Ohio State University, Columbus, 1960.

14. Homans, George C., <u>The Human Group</u>, Harcourt, Brace, New York, 1950.

15. Horne, J. H. and Lupton, Tom, "The Work Activities of Middle Managers--An Exploratory Study," <u>The Journal of Management Studies</u>, Vol. 2 (February 1965), pp. 14-33.

16. Kelly, Joe, "The Study of Executive Behavior by Activity Sampling," <u>Human Relations</u>, Vol. 17 (August 1964), pp. 277-287.

17. Mackenzie, R. Alex, "The Management Process in 3D," <u>Harvard Business Review</u> (November-December 1969), pp. 80-87.

18. Marples, D. L., "Studies of Managers--A Fresh Start?," <u>The Journal of Managerial Studies</u>, Vol. 4 (October 1967), pp. 282-299.

19. Mintzberg, Henry, "Structured Observation as a Method to Study Managerial Work," <u>The Journal of Management Studies</u>, Vol. 7 (February 1970), pp. 87-104.

20. Myers, Charles A. (Editor), <u>The Impact of Computers on Management</u>, The M.I.T. Press, Cambridge, Mass., 1967.

21. Neustadt, Richard E., <u>Presidential Power: The Politics of Leadership</u>, The New American Library, New York, 1964.

22. Papandreou, Andreas G., "Some Basic Problems in the Theory of the Firm," in Bernard F. Haley (editor), <u>A Survey of Contemporary Economics</u>, Vol. II, Irwin, Homewood, Illinois, 1952, pp. 183-219.

23. Sarbin, T. R. and Allen, V.L., "Role Theory," in Gardner Lindzey and Elliot A. Aronson (editors), <u>The Handbook of Social Psychology</u>, Vol. I, Second edition, Addison-Wesley, Reading, Mass., 1968, pp. 488-567.

24. Sayles, Leonard R., <u>Managerial Behavior: Administration in Complex Enterprises</u>, McGraw-Hill, New York, 1964.

25. Stewart, Rosemary, <u>Managers and Their Jobs</u>, Macmillan, London, 1967.

26. Whyte, William F., <u>Street Corner Society</u>, 2nd edition, University of Chicago Press, Chicago, 1955.

QUALITY AND PRODUCTIVITY:
CHALLENGES FOR MANAGEMENT

Glenn E. Hayes

American industry is in an era in which definitions, short-term perspectives, leadership styles, and management strategies are being challenged as obstacles to quality and productivity improvement. This renaissance of interest in quality is occurring at a time when global competition has become a powerful force on U.S. markets. The result has been a stronger management commitment to sharpen business approaches and create new ways to develop and build products of higher intrinsic value. What has been reborn is the idea that quality improvement is a way to realize productivity and profit potential; more and more executives are seeking to tap this source.

However, while quality is being taken much more seriously than it was in the past, even the "best" firms face obstacles that make progress difficult.

In the excitement of change, one might be tempted to believe that verbal commitments can easily be turned into concrete improvements. But achieving continuous improvement still seems to remain an elusive goal. Changing the environment--from one in which management and employes believe that quality ranks third when pitted against cost and schedule, into one where quality is given equal billing--is still a problem in many plants.

Although progress is being made, there is a proclivity to push for short-term gains--cost avoidances, quicker output--and rely on after-the-fact inspection to ensure quality. This imperious but subtle tendency diverts attention away from efforts to produce the required quality effectively; it also reduces the likelihood that the longer-term requirements of customers will be economically met.

This mistaken emphasis--which confuses solace of short-term "progress" with long-term quality and productivity improvement--can eventually become an unyielding component of company culture and thwart real improvement. This is illustrated in Figure 1. Sporadic "successes" (shown by the peaks between A and B)

Figure 1
Long-Term Improvement: Illusion vs. Reality

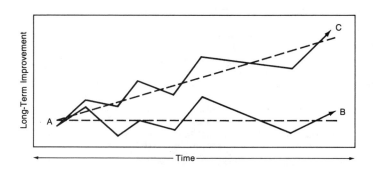

produce the illusion of success, which diverts attention away from the reality that *long-term* improvement is not occurring. This situation is being dealt with by an increasing number of companies, but the tendency to view outputs and profits on a

Reprinted from Quality Progress, October 1985, pp. 42-46, by permission of the publisher.

16

month-to-month or quarter-to-quarter basis continues to hinder long-term improvement.

Figure 2 illustrates the steps companies often pass through as they move toward a long-term perspective on quality and productivity.[1] This hierarchy also provides an indication of a company's cultural stance, management's prevailing philosophy about running the company, and steps that may be taken to improve. (Senior management usually perceives the company as being higher on the staircase than do first-line supervisors and workers.) Here are some factors that influence movement up this staircase.

1. *The cultural posture.* A good quality culture is one in which attitudes and habits are quality-oriented. The genuine desire to perform work right the first time pervades the organization. In companies where good quality cultures have evolved, management has been fundamentally people-oriented. Emphasis has been placed on leadership of people instead of management of things. In poor quality cultures, managing inanimate systems has become a way of life, and there is less regard for employes' concerns, needs, and ideas.

In organizations where good quality cultures exist, quality professionals are regarded as members of the company team, and their advice is usually held in high esteem. Where poor quality cultures are found, quality organizations are typically regarded as roadblocks to meeting delivery promises; there is an adversarial relationship between management and employes, as well as between the quality organization and other departments.

This "us and them" environment, which is found in so many U.S. companies, is only a part of a much broader cultural pattern. The win/lose ethic and the confrontational attitude are deeply ingrained in the way Americans do things. Our challenge is to harness this energy and use it constructively to meet rather than hinder improvement objectives.

2. *The deinstitutionalization of corrective action.* A contagion that has swept across American industry, and has become more or less a fixed value in company culture, is corrective action. Efforts to institutionalize quality improvement will need to be matched by commensurate action to change people's minds about the value of corrective action. Corrective action is so much a part of industrial mentality that people in administrative as well as manufacturing areas expect it, are conditioned to ignore its effects, and even plan for it. Moreover, it is often sufficiently camouflaged that people are not aware that much of what they do is a result of prior work having been done wrong or left unfinished by someone else. Inattention to the magnitude of the corrective action syndrome and a willingness to accept and tolerate doing things over are the first step toward long-term productivity problems.

The phrase "corrective action" is used in two ways: first, as another name for rework; and second, to describe a closed-loop system that goes back to the cause of the problem in order to prevent it from recurring. The second approach is far better than the first, but neither is good, since both depend on problems occurring in the first place.

Corrective actions are normally associated with production departments, where scrap and rework have become targets for reduction, but doing things over has become subtly woven into the attitudes and habits of people in all departments.

17

Figure 2
Up the Staircase to Quality and Productivity Improvement[2]

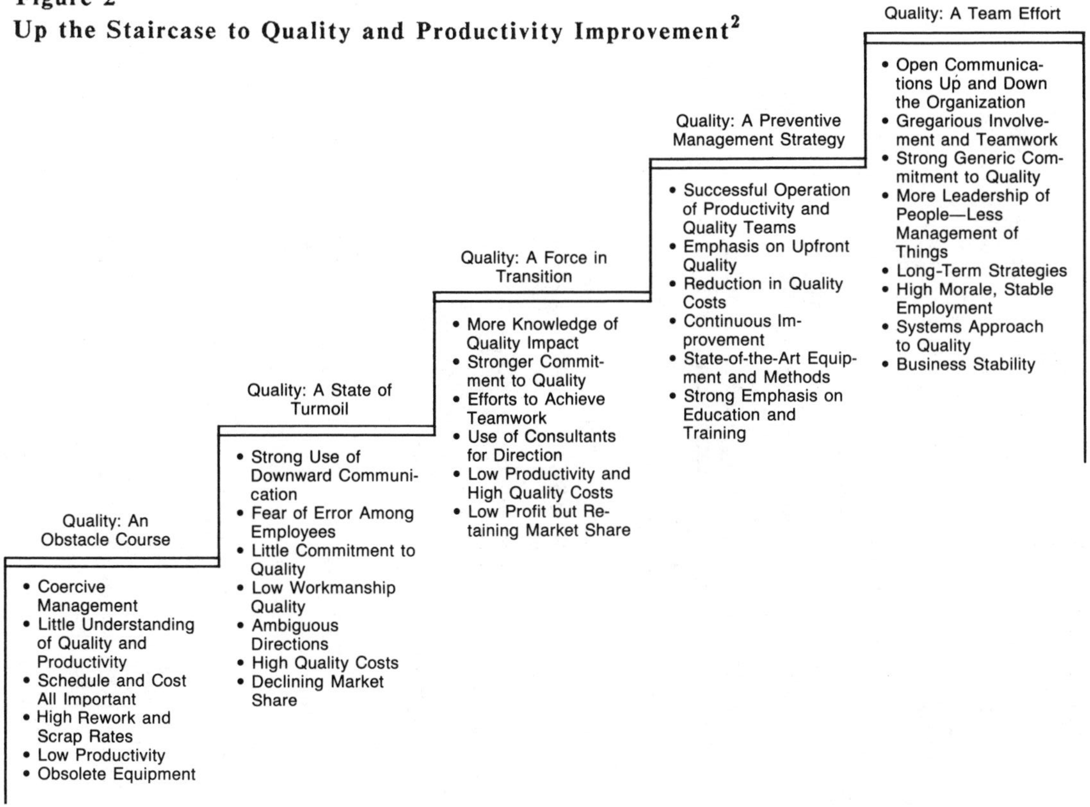

Quality: An Obstacle Course
- Coercive Management
- Little Understanding of Quality and Productivity
- Schedule and Cost All Important
- High Rework and Scrap Rates
- Low Productivity
- Obsolete Equipment

Quality: A State of Turmoil
- Strong Use of Downward Communication
- Fear of Error Among Employees
- Little Commitment to Quality
- Low Workmanship Quality
- Ambiguous Directions
- High Quality Costs
- Declining Market Share

Quality: A Force in Transition
- More Knowledge of Quality Impact
- Stronger Commitment to Quality
- Efforts to Achieve Teamwork
- Use of Consultants for Direction
- Low Productivity and High Quality Costs
- Low Profit but Retaining Market Share

Quality: A Preventive Management Strategy
- Successful Operation of Productivity and Quality Teams
- Emphasis on Upfront Quality
- Reduction in Quality Costs
- Continuous Improvement
- State-of-the-Art Equipment and Methods
- Strong Emphasis on Education and Training

Quality: A Team Effort
- Open Communications Up and Down the Organization
- Gregarious Involvement and Teamwork
- Strong Generic Commitment to Quality
- More Leadership of People—Less Management of Things
- Long-Term Strategies
- High Morale, Stable Employment
- Systems Approach to Quality
- Business Stability

The long-term result is the growth of activities and reliance on functions that are believed to be essential, but are actually parasitic. In many cases, managers ignore the cost implications of the dependence on rework. In shop environments, managers normally make sure that sufficient equipment and people are available to handle corrective action activities adequately. A material review board is established and ample rework centers are provided to correct salvageable parts. Corrective actions are also "encouraged" in fiscal budget planning. For example, "Last year, we spent a little over $400,000 for rework in our department. It looks as if we will have similar problems next year, so we had better put a little more into the budget to make certain we are covered--say $450,000." Or, "Our last year's report shows $700,000 lost in scrap. On the surface, this appears to be high, but we must remember, it would have been higher if the parts reworked had not been salvageable."[3]

More and more firms are establishing goals that combat the proclivity to accept doing things over. For example, the value of an honest quality-associated cost accounting system has been demonstrated. Companies that are enjoying the greatest successes have accomplished several breakthroughs.

    1. Top management is taking the subject of quality-associated costs seriously enough to cause the system to work.

    2. Companies have persevered in efforts to debug the system and establish credibility.

    3. Through education, leadership, and teamwork, unit managers have been convinced that such cost reporting is not a threat to them or their organizations. Everyone is dedicated to making the system work, rather than worrying about how the system will make them look. Supervisors look on this management tool as a way to improve their organizations.

    4. Cost accounting departments are included as members of the quality and productivity team; they do not consider the collection of "quality costs" a heterodox approach to cost accounting methods.

    5. As a direct result of quality cost reporting and control, improvements in quality and productivity are being measured and documented.

    3. *Means can become the end.* A subtle but costly problem in many firms is the efficient conversion of analyses and measurements into improvements.

One of the principal purposes of such departments as quality engineering and industrial engineering is problem solving; many times, however, they find themselves out of phase with this purpose. These groups do a lot of data collection, measurement, and analysis--a necessary first step for improvement. In too many cases, however, these departments ultimately become so involved in the means to an end that the means becomes the end. Analyses beget further data collection, study, and measurement; these, in turn, lead to further investigation-- but no action. Problem solving seems like a treadmill, a closed loop excluding the most important elements--namely, decision and execution.

Why isn't action taken? Some recommendations are scattered in bureaucratic networks; others simply fade away in the face of the predetermined notions of higher authorities. Of course, some proposals will not hold up under close scrutiny by management. Nevertheless, any program for quality and productivity improvement should include a method of continuously assessing both the significance of projects undertaken by problem solvers and the response to recommendations once they have been sent forward.

Some companies have found that a closer organizational and positional bond between quality engineering and industrial engineering makes it easier to carry out solutions to quality and productivity problems. Both functions are in the business of productivity improvement, and teamwork between these organizations not only prevents duplication of effort but also creates synergism between two groups with valuable expertise.

4. *The prevention quandary.* Although the benefits of prevention seem to be generally known, carrying out a prevention-oriented strategy has not proven easy.

Much effort will be spent in vain if attempts are made to implement preventive measures where the foundation blocks of knowledge, commitment, and leadership are not in place. Where company cultures depend on crisis management, for example, preventive techniques will be only partially effective at best. Factors that keep the company on the crisis treadmill are the same as those that hinder the effective execution of preventive strategies.

Ironically, firms that are trying to bear up under the effects of crisis management have the greatest need for preventive strategies. But if crisis management has become the way of life for a company, this energy in motion will resist changes in direction.

Deliberate and systematic actions taken to break the cycle of crisis management may require a great deal of courage and faith. Complaints may even be voiced that a backward step is being taken; although prevention can help a company improve profitability, some will argue that the real need is to drive for greater output, and that time can be better spent striving to get more units out the back door than trying to prevent problems.

A roadblock to prevention is the difficulty of attributing improvements to specific preventive techniques. Prevention always involves a time lapse, the gap between the application and the results. In a society that is action- and results-oriented, this time lapse will always be a deterrent to prevention. Cause-and-effect relationships become fuzzy, and it is difficult to draw a clear line from a preventive action to the consequences of such action. Results are especially difficult to measure if improvements come in oblique forms and cannot be traced to a specific preventive action.

The effects of training provide a good example of these difficulties. In a certification-type program, employes are tested or observed on the job to verify competence; cause-and-effect lines are relatively easy to draw between good and poor performance. However, during such training, behavioral changes may also take place--improving cooperation and teamwork, honoring policies and procedures, or raising quality consciousness. These are very important effects which bring about gains in productivity, but the causes of the change will be obscure.

If prevention is to gain credibility and be regarded as an important long-term mechanism for improvement, the following actions must occur.

    1. Boards of directors, stockholders, and top executives must better understand the potential benefits to be gained from long-term strategies, to allow time for the results of prevention to be realized. An important effect of this longer-term view is that companies would establish overt incentives to take a longer-range view of business dynamics.

2. Quality assurance, industrial engineering, and training departments need to consolidate their efforts to develop measurement indices that will accurately show the effects of their respective preventive efforts. These will, in turn, measure quality, profit, and productivity gains.

3. Managements must be convinced--by financial analyses--to allocate up-front monies necessary to support preventive activities. Without such hard evidence, it is less likely that upper management--operating on the basis of management by exception--will give sufficient credence to the principle that prevention will pay off in dollars and cents.

5. *Quest for teamwork.* While teamwork is now a goal among many U.S. firms, it seems to elude even some of the best managed companies. A teamwork approach has obvious advantages for productivity improvement, but camaraderie is hard to achieve in companies where departments have become silos of private information. In some companies, interdepartmental rivalries have become as heated as rivalries with competing businesses.

High on a management's list of priorities should be the effort to nourish teamwork as an important building block for productivity improvement. The imperative is to convert an "us and them" environment, where it exists, into one which calls upon coadjutant processes for solutions. Where the sense of teamwork has become abstract and remote, the effort will require deliberate and systematic actions to institute changes that will replace suspicion with trust.

Forbearance and persistence, together with overt and continuous evenhanded approaches by management, are needed. Organizational mechanisms such as quality or productivity teams (while some have perished along the way) are being effectively utilized to build team spirit. Collectively small changes originated by teams at the grass-roots level will produce more long-term productivity gains than caveats from senior officials.

Here are four general conditions for successful teamwork.

1. Members of the organization need to have an understanding of, and work toward, a common goal. This, in turn, involves: hearkening to and assisting employes in solving problems, rather than telling and controlling answers; and removing obstacles from employes, so that they can perform their jobs.

2. Team members need to be adequately trained in the jobs they are expected to perform. This means establishing outlets for innovation, helping employes to find better ways to do their work, and taking actions to contribute to employes' development.

3. The organization should be designed so that authority and responsibility are clearly defined, the people best fitted to perform tasks are assigned to them, and clear instructions are given in advance and fully understood. This also means that the management sees to it that suitable resources for the jobs are provided to employes.

4. Employes must also have the freedom to experience the emotions associated with teamwork. This includes demonstrating trust in employes by allowing them to pursue goals without close and anxious supervision, and soliciting their ideas on how to do the job better, rather than giving them the feeling that management's way is the best way.

Many leaders appear to be making progress toward these goals. Their effectiveness is correlated with the degree of commitment they are willing to make to improving teamwork in their organizations.

In the final analysis, commitment to quality and productivity is not enough. It will be through leadership, active involvement by management, and the enrichment of teamwork that commitment will be converted into improvement. Long-range planning, provision of adequate resources, and persistent actions will be required.

References

1. Glenn E. Hayes, Quality and Productivity: The New Challenge (Wheaton, Ill.: Hitchcock Publishing Company, 1985), p. 46.

2. For an analogous approach, see Philip Crosby, Quality is Free (New York: McGraw-Hill, 1979), pp. 38-39.

3. Hayes, Quality and Productivity: The New Challenge, p. 93.

4. "Secrets of America's Best Run Companies," Success, April 1983, p. 43.

THE IDEAS OF FREDERICK W. TAYLOR: AN EVALUATION[1]

Edwin A. Locke
University of Maryland

The ideas and techniques of Frederick W. Taylor are examined with respect to their validity and their acceptance in modern management. With respect to the principle of scientific decision making and techniques such as time study, standardization, goal setting, money as a motivator, scientific selection, and rest pauses. Taylor's views were fundamentally correct and have been generally accepted. Most of the major criticisms that have been made of Taylor are unjustified. Taylor's genius has not been appreciated by many contemporary writers.

Few management theorists have been more persistently criticized than has Frederick W. Taylor, the founder of scientific management, despite his being widely recognized as a key figure in the history of management thought [Wren, 1979]. Taylor and scientific management frequently were attacked in his own lifetime, prompting, among other responses, Gilbreth's Primer [Gilbreth, 1914/1973], and the criticisms have continued to this day.

[1]This paper is based on the Annual Frederick J. Gaudet Memorial Lecture given at the Stevens Institute of Technology, Hoboken, N.J., on April 17, 1980. The author is greatly indebted to J. Myron Johnson of the Stevens Institute and Daniel Wren of the University of Oklahoma for their helpful comments on an earlier draft of this paper, as well as to Marvin Levine for his helpful input on the issue of labor management relations. The preparation of this paper was supported in part by Contract N00014-79-C-0680 between the University of Maryland and the Office of Naval Research.

Reprinted from The Academy of Management Review, 1982, Vol. 7, No. 1, 14-24, by permission of the author and publisher.

The present author agrees with Drucker [1976], although not with all of his specific points, that Taylor has never been fully understood or appreciated by his critics. Many criticisms either have been invalid or have involved peripheral issues, and his major ideas and contributions often have gone unacknowledged.

Wren [1979] did a superb job of showing how Taylor's major ideas permeated the field of management both in the United States and abroad. However, Wren was not concerned primarily with evaluating all of Taylor's techniques or the criticisms of his ideas. Boddewyn [1961], Drucker [1976], and Fry [1976] have made spirited defenses of Taylor, but more by way of broad overviews than in systematic detail. The present paper summarizes Taylor's major ideas and techniques and considers both their validity and their degree of acceptance in contemporary management. In addition, the major criticisms made of Taylor are systematically evaluated.

Taylor's Philosophy of Management

An essential element of Taylor's philosophy of management, as the name of the movement implies, was a scientific approach to managerial decision making [Taylor, 1912/1970b; Sheldon, 1924/1976]. The name was intended to contrast his approach with the unscientific approaches that characterized traditional management practices. By scientific, Taylor meant: based on proven fact (e.g., research and experimentation) rather than on tradition, rule of thumb, guesswork, precedent, personal opinion, or hearsay [Taylor, 1911/1967].

There can be no doubt that this element of Taylor's philosophy is accepted in modern management. This is not to say that all contemporary managers are fully rational decision makers. Clearly this is not the case. However, most would subscribe to the principle of scientific decision making and many actually practice it, at least with respect to some of their decisions. In most business schools there now is a specialized field called management science (which includes operations research), but the scientific approach is reflected in other areas of business as well (e.g., cost accounting). [See Kendall, (1924/1976) for a discussion of Taylor's early influence.] Taylor's goal was to forge a "mental revolution" in management, and in this aim he clearly succeeded. Drucker wrote that "Taylor was the first man in history who actually studied work seriously" [1976, p. 26].

A second element of Taylor's philosophy of management, and the other key aspect of the mental revolution that he advocated, concerned the relationship between management and labor. At the turn of the century, management-labor strife was widespread, violence was not uncommon, and a number of radical labor groups were advocating the violent overthrow of the capitalist system. Many believed that labor-management conflict was virtually inevitable.

Taylor argued that this view was false, that, at root, the interests of both parties were the same. Both would benefit, he argued, from higher production, lower costs, and higher wages, provided that management approached its job scientifically. Taylor believed that there would be no conflict over how to divide the pie as long as the pie were large enough [Taylor, 1912/1970b].

In logic, one cannot argue with Taylor's fundamental premise of a community of interest between management and labor. There were virtually no strikes in plants in which he applied scientific management [Taylor, 1911/1967; 1912/1970a]. Wren [1979] argues that during the 1920s Taylor's hopes for union cooperation in introducing scientific management and in reducing waste were realized to a considerable extent in two industries. Unfortunately this attitude of cooperation ended in the 1930s when unions turned their attention to the passage of prolabor legislation.

In general, management-labor relations now are far more amicable than they were at the turn of the century, but all conflict has not been eliminated. One reason for this is that no matter how big the pie is, there still can be disagreement over how to divide it up. Taylor did not anticipate that as the pie got bigger, aspirations would rise accordingly.

Taylor's Techniques

Time and Motion Study

Before Taylor, there was no objective method for determining how fast a job should be done. Most managers simply used past experience as a guide. Taylor's solution was to break down the work task into its constituent elements or motions; to eliminate wasted motions so the work would be done in the *"one best way"* [Taylor, 1912/1970a, p. 85]--a principle even more strongly emphasized by Frank Gilbreth [1923/1970]; and to time the remaining motions in order to arrive at an expected rate of production (a proper day's work).

Time study now is used routinely in industrialized countries. However, there has been no final solution to the problem of (partially) subjective elements in time study (e.g., fatigue allowances); nor has worker resistance to time study disappeared, although it should be noted that resistance is most likely when there is a lack of trust in management [Bartlem & Locke, 1981]. Such a lack of trust often is earned by practices such as rate-cutting--something that Taylor explicitly warned against.

Standardized Tools and Procedures

Before scientific management, every workman had his own private tool box. This resulted in great inefficiencies because the proper tools were not always used or even owned. Taylor pushed strongly for standardization in the design and use of tools. The tools and procedures were standardized in accordance with what designs that experiments had shown to be most effective in a given context (e.g., the best size and shape for coal shovels).

Like time study, the principle of standardization is now well accepted. Combined with the principle of designing tools to fit people, the technique of standardization has evolved into the science of human engineering. Standardizatiion also has been extended beyond the sphere of tool use to include other types of organizational procedures, especially in large firms.

The Task

Taylor advocated that each worker be assigned a specific amount of work, of a certain quality, each day based on the results of time study. This assigned quota he called a "task" [Taylor, 1911/1967, p. 120]. The term task (which was not original to Taylor) is roughly equivalent to the term goal. Thus, the use of tasks

24

was a forerunner of modern day goal-setting. It is worth noting that Wren's [1979] discussion of scientific management at DuPont and General Motors implies that there is an historical connection between it and the technique of management by objectives (MBO). Pierre DuPont adpated Taylor's cost control ideas in order to develop measures of organizational performance (such as "return on investment") for the DuPont Powder Company. One of his employees, Donaldson Brown, further developed the return on investment concept so that it could be used to compare the efficiency of various departments *within* DuPont. When Pierre DuPont became head of General Motors, he hired Brown and Alfred P. Sloan, who institutionalized Brown's ideas at General Motors. Thus, although the technique of MBO may have been an outgrowth of scientific management, it developed more directly from the concepts of feedback, performance measurement, and cost accounting than from the task concept. Taylor had introduced an interlocking cost and accounting system as early as 1893 [Copley, 1923, Vol. 1].

Drucker acknowledges that Sloan was one of the earliest users of the MBO technique, but the term evidently was coined by Drucker [1954] himself, based not just on his studies at GM but on his work at General Electric with Harold Smiddy [Greenwood, 1980]. At GE, the technique of MBO came to mean objectives set jointly by the manager and his superior rather than simply assigned objectives and/or work measurement.

Another term used widely today is organizational behavior modification (OB Mod); most OB Mod studies merely involve goal-setting with feedback, described in behavioristic terminology [Locke, 1977]. Virtually every contemporary theory of or approach to motivation now acknowledges the importance of goal setting either explicitly or implicitly [Locke, 1978].

The main effect of the post-Taylor research has been to support the validity of his practices. For example, it has been learned that specific challenging goals lead to better performance than do specific, easy goals or vague goals such as "do your best" or "no" goals [Locke, 1968; Locke, Shaw, Saari, & Latham, 1981]. Taylor anticipated these results. The tasks his workers were assigned were, in fact, both specific (quantitative) and challenging; they were set by time study to be reachable only by a trained, "first class" workman [Taylor, 1903/1970]. Remarkably, Alfred P. Sloan himself said: "The guiding principle was to make our standards difficult to achieve, but possible to attain, which I believe is the most effective way of capitalizing on the initiative, resourcefulness, and capabilities of operating personnel" [Odiorne, 1978, p. 15].

Further, it now seems clear that feedback (knowledge of one's progress in relation to the task or goal) is essential for goal setting to work [Locke et al., 1981], just as it is essential to have goals if feedback is to work [Locke et al., 1968]. Again Taylor anticipated these findings. His workers were given feedback at least daily indicating whether or not they had attained their assigned task [Taylor, 1911/1967]. A precursor of evaluative feedback for workers, developed a century before Taylor, was Robert Owen's "silent monitor" technique, described by Wren [1979, p. 72].

The Money Bonus

Taylor claimed that money was what the worker wanted most, and he argued that the worker should be paid from 30 percent to 100 percent higher wages in return for learning to do his job according to scientific management principles, that is, for *"carrying out orders"* [Boddewyn, 1961, p. 105], and for regularly attaining the assigned task.

Although money has been attacked frequently by social scientists from the time of the Hawthorne studies to the present, on the grounds that it is an inadequate motivator, Taylor's claim--that money is what the worker wants most-- was not entirely misguided. A plethora of new incentive schemes have developed since Taylor's time, and new ones are still being tried [Latham & Dossett, 1978], not only for workers but for managers as well. Most labor-management conflicts still involve the issue of wages or issues related to wages, such as seniority, rate setting, layoffs, and fringe benefits. New analyses of the Hawthorne studies indicate that their disparagement of money as a motivator was wrong [Carey, 1967; Franke & Kaul, 1978; Sykes, 1965; Lawler, 1975], and recent books and articles again are advocating the use of money to motivate workers [Lawler, 1971; Locke, 1975; Vough, 1975].

Pay has become a major issue even in the famous Topeka experiment at General Foods, which was intended to stress job enrichment and participation [Walton, 1977], and it is a key element in the still popular Scanlon Plan [Frost, Wakeley & Ruh, 1974], long considered a human relations/organizational development technique. The pendulum now clearly seems to be swinging back toward Taylor's view [Locke, Feren, McCaleb, Shaw & Denny, 1980]. It is notable that one of the most outspoken contemporary advocates of money as a motivator is, like Taylor, an industrial engineer, Mitchell Fein. Fein has developed a new plant-wide incentive system called "Improshare" [Fein, 1977], which is coming into increasingly wide use.

Individualized Work

Taylor was a staunch advocate of individual as opposed to group tasks, as well as individual rewards, because he believed that group work and rewards undermined individual productivity, due to such phenomena as "systematic soldiering." Taylor wrote, "Personal ambition always has been and will remain a more powerful incentive to exertion than a desire for the general welfare" [1912/1976, p. 17]. In this respect, Taylor's views are in clear opposition to the trend of the past four to five decades, which has been toward group tasks.

Nevertheless, Taylor's warnings about the dangers of group work have proven to have some validity. For example, Janis [1972] has demonstrated that groups that become too cohesive are susceptible to groupthink, a cognitive disorder in which rational thinking is sacrificed in the name of unanimity. Latané, Williams and Harkins [1979] have documented a phenomenon called "social loafing," in which people working in a group put out less effort than when working alone even when they claim to be trying their hardest in both cases.

Studies of group decision making indicate that there is no universal superiority of groups over individuals or vice versa. Although a group might outperform the average individual member, the best group member is often superior to the group as a whole [Hall, 1971].

The current view seems to hold that although people may work less hard in groups (as Taylor claimed), the benefits in terms of cooperation, knowledge, and flexibility generally outweigh the costs. Overall, the evidence is not conclusive one way or the other. Most likely the final answer will depend on the nature of the task and other factors.

Management Responsibility for Training

In line with his emphasis on a scientific approach to management, Taylor argued that employees should not learn their skills haphazardly from more experienced workers, who may not be using the "one best way," but from management experts who are thoroughly familiar with the job. There can be no doubt that most contemporary managers fully accept the notion that training new employees is their responsibility. Furthermore, the objective evaluation of training is becoming increasingly common.

Scientific Selection

Taylor advocated selecting only "first class" (i.e., high aptitude) men for a given job because their productivity would be several times greater than that of the average man. Colleague Sanford E. Thompson's use of a measure of reaction time to select bicycle ball bearing inspectors [Taylor, 1911/1967] was one of the earliest efforts at objective selection.

Thompson's selection testing antedated the pioneering work of Hugo Munsterberg [1913] as well as the more systematic attempts at validation of selection tests conducted by American psychologists for the Army during World War I. Since that time, personnel selection has mushroomed enormously and has become a science in its own right. Wren [1979] notes that Taylor's emphasis on scientific selection was an impetus to the development of the fields of industrial psychology and personnel management.

Shorter Working Hours and Rest Pauses

Taylor's experiments with pig iron handlers and ball bearing inspectors determined that fatigue would be reduced and more work would be accomplished if employees were given shorter working hours and/or rest pauses during the day in proportion to the difficulty of the work. The findings with respect to shorter work week were corroborated by the British experiments during World War I [Vernon, 1921] and are now fully accepted. Similarly, the beneficial effects of periodic rest pauses have been documented in numerous experiments. Ryan [1947] summarizes the evidence on both issues.

Criticisms of Taylor

View of Work Motivation

A number of criticisms have been made of Taylor and his ideas. Taylor is frequently criticized for having an oversimplified view of human motivation. Although he never claimed to have a complete view [Taylor, 1911/1967], he did claim that what the worker wanted most was money. Taylor believed that men would not work or follow directions unless they attained some permanent, personal benefit from it. This assumption is fully in accord with the tenets of expectancy theory [Vroom, 1964].

What is the evidence for the power of money as motivator? The present author and his students recently analyzed all available field studies that examined the effectiveness of four motivational techniques: money, goal setting, participation in decision making, and job enrichment [Locke et al., 1980]. It was found that the median performance improvement resulting from individual incentive systems was 30 percent. This figure was far higher than that for any of the other incentives. The median figure for group or plantwide incentive schemes was 18 percent, still higher than for any nonmonetary technique. These findings (which were based mainly on studies of blue collar workers) coincide with the results of numerous recent studies which indicate that extrinsic incentives such as money are more important for blue collar than for white collar employees [Locke, 1976]. This should not be taken to imply that money is unimportant to white collar and professional workers.

Taylor's other major motivational technique was goal setting, that is, assigning specific tasks. A critical incident study by White and Locke (in press) found that goal setting and its equivalents (e.g., deadlines, a heavy work load) were associated with high productivity (and absence of goal setting or goal blockage with low productivity) more frequently than were any other factor. In the Locke et al. [1980] analysis referred to above, goal setting was the second most effective motivational technique. The mean improvement in performance in studies in which workers were assigned specific, challenging goals was 16 percent.

If the effects of Taylor's two main motivators, money and goals--or the task and the bonus, as he called them--are combined, there is an expected or potential perlformance improvement of 46 percent. The figure is very close to the figure of a 40 percent mean performance improvement obtained in studies of individual task and bonus systems [Locke et al., 1980]. A survey of 453 companies [Fein, 1973] found that task and bonus systems combined yielded productivity increases even greater than 40 percent. This figure far exceeds the combined effect of two more recently promulgated motivational techniques, job enrichment and participation [Locke, et al., 1980]. Although Taylor offered nothing approaching a complete theory of human motivation, one must be impressed by the effectiveness of his techniques and by the little that has been added, at least by way of effective techniques, since his time.

Social Factors

The Hawthorne studies [Roethlisberger & Dickson, 1939/1956] were supposed to represent a great enlightenment. They allegedly "discovered" the influence of human relations or social factors on worker motivation. It has been noted that most of the conclusions that the Hawthorne researchers drew from their own data were probably wrong [Franke & Kaul, 1978]. But, beyond this, much of what they said was not even original. Much has been made of the studies in the Bank Wiring Observation room, which found that workers developed informal norms that led to restriction of output. It has been claimed that this discovery refuted Taylor's alleged assumption that workers respond to incentives as isolated individuals. Actually Taylor made no such assumption. In fact, he had identified exactly the same phenomenon as the Hawthorne researchers several decades earlier.

He called it "systematic soldiering." (See also comments by Boddewyn, 1961). Not only did Taylor recognize restriction of output, but one of the chief goals of scientific management was to eliminate it! He viewed soldiering as wasteful and as contrary to the interests of both management and the worker. The main difference between Taylor and Mayo (director of the Hawthorne studies) was that Taylor viewed soldiering as a problem caused by poor management and one that could and should be eliminated by scientific management; Mayo saw it as a reflection of an ineradicable human need.

Nor was Taylor unaware of the effect of social comparisons on worker morale. Discussing the need for the worker to perceive incentive systems as fair, relative to what other workers were getting, he said, "Sentiment plays an important part in all our lives; and sentiment is particularly strong in the workman when he believes a direct injustice is being done him" [Copley, 1923, Vol. 2, p. 133]. Taylor also was aware of social factors at a deeper level. Scientific management itself involved a social revolution in that it advocated replacing management-labor conflict with cooperation.

Authoritarianism

Authoritarianism means the belief in obedience to authority simply because it is authority--that is, obedience for the sake of obedience. Such a doctrine clearly was in total contradiction to everything Taylor stood for. First and foremost he stood for obedience to facts--to reason, to proof, to experimental findings. It was not the rule of authority that he advocated but the rule of knowledge. To quote Taylor's biographer, F. B. Copley, "There is only one master, one boss; namely, knowledge. This, at all events, was the state of things Taylor strove to bring about in industry. He there spent his strength trying to enthrone knowledge as king" [1923, Vol. 1, p. 291].

Taylor did not advocate participation in management matters by his uneducated, manual workers because they did not have the requisite knowledge to do their jobs in the one best way. For example, he shortened the working hours of ball bearing inspectors even when they opposed any such reduction (despite the promise of no loss in pay), because the evidence indicated that their work day was too long [Taylor, 1911/1967]. The positive results vindicated his judgement. Similarly, most workers, when they first heard about the task and bonus system, wanted no part of it. But when Taylor [1903/1947] showed them how such a system would actually benefit them (sometimes, to be sure, accompanied by pressures) most embraced it enthusiastically and performed far better as a result. Taylor was not averse to suggestions from the workers. He wrote, "Every encouragement . . . should be given to him to suggest improvements in methods and in implements" [1911/1967, p. 128]. (See also Gilbreth, 1914/1973.) Fisher quotes Copley on this issue as follows: "If you could prove that yours was the best way, then he would adopt your way and feel very much obliged to you. Frequently he took humble doses of his own imperious medicine" [1925/1976, p. 172].

Specialization of Labor

There is little doubt that Taylor emphasized maximum specialization, not only for workers but for foremen (e.g., functional foremanship) and managers as well. His argument was the traditional one, that specialization decreases learning time and increases competence and skill. To evaluate the criticism that Taylor overemphasized specialization one must ask: How much emphasis is overemphasis?

Advocates of job enrichment have argued with some validity that extreme specialization leads to boredom and low morale and lack of work motivation due to underutilized mental capacity. However, it should be noted that Taylor always argued for a matching of men to jobs in accordance with their capacities. People who do jobs that require very little mental capacity should be people who have very little mental capacity [Taylor, 1903/1947]. Those with more capacity should have more complex tasks to perform (e.g., by being promoted when they master the simple tasks). See Gilbreth [1914/1973] and Taylor [1912/1970a]. In this respect Taylor might very well approve of individualized job enrichment, although, as noted earlier, its effects on performance may be limited. The present author does not agree, however, with Drucker's [1976] claim that Taylor anticipated Herzberg's theory.

There is a potential benefit of job enrichment (e.g., multicrafting and modular working arrangements), however, that Taylor did not foresee. There are fewer and fewer jobs in existence today that stay unchanged for long periods of time. If such jobs exist, they eventually are automated. People are more versatile than machines precisely because of their greater flexibility and adaptability. In times of rapid technological change, such as the present, spending months training a worker for one narrow specialty would not be very cost-efficient. It is more practical to have each worker master several different jobs and to work each day or hour where they are most needed.

With respect to supervision, Taylor's concept of functional foremanship clearly has not been accepted and probably is not very practical.

Men as Machines

The criticism that Taylor's system treated men as machines is related to the previous one. It usually refers to scientific management's requirement of complete uniformity for a given job with respect to the tools and motions used by the workmen (the one best way). As noted earlier, Taylor was not against the workers making suggestions for improvements, provided they first mastered the best known methods. Taylor's well-chosen example of this principle was that of training a surgeon: "He is quickly given the very best knowledge of his predecessors [then] . . . he is able to use his own originality and ingenuity to make *real additions to the world's knowledge, instead of reinventing things which are old*" [1911/1967, p. 126]. The alternative to treating men as machines in the above sense was the prescientific method of management, which allowed men to choose tools and methods based on personal opinions and feelings rather than on knowledge.

It often is forgotten that standardization included the redesign of machines and equipment in order to enable men to become more skilled at the tasks they performed. Taylor applied this principle as much to himself as to others. His unique modifications of the tennis racket and the golf putter for his own use are cases in point. (Both items are on display at the Stevens Institute of Technology.) As noted earlier, he did not force people to fit existing equipment. He, and the Gilbreths (re-)designed equipment to fit people. It might be more accurate to say that Taylor, rather than treating men as machines, helped to develop the science of integrating men with machines.

Exploitation of the Workers

During Taylor's lifetime, socialist Upton Sinclair and others claimed that Taylor's system was exploitative because, although under scientific management the worker might improve his productivity by around 100 percent, his pay was generally increased by a lesser amount. In fairness, they argued, the pay increase should match the productivity increase.

Taylor easily refuted this argument [Fisher, 1925/1976; Copley, 1923, Vol. 1]. He pointed out, for example, that the increase in productivity was not caused by the worker only, but also by management; it was management who discovered the better techniques and designed the new tools, at some cost to themselves. Thus they deserved some of the benefits as well [Taylor, 1911/1967].

Ironically, Lenin, the self-proclaimed enemy of so-called "capitalist exploitation," himself strongly advocated the application of scientific management to Russian industry in order to help build socialism. However, socialist inefficiency, hostility to capitalist ideas, and resistance to change prevented the application of virtually all scientific management techniques in Russia except for the Gantt chart [Wren, 1980]. The Soviets, however, may have been influenced by the Polish manager and theorist Karol Adamiecki, who developed his own scientific management theory independently of Taylor [Wesolowski, 1978].

Antiunionism

The criticism that Taylor was antiunion is true in only one sense. Taylor foresaw no need for unions once scientific management was properly established, especially because he saw the interests of management and labor as fundamentally the same [Copley, 1925/1976]. It is worth noting in this respect that companies that are known for treating their employees well, such as IBM, do not have unions. The belief that unions were unnecessary under the proper type of management did not indicate lack of concern for employee welfare. The leaders of the scientific management movement, including Taylor, showed great concern about the effects of company policies on employee well-being [Sheldon, 1924/1976]. For example, they were constantly preoccupied with eliminating or reducing fatigue. This benevolence, however, did not always characterize the followers of Taylor, who often tried to shortcut the introduction of his methods and engaged in rate-cutting and other deceptive practices.

Dishonesty

The strongest condemnations of Taylor, specifically of Taylor's character, have come in two recent articles [Wrege & Perroni, 1974; Wrege & Stotka, 1978]. The first asserts that Taylor lied about the conduct of the famous pig iron handling experiments at Bethlehem Steel, and the second claims that Taylor plagiarized most of his *Principles of Scientific Mangement* from a colleague, Morris L. Cooke.

As for the pig iron experiments, it seems clear from Wrege and Perroni [1974] that Taylor did stress different things in the three reports that appeared in his writings. However, these descriptions were not contradictory to one another; they differed only in terms of emphasis and in the amount of detail presented. This in itself does not constitute dishonesty. Taylor apparently was in error as to certain details (e.g., the amount of tonnage of iron involved), but this could have involved errors of memory rather than deliberate deception. Nor do these details change the thread of his arguments.

Wrege and Perroni also claim that Schmidt (actual name: Henry Knolle) was not selected scientifically for the job of pig iron handling as claimed, but was simply the only worker who stuck with the task from the beginning to the end of the introductory period. This claim would appear to be true unless James Gillespie and Hartley Wolle, who conducted most of the research, omitted pertinent information in their report. However, if one accepts the idea that by a "first class" workman Taylor meant one who was not just capable but also highly motivated, then the choice of Schmidt was not inconsistent with Taylor's philosophy.

In addition, Wrege and Perroni could find no evidence that local papers had opposed Taylor's experiments as he had claimed. However, it is possible that Taylor was referring to some other paper or papers. Wrege and Perroni do not indicate whether the papers they looked at were the only ones published in the Bethlehem area or surrounding areas at that time.

Wrege and Perroni argue further that Taylor never acknowledged that his "laws of heavy laboring" were based on the work of "two extraordinary workers" [1974, p. 21]. However in *Principles of Scientific Management*, Taylor clearly states that "*a first class laborer*, suited to such work as handling pig iron could be under load only 42 percent of the day and must be free from load 58 percent of the day" [1911/1967, p. 60, footnote 1; italics added]. In short, these laws were specifically *for* extraordinary workers.

Wrege and Perroni claim that Taylor lied about giving the workers rest pauses, because all of the rest periods referred to involved only the return walk after loading the pig iron rather than an actual seated or motionless rest period. However, if one reads Taylor's *Principles* carefully, one notes that he specifically described his laws of heavy laboring in terms of how much of the time the worker can be "under load" [1911/1967, pp. 60-61, footnote 1]. This implies that the return walk was the part not under load. Furthermore, near the end of footnote 1, Taylor states, "Practically the men were made to take a rest, generally by sitting down, after loading ten to twenty pigs. *This rest was in addition to the time which it took them to walk back from the car to the pile*" [1911/1967, p. 61, italics added]. No evidence in Wrege and Perroni's [1974] paper contradicts this assertion; nor do they even mention it.

As to the Wrege and Stotka [1978] claim that Taylor plagiarized most of his *Principles* from a manuscript written by a colleague, Morris Cooke, several facts should be noted. First, Cooke's manuscript was based on a talk written and presented by Taylor himself. Apparently Cooke added to it, but the source of the additional material is not actually known; it could have been from other talks by or discussions with Taylor. Cooke himself gave Taylor credit for this allegedly plagiarized material [Wrege & Stotka, 1978]. Fry argues, "It is ludicrous to accuse Taylor of plagiarizing Cooke if in fact Cooke's material was based on Taylor's own talks" [1976, p. 128]. Second, Taylor published *Principles* with Cooke's full knowledge and apparent consent. Third, Taylor offered Cooke all the royalties lest his book reduce the sales of a similar book Cooke planned to author himself. All of this is hardly consistent with Wrege and Stotka's implication that Taylor was a dishonest exploiter. Actually, the reasons why Cooke agreed to let Taylor be sole author of the manuscript are not known. At most Taylor can be accused of lack of graciousness due to his failure to acknowledge Cooke's editorial work. It is also puzzling why, if Cooke actually wrote most of *Principles*, Wrege, Perroni, and Stotka did not accuse Cooke as well as Taylor of dishonesty in reporting the pig iron experiments.

Wrege and Perroni [1974] also accuse Taylor of not giving credit to Gillespie and Wolle for their work on the Bethlehem studies. Although Taylor did not acknowledge in print every assistant who ever worked with him, in *Principles* he did acknowledge his indebtedness to many colleagues, including Barth, Gilbreth, Gantt, and Thompson. He also used the term "we" when describing the Bethlehem experiments. Thus he was clearly not in the habit of taking all credit for himself, as Wrege and Stotka [1978] charge. Again, however, a footnote acknowledging the work of Gillespie and Wolle would have been appropriate.

In the present author's opinion, not only is the evidence that Taylor was dishonest far from conclusive, it is virtually nonexistent. On the grounds of practicality alone, it seems doubtful that Taylor, who worked and performed experiments with so many different people, would deliberately attempt to distort what was done or who did it and thus leave himself open to exposure by any one of them.

Conclusion

With respect to the issues of a scientific approach to management and the techniques of time and motion study, standardization, goal setting plus work measurement and feedback, money as a motivator, management's responsibility for training, scientific selection, the shortened work week, and rest pauses, Taylor's views not only were essentially correct but they have been well accepted by management. With respect to the issues of management-labor relations and individualized work, Taylor probably was only partially correct, and he has been only partially accepted. These issues are summarized in Table 1.

Table 1
Status of Taylor's Ideas and Techniques
in Contemporary Management

	Valid?	Now Accepted?	Manifested in (outgrowths):
Philosophy			
Scientific decision making	Yes	Yes	Management science: operations research, cost accounting, etc.
Management-labor cooperation	Yes	Partly	Greater management-labor cooperation (but conflict not eliminated)
Techniques			
Time and motion study	Yes	Yes	Widespread use; standard times
Standardization	Yes	Yes	Standardized procedures in many spheres; human engineering

Task	Yes	Yes	Goal setting, MBO, feedback
Bonus	Yes	Increasingly	Proliferation of reward system, Scanlon Plan, Improshare, need to consider money in job enrichment/OD studies
Individualized work	Partly	Partly	Recognition of dangers of groups, groupthink, social loafing, contextual theories of group decision making, (but group jobs sometimes more efficient)
Management training	Yes	Yes	Management responsibility for employee training
Scientific selection	Yes	Yes	Development of fields of industrial psychology and personnel management
Shorter hours; rest pauses	Yes	Yes	40 hour (or less) work week; common use of rest pauses

With respect to criticisms, the accusations regarding the following points are predominantly or wholly false: Taylor's inadequate model of worker motivation, his ignorance of social factors, his authoritarianism, his treatment of men as machines, his exploitation of workers, his antiunionism, and his personal dishonesty. Several of them verge on the preposterous. The accusation of overspecialization seems partly but not totally justified. See Table 2 for a summary of these points.

Table 2
Validity of Criticisms of Taylor's Ideas

Criticism	Valid?	Relevant facts
Inadequate theory of work motivation	Specious, because no complete theory offered	Money and goals are the most effective motivators
Ignored social factors	No	SM designed specifically to facilitate cooperation and to eliminate negative effects of social factors; awareness of sentiments
Authoritarianism	No	Stressed rule of knowledge (the essence of SM)
Overspecialization	Partly	Specialization maximized expertise; matched men to job requirements (but ignored possible benefits of multicrafting)
Treated man as machines	No	Methods based on knowledge, not feelings
Exploitation of workers	No	Management deserves some of the benefits of increased efficiency based on its contribution
Antiunionism	No	Unions not needed under good management
Dishonesty	No	Accusations based on incomplete or false information

Considering that it has been over 65 years since Taylor's death and that a knowledge explosion has taken place during these years, Taylor's track record is remarkable. The point is not, as is often claimed, that he was "right in the context of his time" but is now outdated, but that *most of his insights are still valid today.* The present author agrees with those who consider Taylor a genius [Johnson, 1980]. His achievements are all the more admirable because, although Taylor was highly intelligent, his discoveries were not made through sudden, brilliant insights but through sheer hard work. His metal-cutting experiments, for example, spanned a period of 26 years [Taylor, 1912/1970a]!

Drucker [1976] claims that Taylor had as much impact on the modern world as Karl Marx and Sigmund Freud. This may be true in that Taylor's influence was certainly worldwide and has endured long after his death [Wren, 1979]. Of the three, however, the present author considers Taylor's ideas to be by far the most objectively valid. But the historical figure that Taylor most reminds one of is Thomas Edison [Runes, 1948]--in his systematic style of research, his dogged persistence, his emphasis on the useful, his thirst for knowledge, and in his dedication to truth.

References

1.   Bartlem, C. S. & Locke, E. A. The Coch and Frenth Study: A Critique and Reinterpretation. Human Relations, 1981, 34, pp. 555-566.

2.   Boddewyn, J. Frederick Winslow Taylor Revisited. Academy of Management Journal, 1961, 4, pp. 100-107.

3.   Carey, A. The Hawthorne Studies: A Radical Criticism. American Sociological Review, 1967, 32, pp. 403-416.

4.   Copley, F. B. Frederick W. Taylor: Father of Scientific Management (2 Vols.). New York: Harper & Row, 1923.

5.   Copley, F. B. Taylor and Trade Unions. In De DelMar & R. D. Collins (Eds.), Classics in Scientific Management. University, Ala.: University of Alabama Press, 1976, pp. 52-56. (Originally published, 1925.)

6.   Drucker, P. F. The Practice of Management. New York: Harper, 1954.

7.   Drucker, P. F. The Coming Rediscovery of Scientific Management. Conference Board Record, 1976, 13 (6), pp. 23-27.

8.   Fein, M. Work Measurement and Wage Incentives, Industrial Engineering, 1973, 5, pp. 49-51.

9.   Fein, M. An Alternative to Traditional Managing. Unpublished manuscript, 1977.

10.   Fisher, I. Scientific Management Made Clear. In D. DelMar & R. D. Collins (Eds.), Classics in Scientific Management, University, Ala.: University of Alabama Press, 1976, pp. 154-193. (Originally published, 1925.)

11.   Franke, R. H. & Kaul, J. D. The Hawthorne Experiments: First Statistical Interpretation. American Sociological Review, 1978, 43, pp. 623-643.

12.   Frost, C. F., Wakeley, J. H., & Ruh, R. A. The Scanlon Plan for Organization Development: Identity, Participants, and Equity . East Lansing: Michigan State University Press, 1974.

13.   Fry, L. W. The Maligned F. W. Taylor: A Reply to His Many Critics. Academy of Management Review, 1976, 1 (30), pp. 124-139.

14.   Gilbreth, F. B. Science in Management for the One Best Way to Do Work. In H. F. Merrill (Ed.), Classics in Management. New York: American Management Association, 1970, pp. 217-263.   (Originally published, 1923.)

15.   Gilbreth, F. B. Primer of Scientific Management. Easton, Pa.: Hive Publishing Co., 1973. (Originally published, 1914.)

16.   Greenwood, R. Management by Objectives: As Developed by Peter F. Drucker Assisted by General Electric's Management Consultation Services. Paper presented at the Academy of Management meetings, 1980, Detroit.

17.   Hall, J. Decisions, Decisions, Decisions. Psychology Today, 1971, 5 (6), 51ff.

18.   Janis, I. Victims of Groupthink. Boston: Houghton Mifflin, 1972.

19.   Johnson, M. J. Fred Taylor '83: Giant of Non-Repute. Stevens Indicator, 1980, 97 (2), pp. 4-8.

20.   Kendall, H. P. A Decade's Development in Management Trends and Results of Scientific Management. In D. DelMar & R. D. Collins (Eds.), Classics in Scientific Management. University, Ala.: University of Alabama Press, 1976k, pp. 118-133. (Originally published, 1924.)

21.   Latané, B., Williams, K., & Harkins, S. Social Loafing. Psychology Today, 1979, 13 (4), 104ff.

22.   Latham, G. P. & Dossett, D. L. Designing Incentive Plans for Unionized Employees: A Comparison of Continuous and Variable Ratio Reinforcement Schedules. Personnel Psychology, 1978, 31, pp. 47-61.

23.   Lawler, E. E. Pay and Organizational Effectiveness: A Psychological View. New York: McGraw-Hill, 1971.

24.   Lawler, E. E. Pay, Participation and Organization Change. In E. L. Cass & F. G. Zimmer (Eds.), Man and Work in Society, New York: Van Nostrand Reinhold, 1975, pp. 137-149.

25.   Locke, E. A. Toward a Theory of Task Motivation and Incentives, Organizational Behavior and Human Performance, 1968, 3, pp. 157-189.

26.   Locke, E. A. Personnel Attitudes and Motivation, Annual Review of Psychology, 1975, 26, pp. 457-480.

27.   Locke, E. A. The Nature and Causes of Job Satisfaction. In M. D. Dunnette (Ed.), Handbook of Industrial and Organizational Psychology. Chicago: Rand McNally, 1976, pp. 1297-1349.

28.   Locke, E. A. The Myths of Behavior Mod in Organizations, Academy of Management Review, 1977, 2, pp. 543-553.

29.   Locke, E. A. The Ubiquity of the Technique of Goal Setting in Theories of and Approaches to Employee Motivation. Academy of Management Review, 1978, 3, pp. 594-601.

30.   Locke, E. A., Cartledge, N., & Koeppel, J. Motivational Effects of Knowledge of Results: A Goal-Setting Phenomenon? Psychological Bulletin, 1968, 70, pp. 474-485.

31.   Locke, E. A., Shaw, K. N., Saari, L. M., & Latham, G. P. Goal Setting and Task Performance: 1969-1980. Psychological Bulletin, 1981, 90, pp. 125-152.

32.   Locke, E. A., Feren, D. B., McCaleb, V. M., Shaw, K. M., & Denny, A. T. The Relative Effectiveness of Four Methods of Motivating Employee Performance. In K. Duncan, M. Gruneberg, & D. Wallis (Eds.), Changes in Working Life, Chichester, England: Wiley, 1980, pp. 363-387.

33.   Munsterberg, H. Psychology and Industrial Efficiency. Boston: Houghton Mifflin, 1913.

34.   Odiorne, G. S. MBO: A Backward Glance. Business Horizons, October 1978, pp. 14-24.

35.   Roethlisberger, F. J. & Dickson, W. J. Management and the Worker. Cambridge, Mass.: Harvard University Press, 1956. (Originally published, 1939.)

36.   Runes, D. D. (Ed.) The Diary and Sundry Observations of Thomas Alva Edison, New York: Philosophical Library, 1948.

37.   Ryan, T. A. Work and Effort, New York: Ronald, 1947.

38.   Sheldon, O. Taylor the Creative Leader. In D. DelMar & R. D. Collins (Eds.), Classics in Scientific Management. University, Ala.: University of Alabama Press, 1976, pp. 35-51. (Originally published, 1924.)

39.   Sykes, A. J. M. Economic Interest and the Hawthorne Researchers, Human Relations, 1965, 18, pp. 253-263.

40.   Taylor, F. W. Shop Management (published as part of Scientific Management), New York: Harper, 1947. (Originally published, 1903.)

41.   Taylor F. W. The Principles of Scientific Management, New York: Norton, 1967. (Originally published, 1911.)

42.   Taylor, F. W. Time Study, Piece Work, and the First-Class Man. In H. F. Merrill (Ed.), Classics in Management, New York: American Management Association, 1970, pp. 57-66. (Originally published, 1903.)

43.   Taylor, F. W. The Principles of Scientific Management. In H. F. Merrill (Ed.), Classics in Management. New York: American Management Association, 1970a. (Originally published, 1912.)

44.   Taylor, F. W. What is Scientific Management? In H. G. Merrill (Ed.), Classics in Management. New York: American Management Association, 1970b, pp. 67-71. (Original testimony given, 1912.)

45.   Taylor, F. W. Profit Sharing. In De DelMar & R. D. Collins (Eds.), Classics in Scientific Management. University, Ala.: University of Alabama Press, 1976, pp. 17-20. (Originally written, 1912.)

46.   Vernon, H. N. Industrial Fatigue and Efficiency, New York: Dutton, 1921.

47.   Vough, C. F. Tapping the Human Resource, New York: Wiley, 1964.

48.   Vroom, V. Work and Motivation, New York: Wiley, 1969.

49.   Walton, R. E. Work Innovations at Topeka: After Six Years, Journal of Applied Behavioral Science, 1977, 13 (3), pp. 422-433.

50.   Wesolowski, Z. P. The Polish Contribution to the Development of Scientific Management, Proceedings of the Academy of Management, 1978.

51.   White, F. & Locke, E. A. Perceived Determinants of High and Low Productivity in Three Occupational Groups: A Critical Incident Study. Journal of Management Studies, in press.

52.   Wrege. C. D. & Perroni, A. G. Taylor's Pig-Tale: A Historical Analysis of Frederick W. Taylor's Pig-Iron Experiments. Academy of Management Journal, 1974, 17, pp. 6-27.

53.   Wrege C. D. & Stotka, A. M. Cooke Creates a Classic: The Story Behind F. W. Taylor's Principles of Scientific Management. Academy of Management Review, 1978, 3, pp. 736-749.

54.   Wren, D. A. The Evolution of Management Thought (2nd ed.), New York: Wiley, 1979.

55.   Wren, D. A. Scientific Management in the U.S.S.R., with particular reference to the contribution of Walter N. Polakov, Academy of Management Review, 1980, 5, pp. 1-11.

MINDS AND MANAGERS: ON THE DUAL NATURE OF HUMAN INFORMATION PROCESSING AND MANAGEMENT[1,2]

William Taggart
Daniel Robey
Florida International University

In this paper we present a concept of dual human information processing as an aid to understanding the decision styles and decision strategies of managers. Several threads of thought are woven together: neurological studies of "split-brain" persons, Jung's typology of personality, and philosophical explanations of human duality. The resulting framework differentiates a range of left- to right-hemisphere-dominant decision styles and integrates four decision strategies expressed as approaches to the person and the environment.

For hundreds of years, humanity has been intrigued by the dual nature of human consciousness. In art, philosophy, religion, and recently the behavioral and medical sciences, a dual perspective on the nature of human beings has emerged. From one perspective, people are logical and rational, goal-directed and scientific, technical and analytical. From the other, people are mysterious and intuitive, nonlogical and subjective, artistic and emotional.

These contrasting terms are most often used to describe differences *among* people, but recent neurophysiological research points to the existence of these two types of mind within each person. The two hemispheres of the brain process information in different ways. For most people, verbal and analytical thought processes are located in the left hemisphere, and the right hemisphere is responsible for spatial and intuitive thinking.

Although Barnard recognized the importance of duality over 40 years ago, only recently has its importance to management been examined. Stimulated by management's emerging interest, we present a conceptual framework that integrates several threads of thought: neurological studies in medicine, the psychological typology of Jung, and philosophical explanations of duality. The framework differentiates four basic decision styles that range from a left- to a right-hemisphere-dominant mode. Complementing the decision styles, the framework integrates four decision strategies that suggest alternative managerial approaches to the person and environment.

Approaches to the Study of Human Information Processing

Human information processing (HIP) concerns how people gather and use information in making decisions. Because managers are decision makers, an understanding of HIP in the management context may well be useful. Several

[1] The development of this article was supported in part by a grant from the Florida International University Foundation.
[2] We wish to express our appreciation to Dana Farrow, Tommie Kushner, and Karl Magnusen for their assistance in developing some of the ideas expressed in this paper.

Reprinted from The Academy of Management Review, 1981, Vol. 6, No. 2, 187-95, by permission of the author and publisher.

approaches to the study of HIP can be identified. *One approach* attempts to model the heuristics that individuals use in making choices [Newell & Simon, 1972]. Heuristics become very complex as the task becomes more intricate and as more people and interest groups become involved in the process [Mintzberg, Raisinghani, & Theoret, 1976].

The ultimate aims of this approach are two. The first is simply to build a descriptive model of how people process information, particularly in complex situations. Second, the applied purpose is to provide decision makers with "good" or "efficient" models so that their decisions can improve. As Bowman [1963] has demonstrated, regression weights derived from actual management decisions, when used to guide future decisions, produce a consistency that may be more important than a futile search for optimality. Developing models of decision behavior can thus provide basic findings on human information processing as well as normative decision tools.

A *second approach* to HIP deals with cognitive complexity, the relative complexity within an individual's conceptual system [Schroder, Driver, & Streufert, 1967]. An optimal level of environmental complexity is identified, suggesting that too little or too much environmental complexity results in reduced ability to process information. Individual differences in information processing are recognized: more complex processors are capable of processing more information at the optimal load point than are simpler processors. Research reveals a positive correlation between cognitive complexity and personality variables such as tolerance for ambiguity, and a negative correlation with other variables such as authoritarianism and dogmatism [Streufert, 1972].

Recently, Driver [1979] and Driver and Rowe [1979] have reviewed management research on cognitive complexity and have formulated a revised version of the complexity theory. They identify four decision styles, whereby individuals are typed on the basis of (1) the use of a single or multiple *focus*, and (2) the *amount* of information used (low or high). The four styles are: *decisive* (single focus, low usage), *hierarchic* (single focus, high usage), *flexible* (multiple focus, low usage), and *integrative* (multiple focus, high usage). Experimental studies of decision making show important but tentative differences between the four styles [Driver & Mock, 1975]. The most direct application of this work appears to be in matching managers to decision situations where their natural styles are most effective.

A *third approach* that has found more recent acceptance within management emphasizes the dual nature of HIP. The duality approach differs from the heuristic modeling and cognitive complexity approaches in that it expressly identifies HIP styles that are *qualitatively different*. Some decision makers use logical routines to make decisions and are classified as analytic or systematic. Their nonlogical counterparts use unsystematic, intuitive processes to reach decisions.

A similar distinction has been made in education research to improve communication about curriculum development and test preparation. A taxonomy of educational objectives has been developed around two broad categories: cognitive and affective [Bloom, 1956; Krathwohl, Bloom & Masia, 1964]. The cognitive objectives emphasize developing analytic and systematic capabilities; the affective objectives emphasize unsystematic and intuitive processes. This taxonomy highlights what *should be* two primary emphases in education. However, management education to date has focused on the cognitive aspects of decision making, virtually ignoring the affective.

It is this dual cognitive/affective, analytic/ intuitive concept of HIP that we are dealing with here. In the following sections, we identify both classic and recent interest in dual processing as the basis for our conceptual framework. Of particular interest are the implications that successful management depends on the use of a full range of processing skills. This suggests the need for flexible, situationally dependent styles and strategies for decision making.

A significant concern for the dual perspective is the measurement of individual processing orientations. In a related paper, we [Robey & Taggart, in press] review three basic approaches to such measurement: those that infer style from physiological indicators, those that observe outward behavior directly and self-description inventories. Further practical work with the conceptual framework presented here depends on the assessment of HIP style with combined psychological and physiological measures. This problem constitutes our current research interest.

Tracing Management Interest in HIP

Management interest in a dual classification dates back at least to Barnard's easy "Mind in Everyday Affairs," published as an appendix to his *Functions of the Executive*. Barnard highlighted the logical and nonlogical processes that, woven together, form the decision-making fabric of an organization. He found it convenient to recognize that "mental processes consist of two groups which I shall call 'non-logical' and 'logical'" [1938, p. 302]. By logical process, Barnard meant conscious thinking that can be expressed in words or other symbols. Such thinking is typically referred to as "reasoning." A nonlogical process is one that cannot be expressed in words or described as a thought process, but may be recognized in the result of some action such as a judgment or a decision. In Barnard's view, an effective manager has access to either mode as the situation demands.

Recently, Leavitt [1975a, 1975b] has discussed the consequences of over-emphasizing analytic problem solving in management education. He suggests that the intuitive and emotional aspects of information processing deserve the same attention as the logical and analytic. Leavitt urges moving in the direction of "integrating wisdom and feeling with analysis." Individuals who are capable of such integration "are worth a great deal" to an organization [1975b, p. 20]. Because management education emphasizes the analytic style, which blocks consideration of nonanalytic modes that use intuition and empathy, such integration may be difficult. In Leavitt's opinion, emphasis on the analytic mode breeds suspicion and even hostility toward the opposite, yet complementary style. He believes that an integrated, flexible emphasis would better serve the needs of management education.

Mintzberg has developed this theme further. Citing research in psychology and medicine, Mintzberg contends that individuals who make good *planners* appear to exhibit the strengths of the left hemisphere processor while good *managers* exhibit the strengths of the right. He also suggests that planners and managers would both be more proficient if they could draw at will on the processing style appropriate to the circumstances. Mintzberg states that a major thrust in organizations since Frederick Taylor's work has been to shift management activities out of the intuitive realm into that of conscious analysis. But managers need to overcome this bias and carefully distinguish those activities which should be handled analytically from those "which must remain in the realm of intuition, where, in the meantime, we should be looking for the lost keys to management" [1976, p. 58].

Neurological Evidence of Dual Processing

Substantial clinical evidence for the right/left duality in HIP has grown out of work with "split-brain" surgical patients beginning in the early 1960s. In this surgery, patients suffering from a severe form of epilepsy have the corpus collosum, which connects the two hemispheres of the cerebrum, cut to prevent the onset of seizures. This procedure stops the seizures by eliminating bursts of seizure-inducing neurological transmissions between the two hemispheres of the cerebrum.

After the surgery, patients lead normal lives except that cerebral functioning is impaired under certain conditions. For example, if an object such as a spoon is placed out of sight in the patient's left hand, the patient will not be able to name the object. The left hand "tells" the right hemisphere that a spoon is being held. But the left hemisphere, which is responsible for speech, cannot name the object since the image of the spoon cannot be communicated from the right to the left hemisphere for conversion to words. The patient knows, with one mind, what the object is but cannot verbally express it with the other mind.

A variety of evidence has made it clear that one hemisphere of the cerebrum is enough to sustain an individual's personality or mind. Bogen wrote that "we may conclude that the individual with two intact hemispheres has the capacity for two distinct minds" [1969, p. 157]. Bogen proposed the terms "propositional" for the orientation of the left hemisphere and "appositional" for the right. Left-mode processing is strongly developed and reinforced by Western educational traditions. Bogen believes that as we become better informed about new findings, we can design learning situations for the harmonious development of students' whole minds. In accord with this suggestion, a greater balance between developing left and right hemisphere abilities will enhance management.

A Psychological Foundation for Decision Style

Another conceptual approach to a balanced view of HIP draws from the work of Carl Jung. Jung, one of psychology's classic theorists, provided strong roots for the study of duality in HIP. Jung's theory of personality identifies two dimensions of HIP that seem directly related to right and left brain activity [1971]. Perception (gathering information) and judgment (processing information) are the two dimensions. Perception is achieved by either sensations (S) or intuition (N); judgment is made by either thinking (T) or feeling (F). Pairing a mode of perception with a mode of judgment yields four basic decision styles: sensation/thinking (ST), intuition/thinking (NT), sensation/feeling (SF), and intuition/feeling (NF). These four decision styles are arranged in sequence from left to right along the top of Figure 1. Myers [1976] distinguished these styles in terms of (1) personal focus of attention, (2) method of handling things, (3) tendency to become, and (4) expression of abilities. These characteristics are listed in the left column of Figure 1.

The ST processing style relies on sensing of the environment for perception and rational thinking for judgment. ST processors attend to *facts* and handle them with *impersonal analysis*. They tend to be practical and matter of fact and develop abilities more easily in technical work with facts and objects. In contrast, NF types rely on intuitive perceptions and nonrational feeling for judgment. Such people attend to *possibilities* and handle them with *personal warmth*. They tend to be enthusiastic and insightful, and their abilities are more easily expressed in understanding and communicating.

NT people attend to *possibilities*, as do NF's, but they approach them with *impersonal analysis*, like ST's. NT's are logical and ingenious, and express their abilities easily in theoretical and technical developments. SF people attend to *facts*, as do ST's, but they handle them with *personal warmth*, like NF's. SF's tend to be sympathetic and friendly, and find their abilities best developed in practical help and services for people. Occupationally, the NT is typified by a planner; the ST, a technician; the SF, a teacher; and the NF, an artist.

FIGURE 1
The Range of Decision Styles in Human Information Processing

Left Hemisphere				Right Hemisphere
	←————————————— Decision Style —————————————→			
	ST Sensation/Thinking	NT Intuition/Thinking	SF Sensation/Feeling	NF Intuition/Feeling
Focus of Attention	Facts	Possibilities	Facts	Possibilities
Method of Handling Things	Impersonal Analysis	Impersonal Analysis	Personal Warmth	Personal Warmth
Tendency to Become	Practical and Matter of Fact	Logical and Ingenious	Sympathetic and Friendly	Enthusiastic and Insightful
Expression of Abilities	Technical Skills With Facts and Objects	Theoretical and Technical Developments	Practical Help and Services for People	Understanding and Communicating With People
Representative Occupation	Technician	Planner	Teacher	Artist
	←————————————— Manager —————————————→			

In addition to these characteristic differences in style, Figure 1 suggests two other ideas that are fundamental to our framework. At the top of Figure 1, we suggest a link between left hemisphere domination and the ST type, and one between right hemisphere domination and the NF type. The two intermediate types, NT and SF, can be considered less indicative of hemispheric domination.

The placement of NT to the left of SF suggests that thinking (T) judgment is more characteristic of left hemisphere processors than is intuitive (N) perception. The feeling (F) type, in contrast, is dominated by the right hemisphere, which "pulls" the SF person to the right of the NT. This implies that the second-named element (judgment) takes precedence over the first (perception); in other words, characterization of style depends more on how information is *processed* (judgment) than on how it is *gathered* (perception).

The second idea conveyed by Figure 1 is that managers should be flexible in processing style. This need for flexibility follows from the observations of Barnard, Leavitt, Mintzberg, and Bogen. Because managers face a wide variety of human, technical, and value questions, they are more effective if they can change their style to fit their problems. A manager may need to act like a technician, planner, teacher, or artist, depending on the circumstances.

Consider a manager who has rated a subordinate's performance as marginal. How the manager might handle the situation illustrates the range of styles. An ST manager responds with "Improve your performance or you're fired!" (factual, impersonal, practical). The NT manager's attitude moderates a bit with "If your performance does not improve, you will be transferred to another position" (possibilities, impersonal, ingenious). The SF manager approaches the problem with "You need to change, what can we do to help you?" (factual, personal, sympathetic). And the NF manager suggests "You can improve your performance, let me suggest an approach" (possibilities, personal, insightful). Any one of the responses may be best, depending on situational factors, such as who the subordinate is, the pressure of time, and group norms. The flexible manager recognizes the contingencies and chooses the most appropriate style.

Philosophical Foundations for Dual Processing

The duality we are discussing has not gone unnoticed in the philosophies of either East or West. But the way the two mental processes are perceived and the emphasis placed on each varies according to the two philosophical traditions. The differences between Western and Eastern culture are evident in the divergent accounts of humanity's relation to nature.

Western philosophy, derived from its Greek heritage, assumes the original condition of nature as one of chaos or darkness. The human role is to impose order and shed light on the original chaos or darkness. In contrast, Eastern philosophy takes the original condition of nature to be one of order or integration of the light and the dark. One returns to this original state by letting go and permitting nature's inherent expression rather than by actively intervening.

Typically, Western philosophy seeks to explain how order comes about and how to maintain it. This yields the characteristic Western scientific view of encountering and manipulating things to achieve desired results. The Eastern view reverses the problem to consider how disorder arises and how to avoid it. The classical Chinese notion of *wu wei* or "taking no unnecessary action" expresses this attitude. This Taoist view accepts things as they are, permitting them to express an inherent result [Chan, 1963, pp. 225, 791].

The philosophy of *wu wei* contrasts sharply with the Western attitude that some action must be taken to achieve a desired result. Conceptually, the Western stress on action aligns with the left-hemisphere rational processing style.

Conversely, the Eastern acceptance of things as they are corresponds to the right hemisphere. The Taoist symbol of overlapping light and dark (yang and yin), which we use in the center of Figure 2, symbolizes the inherent unity of hemisphere differentiation. It suggests a holistic, integrated information processor.

Although the integration of active yang and receptive yin principles is most often associated with Eastern thought, Western philosophers have recognized the importance of merging the two sides of man's nature. For example, Nietzche used the Grecian deities Apollo and Dionysus to symbolize duality. Apollo signifies order, restraint, and form--characteristics of the earthbound left hemisphere. Dionysus symbolizes the dynamic interplay that knows no restraints and defies limitations--characteristics of the right hemisphere [1967, pp. 33-47].

Benedict used the Apollonian and Dionysian distinction to contrast two very different American Indian cultures [1934]. Many Indian cultures on the American continent were Dionysian, celebrating their deep bond with nature through elaborate ritual and ceremony freely entered into and freely expressed. In contrast, the Zuni were an Apollonian culture characterized by a single-minded attitude with a restrained middle-of-the-road outlook that distrusted individualism.

The essence of both these cultures is reflected in our current approach to management education. Management *education* stresses Apollonian values and methods, but management *practice* calls for both the Apollonian and the Dionysian. The philosophical position of the manager must integrate these paradoxical opposites by seeking balance. In terms of the Figure 1 range of decision styles, the successful manager must transcend the narrow orientation of one culture or one philosophy.

FIGURE 2
Human Information Processing in Management Decision Making

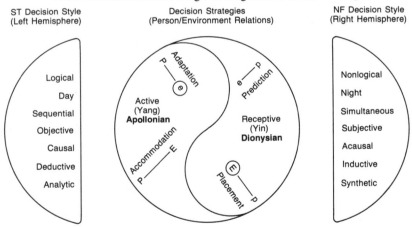

The diverse threads of the previous discussion can be drawn together and the common theme expressed directly. Figure 2 shows the two cerebral hemispheres flanking the Taoist symbol representing different combinations of the active and receptive principles. We have mentioned the physiological, psychological, and philosophical bases for right and left hemisphere information processing. The essence of that discussion is represented by the antonymous adjectives in the two hemispheres. The left hemisphere's orientation to action (the yang principle), as reflected in most Western philosophies, is represented on the left (unshaded) side of the Taoist circle. The right hemisphere's receptivity, the Eastern *wu wei* (the yin principle), is on the right (shaded) side of the circle. The left/right duality provides a basis for organizing management decision strategies with respect to the person and the environment.

From a management perspective, action and nonaction can pertain to both the person and the environment. We have adopted Lewin's [1961] classic formulation that behavior (B) is a function of the interaction of the person (P) and the environment (E), or B = f (P,E). Our framework suggests four management decision strategies: changing both person and environment (P,E), changing the person but not the environment (P,e), changing the environment but not the person (p,E), and changing neither the person nor the environment (p,e).

In Figure 2, we have labeled the left hemisphere action strategies *accommodation* and *adaptation*, and the right hemisphere receptive strategies *placement* and *prediction*. *Accommodation* assumes that we adjust both the person (P) and environment (E) to bring about a desired state. Its complement, *prediction*, takes the person (p) and environment (e) as they are and forecasts the outcomes of their interaction. The middle ground offers two partly active strategies. *Adaptation* treats the environment (e) as given, and changes the person (P) to fit the situation. The other intermediate strategy takes the person (p) as given and accomplishes an objective through *placement* in a selected or designed environment (E).

Adaptation describes the person changing to suit the demands of the environment. It is an active strategy for the person (P) because it involves personal change; however, it is a receptive strategy for the environment (e) because that remains unchanged. Adaptation describes the traditional training functions in management and the less formal processes of socialization and job experience. It assumes that individuals have the capacity to change in directions that the environment requires. It further implies that environmental demands (job requirements) can be meaningfully stated and related to personal characteristics.

Placement refers to the active manipulation of the environment to fit the individual. The person (p) assumes a receptive attitude and does not change, although he or she may be actively involved in changing the environment (E) or in finding a suitable one. In management, placement refers not only to placing persons into jobs that they can do, but also to task and organization design. It is the opposite of training the person to fit the job.

Accommodation reflects a combination of the first two approaches-- adaptation and placement. Management action is maximized through the selective manipulation of person and environment. As interesting as debates between humanists (active P, receptive e) and behaviorists (active E, receptive p) are [Rogers & Skinner, 1956], the accommodation strategy suggests that practicing managers have more to gain from an understanding that behavior results from both the person and the environment.

Accommodation epitomizes the active, logical left hemisphere thought that most characterizes contemporary management. It regards results as sacred and emphasizes purposeful manipulation of both P and E to achieve results. Most modern contingency theorists employ this strategy in their search for the correct

45

fit between people and their environments, with some ultimate criterion (organizational effectiveness, human performance, etc.) at stake.

The fourth strategy shown in the diagram is *prediction*. Unlike the preceding three, prediction assumes a receptive, nonlogical right hemisphere attitude toward the person (p) and the environment (e). Whatever happens, happens. The individual "goes with the flow" and does not manipulate the course of events. A willingness by the individual to harmonize with the situation is implied. Prediction calls for withholding intervention to permit the course of events to find its natural expression.

Because management seems to imply manipulation of things, people, or situations to accomplish goals, prediction is often ignored as a valid strategy. It is useful for managers to know what is going to happen so they can plan active strategies. But prediction, the receptive strategy described here, suggests that knowledge of outcomes is complete in itself and that this knowledge need not be used as the basis for devising active moves. Rather, successful use of this strategy is defined in terms of *understanding one's own position in the flow*--not in terms of using that information to change one's position.

The marginal performance situation, used earlier to illustrate the Jungian styles, can also illustrate the different action approaches implied by the four strategies. Using the left hemisphere accommodation strategy, a manager would seek to modify the subordinate's behavior as well as change the work assignment in an effort to improve the situation. This is characteristic of an active management attitude. Using the adaptation strategy, a manager would focus on changes in the subordinate's behavior while leaving the work content as it is. When the job content is considered acceptable, this approach would be appropriate. The placement strategy would be appropriate if the difficulty lies in the work design and not in the employee's behavior. In this case, performance will improve by adjusting the work to the skills of the employee.

If the manager foresees the unsatisfactory performance is transient and will clear up by itself, then the right hemisphere prediction strategy would be followed. The manager leaves the situation as it is, since the unsatisfactory performance will rectify itself without the subordinate or the job being changed. This last strategy is often overlooked because we tend to assume that a situation will improve only if we actively intervene. The ability to recognize when situations require inaction can conserve an organization's resources.

Implications for Management Education

The educational question raised here is similar to one encountered in leadership theory: Should managers be trained in all styles and learn to apply them, or should situations be tailored to fit the manager's naturally dominant style? There may be nothing "natural" about the analytical decision style acquired through traditional management education. Rather, this style may well be a function of our entire educational process, beginning in kindergarten. Left-hemisphere-dominant teachers breed left-hemisphere-dominant students. However, we each have *two* hemispheres that deserve equal time in our educational experience.

This fact presents a significant challenge to management educators, who have traditionally stressed the left hemisphere analytic style and strategy of processing information. Without exposure to alternative styles and strategies, managers are less likely to see the value of a right-hemisphere approach, even though it may be appropriate to a particular problem. Moreover, there may be many creative, right-hemisphere people who do poorly in traditional business courses and who find unappealing the strictly rational approach to the study of management. These people could more readily see their potential contributions to the managerial world if business schools stressed the full range of HIP styles and strategies.

We are not suggesting that management education should foster basic changes in personality. But we are suggesting that opportunities to explore the full range of decision styles and strategies should be made available in business school curricula. We believe that managers can be more effective if they are aware of several styles and strategies (within a sound theoretical framework), and if they learn to use them appropriately. By widening our educational approach, we are more likely to produce aspiring managers who are effective in both the logical and nonlogical processes about which Barnard wrote so compellingly.

It is neither trite nor exaggerated to say that management is both an art and a science. But accepting this statement as valid presses us to consider how we can develop manager/artists by providing learning experiences to improve right-hemisphere decision skills. At the same time, we must continue to educate managers for success as manager/scientists. This means retaining the left-hemisphere curriculum that we are familiar and comfortable with. Balancing the curriculum to encompass the complete range of processing styles and strategies that our framework suggests is a major challenge for management education in the 1980s.

References

Barnard, C. I., The functions of the executive. Cambridge: Harvard University Press, 1938.

Benedict, R., Patterns of culture. New York: New American Library, 1934.

Bloom, B. S. (Ed.), Taxonomy of educational objectives: Handbook 1: Cognitive domain. New York: David McKay, 1956.

Bogen, J. E., The other side of the brain: II: An appositional mind. Bulletin of the Los Angeles Neurological Societies, 1969, 34, pp. 135-162.

Bogen J. E.; & Bogen, G. M., The other side of the brain. III: The corpus collosum and creativity. Bulletin of the Los Angeles Neurological Societies, 1969, 34, pp. 191-220.

Bowman, E. H., Consistency and optimality in managerial decision making. Management Science, 1963, 9, pp. 310-321.

Chan, W. T., A source book in Chinese philosophy. Princeton, N.J.: Princeton University Press, 1963.

Driver, M. J., Individual decision making and creativity. In S. Kerr (Ed.) Organizational behavior. Columbus, Ohio: Grid Publishing, 1979.

Driver, M. J.; & Mock, T. J., Human information processing, decision style theory, and accounting information systems. Accounting Review, 1975, 50, pp. 490-508.

Driver, M. J.; & Rowe, A. J., Decision-making styles: A new approach to management decision making. In C. L. Cooper (Ed.), Behavioral problems in organizations. Englewood Cliffs, N.J.: Prentice-Hall, 1979.

Jung, C. G., Psychological types (R.F.C. Hall, trans.). Princeton University Press, 1971.

Krathwohl, D. R.; Bloom, B. S.; & Masia, B. B., Taxonomy of educational objectives. Handbook II: Affective Domain. New York: David McKay, 1964.

Leavitt, H. J., Beyond the analytic manager. California Management Review, Spring 1975, 17, pp. 5-12 (a).

Leavitt, H. J., Beyond the analytic manager: Part II. California Management Review, Summer 1975, 17, pp. 11-21 (b).

Lewin K., Field theory in social science. New York: Harper Brothers, 1961.

Mintzberg, H., Planning on the left side and managing on the right. Harvard Business Review, July-August 1976, 54, pp. 49-58.

Mintzberg, H.; Raisinghani, D.; & Theoret, A., The structure of "unstructured" decision processes. Administrative Science Quarterly, 1976, 21, pp. 246-275.

Myers, I. B., Introduction to type. Gainesville, Fla.: AMSA Foundation, 1976.

Newell, A.; & Simon, H. A., Human problem solving. Englewood Cliffs, N.J.: Prentice-Hall, 1972.

Nietzsche, F., The birth of tragedy (W. Kaufman, trans.). New York: Random House, 1967.

Robey, D.; & Taggart, W., Measuring managers' minds: The assessment of style in human information processing. Academy of Management Review, in press.

Rogers, C. R.; & Skinner, B. F., Some issues concerning the control of human behavior: A symposium. Science, 1956, 124, pp. 1057-1066.

Schroder, H. M.; Driver, M. J.; & Streufert, S., Human information processing. New York: Holt, Rinehart & Winston, 1967.

Streufert, S. C., Cognitive complexity: A review. Technical report No. 2. West Lafayette, Indiana: Purdue University, Department of Psychology, 1972.

A LOOK AT PLANNING AND ITS COMPONENTS

Harvey Kahalas

In this paper the author discusses the reasons for long range planning, and some of the inherent problems. He examines the dimensions of planning, single use plans versus standing plans, the need to build flexibility into the plan, and answers the question "Who does the planning?" He states that poor planning can mean organizational suicide.

A plan is any detailed scheme, program or method worked out beforehand for the accomplishment of an objective. Inherent in this definition are three elements. A plan must deal with the future, must involve action, and must identify who is to implement that future action.

Planning is one of the basic tasks of management. If the process of management is divided into four fundamental functions, namely planning, organizing, actuating and controlling, planning becomes the key function. Managers organize, actuate and control to assure that goals are reached according to plans. Planning is not confined to top-level management. Its character and scope will vary with the hierarchical position of the planner within the organization, but unless some planning exists, it is doubtful that the worker is a manager.

Why Plan?

The need for planning stems from the fact that companies must operate in changing environments. Changes in the technological, economic, political, and social climate can have radical effects on the organization. Over 350,000 out of over 2,500,000 American firms go out of existence yearly, many as a result of either failing to predict the opportunities changes might bring or failing to adapt

Reprinted with permission from Managerial Planning, "A Look at Planning and Its Components," Harvey Kahalas, January/February 1982, pp. 13-16.

to those changes. Planning forces the manager to look beyond how things are now to how they might be in the future.

Planning channels efforts toward desired results, and by providing a sequence of efforts, minimizes unproductive behavior. The very act of evolving a plan nurtures a drive to achieve. The process forces the planner to gain a better understanding of each company activity and how they are interrelated. It results in improved utilization of company resources. It facilitates control by giving a manager the tool to measure performance of subordinates. As for the manager himself, planning permits him to provide confident and aggressive leadership. He can truly manage affairs instead of having affairs manage him.

All this is not to imply that planning has no drawbacks. By its very nature, planning is limited by the ability to predict future events. Should actual events turn out to be radically different than those assumed, much of the value of the plan may be lost. Planning can stifle initiative. Not only is it costly, but planning delays action and circumstances may warrant immediate action.

These limitations should not be used as excuses for dismissing the process entirely. While greatly detailed plans can produce a sterile environment in which initiative is stunted, the most effective plans allow room for some flexibility in their implementation. Even when occasions arise that demand immediate action, if that action is to be useful, some thought must be given to what the desired results should be and how best to achieve them given the resources available. Cost is a factor that must be considered in any organizational endeavor. A good plan must be efficient. In other words, it must contribute more to the attainment of company objectives than it costs to formulate and execute. But, one must consider that not planning may prove to be more costly in the long run if corrective measures must be taken to rectify the results of a decision made without proper planning.

Planning Dimensions

Planning can be analyzed along several dimensions. Theorists distinguish between single-use plans which deal with novel, one-time projects and standing plans that are designed to handle repetitive situations. The hierarchical dimension looks at planning in terms of the organizational level involved. The scope of a plan can range from a specific activity of a subsystem to an undertaking that involves the entire organization. Plans can be differentiated by the period of time covered or by the degree of flexibility built into them. Frequently, certain relationships between those dimensions occur. For example, planning done by top management (hierarchical dimension) tends to be more comprehensive (scope) than that done by individuals lower in the corporate chain of command. Long-range plans (time dimension) tend to be less mechanistic (flexible) in order to better deal with environmental changes which usually are larger in quantity and magnitude over a long span versus a short span of time.

Planning and Repetitiveness

The single-use plan deals with a unique, one-time situation. When the goal is achieved, the plan is no longer useful. Single-use plans can vary in scope, running from major projects, programs, special tasks to detailed plans. In the case of a major project, such as the construction of a new plant, success will depend on the integration of more detailed single-use plans.

In contrast to single-use plans, standing plans are established to be used repeatedly. They may be categorized in terms of the degree of detail in which they are stated. Policies are general guides to organizational behavior. As a means of implementing company policies, many more detailed pronouncements, in the form of rules, procedures and methods, are made. For example, a firm may have a policy of promoting from within the organization. Therefore, a procedure is established that requires the personnel department to screen all interested candidates presently employed by the firm before advertising the opening elsewhere.

By creating standing plans, management need not continually invent the wheel. Each time the circumstance arises, a predetermined plan spells out the decision that should be made. It allows the manager to delegate the responsibility for handling the situation to subordinates. A third advantage lies in the fact that similar conditions are handled in the same way throughout the organization.

Standing plans must be carefully designed if they are to achieve the results intended. Vague policy statements that are unsupported by more specific procedures are useless. Overly detailed statements, on the other hand, can lead to the inflexibility of red tape. Furthermore, standing plans must be periodically reexamined to determine if they are still useful.

Planning and the Time Dimension

The period covered by a plan can vary. The cutoff point separating long-range and short-range plans is arbitrary. Generally, plans for a span of two years or less are labelled short-term, while those of five years or more are long-term. Plans encompassing less than five years but more than two are called short- or long-range depending on the organization.

Many factors influence the planning time horizon of a company. Long-range has a different meaning for an electronics firm than for a timber grower. The size of the firm is also a determinant. The larger, more complex company must plan for longer periods, since its very size precludes quick changes in operations. Risk plays a role in that if the risk of a short-term outlook is small, the organization will concentrate on short-range planning. The more accurately a firm can predict conditions and adapt to them, the further into the future the company is willing to project its planning. Another important consideration is the costs involved. A plan should cover a long enough span of time to recover the company's investments in time, effort and money.

Long-range plans should form the framework within which short-range plans, usually concerned with current operations, are formed. Therefore, there should be a high degree of integration between the two. A short-range plan should be adopted only if it contributes to the goals as established by some long-range plans. Problems arise when implementation of the former hinders the latter. For example, buying used equipment to increase production capacity at a minimum of cost (short-range plan) can run counter to a long-range commitment to reduce the amount of factory pollutants. Managers should be continuously aware of the need to view immediate decisions as they may affect long-range plans.

Planning and Scope and Hierarchy

Plans can be categorized according to scope. The narrowest, a functional plan, deals with a specific part of a large endeavor, such as a sales plan. Incorporating a wider range of elements, a project like the construction of a new plant integrates diverse activities. A comprehensive plan includes the other two but is more complex and wider in scope, being more concerned with social, political and legal environmental factors. As the scope of a plan broadens, the level of uncertainty associated with it increases.

Scope and hierarchy are related planning dimensions. Generally, just as the scope of a position in the upper levels of an organization is broader than that in the lower echelons, so are the plans devised by top management.

Plans at a given level of the organization are dependent upon those made at levels above and below it. A sales department plan to increase sales volume by 10% can be directly affected by a corporate plan to discontinue a product line and by individual salesmen's plans not to work overtime. Some planning at lower levels requires guidelines first to be established from above. Corporate sales, forecasts are needed before territorial sales plans can be made. Furthermore, if functional plans are to be integrated, they all must be based on the same premises. The sales and production departments must do their planning based on the same corporate sales forecast if their operations are to run smoothly.

As a manager moves up the organizational ladder, more of his time is spent on planning and less on implementation. It is also desirable that the time span covered by that planning increase with the level of the position held. Typically, top management deals with long-range plans.

Planning and Flexibility

Flexibility is the capacity to make the proper changes when necessary. A scarcity of it can lock a company into a course of action that can lead to ruin, and an overabundance of the quality can produce a company that lacks direction. The degree of flexibility built into a plan can vary. To some extent, the environment may dictate the amount of rigidity. Where political and economic conditions are in constant flux, a firm must have flexible plans to survive, while more stable surroundings may permit less flexibility.

Since there are uncertainties in the best forecast, the greater the amount of flexibility built into a plan, the smaller the danger of losses arising from unexpected events. The ability to change a plan with a minimum of friction and cost is regarded by many managers as the most important principle of planning. However, as in all areas of planning, there is a cost-benefit tradeoff that must be taken into account. Building flexibility into a plan involves cost. The inflexible plan is probably the cheapest if it turns out that having the capability to change was unnecessary. Companies can resolve this dilemma by formulating relatively specific short-term operational plans within the context of more flexible long-range strategic plans.

Besides providing for adaptability within the plan, the planning process itself should be flexible. Once a plan is established, management must periodically review the situation and make any revisions deemed necessary. Planning should, therefore, be a continuous process.

Closely tied to the concept of flexibility is the extent to which operations are spelled out. The degree to which plans are programmed is dependent upon the task involved. The more complex the operation, as in the assembly of a car, or the greater the need for precision, as in the manufacturing of an electronic component, the greater the need for detailed advanced planning. Similarly, where divisions within the organization must be coordinated to accomplish an assignment, there must be more precision and detail in the planning statements. For example, when components of a product are manufactured in separate departments, product schedules must be carefully laid out to insure that parts are ready when needed.

Basic Planning Questions

Successful planning requires the sequential answering of the following "Five W's and How" questions:
1. Why must it be done?
2. What action is necessary?
3. Where will it take place?
4. When will it take place?
5. Who will do it?
6. How will it be done?

The *Why* signals the need for action. Serving as a screening device for the myriad of possible courses of action, it promotes including only those that are necessary in the plan. The answer to *What* provides the types and sequences of activities, and the facilities and equipment needed to perform them. The *Where* response gives the specific site for each phase of the plan. It highlights the need to insure the facilities are ready when needed. The answer to *When* also underscores the importance of timing. It should set up a timetable for each segment of the plan as well as for the entire operation. The *Who* response determines the identify of the person (or persons) to carry out the specified tasks and delineates his (their) duties and responsibilities. The *How* question serves as a check on the plan by forcing a consideration of whether it is complete and achieves what was intended.

Major Planning Steps

Before the actual planning process can begin, there must be an awareness of an opportunity. This problem/opportunity, which necessitates the formulation of a plan, should be clearly and concisely stated.

The first step is establishing objectives. Objectives specify the results to be achieved. To be operational, goals such as "increase sales" should be put into less general terms. Quantification is frequently used to do so.

The second phase calls for obtaining information about the activities involved. While complete information is rarely feasible, knowledge about the courses of action being considered and how they can affect the internal and external workings of the company is essential. Sources of such information include past solutions to problems, practices of other firms, observation, looking over records, and data from research and experiments.

Next, the information must be analyzed and classified. Each piece of data is examined in isolation and then in relation to the entire network of information.

The latter helps to uncover causal relationships. Material on similar topics is then grouped together for simplification.

The fourth step is to establish planning premises and constraints. Premises create the internal and external environment expected when the plan becomes operational. Forecasting is an essential part of the process. It provides an idea of the future directions of environmental factors. Planning premises include basic forecasts of such things as population, prices, costs, markets, public attitudes, and technology. Present company policies or forecast policies not yet made can be planning premises.

Keeping a set of premises for an organization that is both complete and up to date is difficult. Plans are interrelated and interdependent. Thus, every major plan and many minor ones, once adopted, become premises. For example, a decision to penetrate a new geographic market becomes an important premise in determining plans on sales force, advertising, possible expansion of production facilities, distribution channels, etc.

Premises about every aspect of the future environment of a plan is impossible. The set of premises used is limited to those which have the greatest impact on the implementation of a plan. It is to be expected that individuals in an organization will disagree on predictions about the future and on which factors are most crucial to a plan. Therefore, they must first be made to understand and agree to work on the same set of premises if a coordination of efforts is to be achieved. Clearly, a company in which one division manager operates on the assumption that the firm is committed to growth while another plans on the basis of stabilization will find its employees working at cross purposes, leading to confusing and costly operations. A degree of flexibility can be introduced by including several sets of premises under one umbrella and having different sets of plans developed on the basis of each one. Consequently, the company will be ready with a course of action depending upon the actual future conditions.

Not only does the planner face the issue of which premise to use, he must also decide how to make the best use of it. In the case of developing a program for a new product line, the planner may determine that a forecast of that industry's demand is crucial. The problem then becomes how to use that quantitative data in a way that is both meaningful and statistically correct.

The fifth step is to search for alternate plans. Frequently, the problem is not that of being unable to find more than one possible course, but rather reducing the number of them so that the more promising ones can be carefully examined. Mathematical techniques and the computer can be employed to simplify the process.

Next comes making the actual choice of a plan. The final decision may be made by an individual or a group. If analysis of alternative plans shows more than one course has a strong potential for success, the manager may opt for following several approaches to the problem/opportunity.

The seventh phase of the procedure spells out where, by whom, and when the activities should be carried out. In so doing, the components are arranged in the sequence which they are to be performed.

The final step introduces the concept of control. Procedures are set up to check compliance with the plan at various stages of implementation. They are also designed to provide feedback on whether the results actually produced are consistent with the plan.

Who Does the Planning?

All managers plan. The extent to which a given manager plans may vary from one extreme of doing it all personally to the other extreme of delegating the task to a specialized staff.

A manager who does all his own planning tends to produce a practical plan due to his first hand knowledge of the problem in theory and in practice. Since only he is involved in the process, plans can be altered quickly. The arrangement encourages the development of capable managers, but at the price of taking up a large amount of their time. With the need for gathering, analyzing, and evaluating greater quantities of information before a successful planning decision can be made, few organizations can afford to operate in this manner.

An alternative calls for the manager to plan using suggestions from associates. These ideas may be solicited before or after the initial formulation. Feeling that they have contributed, subordinates are more willing to support the plan. However, the approach means a longer planning period. Even if no revisions are needed to incorporate suggestions, some time must be allotted for others to review the program--time that under the first mentioned planning arrangement would be spent in implementation.

A third possibility has the manager presenting his subordinates with only a broad outline of a plan and charging them with providing the necessary details. On the plus side, the system develops the subordinate's planning skills and requires less of the manager's time. It allows those with special technical knowledge to input in those areas of their expertise. On the minus side, planning takes longer and the manager becomes removed from the process.

A fourth course is "bottom-up" planning, in which subordinates plan and managers approve. The manager's contribution to the plan becomes minimal, while the planning skills of subordinates are developed. The danger lies in producing plans that are unrealistic and impractical, since the planners may lack the information and perspective available to those in the upper levels of the organization.

The second approach seems to be the most popular. The best one depends on the circumstances and the individuals involved.

Participation in Planning

The extent and effectiveness of employee participation in planning depends on a number of factors. These include how the manager regards the organization, employee attitudes, and his subordinates. The manager who sees himself in a mechanistic system tends to view planning as his private domain. Similarly, the authoritarian leader or the believer in Theory X does not see the subordinate as a possible source of planning inputs.

The suggestion box system is one method of providing for employee participation in planning. The person who has to deal with a situation "on the line" can have insights into the problem and possible solutions that the staff man does not. Linking the program to an incentive, such as offering a bonus for the best suggestion in a given period, only adds to the motivational value of the scheme.

Many organizations have a basic planning committee made up of the chairman of the board, and the president and vice president of the company. This group is responsible for such things as establishing and enunciating the firm's major goals and plans. Reporting to it are subcommittees or project teams, consisting of a planning committee member and representatives of relevant functional areas of the organization. Project teams study issues brought up by the planning committee, collect pertinent data, evaluate alternative courses of action, and recommend a solution. The planning committee then coordinates and acts on the suggestions of various project teams.

Concluding Comments

Planning is a key managerial concern. Poor planning can mean organizational suicide. Good planning can mean the success that comes from being able to adapt and exploit the changing environment. Both internal and external factors affect the type and the manner of the planning a company conducts.

BUSINESS PLANNING IS PEOPLE PLANNING

David R. Leigh, Manager
Corporate Management Planning & Development,
Robbins & Myers, Inc.
Dayton, Ohio

How Robbins & Myers tied human resources planning to its business plan--and the lessons they learned.

For strategic business planning to succeed it must be tied to human resources planning. Conversely, for human resources planning to succeed, it must be tied to strategic business planning.

The purpose of the following article is to describe how we at Robbins & Myers designed and installed a viable and workable human resources planning process tied to our strategic business plan.

Although different organizations with different businesses and in different situations may require a different approach, there are some basic principles that apply to all human resources planning.

We give our experience to help straighten your path to a successful human resources program. We found that our successes were inevitably the result of following some basic principles. Our failures were--for the most part--related to forays into the frills of human resources planning. (For a corporate overview see box on page 56.)

Know Where You Are Going and Why

Planning is very difficult, especially if it's about the future. The very nature of the job of strategic human resources planning involves a process of anticipating a future which is uncertain and making assumptions to support that uncertainty.

Planners need to keep the following in mind.

Have clear goals. It is imperative that at the beginning of the planning process someone establish appropriate objectives for the system and verify that those objectives relate to the organization.

These goals should certainly include some kind of realistic and objective timetable for the implementation of the total system. This time frame, as we have found, is significantly more than one year.

Clarify your assumptions. Organizations are individual in terms of their position in time, culture, leadership style, marketing goals, growth objectives, etc. So, write down those assumptions related to your own individuality to make human resource planning valid.

These assumptions should not be used to hedge your bets, but rather as a rationale for launching or postponing any human resource planning efforts. Once written, they need to be viewed for accuracy against top management's business strategy.

Some of our assumptions were:

. Robbins & Myers continues to grow at a rate faster than the economy

- human resources could be a greater constraint to growth than capital availability
- major national, global and environmental changes would not have a greater impact on our company than business in general
- each strategy center was responsible for developing its own human resources rather than depending on other parts of the organization to provide future leadership

Some of these assumptions would later prove to be correct; others were not so valid.

Heed the Lessons We Learned

While human resources planning can evolve into a cult within itself, there are some basic guidelines which we found to be true in developing a strategic plan.

Do your research. Research means talking to people in the company early, finding out what they see as needs, and determining what problems they're having that might be helped by human resource planning.

It also means reading the books, talking to the consultants, and visiting other companies--but taking what you read and hear with a grain of salt. You may find, as we did, there are many sources to tell you how to do human resources planning, but there are relatively few who have successfully installed human resources planning in an integrated and systematic way.

Keep it simple. In all the research we conducted, it became quickly apparent that it would be easy to go overboard on this project. Therefore the rule that leaped forward was: keep it simple in the beginning.

Advanced computer models, Markoff modeling, and exotic demand and forecasting techniques may have a place, but not in the initial phase of human resource planning.

Know the business strategy. If the key human resource planner doesn't know the business strategy, don't bother with strategic human resource planning.

We must tie our human resource planning to the company's business needs and to the real problems the company is facing. Otherwise, the plan won't be used or seen as useful by line managers.

Forge a link between the business planning cycle and human resource planning. One of the most important factors in our success was our initial decision to tie human resources planning to our existing business cycle.

In doing so, we accomplished several things. First, line managers were encouraged to address human resource planning at the same time they were thinking of business planning.

Second, we piggybacked on an accepted process that was ingrained as a basic tenant for success in our organization. Third, we formed relationships with the corporate business planning manager working with him to develop an appropriate approach.

Finally, we used the annual strategic business planning manual as the vehicle to introduce human resources planning for the organization.

All these decisions turned out to be fortuitous. It boils down to one basic concept: strategic human resources planning must be tied to business planning to make sense.

Make human resource planning a corporate objective. With our human resource planning system, the president recognized that continued growth of Robbins & Myers might well be constrained by our inability to provide needed human resources for growth.

Since he saw this as more limiting than financial, marketing or production constraints, development of a human resources plan for each division was adopted as a key corporate objective for the fiscal year.

This one decision had more to do with human resources planning getting the attention it needed than any other single decision.

To support this corporate objective, divisional objectives were developed which in turn were included in the objectives for both strategy center managers and human resource managers within the divisions.

Establish a planning horizon. How long is a reasonable timeframe for strategic human resources planning?

We chose three points in time: 1) where we are now; 2) where we expected to be in two fiscal years (approximately 30 months); and 3) where we expected to be at the end of the coming fiscal year.

In larger organizations with stable businesses and where staff turnover is more predictable, longer time frames might be appropriate.

Set a realistic completion date. We probably tried to accomplish too much in too short a time period. More importantly, we did not provide enough face-to-face education to accomplish idea acceptance and commitment for a full response in the early stages.

On the other hand, the rapid growth rate of the organization provided significant logic and reason for the fast start-up.

Get the organization's attention. How do you get attention? From the beginning, it's a question of ownership. Whose program is this?

To the extent possible, your preliminary research contacts and foundation building should attempt to minimize the image of a "personnel department" or "corporate" program, if at all possible.

To eliminate it altogether is neither realistic nor pragmatic; but to the extent possible, minimizing a corporate image is an important part of the process.

Get support from all areas. To get strong support from the operating areas, organize the process to give line managers something they want. The challenge here involves timing the introduction of human resources planning with visible needs.

For example, you might tie the project into a request for related information from a line manager or division president.

Next is support from the top. Is there any personnel-related proposal that does not say support from the top is essential for success?

The top person in the organization must have an appreciation and see a need for human resources planning. We had this support, and it was invaluable.

The top person must also have a high respect for the human resources function and its previous contributions to the organization. If your group is seen as a personnel department whose primary job is that of record keeper, forget any broad human resources planning effort for the moment. It is imperative that the department's past history demonstrate support and contribution to the business success of the company.

Get key people involved in the process. Considerable efforts were taken to involve the individual plant human resources managers in the continuing process of developing and implementing the human resources system.

Although initial design was done primarily at the corporate level, there was a great deal of communication with the division human resources managers. In making this decision, we placed our human resources eggs in the baskets of our field human resources people for implementation. In most cases, this worked well. In a few, it did not.

Also built into the system was the inclusion of the local human resources manager in the business planning process. Where this had not been done previously, the human resources plan was instrumental in getting the person in this position involved in business planning.

Our program was most successful in those areas where the local human resources people were significantly involved in the business planning process.

However, by not sufficiently involving vice presidents and line managers, we may have made some initial mistakes. The corporate group funneled most of the information concerning the plans to the local human resources persons and initiated relatively little direct contact with line management.

This approach was in keeping with a more decentralized approach. But, if we were starting again, we might place additional emphasis on initial face-to-face contact with key line managers.

Provide sufficient structure and detail. The question of how much structure should be in the initial plan was raised frequently during the whole process.

Because this was our first attempt at corporate-wide strategic human resources planning, we elected to provide considerable detail during the first year. This decision was based primarily on the assumption that many of the managers involved had little or no formal exposure to human resources planning principles.

Our decision to provide significant detail was defensible on the basis of the need for direction and information. However, this decision also created a problem situation for the more autonomous and creative managers who challenged the degree of structure in the system.

The degree of structure was modified for the second year to allow more freedom for those managers who wished it.

Our Steps in the Planning Process

So what did we do? Our planning model is on an annual cycle starting in September, the first month of our fiscal year. At that time, material is sent to the human resources managers and key line managers and included as a separate chapter in the strategic planning manual.

These materials provided each of the strategy center managers with background material, assumptions, objectives, and a human resources calendar defining each section of the program, what was to be accomplished and the due dates.

We then identified the following steps to be taken in developing the human resources plan in accordance with the business plan:

Identify the strategic human resources issues. The first basic step in the process was the identification and analysis of the strategic human resources issues that related to the accomplishment of the business plan.

We provided sample issues on both a national and local basis. It was the responsibility of the strategy center manager to develop the relevant issues that would either constrain or possibly enhance the achievement of the business plan *before* it was formally proposed and approved.

Conduct an organizational analysis. The basic premise was that the form should follow function. Any change in the strategic direction for the business could well include organizational changes.

Thus, the second step in the program was an organizational analysis and the development of an organizational plan for one and two future fiscal years. These plans were developed by the strategy center based upon the changes in organizational structure seen as appropriate according to their strategic plans.

Forecast staffing requirements. Once additional slots and positions were identified in the organizational analysis, the next step included forecasting and staffing.

Each location made a basic forecast of *new* positions based upon probability and those positions with probabilities of more than 70% turnover.

In the first year we did not attempt to forecast normal turnover for two reasons. One, we were placing our emphasis on key positions that were highly predictable; and two, normal turnover is hard to predict accurately when you have small numbers of people in most classifications and strategy centers.

Once key staffing needs were identified, staffing tables were developed at both discipline and organizational levels to show the total number of people needed to fulfill the projected business plans.

Following the submission of the organizational and forecasting material, the corporate human resources staff analyzed projections, raised clarifying questions and summarized the data.

Develop succession plans. From that point, the managers developed individual succession plans for the key positions. This involved identifying replacements for the replacements.

Identify training requirements. Training managers also analyzed organizational and operational problems in light of the training requirements for the future.

Training proposals were presented by each group, and this information was then used at a corporate level to help establish training objectives and develop programs, including accelerated experience and affirmative action programs.

Identify individual development plans for key people. A final segment provided by the human resources staff was the identification of individual development plans for the key people who had been singled out in the succession planning process.

These individual development plans were presented in writing and then monitored throughout the year. Individual plans were limited to key people during the first year and were kept to a maximum of 5-to-10% of the exempt work force.

Present the plan for organizational review. The organizational review is the key end point in this planning process. Each division president makes a presentation to the president of the organization, the vice president of human resources, and the manager of corporate management planning and development.

In this presentation, the division president summarizes the human resources plan, including the issues, organizational changes, relevant forecasting information, and individual development plans for key personnel.

Human Resources Planning: A Flowchart

Robbins & Myers
Dayton, Ohio

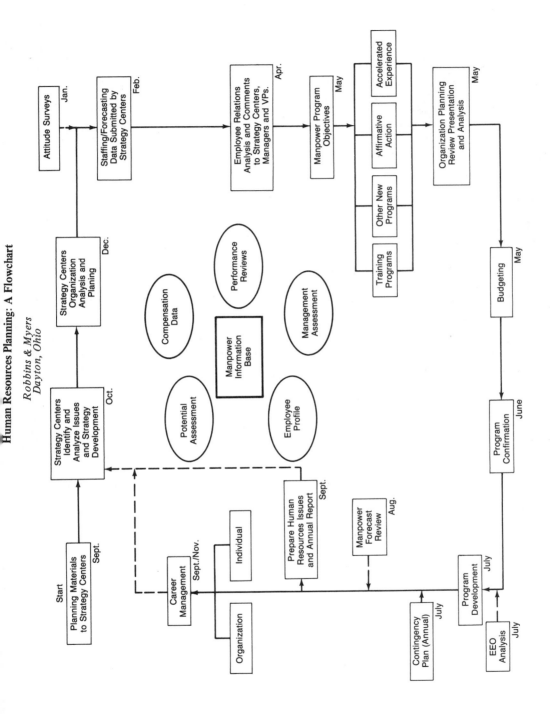

The organizational review is an opportunity to clarify and question the proposed plan. The manager's planning process is then confirmed so that he or she may proceed.

Develop a budget. After the organizational review, a budget is developed. If complete organization staffing tables have been prepared by location management, the staff budgeting becomes an easy process.

The budgeting of programs and other expenses at the corporate level is then done much more appropriately and accurately than in the past. Development programs can then be budgeted at local and corporate levels.

Conduct a follow up. During June and July, prior to the September start of the fiscal year, program confirmations are made, program development starts for the following year, EEO plans are developed, and manpower forecasts made the previous February are reviewed for accuracy. Thus, recruiting plans can be developed for both college and corporate-level recruiting systems.

The plan then recycles so that the following September or October, the whole process is repeated again in sequence with the business planning cycle.

One note should be made. During the first year, the career management section was not implemented. At the time it was felt that adding that additional element to the implementation of the program was well beyond the capabilities of the system.

In the second year of the program, we implemented the career management section on a division basis with each division selecting appropriate career management elements to fit its particular business cycle.

The model also includes a database that feeds information into the various elements of the program and becomes the source for determining what decisions are made at various points in the process.

Reviewing Our Initial Results

What do we feel we achieved? First, we identified a human resources system that was a logical outgrowth of the business planning cycle. We established in the minds of management that human resources planning is a continuing process that develops from the business plan.

Secondly, we implemented a system that worked surprisingly well for a first effort. Finally, we were able to modify elements of the program based on line management's experience and provide an improved process for the second year.

THE ETHICS OF MBO

Charles D. Pringle
University of Houston at Clear Lake City
Justin G. Longenecker
Baylor University

Despite the widespread adoption of Management by Objectives (MBO), and its extensive coverage in the literature, few questions have been raised regarding the ethical issues involved in this form of management. Points in the MBO process that are particularly likely to create ethical problems for organizational members are identified, and some means that management can use to increase the likelihood that its MBO program will be conducted in an ethical manner are suggested.

Since Drucker [1954] first coined the term "Management by Objectives" (MBO), a wide variety of organizations--profit and nonprofit, large and small--have adopted this planning technique in various forms. One writer, Odiorne, estimates that "MBO is *the* dominant form of management in large corporations and in government" [1979, p. v].

Although the MBO concept encompasses planning, motivation, management development, control, and performance appraisal, it is the last application that provides much of the impetus for current organizational adoptions of MBO. A number of court rulings and decisions of the Equal Employment Opportunity Commission emphasize that performance appraisals must be based on clear, job related standards that are nondiscriminatory. One U.S. Supreme Court ruling (*Albemarle Paper Company v. Moody*, 1975), for example, held that subjective supervisory ratings were an insufficient defense against charges of discrimination because such ratings failed to evaluate employees against specific job performance criteria.

An incentive for federal agencies to adopt MBO came from the Civil Service Reform Act of 1978. Among its provisions, this act requires that actual job performance--rather than length of service--be used to grant or deny merit pay raises to certain categories of government employees. The National Aeronautics and Space Administration, for example, replaced its subjective performance appraisal system with MBO in 1980 in an attempt to link pay to performance and to demonstrate objectivity, fairness, and a meaning to rating differences.

Is MBO Inherently Ethical?

Despite the widespread adoption of MBO and its extensive coverage in the literature, few explicit questions have been raised about the ethical issues involved in this form of management. A review of the academic literature and material written for practitioners suggests that most writers assume that MBO, properly implemented, is inherently ethical; few of them address the issue. But precisely

Reprinted from The Academy of Management Review, 1982, Vol. 7, No. 2, 305-12, by permission of the author and publisher.

what constitutes proper implementation is subject to some debate [McConkie, 1979]. Furthermore, comments from scores of engineers, nurses, teachers, and other professionals enrolled in night division MBA courses lead to the disturbing conclusion that MBO is quite capable of posing ethical problems for organizational members.

Unethical acts in organizational life typically are viewed as individual failures to conform to some moral principle. And, indeed, they are. Such a view is incomplete, however, in failing to recognize the systemic forces (including cultural norms) that also influence such behavior. Allen has pointed out the weakness of concentrating exclusively on individual behavior in evaluating ethical performance:

> Blaming individual victims is more or less pointless. . . . It would be much more helpful to focus a significant percentage of our energies on finding out what in the situation had encouraged the behavior that concerned us [1980, p. 32].

Managerial systems are significant parts of organizational cultures. They may stimulate or discourage ethical performance. Because MBO is a widely used managerial system, its impact on organizational ethics may be far reaching. It is appropriate, therefore, to examine its moral dimensions.

Ethical problems in MBO programs are most likely to arise as a result of the goal setting and performance appraisal processes. These "clearly constitute the heart and flow of Management by Objectives" [McConkie, 1979, p. 29]. Hence, this examination will concentrate on these particular processes.

Setting Objectives

In the goal setting phase of MBO, two areas are particularly likely to create ethical problems for organizational members: the process of determining the actual objectives for subordinates and various characteristics of the objectives themselves.

Subordinates' Objectives

The goal setting process of MBO is often conceptualized as a form of participative management in which the superior and subordinate first discuss and then jointly establish objectives for the subordinate. McConkie indicates that only 2 of the 40 authorities on MBO whose works he surveyed "suggest anything other than involving subordinates in goal setting from the initial stages" [1979, p. 32]. Recent studies of MBO participants [Hollman, 1976; Stein, 1979] also emphasize the importance subordinates place on participation. Certainly, in view of the value attached to individual worth by society, a management system that gives organizational members a greater voice in setting their own goals seems ethical and congruent with societal values.

Obviously, individual differences among subordinates must be considered. Not all employees desire to participate equally. Although a minor problem may exist in forcing participation on unwilling participants, the larger issue concerns the extent to which individuals who wish to participate--and are led to believe that MBO is a participative system--are denied a voice in establishing their own objectives. The present authors' experience indicates that part time MBA students involved in MBO programs at work express some cynicism when MBO is presented in class as a form of participative management. In many of their organizations, which purport to practice MBO, objectives are formulated at the top and passed down with little or no discussion. These objectives then become "theirs," and they are evaluated on how well they attain them.

Carroll and Tosi [1973] report on an unpublished study by Stein who, after interviewing several hundred managers in an MBO program, concluded that managers may feel forced to accept objectives that they honestly feel are unrealistic or undesirable because they are unable to argue effectively against them. If the objectives are to be used to evaluate subordinates' performance, and pay and progress up the organizational ladder are based primarily on the degree to which the objectives are attained, then is it not ethical at least to involve the subordinates in formulating those objectives?

The answer to this question by ardent supporters of MBO is not clear. McConkey believes, at one extreme, that "the real value of MBO is participation in the objective-setting process, not the objectives themselves" [1976, p. 169]. But, if the objectives are not important, then the entire process is a sham to be taken seriously by no one. As Pinder puts it:

> MBO programs are often simply legitimized systems of phony participation, in which the fiction is maintained that the subordinate is making a real input into planning work objectives and procedures. Such situations smack of Machiavellianism and are quickly self-defeating [1977, p. 388].

At the other extreme, Odiorne, a major advocate of MBO as a system of management, argues that whether participative or autocratic means are used to establish the subordinates' objectives is immaterial because "the system is really neutral to such value judgments" [1979, p. 286].

> These days some managers and professionals seem to expect to be invited to participate in goal setting. If you have no reason to think subordinates will withhold effort or try to deceive the organization, then let them participate. In those rare cases where you suspect some serious foot-dragging, don't let any false lust for participative management deter you from *imposing* goals. Breaking a general rule about allowing participation can be done if there is good reason [Odiorne, 1979, p. 113].

But management systems are not neutral to value judgments. If MBO is to be introduced properly into an organization, the reasons for the system (i.e., the benefits to the organization and its employees) and the effects of the system on the participants should be fully discussed with all organizational members. Once the appropriate groundwork has been laid and the employees have learned to set objectives then it seems unethical not to permit them to participate in establishing their objectives, because participation is an integral part of MBO. If the MBO process is to be ethical, it must concern itself not only with the objectives themselves, but the means by which they are set.

The problems resulting from management pressures on subordinates to quantify objectives in order to make them measurable and verifiable are well known. In a survey of 428 lower and middle level managers in 10 organizations in business and government, Stein [1979] found that the most oft-mentioned problem in these MBO programs was the pressure to write measurable objectives even if unrealistic quantitative goals resulted.

Forcing subordinates to quantify their objectives, however, requires them to be evaluated on something decidedly less than their full performance. As Levinson states: "The greater the emphasis on measurement and quantification, the more likely the subtle, nonmeasurable elements of the task will be sacrificed" [1970, p. 127]. The "subtle, nonmeasurable elements" that may be sacrificed include such qualities as concern for others, adherence to moral principles, and commitment to fair play. Quantification per se does not require a neglect of other factors. However, a system such as MBO that stresses quantitative goals turns the spotlight on the numbers and leaves other values in the shadows.

Quantitative goals all too easily give rise to "Catch-22" situations in which the subordinate who meets his or her goals is informed that next year's objectives must be even higher. As Muczyk pointedly asks: "How many managers will accept as a satisfactory goal the maintenance of last year's level?" [1979, p. 54]. Although progress is expected in most jobs, subordinates may feel that the highly lauded MBO program gives their superiors an unethical ratchet.

Those who feel pressured to meet quantitative goals by neglecting important values also may experience guilt in their personal lives. Individuals who enter certain professions or careers hoping to enrich the lives of others and improve the world about them may eventually find themselves sacrificing their idealism as the pressure to meet more quantifiable goals intensifies and consumes most of their working hours. Over time, as the major motivation for their career becomes displaced, they may be plagued by guilt feelings as they grow increasingly disillusioned over the directions their lives have taken. For instance, human service professionals who are faced with heavy case workloads find it more difficult to maintain their idealism, commitment, and compassion and are more likely to experience "burnout" than are workers with lighter caseloads [Cherniss, 1980, pp. 161-163].

Compounding the problem is the emphasis that quantitative goals are likely to place on subordinate job performance, while little, if any emphasis is given the employee's personal goals. Performance objectives stress activities related to the subordinate's job assignment; personal goals focus on improving the individual's interpersonal skills, technical skills, and preparation for advancement [Carroll & Tosi, 1973]. When the former are emphasized at the expense of the latter, the subordinate may conclude that he or she is being used by the organization to further its goals. "Why should an individual be expendable for someone else and sacrifice himself for something that is not part of his own cherished dreams?" [Levinson, 1970, p. 130].

In their analysis of Tenneco's goal setting program, Ivancevich, McMahon, Streidl, and Szilagyi [1978] caution that personal development goals must not be relegated to a "second-class citizenship" because they may play an important role in improving the quality of work life for organizational members. Subordinates improving the quality of work life for organizational members. Subordinates themselves feel this need. Interviews with 48 managers in one MBO program indicated that one-third believed the program would be improved by the inclusion of personal objectives in addition to performance goals [Carroll & Tosi, 1973].

Goals that emphasize only part of the individual's job, then, may not be considered fair by the subordinate. But, the fairness question has yet another dimension. In most organizational systems, one's job performance reflects more than the efforts and ability of that person. The more an individual's effectiveness depends on the performance of others, the less that individual can be held responsible for the outcome of her or his efforts [Levinson, 1970]. For this reason, some theorists have suggested that the manager and subordinates act as a team in setting, first, group objectives and then individual objectives to increase cooperation and helping behavior within the unit [Likert & Fisher, 1977]. The extent to which this mode of objective setting has been adopted is not clear.

Even if all of these problems can be overcome and the subordinate, in collaboration with his or her superior, is able to formulate an acceptable, comprehensive, fair set of objectives, appropriate behavior will not necessarily follow. Odiorne maintains that "activity will follow goals at the same level of excellence. Bad goals produce worthless activity. Good goals produce rewarding activity" [1979, p. 110]. But "good" goals such as higher profits, increased sales, greater market share, or a job promotion can be attained through patently unethical means.

Performance Appraisal

Emphasis on ends rather than means is, at once, MBO's greatest potential strength and weakness. Concentration on goal attainment contributes to the fairness of the system by lending an air of rational objectivity to performance appraisal. As an added plus, emphasis on specific goals helps subordinates know exactly what is expected of them and in what direction to channel their efforts. This knowledge may well decrease job ambiguity, a source of stress for some individuals.

Concentration on ends rather than means in performance appraisal also is commendable because of the greater autonomy granted to members of the organizations. Any system that permits and encourages maturity and independence on the part of organizational members shows practical respect for the worth and dignity of people. The greater freedom accorded by MBO, therefore, represents an advancement in the attainment of this important value.

On the other hand, appraisal based primarily on ends may produce overwhelming pressure on subordinates to attain the objectives.

The practice of setting very difficult goals and then applying pressure to reach these goals creates conditions favorable to producing unethical behavior. Is it always clear to personnel that they are expected to attain goals only within the confines of ethical performance? Or, is the emphasis upon goals so intense that attention is directed to the goals and not to means of achieving those goals? [Longenecker & Pringle, 1981, p. 89].

67

Levinson terms the typical method of practicing performance appraisal under MBO a "reward-punishment psychology that serves to intensify the pressure on the individual" [1970, p. 134]. Once the employee's goals have been approved by the superior, the goals then become the subordinate's "own." As Levinson so colorfully puts it: "Presumably, he has committed himself to what he wants to do. He has said it and he is responsible for it. He is thereafter subject to being hoisted on his own petard" [1970, p. 128].

There are myriad instances of employees using unethical means to attain goals regarded as extremely important by their superiors. Three examples will suffice:

(1) The infamous Equity Funding scandal in the early 1970s revolved around a situation in which a chief executive established such high growth objectives that subordinates began to falsify records and create fictitious insurance policies for nonexistent people.

(2) Plant supervisors at a Chevrolet truck plant in Michigan who were having problems meeting their weekly production goals complained to their superior that the goals were predicated on the unrealistic assumption that everything would go perfectly. Their superior replied: "I don't care how you do it--just do it." To "do it," the supervisors installed a secret control box that sped up the assembly line and increased production. The assembly line workers, however, discovered the secret mechanism. The supervisors were temporarily suspended and later transferred, and the company had to award $1 million in back pay to the United Auto Workers [Getschow, 1979, p. 26].

(3) A scandal erupted at H. J. Heinz Company in 1979 when middle managers chose to falsify reports in the "pressure-cooker" atmosphere of the company's U.S.A. division. As one former marketing official stated it: "When we didn't meet our growth targets, the top brass really came down on us. And everybody knew that if you missed the targets enough, you were out on your ear" [Getschow, 1979, p. 1].

Surveys report similar conclusions. Carroll found that over 64 percent of the 238 American business executives he surveyed across a number of industries "agreed" or "somewhat agreed" with the statement that "managers today feel under pressure to compromise personal standards to achieve company goals" [1975, p. 77]. An in-house survey of Pitney Bowes [1977] managers revealed that 59 percent of them regarded pressure to compromise personal ethics to achieve corporate goals as a problem.

The behavior of superiors is the most important factor influencing unethical decisions in organizations, according to a survey of 1,2227 *Harvard Business Review* readers [Brenner & Molander, 1977]. Hence, it may be that a strong, ethical stand by the chief executive officer (CEO) is a necessary, but insufficient, condition for ethical behavior among subordinates. A survey of presidents and CEOs of the *Fortune* 500 companies revealed that 34 percent of the 237 respondents felt that the best way a president can have a real impact on the ethical climate of the corporation is through setting reasonable goals "so that subordinates are not pressured into unethical actions" [Dagher & Spader, 1980, p. 56]. Of course, a CEO may state that he or she subscribes to a rigid code of ethics and expects such behavior from all members of the organization. At the same time the CEO may be setting goals for his or her subordinate manager "that cannot be achieved without deviating from that standard. The executive can further state that if these goals can't be achieved, it is because the manager does not know how to manage" [Dagher & Spader, 1980, p. 56].

Ethical performance appraisal requires a concern for the means of attaining the objectives as well as the degree to which they are reached.

> The means used to accomplish goals must be evaluated. It is obviously of great importance that the organization not reward behavior that is unethical, illegal, or that creates future or other current problems for the organization. A manager might achieve his goals at the expense of creating ill will or future problems for the organization or by contributing to the nonaccomplishment of the goals of others [Carroll & Tosi, 1973, p. 118].

Recognizing the problem, McConkey recommends that results-oriented evaluations not be formally introduced until two or three years after MBO has been implemented. "This helps keep positive emphasis on the system as a way of managing rather than having it generate distrust and fear because the manager is worrying about being evaluated while he is learning how to apply the system" [1976, p. 152]. But, it must be added, even these results-oriented evaluations must be concerned with the means used to attain the results.

Broader Implications

Although MBO involves some positive ethical values, it can, potentially, produce ethical problems of two types: (1) the process of setting objectives and various characteristics of the objectives themselves give rise to important ethical implications for subordinates; and (2) performance appraisals that heavily emphasize goal attainment can create pressures that encourage subordinates to reach their goals regardless of the means they employ. There is an even larger issue. An MBO program that is not well planned, thoroughly discussed--in advance--with all participants, and ethically conducted is simply a unilateral attempt by top management to increase worker productivity. Such charades are doomed to failure. Furthermore, the failure itself has ethical implications.

Failed--and failing--MBO programs are likely to create or enhance adversary relationships between superior and subordinate, thereby increasing distrust and job dissatisfaction. Participants understandably become skeptical of management theory and leery of any new program that management attempts to foist upon them in the future. Such skepticism leads to self-fulfilling prophecies that doom even sound, well-conceived efforts. Carroll and Tosi report such a problem at one company:

> Many managers at Black & Decker did not initially have a positive reaction to the new MBO program and felt that it was simply another fad that would be soon forgotten, because they had experienced new programs in the past that were later abandoned. Our interview results suggested that this negative reaction based on past experiences may have significantly influenced the manner in which certain managers carried out the goal-setting and performance-review process [1973, pp. 126-127].

69

Is Ethical MBO Attainable?

Donaldson and Waller [1980] point out that no behavioral act is necessarily free of moral implications. Certainly, the adoption and implementation of MBO comprise a series of acts fraught with ethical considerations. MBO has serious and powerful effects on the lives of its participants. How, then, is it possible for management to ensure that its MBO program is conducted in an ethical manner?

Organizational Priorities

The first action management must take is to create and foster a climate in which ethical behavior is not only encouraged but expected. All too often, technical and economic matters take priority over ethical behavior, frequently through simple lack of any managerial statement regarding ethical standards. Top management must make it clear that the manner in which goals are established, the characteristics of those goals, and the means used to attain the goals must be within ethical guidelines. Fletcher L. Byrom, Chairman of the Board of Koppers Company, commented as follows on his efforts to clarify organizational priorities:

> The thing we as a corporation wanted to do was to remove what might be considered by some to be an ambiguity between economic performance and ethical conduct.... And we wanted to make it clear that we did not expect anybody to do something that was inconsistent with their ethical standards under the guise that it was for the benefit of the Company [Steiner, 1978].

Weber refers to this process of clarifying the role of ethics within the organization as "institutionalizing" ethics, a process he defines as "getting ethics formally and explicitly into daily business life, making it a regular and normal part of business" [1981, p. 47]. This process begins with policy making at the top management level and ultimately integrates ethics "into all daily decision making and work practices for all employees [1981, p. 47]. One means of accomplishing this end is to develop and disseminate a code of ethics to organizational members.

Code of Ethics

Ethical codes often are criticized as ineffective and immaterial. When properly used, they can provide an explicit statement of behavioral expectations. A well conceived code of ethics can be used to express the standards supported by organizational leaders. These standards should include clear statements of top management's expectations regarding the ethics of establishing and attaining goals.

A majority of the respondents to the *Harvard Business Review* survey [Brenner & Molander, 1977] believed that an ethical code would help executives define the limits of acceptable conduct and refuse unethical requests. For such a code to be effective, organizational members must be convinced that top management takes the code seriously, and the code should be made a part of the orientation program for new employees. Over time, as top managers demonstrate through their daily behavior adherence to ethical norms, lower level participants are likely to conform. Conformity to ethical norms can be strengthened further through the reinforcement of ethical behavior.

Behavioral Reinforcement

Without enforcement, no code is likely to be taken seriously. Fred T. Allen, Chairman and CEO of Pitney Bowes, urges rigorous application of ethical codes:

> How should the corporation respond to the individual who is guilty of violating its ethical code? From the pinnacle of the corporate pyramid to its base, immediate punitive action, commensurate with the degree of transgression, is the only choice. The corporation thus says in the clearest terms that it will not tolerate corporate wrongdoing of any kind by anyone [Allen, n.d., p. 23].

Punishment of a manager for unethical actions is quickly communicated throughout the organization. Payne suggests that "organization members learn vicariously from the ways in which deviates are reinforced" [1980, p. 413].

In the opposite vein, highly ethical behavior should be positively reinforced. This process can be accomplished most effectively by making judgments of adherence to the organization's ethical code a regular part of the performance appraisal process. The means used by subordinates to attain their goals should be an integral part of appraisals.

On a broader scale, Hegarty and Sims, in an intriguing laboratory experiment, demonstrated that "individual behavior is controlled not only by the consequences of the behavior (reinforcement), but by the stimulus environment present prior to the occurrence of the behavior" [1978, p. 54]. They hypothesize, based on their findings, that if top management's statement of ethical policy is strong and explicit, ethical behavior within the organization will increase, which will reduce the need to engage in heavy "after-the-fact" control activities.

A Suggested Ethical Criterion

As the ethical criterion of organizational relationships, Donaldson and Waller [1980] offer the traditional Golden Rule--do unto others as you would have them do unto you. (If the Golden Rule terminology is objectionable to some, then Donaldson and Waller suggest calling it the "Prescriptive Groundrule.")

This criterion can be operationalized through psychological role-reversal to test the ethical legitimacy of behavioral relationships between A (a superior) and B (a subordinate).

> The legitimacy of the relationship does not depend on A's imagining himself in B's position with A's own values; it does depend on A's imagining himself in B's position with B's values. We transfer B's values to A, and *vice versa*, because their respective values are part of the structure of the situation. This can be generalized to an indefinitely large number of people [Donaldson & Waller, 1980, p. 50].

This conceptual framework certainly provides a starting point. Few managers, for instance, would appreciate: being placed under an MBO system that was not previously discussed with them, having "their" objectives dictated to them, being evaluated solely on the attainment of goals that are quantifiable, and having overwhelming pressure placed on them to reach their objectives regardless of the means used.

Conclusion

The foregoing analysis indicates that the goal setting and performance appraisal processes involved in MBO are susceptible to ethical problems. Hence, the first step in developing an ethical MBO program is an awareness of this susceptibility. The MBO processes that are particularly vulnerable to unethical behavior have been examined.

To reduce the likelihood that unethical behavior will occur, it is suggested that top management: place ethical behavior high on its list of organizational priorities, develop a clear statement of behavioral expectations, and appropriately reinforce employee behavior.

MBO is not inherently ethical, but ethical MBO is attainable. It is hoped that academicians, consultants, and practitioners will become more conscious of-- and responsive to--the ethics of MBO.

References

Albemarle Paper Company v. Moody, 422 U.S. 405 (1975), 10 FEP Cases 1181.

Allen, F. T. Business ethics, The management of international corporate citizenship, Top Management Report. Washington: International Management and Development Institute, n.d.

Allen, R. F. The Ik in the office. Organizational Dynamics, 1980, 8 (3), 27-41.

Brenner, S. N., & Molander, E. A. Is the ethics of business changing? Harvard Business Review, 1977, 55 (1), 57-71.

Carroll, A. B. Managerial ethics: A post-Watergate view. Business Horizons, 1975, 18 (2) 75-80.

Carroll, S. J., Jr., & Tosi, H. L., Jr. Management by objectives: Applications and research. New York: Macmillan, 1973.

Cherniss, C. Professional burnout in human service organizations. New York: Praeger, 1980.

Dagher, S. P., & Spader, P. H. Poll of top managers stresses education and leadership-by-example as strong forces for higher standards. Management Review, 1980, 69 (2) 54-57.

Donaldson, J., & Waller, M. Ethics and organization. Journal of Management Studies, 1980, 17, 34-55.

Drucker, P. F. The practice of management. New York: Harper & Row, 1954.

Getschow, G. Some middle managers cut corners to achieve high corporate goals. Wall Street Journal, November 8, 1979, pp. 1, 26.

Hegarty, W. H. & Sims, H. P., Jr. Organizational philosophy related to unethical decision behavior: An experiment. Proceedings of the Eastern Academy of Management, 1978, 53-55.

Hollmann, R. W. Supportive organizational climate and managerial assessment of MBO effectiveness. Academy of Management Journal, 1976, 19, 560-576.

Ivancevich, J. M., McMahon, J. T., Streidl, J. W., & Szilagyi, A. D., Jr. Goal setting: The Tenneco approach to personnel development and management effectiveness. Organizational Dynamics, 1978, 6 (3), 58-80.

Levinson, H. Management by whose objectives? Harvard Business Review, 1970, 48 (4), 125-134.

Likert, R., & Fisher, M. S. MBGO: Putting some team spirit into MBO. Personnel, 1977, 54 (1), 40-47.

Longenecker, J. G., & Pringle, C. D. Management. 5th ed. Columbus, Ohio: Charles E. Merrill, 1981.

McConkey, D. D. How to manage by results. 3rd ed. New York: AMACOM, 1976.

McConkie, M. L. A clarification of the goal setting and appraisal processes in MBO. Academy of Management Review, 1979, 4, 29-40.

Muczyk, J. P. Dynamics and hazards of MBO application. Personnel Administrator, 1979, 24 (5), 51-62.

Odiorne, G. S. MBO II: A system of managerial leadership for the 80s. Belmont, Cal.: Fearon Pitman, 1979.

Payne, S. L. Organizational ethics and antecedents to social control processes. Academy of Management Review, 1980, 5, 409-414.

Pinder, C. C. Concerning the application of human motivation theories in organizational settings. Academy of Management Review, 1977, 2, 384-397.

Pitney Bowes. Management report. Stamford, Conn.: February 9, 1977.

Stein, C. I. Objective management systems: Two to five years after implementation. Personnel Journal, 1979, 54, 525-528ff.

Steiner, J. B. A conversation with Fletcher L. Byrom, transcript of an interview. Center for the Study of Business and Society, California State University, Los Angeles, 1978.

Weber, J. Institutionalizing ethics into the corporation. MSU Business Topics, 1981, 29 (2), 47-52.

SOCIO-POLITICAL FORECASTING:
A NEW DIMENSION TO STRATEGIC PLANNING

Ian H. Wilson

As with any current fancy, there is the danger that management's romance with socio-political forecasting will turn out to be a short-lived affair, weakened by lack of substantive contribution to business planning and crushed by the exaggerated claims of a few enthusiastic proponents.

This would be a pity, if it happened. The need for this new dimension to strategic planning is real and, to a large extent, recognized by managers. What is mainly lacking is an armory of analytical tools and techniques that are available to, say, economic and technological forecasting. And these take time, skill and discipline to develop. Now is the time, then, for a serious evaluation--by managers and forecasters alike--of the progress to date, the potential to be realized, and the programs of research and action to be implemented.

Social Change and the Need for Forecasting

The instincts of those pioneering companies which turned, in the late Sixties, toward some experimentation with social forecasting were right. Something basic *is* changing on the social scene, something that will have profound impact on business, something to which business needs time to adjust. And the hope was, and is, that this forecasting will provide the necessary lead time for companies to develop their "strategies of adjustment."

Reprinted from University of Michigan Business Review, July 1974, Vol. 26, No. 4, 15-25, with permission of the publisher.

What are these changes? It is perhaps misleading, in an age and world of discontinuous change, to single out any one particular trend but, for purposes of this article, we can focus on the phenomenon of changing societal values and expectations and the resulting increased politicizing of our economy.

The years 1965-70 were a watershed in U.S. history. The analogy is apt for, since then, the streams of our social thinking have started to flow in quite different directions. We need only to consider the changing values inherent in our new perceptions about the right relationship between man and woman, the majority and minorities, the individual and institutions, the economy and ecology, business and society. Among the consequences of these value shifts will be a re-writing of society's "charter of expectations" of corporate performance, and a shaking of what I have termed the "seven pillars of business," those basic values that we have up to now considered to be eternal verities undergirding our business system--growth; technology; profit; private property (as it applies to corporations); managerial authority; "hard work"; company loyalty.

Clearly, expectations are on the march and institutions must scurry to keep up with them. By 1970 it was obvious that business could no longer be satisfied with a complacent "other things being equal" formulation to cover the areas of its planning that lay outside traditional economic and technological forecasting. The impact of the various "movements" of the period broke suddenly and forcefully on the unprotected flanks of many companies, causing major disruptions in their plans of action. Lacking strategies to deal with these unexpected forces, companies were forced back on hastily improvised tactics that did little more than stave off one assault before another came.

Such a course of reluctant and belated *reaction* is the antithesis of corporate enterprise and initiative on which companies pride themselves and which is an essential prerequisite for the future vitality and legitimacy of the corporation. If business is to reverse this situation and engage in *proactive* strategies to deal with changing social and political forces, it seems logical to conclude that it must, as one condition for success, expand its forecasting system to include these new factors.

A Critique of Objections

Up to this point there would most probably be general agreement with this line of reasoning: the need is apparent and managers are aware, if not of the rewards for success, at least of the penalties for failure. Where uncertainty, and perhaps disagreement, sets in is over the feasibility, scope and effectiveness of any formal venture into socio-political forecasting. The feeling is widespread that there is a basic incompatibility between the "soft" data of social and political analyses and the "hard" data of economic and technological forecasting: that the key strategic issues for business will be almost exclusively economic and financial; and that there is no satisfactory way of making socio-political forecasting contribute effective inputs into the strategic planning process.

Yet experience suggests that each one of these assumptions is subject to rebuttal. And the rebuttals are, of course, inter-linked in their rationale.

First, the "hardness" of economic and technological forecasting data seems to be an assumption based on the fact that these data can be more easily quantified. Just how "hard" the data really may be is subject to question when one considers, for instance, the record in economic forecasting. This is said, *not* to damn economic forecasting, but simply to call in question the validity of this alleged dichotomy between "hard" and "soft" data. Forecasts, in *any* classification, may be "right" or "wrong"--which is surely an important and valid difference. But I think we should lay to rest any objection to socio-political forecasting that is based on a supposed incompatibility of data with the more traditional inputs to corporate planning.

A somewhat similar dichotomy appears to underlie the second objection which states, in effect, that the central issues for business will remain economic (market conditions, costs of labor and materials, etc.) and financial (cash flow, availability of capital, etc.), while social and political factors will be peripheral. Admittedly, the rebuttal involves a somewhat circular argument: namely, socio-political forecasting so far undertaken indicates the key importance to business of certain social and political issues which, in turn, argues the case for more such forecasting in the future. For instance, a priority analysis of social pressures on the corporation, undertaken in 1972 for the Public Issues Committee of General Electric's Board of Directors, highlighted the following key corporate issues of the future:

1. Constraints on corporate growth--a spectrum of issues ranging from national growth policy through economic controls and environmental protection to questions of antitrust policy and industrial structure.
2. Corporate governance--including matters of accountability, personal liability of managers and directors, board representation, and disclosure of information.
3. Managing the "new work force"--dealing with the growing demands for job enlargement, more flexible scheduling, more equality of opportunity, greater participation and individualization.
4. External constraints on employee relations--the new pressures from government (EEO, health and safety, "federalization" of benefits), unions (coalition bargaining) and other groups (class-action suits, "whistle-blowing").
5. Problems and opportunities of business-government partnership-- including a redefinition of the role of the private sector in public problem-solving.
6. "Politicizing" of economic decision-making--the growing government involvement in corporate decisions through consumerism, environmentalism, industrial reorganization, inflation control, etc.

It is quite beside the point to argue whether this (or some comparable) listing of issues is *more* or *less* important than economic, financial and technological issues. All that is needed is agreement that they are, and will be, *as* important and central to a corporation, and therefore deserve the same careful forecasting, monitoring and analysis that we now give to the state of the economy, the growth (or decline) of markets and the flow of funds.[1]

What, then, of the third objection? Are socio-political forecasts and analyses doomed forever to be interesting "coffee-table studies" and nothing more? Is it really true that there is no way of placing them in the mainstream of corporate planning? Here perhaps the best answer is provided by our early and, I think, promising experience at General Electric.[1]

Socio-Political Forecasting at General Electric

Socio-political forecasting emerged as a separate operation in General Electric in May, 1967, with the establishment of Business Environment Studies (BES) in the corporate-level Personnel and Industrial Relations component. (In retrospect, there is some organizational logic to the fact that this "people-oriented" forecasting grew up in the "people function" of the corporation.) At that time, with social and political change already starting to accelerate, it seemed to us that the Relations function of the business was in as much need of a forecasting operation and a futures dimension, in order to do an intelligent job of long-range planning, as were the marketing and technical functions of the company.

Personnel and industrial relations policies and practices are no exceptions to the general rule of institutional inertia. Indeed, the probability is that systemic change occurs more slowly here than in other areas of the business, if for no other reason than that it is inherently more sensitive and difficult a task to deal with people than with technologies. In this area above all, therefore, companies need lead time for strategies of adjustment. 1967 was, in other words, not too soon to be thinking about the relations policies that might be needed in 1974.

The area of our search lay in the broad sweep of social, political and economic trends in the United States over the next ten years or so (our original time-horizon was 1980). The tasks of the new BES operations were to identify and monitor these trends; to analyze them to determine their implications for relations planning and, hopefully, to catalyze those strategies of adjustment of which I have written. The last element of the task is, in a sense, the crucial one, for there is little point to gaining lead time if it is not put to good use.

The initial BES effort was a broad survey of the whole prospective business environment of the Seventies. In an effort to "make sense of change," to see a pattern in the kaleidoscope of prospective events, the BES group viewed social change as the interaction of eight developing forces for change:

1. Increasing affluence

2. Economic stabilization

3. Rising levels of education

4. Changing attitudes toward work and leisure

5. Increasing pluralism and individualism

6. Emergence of the post-industrial society

7. Growing interdependence of institutions

8. The urban/minority problem

This broad survey can be likened to a single 360° sweep of the early warning system radar, revealing a number of ill-defined "blips" on the screen. If left there, the survey might justifiably have been relegated to the "interesting, but ineffective" category of studies.

It was, however, only a beginning. It provided us with a frame of reference and a perspective on the future. More important, it established the priorities for more detailed studies and analyses. To continue the radar analogy, these subsequent studies examined the "blips" on the screen in greater detail in an effort to determine the exact nature, trajectory and impact points of the incoming "missiles." It was these studies (for example, on the future minority environment; women's rights in the Seventies, prospects for inflation) that, by focusing more sharply on specific policy implications, started to make the hoped-for contribution toward making personnel and industrial relations planning a more proactive affair. One indicator: whereas the minority study (1969), though focusing on the future, barely enabled us to keep pace with events, the women's rights study (1970) gave us enough of a jump on events that our own affirmative action guidelines on equal employment opportunity for women were published a year before the Federal guidelines.[2]

A "Four-Sided Framework" for Planning

Two years' experience with this new venture convinced us of its potential value to personnel relations planning. However, it became increasingly clear that many of the questions raised by our studies simply could not be answered within the framework of the personnel function. The implications of trend-analysis spilled over into matters of the social purpose of business, the structure and governance of the corporation, business-government relationships, production processes and market orientation. They could fit comfortably in only one frame of reference--corporate planning as a whole.

It would, however, have to be a different type of corporate planning from the past. Typically, corporate planning has based its strategies on inputs derived from economic forecasting (predictions about GNP, consumer and government spending, savings and investment, market analyses, etc.) and technological forecasting (assessments of "state of the art" developments, expected outputs from one's own and competitors' laboratories). The planning parameters of the past (and present) can, therefore, be conceptually represented by the model in Figure 1. Certainly these inputs have been, and will continue to be, vital to the planning process: change--and, therefore, forecasting--in these fields is becoming more complex and more needed. However, these inputs, our studies suggested, would no longer suffice, as the "exposed flanks" in this diagram might lead one to guess.

The typical business now finds itself the focal point for a bewildering array of external forces that impact on it from every angle. The larger the company, the more likely is this to be true. There is virtually no major trend in the social, political and economic arena, at home and abroad, that does not affect in some way the operations or future growth of the large corporation. To create an "early warning system" on only two fronts--economic and technological--is, therefore, apt to leave a company highly vulnerable to attack from an unexpected quarter. Managers have been too ready to pretend that other factors were adequately covered by generalized assessments of the conventional and obvious political events--war, an election, or international trade agreements--or to rely on the caveat "other things being equal," which in the circumstances of today is a highly unsatisfactory (and unbusinesslike) treatment of vital factors.

If we have learned one lesson from the disruptions of accelerating change in the past decade, we should by now have recognized that "other things" have an uncomfortable habit of *not* being "equal." To look no further than at the outbursts in our cities and on our campuses, at the surge of a heightened ecological consciousness, at the proliferation of legislation on product safety, equal employment opportunity and occupational health, it should be obvious that social moods, personal attitudes, and political action have become dynamic and determinative forces for business.

Figure 1

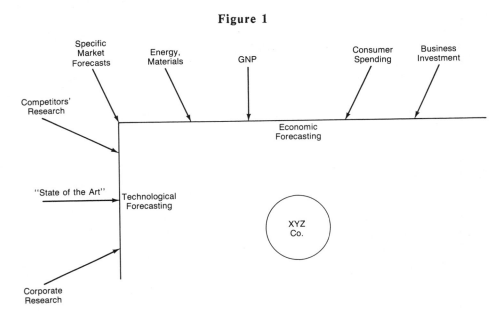

The planning model for the future, therefore, will be more nearly represented by the four-sided framework illustrated in Figure 2.

An approximation of this model was, in fact, incorporated as one element in the revamping of General Electric's strategic planning system in 1970. The starting point for the planning cycle is now the long-term environmental forecast. This establishes the basic premises from which can be deduced the strategies and policies that are likely to produce the best "fit" between the company and the future business environment. And it is in this larger context of environmental forecasting that socio-political forecasting finds its natural place.

Some Key Elements in the Process

Socio-political forecasting is nothing if not an art. By any standard, it is still far from being a science. However, even lacking the precision and instruments of science, it is evolving its own beginning processes, methodologies and discipline. Four key elements in the process bear examination:

1. *Continuous and comprehensive monitoring.* The paradox of forecasting in what Max Ways once called an "era of radical change" is that it becomes at once more necessary and more difficult. In a relatively stable society, in which tomorrow will predictably be pretty much like today, forecasting is relatively easy; but, by the same token, it is scarcely necessary since today's way of doing things will still be valid tomorrow. The more rapid, complex and pervasive change

becomes, the more essential it is to try to "get a fix on the future." But, of course, the difficulties of forecasting increase geometrically with the number of sources of change.

Figure 2

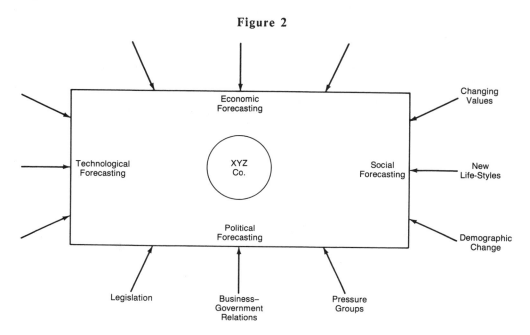

The salient characteristics of a good monitoring system are continuity and comprehensiveness. A non-repetitive scanning of the environment ("We did our 1980 study in 1970--and that's it!") will soon become an erroneous input to planning. Even a long-term forecast requires continuous updating, granted the rapidity of change and the present state of the art.

Whether the monitoring is actually done by company personnel or outside consultants remains a matter of choice. Probably the best self-operated system is, in fact, an industry-wide effort among life insurance companies, under the leadership of the Institute of Life Insurance (ILI). Their Trend Analysis Program (TAP) operates on the basis of a matrix, one axis of which is categories of publications (general press, business publications, academic journals, etc.), the other being segments of the environment (social change, technology, politics, etc.). "Monitors" are nominated to the Program by individual companies, and each is then assigned to a particular cell of the matrix to monitor a publication (or a set of them) for evidence of trends in that segment of the environment. Monitors' reports are collected, analyzed and synthesized into periodic reports by ILI, which distributes them to participating companies.

Most companies will find it imperative to supplement their own efforts, either by participating in a cooperative effort such as TAP or by purchasing monitoring services from outside organizations. Among the better known organizations are the Hudson Institute (Corporate Environment Program), the Futures Group ("Scout"), Institute for the Future ("Project Aware") and Daniel

Yankelovich, Inc. ("Monitor," "Corporate Priorities")--However achieved, comprehensiveness must be a goal--and there is a large environment to monitor.

2. *Analyzing for critical business implications.* However the monitoring is done, the critical job of particularizing the findings to significance for a single company must, I think, be done internally. Only in this way can it become part of the thinking process of the management system of that company.

Here I would like to stress the importance of seeing *patterns* in trends and events. It is not sufficient merely to identify and monitor hundreds, maybe thousands, of separate items of change; to do only that would saturate the planning system with data. I appreciate that there is a very fine dividing line between objectively trying to find patterns in the trends, and subjectively imposing one's own pattern on them. Nevertheless, I think we must make this attempt and tread this fine line. I stress this need to see patterns in change because of its importance in enabling us to:

    a.   see the significance of isolated events;

    b.   analyze the cross-impacts of one trend on another (or others);

    c.   improve management's understanding of the probable future course of events.

Bringing the generalized forecast down to specific implications for a particular business may prove to be the most difficult part of all. We are all most apt to be blind in matters that closely affect us. But however difficult the exercise may be, we must make a thoroughgoing and conscientious effort to answer, in precise terms, the crucial questions: "What does this trend mean for me? For my work? For my company?" This exercise may be particularly difficult for managers because many of the implications will seem to challenge and even undermine some of their basic assumptions and values. These implications are, therefore, most apt to be set aside as mistaken interpretations, as "unthinkable," or as inconsistent with past experience and future forecasts along "traditional" lines. Yet it is precisely these seeming "wild cards" that our research must seek to uncover and evaluate.

3. *Developing tools and techniques.* As already noted, socio-political forecasting lacks the armory of analytical tools and techniques possessed by older forecasting disciplines. Trend projections, Delphi forecasting, scenarios, and "cross-impact analysis" are useful starts on forecasting methodologies, but the need for more tools remains great. With an acute awareness of their limitations and relative lack of sophistication, I offer for consideration two tools that we have found to be of some value.

(a) *Probability-Diffusion Matrix*

In predicting developments over a decade it is more meaningful to talk in terms of degree of relative probability, than of certainty or "inevitability." In the final analysis, assigning probability to a trend or future event is a matter of judgment after weighing the known data and cross-checking with informed opinion. A further cross-check can be run by plotting the predictions along a probability axis so that their relative positions are made apparent.

It is also helpful to assess the probable "diffusion" of a trend or event--that is, the extent to which it is uniformly distributed over the population to which it applies (world, U.S.A., an industry, etc.) or relatively confined to a segment of that

Figure 3

Probability/Diffusion Matrix for Events and Trends
Occurring in U.S. and World by 1980

Diffusion: High ← → Low

Probability: Low ← → High

Items in matrix:
- Thermonuclear War
- Rising Level of Education
- 3 + % Inflation
- 35-hr. Work Week
- Retirement at 55
- 3.5-5% Unemployment
- More Business-Government Partnerships
- $3,600 Per Capita Income
- Regional Conflicts
- Detroit-Type Riots
- Strikes Outlawed

population. Again, plotting the predictions along a diffusion axis makes explicit, in a coordinated fashion, the relative weightings assigned in separate judgments.

Combining these two axes into a probability/diffusion matrix, as is done in Figure 3, serves as a check on the internal consistency of a relatively large number of predictions, from two viewpoints. By itself, such a matrix adds little to a scientific approach to environmental forecasting, but it does provide a way of looking at the future that may perhaps be helpful.

The plottings made in this matrix are largely for purposes of illustration, and not to be taken as final judgments. To the extent that they provoke debate, they will have at least demonstrated the value of making judgments clearly explicit so that planned action can more surely be taken.

(b) "Values Profile"

As we have already noted, changes in value systems may be the major determinants of social and political trends in the future, and business planning would be well advised to try to get a fix on these changes as one essential element in its forecasting system. One way of systematizing analysis of value trends is to develop a "values profile" (Figure 4). Like the probability/diffusion matrix, this chart should be viewed, not as a precise scientific measurement, but merely as a useful way of looking at the future. Like the matrix, too, it contains plottings that are meant to be indicative--pointing the way to a more comprehensive study--rather than definitive.

To point up the possible attitudinal changes as dramatically as possible, the chart has been made up of contrasting pairs of values (to a greater or lesser extent, that is, enhancement of one value implies a diminution of the other--e.g., war vs. peace; conformity vs. pluralism). Each society and generation has tended to seek its own new balance between these contrasting pairs, with the weight shifting from one side to the other as conditions and attitudes change.

The chart also emphasizes the value changes likely to be most prevalent among the trend-setting segment of the population (young, well-educated, relatively affluent, "committed"). These are the people among whom companies recruit the managerial and professional talent they require.

The chart presents two value profiles--one representing the approximate balance struck by these trend-setters in 1969 (when our initial study was undertaken) between each pair of values; the other indicating the hypothetical balance that might be struck in 1980. It is important to stress that the chart attempts to predict value changes, *not* necessarily events. Even though trend-setters may value, say, arms control agreements, events may lag behind their influence (e.g., due to political thinking of the electorate as a whole) or lie outside their control (e.g., regional wars among developing nations).

4. *Integrating with other forecasts.* The essence of environmental forecasting, as has been mentioned, is the integration of the various conventional and non-conventional types of forecasting. The four-sided framework implies only four sets of inputs to the process; but this is merely a conceptual approach, and ideally the number should be higher. When the long-term environmental forecast was first undertaken in 1971 for our strategic planning, the number of initial inputs was set at nine (see Figure 5)--geopolitical/defense, international economic, social, political, legal, economic, technological, manpower and financial. In each of

these, separate "tunnel visions" of specific aspects of the future we tried to (a) give a brief historical review (1960-70) as a jumping-off point for our analysis of the future; (b) analyze the major future forces for change--a benchmark forecast for

Figure 4
Profile of Significant Value-System Changes: 1969-1980
as seen by General Electric's Business Environment Section

War (Military Might)	Peace (Economic Development)
Nationalism	Internationalism
Federal Government	State/Local Government
Public Enterprise	Private Enterprise
Organization	Individual
Uniformity/Conformity	Pluralism
Independence	Interdependence
Sociability	Privacy
Materialism	Quality of Life
Status Quo/Permanence/Routine	Change/Flexibility/Innovation
Future Planning	Immediacy
Work	Leisure
Authority	Participation
Centralization	Decentralization
Ideology/Dogma	Pragmatism/Rationality
Moral Absolutes	Situation Ethics
Economic Efficiency	"Social Justice"
Means (Especially Technology)	Ends (Goals)

——— 1969 Values Profile

— — 1980 Values Profile

1970-80; (c) identify the potential discontinuities, i.e., those events which might have low probability, but high significance for General Electric; and (d) raise the first-order questions and policy implications suggested by these forecasts.

These were, by definition, *segmented* views of the future, and so inadequate as a final product. We proceeded to a "cross-impact analysis," selecting from the hundreds of trends/events in those nine environmental "slices" the 75 or so that had the highest combined rating of probability and importance. (Some events that were quite probable had little significance for General Electric; while others of low probability would have critical importance for the Company, should they occur.) On these 75 trends/events, we performed the sort of cross-impact analysis developed by Theodore J. Gordon, asking "If event A occurs, what will be the impact on the other 74? Will the probability of their occurrence increase? Decrease? Remain the same?" In effect, this process enabled us to build sets of "domino chains," with one event triggering another, and then to construct a small number of consistent configurations of the future.

The final step in the environmental forecasting process was the development of scenarios as an integrative mechanism for our work, pulling together the separate forecasts of the nine "slices," and blending quantitative and qualitative data. I must stress that we developed multiple scenarios; we did *not* take a single view of the future. In fact, we ended up with four possibilities:

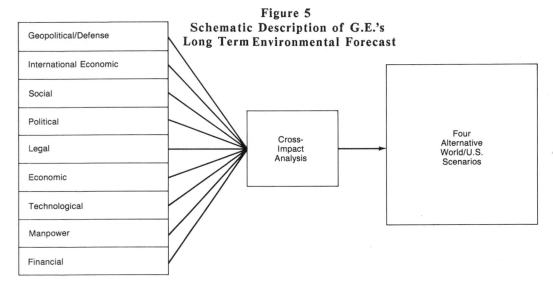

Figure 5
Schematic Description of G.E.'s
Long Term Environmental Forecast

--A benchmark forecast, which combined the "most probable" developments from the nine environmental "slices."
--Three variants which, in effect, were derived from varying combinations of discontinuities.

Significantly, I think, we rated even the benchmark forecast no more than a 50 percent probability. That, at least, is a measure of our own uncertainty about the future.

Conclusion

When all is said and done, of course, the element of chance or surprise will always remain. Indeed, one certain prediction is that managers will have to learn how to live with, and manage, uncertainty. However, within a framework of four (or nine) environmental parameters, business plans can be formulated with greater assurance that the major predictable environmental factors have been taken into consideration. With anything less, an otherwise sound strategy will remain vulnerable to the new discontinuities of our age.

Footnotes

[1] One overclaim that must be guarded against is the reasoning that political decisions will be the major determinants of the economy, and that political forecasting is the crucial input to planning. As in any system it is the interaction of all trends and factors that determines the outcomes, so I would argue that it is futile to argue for the primacy of any one type of forecasting.

[2] Even this could not, of course guarantee immunity from EEOC complaints and lawsuits as recent events have demonstrated.

TRENDS IN ORGANIZATIONAL DESIGN

Keith Davis
Arizona State University

From time to time it is appropriate to back away from a current situation in order to examine it in broader perspective. In this manner we can get a better understanding of the significance of events around us. The following discussion has that purpose. It seeks to understand the directions in which organizational design is moving. As used in this discussion the term "organizational design" refers both to the design of the job, such as the number of work elements performed, and design of the organizational environment itself, such as rigidity of structure, communication systems, and amount of control.

Classical Organizational Design

Classical organizational design dominated management thinking for the first half of the twentieth century. It had its origins in the ideas of Adam Smith, who in 1776 in the *Wealth of Nations* [18] presented a discussion of pinmakers to show how division of labor could improve productivity a hundredfold or more. However, it was not until the early 1900s that the full philosophy of classical design was presented by Frederic W. Taylor [19] and Henri Fayol. [5] As it evolved from Taylor and Fayol, classical design used full division of labor rigid hierarchy, and standardization of labor to reach its objectives. The idea was to lower costs by using unskilled repetitive labor that could be trained easily to do a small part of a job. Job performance was tightly controlled by a large hierarchy that strictly enforced *the one best way of work.*

In spite of our tendency occasionally to think otherwise, the classical design did gain substantial improvements. There were remarkable increases in economic productivity, something which was sorely needed by an impoverished world. *The difficulty was that these gains were achieved at considerable human costs.* There was excessive division of labor and overdependence on rules, procedures, and hierarchy. The worker became isolated from his fellow workers. The result was higher turnover and absenteeism. Quality declined, and workers became alienated. Conflict arose as workers tried to improve their lot. Management's response to this situation was to tighten the controls, to increase the supervision, and to organize more rigidly. These actions were calculated to improve the situation, but they only made it worse. Management made a common error by treating the *symptoms* rather than the causes of the problems. The job itself simply was not satisfying.

It took management--and academicians--some time to recognize the nature and severity of the problem. In 1939 Roethlisberger and Dickson published their powerful behavioral interpretation of management. [17] Then in 1949 Douglas McGregor in his insightful way warned, "Practically all the means of need-satisfaction which workers today obtain from their employment can be utilized *only after they leave their jobs.*" [16, p. 117; italics in original] He pointed

Reprinted from Academy of Management Proceedings, 33rd Annual Meeting, Boston, MA, 1973, pp. 1-6, by permission of the author and publisher.

out that all of the popular personnel devices of the time, such as vacations and insurance benefits, were satisfactions received off the job.

A few years later in 1957 Chris Argyris charged that poor organizational design established a basic incongruence between formal organizations and the workers' drives for self-actualization. Organizations tend to ignore the potential of people, he claimed. They fail to encourage self-development in areas that are meaningful to each individual. They do not encourage responsibility and innovation. They do not develop and employ the whole man. At lower levels the workers become alienated, frustrated, and unproductive, and they fight the company with a certain sense of social justice. The problem is also severe at management levels, because the situation lacks trust, openness, and risk taking. The frustrated manager often abdicates his independence, becoming a servile "organization man" in the words of William H. Whyte. [23]

Another straw in the wind for change was the famous need hierarchy presented by A.H. Maslow. [15, pp. 370-396] His hierarchy suggested that as society made social and economic progress, new needs of employees would arise. In turn, these new needs require new forms of job and organizational design. The problem was not so much that the work itself had changed for the worse, but rather *the employees were changing.* Design of jobs and organizations had failed to keep up with widespread changes in worker aspirations and attitudes. Employers now had two reasons for redesigning jobs and organizations.

1. Classical design originally gave inadequate attention to human factors.
2. The needs and aspirations of employees themselves were changing.

Humanistic Organizational Design

In taking corrective action the most obvious direction for management to go was to swing the pendulum away from mechanistic classical design toward a more behavioral, participative, humanistic design, also called organic design by Burns and Stalker. [4] The new design furnished a wide variety of humanistic options, such as the following:

Classical Design	Humanistic Design
Closed system	Open system
Job specialization	Job enlargement
Centralization	Decentralization
Authority	Consensus
Tight hierarchy	Loose project organization
Technical emphasis	Human emphasis
Rigid procedures	Flexible procedures
Command	Consultation
Vertical communication	Multidirectional communication
Negative environment	Positive environment
Maintenance needs	Motivational needs
Tight control	Management by objectives
Autocratic approach	Democratic approach

The objective was to make the job environment supportive of the employee rather than threatening to him. The job should be a place that stimulates his drives and aspirations and helps him to grow as a whole person. Work should be psychologically rewarding as well as economically rewarding. By the 1950s organizations were moving gradually in this direction.

In addition to Maslow, McGregor, Argyris, and Roethlisberger already mentioned, the following persons made significant contributions to humanistic organizational design. Rensis Likert [14] emphasized organizational development and offered four categories called Systems 1, 2, 3, and 4, to describe the move from authoritarian management (System 1) to participative management (System 4). Organizational development was used to help organizations gradually move toward System 4, which was considered the ideal system.

Blake and Mouton [3] offered organizational development in the form of a managerial grid which emphasized leadership style. It was perceived that the leader sets the environmental structure and climate for his work group; consequently, the most effective way to move toward humanistic design is through the leadership structure of the organization. By using the grid, various managerial styles may be identified in order to discuss both existing styles which need correction and more idealized styles.

Herzberg [10] took an unusual and controversial approach by emphasizing a difference between maintenance and motivational factors. Herzberg identified some job conditions that operate primarily to dissatisfy employees when the conditions are absent, but when present do not motivate employees in a strong way. These are dissatisfiers or maintenance factors, because they maintain the employee ready for effective motivation. These maintenance factors arise primarily from the "job context" or environment, such as pension, vacations, wages and interpersonal relations. Another set of conditions operate primarily to build strong motivation and high job satisfaction, but their absence rarely proves dissatisfying. These are satisfiers or motivational factors. They arise primarily from the job content itself, such as achievement, growth, and responsibility. The Herzberg model provoked much controversy about its correctness, but regardless it has been an effective vehicle to convince managers of significant distinctions in types of rewards offered by management.

Bennis [2] presented the fundamental ideal of humanistic democracy and insisted that in the work place "democracy is inevitable." According to this line of reasoning, democracy is inevitable because it is the only form which provides the flexibility and decentralization which large, complex organizations require. In the complex organization the top executive cannot know enough about all functions of the organization to make effective decisions. He must depend on extensive horizontal communication and functional expertise to guide him. Democratic, humanistic organizational systems are the most effective for this situation. They are a decision-making necessity and also a behavioral necessity, because they provide the optimal environment for today's knowledge workers.

Without question, humanistic designs were an improvement; however, a funny thing happened on the way to this proposed utopia. Just as classical design generated excesses, so did humanistic design. The model builders forgot that the behavioral system in an organization is part of several larger systems, such as the technological system and the economic system. If decisions are made in terms of only the behavioral system, the situation becomes unbalanced and the same kinds of rigidities develop that the classicists caused.

A prime example of the descent from humanistic utopia to worldly reality is the experience of Non-Linear Systems, Inc., of San Diego. In the 1960s it changed its organizational design to the behavioral model, entirely eliminating assembly lines and time cards. As the company grew, it was hailed as the harbinger of the future. One behavioral scientist commented about his associates. "There was so much excitement it was almost seductive." The excitement died when the company met a business slump and the new system was unable to endure adversity. Sales dropped nearly fifty percent and profits disappeared. In order to restore profitability the president took a more controlling, classical role. He commented, "I may have lost sight of the purpose of business, which is not to develop new theories of management." And he added a comment about the rigidities of the humanistic model, "We didn't take into account the varied emotional and mental capacities of our employees when we changed the assembly line." [21, pp. 99-100]

Contingency Organizational Design

The move toward a more system-wide way of thinking about organizations is producing a swing toward contingency or situational designs in the 1970s. This is clearly the design emphasis of the future because it escapes narrow perspectives that have restricted earlier approaches. It is still strongly humanistic, but it is more complete than that, because it includes all situational factors including the technology and economic environment. *Contingency organization design* means that different environments require different organizational relationships for optimum effectiveness. [9, p. 59] No longer is there a "one best way" whether it is classical or behavioral.

Contingency management, for example, means that job enrichment should be applied with the realization that some employees do not want their jobs enriched. Some prefer easier and more routine work. Some are troubled by a challenge. Others prefer a friendly situation and are not much concerned about job content. Each person and situation is different. Many organizations have policies and procedures that reflect a single value system based on the belief that all employees want the same work environment and fringe benefits; consequently, these firms are not able to adjust situationally to different conditions. [11, pp. 8-23]

Early research evidence of contingency design was provided by Woodward in 1965. [24] She studied 100 firms in England to determine that structural variables were related to economic success. Firms were classified according to three types of production technology: unit, mass, and continuous process production. Research disclosed that the effective form of organization varied according to the firm's technology. Mass production was more successful with classical design, while unit and process production were more successful when they used humanistic designs.

Fiedler probably provided the name for the contingency approach, with his studies of leadership published in 1967. [6] He showed that an effective leadership pattern is dependent on the interaction of a number of variables including task structure and leadership position power. Generally, a more classical approach is effective when conditions are substantially favorable or unfavorable for the leader, but a more behavioral approach is better in the intermediate zone of favorability. The intermediate conditions are the ones most commonly found in organizations.

Lawrence and Lorsch [13] popularized the contingency approach with their study of organizations in stable and changing environments in 1967. They showed that in certain stable environments the classical forms tend to be more effective. In changing environments the opposite is true. More humanistic forms are required to permit organizations to respond effectively to their unstable environment.

Since contingency design deals with a large number of variables, it is not easy to apply, but some experimental applications have produced excellent results. For example, in the Treasury Department of American Telephone and Telegraph Company, educated and intelligent women handle correspondence with stockholders. Originally they worked in a highly structured environment under close supervision in order to assure a suitable standard of correspondence. Under these conditions, quality of work was low and turnover was high. The job design was too routine and lacking in challenge.

Using a control group and a test group, the jobs of the test group were enriched as follows: (1) the women were permitted to sign their own names to the letters they prepared; (2) the women were held responsible for the quality of their work; (3) they were encouraged to become experts in the kinds of problems that appealed to them; and (4) subject matter experts were provided for consultation regarding problems.

The control group remained unchanged after six months, but the test group improved by all measurements used. The measures included turnover, productivity, absences, promotions from the group, and costs. The quality measurement index climbed from the thirties to the nineties.

American Telephone and Telegraph Company also has achieved excellent results in other job enrichment efforts. In the directory-compilation function, name omissions dropped from 2 to 1 percent. In frame wiring, errors declined from 13 to 0.5 percent, and the number of frames wired increased from 700 to over 1,200. [7; 8]

Equally successful results have been achieved at Emery Air Freight using the behavioral modification ideas of B.F. Skinner. The company made design changes in the communication system in order to provide positive reinforcement for workers. In this situation the company had been using large containers to reduce handling costs for forwarding small packages. The company has a standard of 90 percent use of the containers for small packages, but research showed that actual utilization was only 45 percent.

The communication system was redesigned to give workers daily feedback on how near they came to the 90 percent goal. Furthermore, supervisors provided positive verbal reinforcement. The result was that when the new communication design was applied, *in a single day* use of large containers increased to 95 percent. As this design was applied to other facilities throughout the nation, use of large containers at these facilities also rose to 95 percent in a single day. The high performance level was maintained for three years following the new design. [22, pp. 64-65]

A more complete effort was the organizational design of a new General Foods Corporation pet food plant to incorporate appropriate behavioral and system ideas. The new plant offers a completely different way of work compared with a traditional dog food plant. Work is performed by autonomous teams of 7-14 persons. Most support functions are integrated within the teams, meaning that very little staff is provided. Job design is used to enlarge jobs to increase the challenge in them. Decision making is decentralized, and group leaders encourage team members to make as many decisions as possible. Full feedback about performance is given to all members. [20, pp. 70-81]

The result compared with other plants is that absenteeism and turnover are reduced and productivity has increased. Furthermore, rework of faulty quality material has been reduced 90 percent. The plant definitely shows superior results compared with conventionally designed plants, although it is too new to be sure whether these results will last indefinitely. [12, p. 54]

Although experimental contingency design efforts have had remarkable success, they do not signal a quick coming of utopia at work. Classical design and strict behavioral design gave easy answers, but contingency design is difficult to apply. Much about the workplace is still unknown. We also know relatively little about people and the social systems in which they interact. The road ahead is going to be a rocky one. If predictions are appropriate at this point, my opinion is that progress in organizational design will be slower than most experts think. It is easy to theorize about how to redesign organizations and jobs, but actual practice is much more difficult. Furthermore, changes in design assume certain changes in the way managers think, and we all know that attitudes and frameworks change very slowly. Traditional ways of work and organizational design have been entrenched for centuries, and they will not change easily.

Meanwhile, the worker is changing, and the resulting psychological dissonance between him and his job is likely to grow worse before it becomes better. There will be other Lordstown-type demonstrations and many smaller conflicts as society wrestles with whether organizational design can be restructured to increase productivity and employee fulfillment. In all this turmoil, however, the important point to remember is that we are making progress. We are moving toward more contingency design with enriched jobs and open organizational systems.

References

1.   Argyris, Chris, Personality and Organization: The Conflict Between the System and the Individual (New York: Harper & Row, Publishers, Inc., 1957).
2.   Bennis, Warren G., Changing Organizations: Essays on the Development and Evolution of Human Organization (New York: McGraw-Hill Book Company, 1966).
3.   Blake, Robert R., and Jane S. Mouton, The Managerial Grid (Houston: Gulf Publishing Company, 1964).
4.   Burns, Tom and G. M. Stalker, The Management of Innovation (London: Tavistock Publications, 1961).
5.   Fayol, Henri, General and Industrial Management (1916) trans. by Constance Storrs (New York: Pitman Publishing Corporation, 1949).
6.   Fiedler, Fred E., A Theory of Leadership Effectiveness (New York: McGraw-Hill Book Company, 1967).
7.   Ford, Robert N., Motivation through the Work Itself (New York: American Management Association, 1969).
8.   Gellette, Malcolm B., "Work Itself as a Motivator," speech at annual meeting, Western Division, Academy of Management, Salt Lake City, Utah (March 20, 1970).
9.   Hellriegel, Don, and John W. Slocum, Jr., "Organizational Design: A Contingency Approach," Business Horizons, Vol. XVI, No. 2 (April, 1973), pp. 59-68.
10. Herzberg, Frederick, Bernard Mausner, and Barbara Synderman, The Motivation to Work (New York: John Wiley & Sons, Inc., 1959).
11. Hughes, Charles L. and Vincent S. Flowers, "Shaping Personnel Strategies to Disparate Value Systems," Personnel, Vol. 50, No. 2 (March-April, 1973), pp. 8-23.
12. "Latest Moves to Fight Boredom on the Job," U.S. News & World Report (December 25, 1972), pp. 52-54.
13. Lawrence, Paul R., and Jay W. Lorsch, Organization and Environment: Managing Differentiation and Integration (Boston: Harvard Graduate School of Business Administration, 1967).
14. Likert, Rensis, The Human Organization: Its Management and Value (New York: McGraw-Hill Book Company, 1967).
15. Maslow, A. H., "A Theory of Human Motivation," Psychological Review, Vol. 50 (1943), pp. 370-396.

16. McGregor, Douglas, "Toward a Theory of Organized Human Effort in Industry," in Arthur Kornhauser, editor, Psychology of Labor-Management Relations (Champaign, Ill.: Industrial Relations Research Association, 1949), pp. 111-122.

17. Roethlisberger, F. J., and W. J. Dickson, Management and the Worker (Cambridge, Mass.: Harvard University Press, 1939).

18. Smith, Adam, An Inquiry into the Nature and Causes of the Wealth of Nations (1776) (New York: Modern Library, Inc., 1937).

19. Taylor, Frederick W., The Principles of Scientific Management (New York: Harper & Brothers, 1911).

20. Walton, Richard E., "How to Counter Alienation in the Plant," Harvard Business Review, Vol. 50, No. 6 (November-December, 1972), pp. 70-81.

21. "Where Being Nice to Workers Didn't Work," Business Week (January 20, 1973), pp. 99-100.

22. "Where Skinner's Theories Work," Business Week (December 2, 1972), pp. 64-65.

23. Whyte, William H., Jr., The Organization Man (New York: Simon and Schuster, Inc., 1956).

24. Woodward, Joan, Industrial Organization: Theory and Practice (London: Oxford University Press, 1965).

STRUCTURE IS NOT ORGANIZATION

Robert H. Waterman, Jr.
Thomas J. Peters
and
Julien R. Phillips

Diagnosing and solving organizational problems means looking not merely to structural reorganization for answers but to a framework that includes structure and several related factors.

The Belgian surrealist René Magritte painted a series of pipes and titled the series *Ceci n'est pas une pipe*: this is not a pipe. The picture of the thing is not the thing. In the same way, a structure is not an organization. We all know that, but like as not, when we reorganize what we do is to restructure. Intellectually all managers and consultants know that much more goes on in the process of organizing than the charts, boxes, dotted lines, position descriptions, and matrices can possibly depict. But all too often we behave as though we didn't know it; if we want change we change the structure.

Early in 1977, a general concern with the problems of organization effectiveness, and a particular concern about the nature of the relationship between structure and organization, led us to assemble an internal task force to review our client work. The natural first step was to talk extensively to consultants and client executives around the world who were known for their skill and experience in organization design. We found that they too were dissatisfied with conventional approaches. All were disillusioned about the usual structural solutions, but they were also skeptical about anyone's ability to do better. In their experience, the techniques of the behavioral sciences were not providing useful alternatives to structural design. True, the notion that structure follows strategy (get the strategy right and the structure follows) looked like an important addition to the organizational tool kit; yet strategy rarely seemed to dictate unique structural solutions. Moreover, the main problem in strategy had turned out to be execution: getting it done. And that, to a very large extent, meant *organization*. So the problem of organization effectiveness threatened to prove circular. The dearth of practical additions to old ways of thought was painfully apparent.

Outside Explorations

Our next step was to look outside for help. We visited a dozen business schools in the United States and Europe and about as many superbly performing companies. Both academic theorists and business leaders, we found, were wrestling with the same concerns.

Our timing in looking at the academic environment was good. The state of theory is in great turmoil but moving toward a new consensus. Some researchers continue to write about structure, particularly its latest and most modish variant, the matrix organization. But primarily the ferment is around another stream of ideas that follow from some startling premises about the limited capacity of decision makers to process information and reach what we usually think of as "rational" decisions.

The stream that today's researchers are tapping is an old one, started in the late 1930s by Fritz Roethlisberger and Chester Barnard, then both at Harvard (Barnard had been president of New Jersey Bell). They challenged rationalist theory, first--in Roethlisberger's case--on the shop floors of Western Electric's Hawthorne plant. Roethlisberger found that simply *paying attention* provided a stimulus to productivity that far exceeded that induced by formal rewards. In a study of workplace hygiene, they turned the lights up and got an expected productivity increase. Then to validate their results they turned the lights down. But something surprising was wrong: productivity went up again. Attention, they concluded, not working conditions per se, made the difference.

Barnard, speaking from the chief executive's perspective, asserted that the CEO's role is to harness the social forces in the organization, to shape and guide values. He described good value-shapers as *effective* managers, contrasting them with the mere manipulators of formal rewards who dealt only with the narrower concept of *efficiency*.

Barnard's words, though quickly picked up by Herbert Simon (whom we'll come back to later), lay dormant for thirty years while the primary management issues focused on decentralization and structure--the appropriate and burning issue of the time.

But then, as the decentralized structure proved to be less than a panacea for all time, and its substitute, the matrix, ran into worse trouble, Barnard's and Simon's ideas triggered a new wave of thinking. On the theory side, it is exemplified by the work of James March and Karl Weick, who attacked the rational model with a vengeance. Weick suggests that organizations learn--and adapt--very slowly. They pay obsessive attention to internal cues long after their practical value has ceased. Important business assumptions are buried deep in the minutiae of organizational systems and other habitual routines whose origins have been long obscured by time. March goes further. He introduced, only slightly facetiously, the garbage can as an organizational metaphor. March pictures organizational learning and decision making as a stream of choices, solutions, decision makers, and opportunities interacting almost randomly to make decisions that carry the organization toward the future. His observations about large organizations parallel Truman's about the presidency: "You issue orders from this office and if you can find out what happens to them after that, you're a better man than I am."

Other researchers have accumulated data which support this unconventional view. Henry Mintzberg made one of the few rigorous studies of how senior managers actually use time. They don't block out large chunks of time for planning, organizing, motivating, and controlling as some suggest they should. Their time, in fact, is appallingly but perhaps necessarily fragmented. Andrew Pettigrew studied the politics of strategic decision and was fascinated by the inertial properties of organizations. He showed that organizations frequently hold onto faulty assumptions about their world for as long as a decade, despite overwhelming evidence that it has changed and they probably should too.

In sum, what the researchers tell us is: "We can explain why you have problems." In the face of complexity and multiple competing demands, organizations simply can't handle decision making in a totally rational way. Not surprisingly, then, a single blunt instrument--like structure--is unlikely to prove the master tool that can change organizations with best effect.

Somewhat to our surprise, senior executives in the top-performing companies that we interviewed proved to be speaking very much the same language. They were concerned that the inherent limitations of structural approaches could render their companies insensitive to an unstable business environment marked by rapidly changing threats and opportunities from every quarter--competitors, governments, and unions at home and overseas. Their organizations, they said, had to learn how to build capabilities for rapid and flexible response. Their favored tactic was to choose a temporary focus, facing perhaps one major issue this year and another next year or the year after. Yet at the same time, they were acutely aware of their people's need for a stable, unifying value system--a foundation for long-term continuity. Their task, as they saw it, was largely one of preserving internal stability while adroitly guiding the organization's responses to fast-paced external change.

Companies such as IBM, Kodak, Hewlett-Packard, GM, Du Pont, and P&G, then, seem obsessive in their attention to maintaining a stable culture. At the same time, these giants are more responsive than their competitors. Typically, they do not seek responsiveness through major structural shifts. Instead, they seem to rely on a series of temporary devices to focus the attention of the entire organization for a limited time on a single priority goal or environmental threat.

Simon as Exemplar

Thirty years ago, in *Administrative Behavior*, Herbert Simon (a 1977 Nobel laureate) anticipated several themes that dominate much of today's thinking about organization. Simon's concepts of "satisficing" (settling for adequate instead of optimal solutions) and "the limits of rationality" were, in effect, nails in the coffin of economic man. His ideas, if correct, are crucial. The economic man paradigm has not only influenced the economists but has also influenced thought about the proper organization and administration of most business enterprises--and, by extension, public administration. Traditional thought has it that economic man is basically seeking to maximize against a set of fairly clear objectives. For organization planners the implications of this are that one can specify objectives, determine their appropriate hierarchy, and then logically determine the "best" organization.

Simon labeled this the "rational" view of the administrative world and said, in effect, that it was all right as far as it went but that it had decided limits. For one, most organizations cannot maximize--the goals are really not that clear. Even if they were, most business managers do not have access to complete information, as the economic model requires, but in reality operate with a set of relatively simple decision rules in order to *limit* the information they really need to process to make most decisions. In other words, the rules we use in order to get on with it in big organizations limit our ability to optimize anything.

Suppose the goal is profit maximization. The definition of profit and its maximization varies widely even within a single organization. Is it earnings growth, quality of earnings, maximum return on equity, or the discounted value of the future earnings stream--and if so, at what discount rate? Moreover, business organizations are basically large social structures with diffuse power. Most of the individuals who make them up have different ideas of what the business ought to be. The few at the top seldom agree entirely on the goals of their enterprise, let alone on maximization against one goal. Typically, they will not push their views so hard as to destroy the social structure of their enterprise and, in turn, their own power base.

All this leaves the manager in great difficulty. While the research seems valid and the message of complexity rings true, the most innovative work in the field is descriptive. The challenge to the manager is how to organize better. His goal is organization effectiveness. What the researchers are saying is that the subject is much more complex than any of our past prescriptive models have allowed for. What none has been able to usefully say is, "OK, here's what to to about it."

The 7-S Framework

After a little over a year and a half of pondering this dilemma, we began to formulate a new framework for organizational thought. As we and others have developed it and tested it in teaching, in workshops, and in direct problem solving over the past year, we have found it enormously helpful. It has repeatedly demonstrated its usefulness both in diagnosing the causes of organizational malaise and in formulating programs for improvement. In brief, it seems to work.

Our assertion is that productive organization change is not simply a matter of structure, although structure is important. It is not so simple as the interaction between strategy and structure, although strategy is critical too. Our claim is that effective organizational change is really the relationship between structure, strategy, systems, style, skills, staff, and something we call superordinate goals. (The alliteration is intentional: it serves as an aid to memory.)

Our central idea is that organization effectiveness stems from the interaction of several factors--some not especially obvious and some underanalyzed. Our framework for organization change, graphically depicted in the exhibit above, suggests several important ideas:

.   First is the idea of a multiplicity of factors that influence an organization's ability to change and its proper mode of change. Why pay attention to only one or two, ignoring the others? Beyond structure and strategy, there are at least five other identifiable elements. The division is to some extent arbitrary, but it has the merit of acknowledging the complexity identified in the research and segmenting it into manageable parts.

. Second, the diagram is intended to convey the notion of the interconnectedness of the variables--the idea is that it's difficult, perhaps impossible, to make significant progress in one area without making progress in the others as well. Notions of organization change that ignore its many aspects or their interconnectedness are dangerous.

. In a recent article on strategy, *Fortune* commented that perhaps as many as 90 percent of carefully planned strategies don't work. If that is so, our guess would be that the failure is a failure in execution, resulting from inattention to the other S's. Just as a logistics bottleneck can cripple a military strategy, inadequate systems or staff can make paper tigers of the best-laid plans for clobbering competitors.

A NEW VIEW OF ORGANIZATION

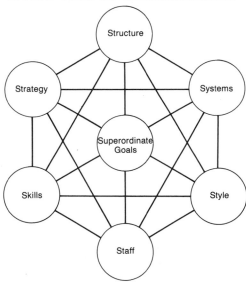

. Finally, the shape of the diagram is significant. It has no starting point or implied hierarchy. A priori, it isn't obvious which of the seven factors will be the driving force in changing a particular organization at a particular point in time. In some cases, the critical variable might be strategy. In others, it could be systems or structure.

Structure

To understand this model of organization change better, let us look at each of its elements, beginning--as most organization discussions do--with structure. What will the new organization of the 1980s be like? If decentralization was the trend of the past, what is next? Is it matrix organization? What will "Son of Matrix" look like? Our answer is that those questions miss the point.

To see why, let's take a quick look at the history of structural thought and development. The basic theory underlying structure is simple. Structure divides tasks and then provides coordination. It trades off specialization and integration. It decentralizes and then recentralizes.

The old structural division was between production and sales. The chart showing this was called a functional organization. Certain principles of organization, such as one-man/one-boss, limited span of control, grouping of like activities, and commensurate authority and responsibility, seemed universal truths.

What happened to this simple idea? Size--and complexity. A company like General Electric has grown over a thousandfold in both sales and earnings in the past eighty years. Much of its growth has come through entry into new and diverse businesses. At a certain level of size and complexity, a functional organization, which is dependent on frequent interaction among all activities, breaks down. As the number of people or businesses increases arithmetically, the number of interactions required to make things work increases geometrically. A company passing a certain size and complexity threshold must decentralize to cope.

Among the first to recognize the problem and explicitly act on it was Du Pont in 1921. The increasing administrative burden brought about by its diversification into several new product lines ultimately led the company to transform its highly centralized, functionally departmental structure into a decentralized, multidivisional one. Meanwhile, General Motors, which has been decentralized from the outset, was learning how to make a decentralized structure work as more than just a holding company.

However, real decentralization in world industry did not take place until much later. In 1950, for example, only about 20 percent of the *Fortune 500* companies were decentralized. By 1970, 80 percent were decentralized. A similar shift was taking place throughout the industrialized world.

Today three things are happening. First, because of the portfolio concept of managing a business, spun off from General Electric research (which has now become PIMS), companies are saying, "We can do more with our decentralized structure than control complexity. We can shift resources, act flexibly--that is, manage strategically."

Second, the dimensions along which companies want to divide tasks have multiplied. Early on, there were functional divisions. Then came product divisions. Now we have possibilities for division by function, product, market, geography, nation, strategic business unit, and probably more. The rub is that as the new dimensions are added, the old ones don't go away. An insurance company, for example, can organize around market segments, but it still needs functional control over underwriting decisions. The trade-offs are staggering if we try to juggle them all at once.

Third, new centralist forces have eclipsed clean, decentralized divisions of responsibility. In Europe, for example, a company needs a coherent union strategy. In Japan, especially, companies need a centralized approach to the government interface. In the United States, regulation and technology force centralization in the interest of uniformity.

This mess has produced a new organization form: the matrix, which purports, at least in concept, to reconcile the realities of organizational complexity with the imperatives of managerial control. Unfortunately, the two-dimensional

97

matrix model is intrinsically too simple to capture the real situation. Any spatial model that really did capture it would be incomprehensible.

Matrix does, however, have one well-disguised virtue: it calls attention to the central problem in structuring today. That problem is not the one on which most organization designers spend their time--that is, how to divide up tasks. It is one of emphasis and coordination--how to make the whole thing work. The challenge lies not so much in trying to comprehend all the possible dimensions of organization structure as in developing the ability to focus on those dimensions which are currently important to the organization's evolution--and to be ready to refocus as the crucial dimensions shift. General Motors' restless use of structural change--most recently the project center, which led to their effective downsizing effort--is a case in point.

The General Motors solution has a critical attribute--the use of a temporary overlay to accomplish a strategic task. IBM, Texas Instruments, and others have used similar temporary structural weapons. In the process, they have meticulously preserved the shape and spirit of the underlying structure (e.g., the GM division or the TI Product Customer Center). We regularly observe those two attributes among our sample of top performers: the use of the temporary and the maintenance of the simple underlying form.

We speculate that the effective "structure of the eighties" will more likely be described as "flexible" or "temporary"; this matrix-like property will be preserved even as the current affair with the formal matrix structure cools.

Strategy

If structure is not enough, what is? Obviously, there is strategy. It was Alfred Chandler who first pointed out that structure follows strategy, or more precisely, that a strategy of diversity forces a decentralized structure.[1] Throughout the past decade, the corporate world has given close attention to the interplay between strategy and structure. Certainly, clear ideas about strategy make the job of structural design more rational.

By "strategy" we mean those actions that a company plans in response to or anticipation of changes in its external environment--its customers, its competitors. Strategy is the way a company aims to improve its position vis-a-vis competition-- perhaps through low-cost production or delivery, perhaps by providing better value to the customer, perhaps by achieving sales and service dominance. It is, or ought to be, an organization's way of saying: "Here is how we will create unique value."

As the company's chosen route to competitive success, strategy is obviously a central concern in many business situations--especially in highly competitive industries where the game is won or lost on share points. But "structure follows strategy" is by no means the be-all and end-all of organization wisdom. We find too many examples of large, prestigious companies around the world that are replete with strategy and cannot execute any of it. There is little if anything wrong with their structures; the causes of their inability to execute lie in other dimensions of our framework. When we turn to nonprofit and public-sector organizations, moreover, we find that the whole meaning of "strategy" is tenuous-- but the problem of organizational effectiveness looms as large as ever.

Strategy, then, is clearly a critical variable in organization design--but much more is at work.

Systems

By systems we mean all the procedures, formal and informal, that make the organization go, day by day and year by year: capital budgeting systems, training systems, cost accounting procedures, budgeting systems. If there is a variable in our model that threatens to dominate the others, it could well be systems. Do you want to understand how an organization really does (or doesn't) get things done? Look at the systems. Do you want to change an organization without disruptive restructuring? Try changing the systems.

A large consumer goods manufacturer was recently trying to come up with an overall corporate strategy. Textbook portfolio theory seemed to apply: Find a good way to segment the business, decide which segments in the total business portfolio are most attractive, invest most heavily in those. The only catch: Reliable cost data by segment were not to be had. The company's management information system was not adequate to support the segmentation.

Again, consider how a bank might go about developing a strategy. A natural first step, it would seem, would be to segment the business by customer and product to discover where the money is made and lost and why. But in trying to do this, most banks almost immediately come up against an intractable costing problem. Because borrowers are also depositors, because transaction volumes vary, because the balance sheet turns fast, and because interest costs are half or more of total costs and unpredictable over the long term, costs for various market segments won't stay put. A strategy based on today's costs could be obsolete tomorrow.

One bank we know has rather successfully sidestepped the problem. Its key to future improvement is not strategy but the systems infrastructure that will allow account officers to negotiate deals favorable to the bank. For them the system *is* the strategy. Development and implementation of a superior account profitability system, based on a return-on-equity tree, has improved their results dramatically. "Catch a fish for a man and he is fed for a day; teach him to fish and he is fed for life": The proverb applies to organizations in general and to systems in particular.

Another intriguing aspect of systems is the way they mirror the state of an organization. Consider a certain company we'll call International Wickets. For years management has talked about the need to become more market oriented. Yet astonishingly little time is spent in their planning meetings on customers, marketing, market share, or other issues having to do with market orientation. One of their key systems, in other words, remains *very* internally oriented. Without a change in this key system, the market orientation goal will remain unattainable no matter how much change takes place in structure and strategy.

To many business managers, the word "systems" has a dull, plodding, middle-management sound. Yet it is astonishing how powerfully systems changes can enhance organizational effectiveness--without the disruptive side effects that so often ensue from tinkering with structure.

Style

It is remarkable how often writers, in characterizing a corporate management for the business press, fall back on the word "style." Tony O'Reilly's style at Heinz is certainly not AT&T's, yet both are successful. The trouble we have with style is not in recognizing its importance, but in doing much about it. Personalities don't change, or so the conventional wisdom goes.

We think it important to distinguish between the basic personality of a top-management team and the way that team comes across to the organization. Organizations may listen to what managers say, but they believe what managers do. Not words, but patterns of actions are decisive. The power of style, then, is essentially manageable.

One element of a manager's style is how he or she chooses to spend time. As Henry Mintzberg has pointed out, managers don't spend their time in the neatly compartmentalized planning, organizing, motivating, and controlling modes of classical management theory.[2] Their days are a mess--or so it seems. There's a seeming infinity of things they might devote attention to. No top executive attends to all of the demands on his time; the median time spent on any one issue is nine minutes.

What can a top manager do in nine minutes? Actually, a good deal. He can signal what's on his mind; he can reinforce a message; he can nudge people's thinking in a desired direction. Skillful management of his inevitably fragmented time is, in fact, an immensely powerful change lever.

By way of example, we have found differences beyond anything attributable to luck among different companies' success ratios in finding oil or mineral deposits. A few years ago, we surveyed a fairly large group of the finders and nonfinders in mineral exploration to discover what they were doing differently. The finders almost always said their secret was "top-management attention." Our reaction was skeptical: "Sure, that's the solution to most problems." But subsequent hard analysis showed that their executives *were* spending more time in the field, *were* blocking out more time for exploration discussions at board meetings, and *were* making more room on their own calendars for exploration-related activities.

Another aspect of style is symbolic behavior. Taking the same example, the successful finders typically have more people on the board who understand exploration or have headed exploration departments. Typically they fund exploration more consistently (that is, their year-to-year spending patterns are less volatile). They define fewer and more consistent exploration targets. Their exploration activities typically report at a higher organizational level. And they typically articulate better reasons for exploring in the first place.

A chief executive of our acquaintance is fond of saying that the way you recognize a marketing-oriented company is that "everyone talks marketing." He doesn't mean simply that an observable preoccupation with marketing is the end result, the final indication of the company's evaluation toward the marketplace. He means that it can be the lead. Change in orientation often starts when enough people talk about it before they really know what "it" is. Strategic management is not yet a crisply defined concept, but many companies are taking it seriously. If they talk about it enough, it will begin to take on specific meaning for their organizations--and those organizations will change as a result.

This suggests a second attribute of style that is by no means confined to those at the top. Our proposition is that a corporation's style, as a reflection of its culture, has more to do with its ability to change organization or performance than is generally recognized. One company, for example, was considering a certain business opportunity. From a strategic standpoint, analysis showed it to be a winner. The experience of others in the field confirmed that. Management went ahead with the acquisition. Two years later it backed out of the business, at a loss. The acquisition had failed because it simply wasn't consistent with the established corporate culture of the parent organization. It didn't fit their view of themselves. The will to make it work was absent.

Time and again strategic possibilities are blocked--or slowed down--by cultural constraints. One of today' more dramatic examples is the Bell System, where management has undertaken to move a service-oriented culture toward a new and different kind of marketing. The service idea, and its meaning to AT&T, is so deeply embedded in the Bell System's culture that the shift to a new kind of marketing will take years.

The phenomenon at its most dramatic comes to the fore in mergers. In almost every merger, no matter how closely related the businesses, the task of integrating and achieving eventual synergy is a problem no less difficult than combining two cultures. At some level of detail, almost everything done by two parties to a merger will be done differently. This helps explain why the management of acquisitions is so hard. If the two cultures are not integrated, the planned synergies will not accrue. On the other hand, to change too much too soon is to risk uprooting more tradition that can be replanted before the vital skills of the acquiree wither and die.

Staff

Staff (in the sense of people, not line/staff) is often treated in one of two ways. At the hard end of the spectrum, we talk of appraisal systems, pay scales, formal training programs, and the like. At the soft end, we talk about morale, attitude, motivation, and behavior.

Top management is often, and justifiably, turned off by both these approaches. The first seems too trivial for their immediate concern ("Leave it to the personnel department"), the second too intractable ("We don't want a bunch of shrinks running around, stirring up the place with more attitude surveys").

Our predilection is to broaden and redefine the nature of the people issue. What do the top-performing companies do to foster the process of developing managers? How, for example, do they shape the basic values of their management cadre? Our reason for asking the question at all is simply that no serious discussion of organization can afford to ignore it (although many do). Our reason for framing the question around the development of managers is our observation that the superbly performing companies pay extraordinary attention to managing what might be called the socialization process in their companies. This applies especially to the way they introduce young recruits into the mainstream of their organizations and to the way they manage their careers as the recruits develop into tomorrow's managers.

The process for orchestrating the early careers of incoming mangers, for instance, at IBM, Texas Instruments, P&G, Hewlett-Packard, or Citibank is quite different from its counterpart in many other companies we know around the world. Unlike other companies, which often seem prone to sidetrack young but expensive talent into staff positions or other jobs out of the mainstream of the company's business, these leaders take extraordinary care to turn young managers' first jobs into first opportunities for contributing in practical ways to the nuts-

and-bolts of what the business is all about. If the mainstream of the business is innovation, for example, the first job might be in new-products introduction. If the mainstream of the business is marketing, the MBA's first job could be sales or product management.

The companies who use people best rapidly move their managers into positions of real responsibility, often by the early- to mid-thirties. Various active support devices like assigned mentors, fast-track programs, and carefully orchestrated opportunities for exposure to top management are hallmarks of their management of people.

In addition, these companies are all particularly adept at managing, in a special and focused way, their central cadre of key managers. At Texas Instruments, Exxon, GM, and GE, for instance, a number of the very most senior executives are said to devote several weeks of each year to planning the progress of the top few hundred.

These, then, are a few examples of practical programs through which the superior companies manage people as aggressively and concretely as others manage organization structure. Considering people as a pool of resources to be nurtured, developed, guarded, and allocated is one of the many ways to turn the "staff" dimension of our 7-S framework into something not only amenable to, but worthy of practical control by senior management.

We are often told, "Get the structure 'right' and the people will fit" or "Don't compromise the 'optimum' organization for people considerations." At the other end of the spectrum we are earnestly advised, "The right people can make any organization work." Neither view is correct. People do count, but staff is only one of our seven variables.

Skills

We added the notion of skills for a highly practical reason: It enables us to capture a company's crucial attributes as no other concept can do. A strategic description of a company, for example, might typically cover markets to be penetrated or types of products to be sold. But how do most of us characterize companies? Not by their strategies or their structures. We tend to characterize them by what they do best. We talk of IBM's orientation to the marketplace, its prodigious customer service capabilities, or its sheer market power. We talk of Du Pont's research prowess, Procter & Gamble's product management capability, ITT's financial controls, Hewlett-Packard's innovation and quality, and Texas Instruments' project management. These dominating attributes, or capabilities, are what we mean by skills.

Now why is this distinction important? Because we regularly observe that organizations facing big discontinuities in business conditions must do more than shift strategic focus. Frequently they need to add a new capability, that is to say, a new skill. The Bell System, for example, is currently striving to add a formidable new array of marketing skills. Small copier companies, upon growing larger, find that they must radically enhance their service capabilities to compete with Xerox. Meanwhile Xerox needs to enhance its response capability in order to fend off a host of new competition. These dominating capability needs, unless explicitly labeled as such, often get lost as the company "attacks a new market" (strategy shift) or "decentralizes to give managers autonomy" (structure shift).

Additionally, we frequently find it helpful to *label* current skills, for the addition of a new skill may come only when the old one is dismantled. Adopting a newly "flexible and adaptive marketing thrust," for example, may be possible only if increases are accepted in certain marketing or distribution costs. Dismantling some of the distracting attributes of an old "manufacturing mentality" (that is, a skill that was perhaps crucial in the past) may be the only way to insure the success of an important change program. Possibly the most difficult problem in trying to organize effectively is that of weeding out old skills--and their supporting systems, structures, etc.--to ensure that important new skills can take root and grow.

Superordinate Goals

The word "superordinate" literally means "of higher order." By superordinate goals, we mean guiding concepts--a set of values and aspirations, often unwritten, that goes beyond the conventional formal statement of corporate objectives.

Superordinate goals are the fundamental ideas around which a business is built. They are its main value. But they are more as well. They are the broad notions of future direction that the top management team wants to infuse throughout the organization. They are the way in which the team wants to express itself, to leave its own mark. Examples would include Theodore Vail's "universal service" objective, which has so dominated AT&T; the strong drive to "customer service" which guides IBM's marketing; GE's slogan, "Progress is our most important product," which encourages engineers to tinker and innovate throughout the organization; Hewlett-Packard's "innovative people at all levels in the organization"; Dana's obsession with productivity, as a total organization, not just a few at the top; and 3M's dominating culture of "new products."

In a sense, superordinate goals are like the basic postulates in a mathematical system. They are the starting points on which the system is logically built, but in themselves are not logically derived. The ultimate test of their value is not their logic but the usefulness of the system that ensues. Everyone seems to know the importance of compelling superordinate goals. The drive for their accomplishment pulls an organization together. They provide stability in what would otherwise be a shifting set of organization dynamics.

Unlike the other six S's, superordinate goals don't seem to be present in all, or even most, organizations. They are, however, evident in most of the superior performers.

To be readily communicated, superordinate goals need to be succinct. Typically, therefore, they are expressed at high levels of abstraction and may mean very little to outsiders who don't know the organization well. But for those inside, they are rich with significance. Within an organization, superordinate goals, if well articulated, make meanings for people. And making meanings is one of the main functions of leadership.

Conclusion

We have passed rapidly through the variables in our framework. What should the reader have gained from the exercise?

We started with the premise that solutions to today's thorny organizing problems that invoke only structure--or even strategy and structure--are seldom adequate. The inadequacy stems in part from the inability of the two-variable model to explain why organizations are slow to adapt to change. The reasons often lie among our other variables: systems that embody outdated assumptions, a management style that is at odds with the stated strategy, the absence of a superordinate goal that binds the organization together in pursuit of a common purpose, the refusal to deal concretely with "people problems" and opportunities.

At its most trivial, when we merely use the framework as a checklist, we find that it leads into new terrain in our efforts to understand how organizations really operate or to design a truly comprehensive change program. At a minimum, it gives us a deeper bag in which to collect our experiences.

More importantly, it suggests the wisdom of taking seriously the variables in organizing that have been considered soft, informal, or beneath the purview of top management interest. We believe that style, systems, skills, superordinate goals can be observed directly, even measured--if only they are taken seriously. We think that these variables can be at least as important as strategy and structure in orchestrating major change; indeed, that they are almost critical for achieving necessary, or desirable, change. A shift in systems, a major retraining program for staff, or the generation of top-to-bottom enthusiasm around a new superordinate goal could take years. Changes in strategy and structure, on the surface, may happen more quickly. But the pace of real change is geared to all seven S's.

At its most powerful and complex, the framework forces us to concentrate on interactions and fit. The real energy required to redirect an institution comes when all the variables in the model are aligned. One of our associates looks at our diagram as a set of compasses. "When all seven needles are all pointed the same way," he comments, "you're looking at an *organized* company."

Footnotes

[1]   Alfred D. Chandler, Jr., Strategy and Structure: Chapters in the History of the American Industrial Enterprise (Cambridge, Mass.: MIT Press, 1962).

[2]   Henry Mintzberg, "The Manager's Job: Folklore and Fact," Harvard Business Review, July/August 1975; 49-61.

EVOLUTION TO A MATRIX ORGANIZATION[1]

Harvey F. Kolodny
University of Toronto

An evolutionary model is proposed to illustrate the development of a matrix organization through function, project, product/matrix, and matrix stages. The structural and behavioral characteristics that accompany each of the stages are identified and discussed. Some of the strategic and environmental conditions that determine the different stages are postulated.

Matrix organizations have become common in a wide variety of organization sectors. From a restricted beginning in the aerospace industry, matrix applications have proliferated and now flourish in multinational corporations, financial institutions, hospitals and health-care agencies, and governmental and educational institutions. Effective management of a matrix organization calls for the use of behavioral skills and structural mechanisms in ways that contrast sharply with those of traditional forms of organizations. Nevertheless, most matrix organizations arise out of these traditional forms. This article develops a model of the evolutionary process.

John Mee [1964] offered one of the earliest attempts to define matrix organization, suggesting that it functioned as a "web of relationships." Since then, many authors have struggled to define this new form [Shull, 1965; Cleland & King, 1968; Delbecq, Shull, Filley, & Grimes, 1969; Ansoff & Brandenburg, 1971; Galbraith, 1971; Kingdon, 1973; Knight, 1976; and Davis & Lawrence, 1977]. However, consensus about a definition of matrix organization has been slow in coming. Most investigators of matrix organization designs have been content to follow Mee's lead and describe the form in terms of how it works--for example, as a "business organized by means of coordination functions" [Corey & Starr, 1971, p. 3].

Agreement about the term "matrix" itself, as used in management, hasn't fared much better. Some forms of team management are referred to as matrix management, as are many instances of resource sharing. The same can be said of program and project management. Extensive application of matrix designs in multinational corporations has given rise to terms such as "grid structure" [Stopford & Wells, 1972], "multidimensional structure" [Goggin, 1972], and "global matrix" [Davis, 1976].

The difficulty in defining and naming the form arises because matrix organization represents a range of possible structural arrangements and accompanying behaviors, many of which are best described in process terms. Galbraith [1972] made this clear when he proposed a Guttman-type scale of continuously increasing complexity in the coordination devices of organizations:

. rules and programs
. hierarchy
. plans

[1] I would like to thank Robert House for his comments on an earlier draft of this article.

Reprinted from The Academy of Management Review, 1979, Vol. 4, No. 4, 543-53, by permission of the author and publisher.

- direct contact
- liaison
- task force
- teams
- integrators
- integrating departments
- matrix organization

Depending on the information-processing demands of its environment, an organization might appear anywhere on the scale. Those whose primary coordination methods are at the top of the list are classified as conventional function or product forms. Those using the top methods and some of the lower ones as well tend toward the matrix end of the continuum, but it is probably not appropriate to refer to them as matrix organizations; another item to describe "matrix-tending" organizations would be useful.

Some authors have suggested an alternative evolutionary perspective. They view matrix organization as a transient condition, a type of coordination that an organization adopts on its way from one form to another. Prahalad [1976] takes this position. He illustrates how a multinational corporation swings from area domination through matrix structure to product domination as the locus of relative power in the organization shifts. Khandwalla also proposes a dissenting view. He takes exception to conceptualizing matrix structure as a pure organization form, preferring to categorize it as a hybrid product-function form, "a combination of the principle of specialized departments with the principles of self-sufficient, more or less autonomous units or divisions" [1977, p. 495].

I do not deny the alternative perspective--namely, that a matrix may be a transitional form that organizations adopt while changing their response from one environmental pressure to another. Rather, my intent is to describe the structural and behavioral changes that take place at each of the stages an organization goes through in becoming a matrix organization. These structures and behaviors are difficult to put in place. It takes time to learn them. An evolutionary path, of the type described here, may facilitate learning.

Not all organizations follow an evolutionary path to its logical conclusion. Some stop along the way because they have found the appropriate form for their situation. Others skip stages or go directly to the last stage. It is a feasible action: there are many successful matrix organizations that serve as witness to this possibility [Curtis & Neuhauser, 1974; Davis & Lawrence, 1977, p. 211].

However, learning new behaviors takes time. For those who take giant steps, the price in human dislocation can be high, not only for the obvious victims of the accelerated change rate, but for the managers and changers themselves. They may be forced to adapt themselves more rapidly than their cognitive and emotional understanding can keep pace. They may also pay a heavy psychological penalty for too rapid a rate of change; and it will show in the difficulties in managing the matrix structure years after the design has been put in place [Kolodny & Lawrence, 1975].

There may be many paths to a particular end [Bertalanffy, 1968]. However, there is no significant empirical evidence as yet to suggest that shortcuts along the evolutionary path necessarily get the organization and its *total* behavioral and structural support systems to the appropriate form any faster than does a step-by-step approach.

Stages of Evolution

Matrix as an Evolutionary Structural Form

Research into the evolution of organizations is sparse [Starbuck, 1965]. Some theorists have concentrated on internal characteristics of the organization as determinants of change. Greiner [1972], for example, points to a series of crises of "control" that move organizations from one stage through another. Using a function/dysfunction [Merton, 1949] type of argument, Greiner shows each stage to be a consequence of the previous stage and a cause, a precipitating crisis, for the next one.

Chandler [1962] advanced the idea of an external determinant in his classic study of the historical evolution of major American companies. Proposing the hypothesis that "structure follows strategy," his study identified strategy as an intervening variable between environment and organization structure, with complexity in the product-market sectors identified as the key external variable in the strategy/structure decision. Building on Chandler's data, Scott [1971] developed a three-stage model of how organizations develop under the pressure of increasing complexity: from (1) an entrepreneurial stage to (2) a single product or functionally organized stage to (3) a divisionalized stage based on diversification.

Contingency theorists maintain that it is attributes of the environment and technology that determine structure [Burns & Stalker, 1961; Woodward, 1965; Lawrence & Lorsch, 1967]. With the exception of Child [1972], they have tended to ignore the possibility of an intervening variable such as strategy. Strategy, as an intervening variable, can account for some of the debate about perceived versus objective environments [Duncan, 1972]. Strategic decisions can delimit environmental sectors and create a closer relationship between "perceived" environmental characteristics and "real" ones. With or without the intervening variable, it follows from their prescriptions that each stage an organization moves through in evolving toward a matrix organization should be commensurate with the demands of the environment at that particular stage. If not, an environment-organization mismatch results. This mismatch gives rise to the crises that Greiner [1972] refers to as the triggers of a subsequent stage of development. These crises show up both as economic warnings and as behavioral signals to the organization's management that corrective action must be taken to re-align the organization to its environment.

I take a similar position: environmental conditions determine the stages most organizations follow in evolving to a matrix design, but strategic considerations can serve to delimit the relevant environment and provide a tighter definition of the determining conditions for each stage. These conditions are described in the last section of this article.

Most matrix designs combine two of the three dominant organization forms in our society: function, product, and area. I examine the evolution from a functional or specialist organization basis to a combined function-and-product matrix form. The evolutionary mode presented here has four distinct stages: function, project, product/matrix, and matrix. If one accepts the viewpoint of those who see the matrix stage as a transitional form that takes an organization from a centralized to a decentralized structure, the model has an additional "divisionalized" stage beyond the matrix stage [Davis & Lawrence, 1977].

107

Galbraith [1971] provided an early descriptive example of how an organization evolves from a functional to a matrix form. The process begins with the organization's inability to respond in timely fashion to problems in its environment: variations required in the product lines, uncertainty in the competitive marketplace, complexity in the product-market relationships, and technological changes that threaten critical products with obsolescence. More often than not these environment-stimulated problems cut across departments in the organization. They demand complex and frequently interdependent responses from these different segments. The vertically structured hierarchy cannot cope with the horizontal coordinating requirements quickly enough. The organizational answer is to decentralize decision making around a specific task and to assign that task to a specific coordinator, often called a project manager.

This action usually takes some of the pressure off the top of the organization and the philosophy soon gets extended to other tasks, activities, and projects. In essence, the organization acknowledges that a second orientation, one that is concerned with task coordination, cost, delivery, and performance is too important to be treated as a secondary concern by the functional managers, whose primary orientation is to their specialist activities. The organization learns that explicit structural actions must be taken to ensure that the management of its projects (and sensitivity to the clients who are concerned about them) is not reduced to too low a level of priority because of the traditional specialist orientations of the functional managers.

Project organization decentralizes decision making to the level of the project team-leader or project manager. This is the level where knowledge relevant to the decision issues can be brought together [Davis, 1951] and where a close monitoring of activities is possible. Project managers acquire and assemble the relevant resources; they plan, organize, and control the tasks and activities; and they take responsibility for the results of their projects or tasks [Flaks & Archibald, 1968]. Through project organization it becomes possible to handle the large amounts of information that otherwise overload the vertical hierarchy.

Yet the choice of a project form of organization also results in more centralized control over the project. This is precisely what the functional organization was no longer able to provide. Centralization, sometimes through control systems, sometimes through physical location rearrangements, and often just through the superordinate role of the project manager, serves as a way to integrate and resolve the conflicting opinions that inevitably come about when different persons or groups are assembled to serve on a task group or project team. PERT, CPM, and a variety of network and control methods serve as procedural frameworks for some of these centralizing tendencies in project organization systems [Malcolm, Roseboom, Clark, & Fazer, 1959; Weist, 1977].

Despite decentralized decision making and tight local control, the project or task seldom achieves complete autonomy [Middleton, 1967]. Many projects are just not large enough to contain all their own resources. Furthermore, each project is unique and moves through different stages. At each of these stages a project requires a different set of resources. The need to share resources becomes a clear requirement of the situation. Resource sharing is accomplished through decentralized support of the projects, support that can come from a variety of sources: functional   units   within   the   organization,   outside   consultants, subcontractors, suppliers, customers, and the like. The project organization design places a premium on the ability to support projects flexibly and adaptively.

In this brief scenario, we see the three conditions for matrix structure developing [Lawrence, Kolodny, & Davis, 1977]. Two orientations are explicitly recognized, though they may not yet be viewed as of equal importance. The organization uses its smaller project groupings to increase its capacity to process information, which requires decentralizing many of its activities.   Finally, coordinating mechanisms are developed to share needed resources flexibly and to organize a cohesive response (teams or projects) to the demands of an ever-changing environment.

It is instructive at this point to examine how project organization differs from functional or classical management structures. Project organization goes beyond conventional bureaucratic assumptions [Massie, 1965] by (1) using horizontal coordination as well as vertical; (2) providing, in the form of project managers, alternative authority figures to those with hierarchical position power, (3) focusing on tasks that are of limited duration and not conducive to the bureaucratic strengths of increasing efficiency through repetition and working down the learning curve; and (4) delegating decisions downward to autonomous units rather than bucking them constantly up the hierarchy.

Project organization is a stage of unfreezing bureaucratic behavior, a stage anticipating movement to a new kind of behavior. It is a period when learning new behavior begins for the organization's members. Changes in processes and behaviors, rather than structural changes, best characterize this stage.

The next stage is a "changing" stage, one in which the behaviors unfrozen in the project organization phase are shaped to a different pattern.   Figure 1 illustrates the process. Just before this next stage, there is a time to choose whether the tasks of the organization will remain temporary, with the design unfrozen into a permanent project organization form, or whether the tasks undertaken will become permanent ones and the organization continue on its evolution toward matrix.

The belief expressed by the design emphasis in Figure 1 is that structural mechanisms are used to reinforce and to induce desired behavior. The sequence proposed begins with behaviors that are initially frozen and maintained by a bureaucratic structure. They are then unfrozen by relaxing these bureaucratic constraints through the introduction of project organization. The new and desired behaviors are subsequently induced or reinforced through the use of structural mechanisms (which are described next). Finally, in the matrix stage, the design emphasizes both structural and behavioral mechanisms.

Ultimately, matrix organization is a way of behaving. When the members of the organization learn the required behaviors, the organization's structural mechanisms become relatively redundant. They exist to reinforce and to induce desired behavior in new members; but they take a background role to the stronger effects of the learned new behaviors.

Product/Matrix Organization

The second step on the evolutionary road to matrix structure differs from the previous stage on several counts: the task activities are permanent, and the primary organizational emphasis is on building the structural devices that will shape and maintain the new and desired behavior patterns. It is a stage where the support systems that accompany the organization design are put in place and learned. It is also a time when the individuals in the organization acquire enough understanding of how the system works to begin making their own decisions, based on the data of experienced or observed behaviors.

Project organization aims to complete a temporary task in a fixed amount of time, for a predetermined cost, and according to a tightly specified set of performance standards. In the end, project managers aim to put themselves out of business. Product/matrix organization, in contrast, takes an idea or a product or a particular kind of technology and aims to develop it so it can grow "as large and as long and as profitable as possible" [Kolodny & Lawrence, 1974]. A product manager becomes a "mini-general-manager," a person responsible for the complete business, for its profit and loss, for its success or failure, and for its future potential as well as its current operations.

FIGURE 1
Stages of Evolution to a Matrix

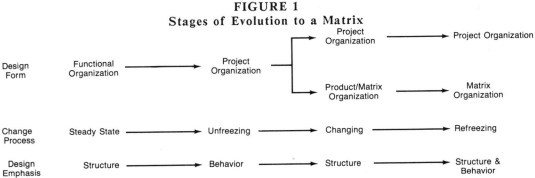

In the stage called product/matrix organization, some or all of the following support systems are put in place:

Dual evaluation/reward systems. Both superiors of a "two-boss" manager are encouraged to contribute to the employee's evaluation and to jointly sign performance appraisals; differential reward or recognition credits (e.g., offices or titles) are given to the product and project managers (vs. the functional managers) to increase the authority of the product side of the organization [Harmer, Gibson, & Lorsch, 1971; Kolodny & Lawrence, 1974; Lawrence et al., 1977].

Dual accounting/control systems. Control over costs is exercised in both the functional and product sides of the organization and a dual set of accounts is developed; functional cost structures and manhour rates are opened up for product management challenge during budget negotiations [Kolodny, 1976].

Comprehensive team-building and interpersonal skill development programs. For further discussion, see Thompson and Lorsch [1967], Kingdon [1973], and Davis and Lawrence [1977].

Extensive information dissemination. A cascading series of regular formal meetings held on both sides of the organization ensures that both receive the same information [Kolodny, 1976].

Strategic and operating systems. New planning systems are devised to allow product managers to be responsible for both operating and strategic performance [Vancil, 1974].

110

Role re-assessment. Job descriptions, particularly those for two-boss people, are written so as to be low in specificity of roles and of tasks [Kolodny & Lawrence, 1975].

Extensive physical space re-orientation. Product groups acquire clearly identified physical territory; key two-boss managers often maintain two or more desks, one in each of their "homes;" functional personnel physically move their locations as they phase in and out of projects or programs; organizations formulate explicit rules about transfers and time limits for functional people co-located with project groups [Kolodny, 1976].

Matrix Organization

For organizations evolving from functional to product forms or from centralized to divisionalized forms the stages are clear. However, when organizations have some systems centralized and others decentralized [Perrow, 1977] the distinction between stages requires a closer examination of the support mechanisms: the control systems, the reward systems, profit and loss responsibility, and so on. Furthermore, when an organization moves from a product/matrix organization to a matrix organization, where the differences are more behavioral than structural, the distinctions between stages become increasingly difficult to specify.

Most of the processes and behaviors that reach maturity under the matrix structure existed to some extent in the project and product/matrix stages. For example, the balance of power that is always evident in a mature matrix is first evident as a dilution of functional power under project organization. In the product/matrix structure it surfaces as a trend in the direction of increasing authority, responsibility, and power for the product manager. Also, the team participation that begins with project organization is elaborated to become an everyday way of life when the organization reaches the matrix stage. In fact, for many in the matrix, multi-team membership becomes normal. Hence, distinguishing explicit stages in an evolutionary process where the discriminating characteristics are primarily behavioral is a problematic undertaking. Nevertheless, under matrix organization one can expect to see some or all of the following:

High flexibility and adaptability. Not only do projects and products phase in and out, but new functional groups develop either out of new demands (e.g., if computers are built into the products, then computer programming might surface as a new function) or as existing functional groupings become more differentiated [Kolodny, 1976]. The organization becomes increasingly morphogenic [Buckley, 1967]. It grows and acquires and divests itself of different organizational units. And it recombines resources in a wide and unanticipated variety of ways.

Intensive boundary transactions. Not only do the product managers acquire the right to subcontract outside the organization for services that could be supplied in-house (but in some way do not meet the requirements of the product groups), but also functional groups acquire equivalent rights to sell their services outside [Kolodny, 1976]. In effect, the matrix organization transacts far more extensively across its many boundaries with the environment than it did as a functional or project or product/matrix organization. Not only are there a larger number of product/project and functional managers in intensive interaction with their local environments, but because much of the decision making has been decentralized to the level of these managers, top management has more time to interact with the external forces it faces for the organization as a whole. The result is that more managers are carrying out the boundary transactions that are normally considered the primary functions of management [Rice, 1963]. The mature matrix organization approaches more and more the ideal of an open system [Bertalanffy, 1968]. Scott [1971] illustrates a similar phenomenon, observing that the number of transactions across an organization's boundary increases as it grows from entrepreneurial to functional to product forms.

Resources sharing, multiple team membership, and interpersonal skill development. As a kaleidoscope recombines its elements into different forms that stay within the confines of the kaleidoscope, so does the matrix provide a framework in which its members combine and recombine into a complex variety of teams, task forces, projects, programs, product groupings, functional homes, and a variety of ad hoc arrangements that overwhelm the ability of any organization chart to capture [Gabarro & Lorsch, 1968; Galbraith, 1970; Galbraith, 1971]. Matrix members complain of the continuous process of meetings but through them learn the collaborative skills needed to function in an ever-interacting environment. They also learn to resolve conflicts because each team is multidisciplinary and differences in orientation must be managed [Lawrence & Lorsch, 1967]. They learn interpersonal and communication skills because the multiple team memberships allow time enough only for clear and unambiguous communication and no time to resolve problems that are a consequence of emotional or personality differences [Thompson & Lorsch, 1968; Davis & Lawrence, 1977]. They learn problem-solving and group-process skills as consensus decision making replaces individual and authority-based decisions. As members come to value the different inputs to a task, they also come to realize that these inputs cannot be used effectively unless the team members acquire participative skills.

Balance-of-power issues pervade every decision. Both orientations of the matrix are important to the business of the organization and the balance between them must be continuously monitored and adjusted. Environmental changes constantly unbalance the system and the chief executive officer must decide how much unbalance is appropriate given the particular external conditions. If economic times are tight, power shifts to the product side, which is more closely concerned with profit and loss and short-term performance. If the economy is benevolent, the emphasis shifts to new developments in the subenvironments of the functional areas, since competitors will also be examining the new technologies and new developments that will ultimately allow projects and programs to formulate innovative responses to their product-market sectors. The internal workings of the matrix is a web of relationships, a battleground on which the representatives of the different orientations advance and retreat as changes in the environment cause the focus to shift from one to the other. In the process, the actors (the matrix managers and the two-boss persons) "learn to learn" from the continuously changing situations they encounter. The design becomes more a "logic of change" and less a

112

"logic of control." (I am indebted to Eric Rhenman for this concept of a logic of change.)

Pro-active behavior. Functional managers in the matrix "unlearn" reactive behavior and learn, instead, to go to product and project managers in anticipation of their needs [Kolodny & Lawrence, 1974; Kolodny, 1976]. No longer the exclusive repository of a functional skill, because product managers can buy services outside, the functional managers learn to sell their services. The increased responsiveness makes the matrix more of a marketplace: negotiations are constantly being conducted with respect to the assignment and priorities of people, equipment, facilities, and other resources. At the same time, product managers become increasingly pro-active about their subenvironments. Already engaged in the task of fitting their product/project technology or specialist skills to their particular market or customer segments, they take the additional step of attempting to reduce uncertainty [Thompson, 1967] or equivocality [Weick, 1969] in their subenvironment. Hence we see aerospace program managers who take offices in the client's plant or bring the client into their facility [Barlow, 1969]. We see human service coordinators who engage a client's "social network" to support the client with at least some minimal level of structure and stability [Curtis, 1974]. And we see program managers in schools of education who co-opt both of their key environments by bringing into their faculty school teachers as adjunct professors, and professors from other faculties and departments within their university [Overing, 1973].

Career Planning. The dual career ladders that marked technical and managerial trajectories in high-technology organizations [Kornhauser, 1962] are elaborated as career options become available in the product side of organizations. The upward course of successful managers is more often than not punctuated with service on both sides of the organization [Lane & Morley, 1975]. Individual career planning [Van Maanen & Schein, 1977] and aggregate career considerations become central organization issues. The product managers who serve as "mini-general-managers" of today are prime candidates for divisional and top management positions of tomorrow. The pro-activity they learn, when injected into a functional department, can invite changes in those departments in a way that accelerates the normally slow evolutionary process to a mature matrix organization.

It is worthwhile to examine the process whereby the organizational devices in a mature matrix organization become consistent with each other and congruent with the design. As functional managers become pro-active and go to the product/project managers, the latter have less need to look inward on the organization. They have more time to focus on the boundary management problems, the interface between their product groups and the relevant customer/market segment. As product managers pay more attention to their individual businesses, the CEO finds less need to be concerned about how those individual businesses are being managed. The CEO finds more time to do the primary CEO job: managing the long-range concerns of the organization, and scanning and being sensitive to aggregate environmental changes. This necessarily means more interaction with the functional managers who hold the organizational responsibility for appropriate development of longer-term resources.

With this re-assessment of functional manager relevance on the part of the CEO, and with increased confidence from the product managers that the functional managers will be doing the job well, the mature matrix organization becomes increasingly self-supporting (Figure 2). The words of one CEO emphasize this outcome: "The necessity for product managers to go bashing functional managers has largely disappeared. The system has become supportive. I know that we'll all live longer for it. It's now a real beauty to observe. You can see people anticipating, talking to others about a need that they can see others are going to have, and asking how they can help" [Kolodny & Lawrence, 1974, p. 16].

FIGURE 2
The Self-Supporting Matrix

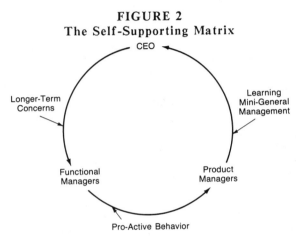

The Determinants of the Stages of Evolution

I have claimed that there is an evolutionary pattern to the development of matrix organization. If structure is externally determined, as contingency theory maintains, then each of the stages in the evolution toward matrix should be identified with different determining conditions. The contingent paradigm, however, has not achieved much consensus about just what it is that structure depends on. Environmental conditions, and its many derivatives (uncertainty, variability, complexity, product-market relationships, interconnectedness, rate of change of new products) engage the research preoccupation of one set of authors [Duncan, 1972; Jurkovich, 1974; Downey, Hellriegel, & Slocum, 1975]. Technology and its variations (technological complexity, technical specificity, line control to workflow, workflow integration) have been the focal independent variable for another school of researchers [Woodward, 1965; Khandwalla, 1974]. Strategy and strategic choice are the determinants of structure for some [Chandler, 1962; Child, 1972]. Information-processing requirements determine organizational arrangements for others [Galbraith, 1972]. And still another group clings doggedly to size as the most explanatory of the independent variables [Hickson, Pugh, & Pheysey, 1969].

Given the lack of consensus associated with this contingent paradigm, it becomes a fool's errand to try to predict the determinants of the different stages an organization will pass through on its evolutionary journey to a matrix form. Nevertheless, fools do rush in. Table 1 takes a coarse cut at identifying the strategic and environmental contingencies that might properly locate an organization in the function, project, product/matrix, or matrix stage. Because the last stage, matrix, is held to be a mature version of product/matrix, the determinants of the latter will resemble those of the former.

To understand that the path to matrix is an evolutionary one is to understand that the implementation of a matrix organization takes time. There are new values that must be understood [Davis, 1967; Tannenbaum & Davis, 1969] and there are new behaviors that must be learned [Thompson & Lorsch, 1967; Kingdon, 1973; Davis & Lawrence, 1977]. The understanding and learning can come about through experience, but the process is slow and each of the stages may take years.

The process can be accelerated with a careful program of training and development [Davis & Lawrence, 1977, chap. 5], but even then, it will take several years. However, I believe that those organizations that embark on the matrix path without undertaking explicit training and development along the way will find their evolutionary progress stunted at some point--not because that point was the appropriate place for them to stop, but because old behaviors will ultimately constrain the desired new ones [Argyris, 1967].

TABLE 1
Determinants of the Stages of Matrix Organization

Form	Determinants
Function	1. Efficiency is a success criterion 2. Competitive advantage is along a single parameter (technology, price, performance, delivery) 3. Markets are relatively predictable 4. Narrow range of products with long time horizons
Project	1. Several simultaneous success criteria (performance, cost, price, schedule, technology, efficiency) 2. Moderate market change 3. Differentiated clients and markets 4. Moderate number of products (projects) 5. Specified time horizons for each client or project 6. Interconnectedness between outside and local organization
Product/Matrix	1. Innovation is a success criterion 2. Differentiated products, markets, customers 3. High variability and uncertainty in product-market mix 4. Time horizons for product vary from medium to long
Matrix	Same as product/matrix

It does not follow that every organization embarking on this journey should aspire to a mature matrix design. For many, the form won't fit. Project or product/matrix may be all their environments call for. Knowing how much is

115

needed is a difficult assessment. Those who are familiar with matrix organizations know that the successful ones are *always* led by a CEO who understands how to make them work.

References

Ansoff, H. I., & Brandenburg, R. G. A language for organization design: Parts I & II, <u>Management Science</u>, 1971, 17(12), B-705-B-731.

Argyris, Chris. Today' problems with tomorrow's organizations, <u>The Journal of Management Studies</u>, 1967, 4(1), 31-55.

Barlow, Edward J. The optimum balance between program organizations and functional organizations to promote technology transfer, <u>IEEE Transactions on Engineering Management</u>, 1969, 16(3), 116-121.

Bertalanffy, Ludwig von. <u>General systems theory: Foundations, development, applications</u>. New York: Braziller, 1968.

Buckley, Walter. <u>Sociology and modern systems theory</u>. Englewood Cliffs, N.J.: Prentice-Hall, 1967.

Burns, Tom, & Stalker, G. H. <u>The management of innovation</u>. London: Tavistock, 1961.

Chandler, Alfred D. <u>Strategy and structure: Chapters in the history of the industrial enterprise</u>. Cambridge, Mass.: MIT Press, 1962.

Child, John. Organizational structure, environment, and performance: The role of strategic choice, <u>Sociology</u>, 1972, 6, 1-22.

Cleland, David I. & King, William R. <u>Systems analysis and project management</u>. New York: McGraw-Hill, 1968.

Corey, E. Raymond & Star, Steven H. <u>Organization strategy: A marketing approach</u>. Boston: Harvard University Graduate School of Business Administration, Division of Research, 1971.

Curtis, Robert W. Team problem solving in a social network, <u>Psychiatric Annals</u>, 1974.

Curtis, Robert, & Neuhauser, Duncan. <u>Providing specialized coordinated human service to communities: The organizational problem and a potential solution</u>. Working paper, Taunton Area, Massachusetts Department of Human Resources, 1974.

Davis, R. C. <u>The fundamentals of top management</u>. New York: Harper & Bros., 1951.

Davis, Sheldon A. An organic problem-solving method of organizational change, <u>Journal of Applied Behavioral Science</u>, 1967, 3(1), 3-21.

Davis, Stanley M. Trends in the organization of multinational corporations, <u>Columbia Journal of World Business</u>, 1976, 11(2), 59-71.

Davis, Stanley M., & Lawrence, Paul R. <u>Matrix</u>. Reading, Mass.: Addison-Wesley, 1977.

Delbecq, Andre L., Shull, Fremont A., Filley, Alan C., & Grimes, Andrew J. Matrix organization: A conceptual guide to organizational variation, <u>Wisconsin Business Papers</u>, 1969, September, No. 2. Madison University of Wisconsin Bureau of Business Research & Service.

Downey, H. Kirk, Hellriegel, Don H., & Slocum, John W. Jr. Environmental uncertainty: The construct and its application, <u>Administrative Science Quarterly</u>, 1975, 20(4), 613-629.

Duncan, Robert B. Characteristics of organizational environments and perceived environmental uncertainty, <u>Administrative Science Quarterly</u>, 1972, 17, 313-327.

Flaks, Marvin, & Archibald, Russel D. The electronic engineer's guide to project management, <u>Electronic Engineer</u>, 1968, April-August, parts 1-5.

Gabarro, John J., & Lorsch, Jay W. <u>Northern Electric Company, Ltd.</u>, (A), (B), (C), and (D) (ICCH 9-413-062, 063, 064, 065). Boston: Intercollegiate Case Clearing House, 1968.

Galbraith, Jay R. Environmental and technological determinants of organization design. In Jay W. Lorsch & Paul R. Lawrence (Eds.), <u>Studies in organization design</u>. Homewood, Ill.: Irwin, 1970, 113-139.

Galbraith, Jay R. Matrix organization design, <u>Business Horizons</u>, 1971, 14(1), 29-40.

Galbraith, Jay R. Organization design: An information processing view. In Jay W. Lorsch & Paul R. Lawrence (Eds.), <u>Organization planning: Cases and concepts</u>. Homewood, Ill.: Irwin, 1972, 49-74.

Goggin, William C. How the multidimensional structure works at Dow Corning, <u>Harvard Business Review</u>, 1974, 52(1), 54-65.

Greiner, L. E. Evolution and revolution as organizations grow, <u>Harvard Business Review</u>, 1972, 50(4), 37-46.

Harmer, Richard, Gibson, Cyrus, & Lorsch, Jay. <u>Product management at United Brands</u> (ICCH 9-471-049). Boston: Intercollegiate Case Clearing House, 1971.

Hickson, David J., Pugh, D. S., & Pheysey, Diana C. Operations technology and organization structure: An empirical reappraisal, <u>Administrative Science Quarterly</u>, 1969, 14(3), 378-397.

Jurkovich, Ray. A core typology of organizational environments, <u>Administrative Science Quarterly</u>, 1974, 19(3), 380-394.

Khandwalla, Pradip N. Mass output orientation of operations technology and organizational structure, <u>Administrative Science Quarterly</u>, 1974, 19(1), 74-97.

Khandwalla, Pradip N. <u>The design of organizations</u>. New York: Harcourt, Brace, Jovanovich, 1977.

Kingdon, Donald Ralph. <u>Matrix organization: Managing information technologies</u>. London: Tavistock, 1973.

Knight, Kenneth. Matrix organizations: A review, <u>The Journal of Management Studies</u>, 1976, 13(2), 111-130.

Kolodny, Harvey F. <u>Matrix organization design, implementation, and management</u>. Unpublished doctoral dissertation. Harvard University, 1974.

116

Kolodny, Harvey F., & Lawrence, Paul R. Canadian Marconi Company - Avionics Division (ICCH 9-474-158). Boston: Intercollegiate Case Clearing House, 1974.

Kolodny, Harvey F. & Lawrence, Paul R. Diamond Instrument Company (ICCH 9-474-071). Boston: Intercollegiate Case Clearing House, 1975.

Kornhauser, W. Scientists in industry: Conflict and accommodation. Berkeley: University of California Press, 1962.

Lane, Henry W., & Morley, Eileen. Neiman-Marcus (ICCH 1-475-077). Boston: Intercollegiate Case Clearing House, 1975.

Lawrence, Paul R., Kolodny, Harvey F., & Davis, Stanley M. The human side of the matrix, Organizational Dynamics. 1977, 6(1), 43-61.

Lawrence, Paul, & Lorsch, Jay W. Organization and environment: Managing differentiation and integration. Boston: Harvard University Graduate School of Business Administration, Division of Research, 1967.

Malcolm, Donald, Roseboom, John, Clark, Charles E., & Fazer, Willard. Applications of a technique for research and development program evaluation, Operations Research, 1959, 7(5), 646-669.

Massie, J. L. Management theory. In J. G. March (Ed.), Handbook of organizations. Chicago: Rand McNally, 1965.

Mee, John F. Ideational items: Matrix organization, Business Horizons, 1964, 7, 70-72.

Merton, Robert. Social theory and social structure. New York: Free Press, 1949.

Middleton, C. J. How to set up a project organization, Harvard Business Review, 1967, 45(2), 73-82.

Overing, Robert. Toward a redefinition of teacher education, Interchange, 1973, 4(2/3), 19-27.

Perrow, Charles. The bureaucratic paradox: The efficient organization centralizes in order to decentralize, Organizational Dynamics, 1977, 5(4), 3-14.

Prahalad, C. K. Strategic choices in diversified MNCs, Harvard Business Review, 1976, 54(4), 67-78.

Rice, A. K. The enterprise and its environment. London: Tavistock, 1963.

Scott, Bruce R. Stages of corporate development - Part 1 (ICCH 4-37-294). Boston: Intercollegiate Case Clearing House, 1971.

Scull, Fremont A. Matrix structure and project authority for optimizing organizational capacity (Bus. Sci. Monograph 1). Carbondale, Ill.: Souther Illinois University Business Research Bureau, 1965.

Starbuck, W. H. Organizational growth and development. In J. G. March (Ed.), Handbook of organizations. Chicago: Rand McNally, 1965.

Stopford, John M., & Wells, Louis T. Managing the multinational enterprise. New York: Basic Books, 1972.

Tannenbaum, Robert, & Davis, Sheldon A. Values, man, and organizations, The Industrial Management Review, 1969, 10(2), 67-86.

Thompson, James D. Organizations in action. New York: McGraw-Hill, 1967.

Thompson, Paul H., & Lorsch, Jay W. The TRW systems group, (A), (B), and (C) (ICCH 9-414-013, 014, 015). Boston: Intercollegiate Case Clearing House, 1967.

Vancil, Richard. Texas Instruments, Incorporated (ICCH 9-172-054). Boston: Intercollegiate Case Clearing House, 1974.

Van Maanen, John, & Schein, Edgar H. Career development in J. Richard Hackman & J. Lloyud Suttle (Eds.), Improving life at work: Behavioral science approaches to organizational change. Santa Monica, Calif.: Goodyear, 1977, 30-95.

Weick, Karl E. The social psychology of organizing. Reading, Mass.: Addison-Wesley, 1969.

Weist, Jerome D. Project network models: Past, present, and future, Project Management Quarterly, 1977 7(4), 27-36.

Woodward, Joan. Industrial organization: Theory and practice. London: Oxford University Press, 1965.

ORGANIZATION DESIGN: AN INFORMATION PROCESSING VIEW

Jay R. Galbraith
European Institute for Advanced Studies

The Information Processing Model

A basic proposition is that the greater the uncertainty of the task, the greater the amount of information that has to be processed between decision makers during the execution of the task. If the task is well understood prior to performing it, much of the activity can be preplanned. If it is not understood, then during the actual task execution more knowledge is acquired which leads to changes in resource allocations, schedules, and priorities. All these changes require information processing *during* task performance. Therefore *the greater the task uncertainty, the greater the amount of informatiion that must be processed among decision makers during task execution in order to achieve a given level of performance.* The basic effect of uncertainty is to limit the ability of the organization to preplan or to make decisions about activities in advance of their execution. Therefore it is hypothesized that the observed variations in organizational forms are variations in the strategies of organizations to 1) increase their ability to preplan, 2) increase their flexibility to adapt to their inability to preplan, or, 3) to decrease the level of performance required for continued viability. Which strategy is chosen depends on the relative costs of the strategies. The function of the framework is to identify these strategies and their costs.

The Mechanistic Model

This framework is best developed by keeping in mind a hypothetical organization. Assume it is large and employs a number of specialist groups and resources in providing the output. After the task has been divided into specialist subtasks, the problem is to integrate the subtasks around the completion of the global task. This is the problem of organization design. The behaviors that occur in one subtask cannot be judged as good or bad *per se*. The behaviors are more effective or ineffective depending upon the behaviors of the other subtask performers. There is a design problem because the executors of the behaviors cannot communicate with all the roles with whom they are interdependent. Therefore the design problem is to create mechanisms that permit coordinated action across large numbers of interdependent roles. Each of these mechanisms, however, has a limited range over which it is effective at handling the information requirements necessary to coordinate the interdependent roles. As the amount of uncertainty increases, and therefore information processing increases, the organization must adopt integrating mechanisms which increase its information processing capabilities.

1. *Coordination by Rules or Programs*
For routine predictable tasks March and Simon have identified the use of

rules or programs to coordinate behavior between interdependent subtasks [March and Simon, 1958, Chap. 6]. To the extent that job related situations can be predicted in advance, and behaviors specified for these situations, programs allow an interdependent set of activities to be performed without the need for inter-unit communication. Each role occupant simply executes the behavior which is appropriate for the task related situation with which he is faced.

2. *Hierarchy*

As the organiztion faces greater uncertainty its participants face situations for which they have no rules. At this point the hierarchy is employed on an exception basis. The recurring job situations are programmed with rules while infrequent situations are referred to that level in the hierarchy where a global perspective exists for all affected subunits. However, the hierarchy also has a limited range. As uncertainty increases the number of exceptions increases until the hierarchy becomes overloaded.

3. *Coordination by Targets or Goals*

As the uncertainty of the organization's task increases, coordination increasingly takes place by specifying outputs, goals or targets [March and Simon, 1958, p. 145]. Instead of specifying specific behaviors to be enacted, the organization undertakes processes to set goals to be achieved and the employees select the behaviors which lead to goal accomplishments. Planning reduces the amount of information processing in the hierarchy by increasing the amount of discretion exercised at lower levels. Like the use of rules, planning achieves integrated action and also eliminates the need for continuous communication among interdependent subunits as long as task performance stays within the planned task specifications, budget limits and within targeted completion dates. If it does not, the hierarchy is again employed on an exception basis.

The ability of an organization to coordinate interdependent tasks depends on its ability to compute meaningful subgoals to guide subunit action. When uncertainty increases because of introducing new products, entering new markets, or employing new technologies these subgoals are incorrect. The result is more exceptions, more information processing, and an overloaded hierarchy.

Design Strategies

The ability of an organization to successfully utilize coordination by goal setting, hierarchy, and rules depends on the combination of the frequency of exceptions and the capacity of the hierarchy to handle them. As the task uncertainty increases the organization must again take organization design action. It can proceed in either of two general ways. First, it can act in two ways to reduce the amount of information that is processed. And second, the organization can act in two ways to increase its capacity to handle more information. The two methods for reducing the need for information and the two methods for increasing processing capacity are shown schematically in Figure 1. The effect of all these actions is to reduce the number of exceptional cases referred upward into the organization through hierarchical channels. The assumption is that the critical limiting factor of an organizational form is its ability to handle the non-routine, consequential events that cannot be anticipated and planned for in advance. The non-programmed events place the greatest communication load on the organization.

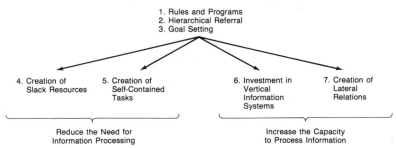

FIGURE 1
Organization Design Strategies

1. Rules and Programs
2. Hierarchical Referral
3. Goal Setting

4. Creation of Slack Resources
5. Creation of Self-Contained Tasks
6. Investment in Vertical Information Systems
7. Creation of Lateral Relations

Reduce the Need for Information Processing

Increase the Capacity to Process Information

1. *Creation of Slack Resources*

As the number of exceptions begin to overload the hierarchy, one response is to increase the planning targets so that fewer exceptions occur. For example, completion dates can be extended until the number of exceptions that occur are within the existing information processing capacity of the organization. This has been the practice in solving job shop scheduling problems [Pounds, 1963]. Job shops quote delivery times that are long enough to keep the scheduling problems within the computational and information processing limits of the organization. Since every job shop has the same problem, standard lead times evolve in the industry. Similarly budget targets could be raised, buffer inventories employed, etc. The greater the uncertainty, the greater the magnitude of the inventory, lead time or budget needed to reduce an overload.

All of these examples have a similar effect. They represent the use of slack resources to reduce the amount of interdependence between subunits [March and Simon, 1958; Cyert and March, 1963]. This keeps the required amount of information within the capacity of the organization to process it. Information processing is reduced because an exception is less likely to occur and reduced interdependence means that fewer factors need to be considered simultaneously when an exception does occur.

The strategy of using slack resources has its costs. Relaxing budget targets has the obvious cost of requiring more budget. Increasing the time to completion date has the effect of delaying the customer. Inventories require the investment of capital funds which could be used elsewhere. Reduction of design optimization reduces the performance of the article being designed. Whether slack resources are used to reduce information or not depends on the relative cost of the other alternatives.

The design choices are: 1) among which factors to change (lead time, overtime, machine utilization, etc.) to create the slack, and 2) by what amount should the factor be changed. Many operations research models are useful in choosing factors and amounts. The time-cost trade off problem in project networks is a good example.

2. *Creation of Self-Contained Tasks*

The second method of reducing the amount of information processed is to change the subtask groupings from resource (input) based to output based categories and give each group the resources it needs to supply the output. For example, the functional organization could be changed to product groups. Each group would have its own product engineers, process engineers, fabricating and assembly operations, and marketing activities. In other situations, groups can be created around product lines, geographical areas, projects, client groups, markets, etc., each of which would contain the input resources necessary for creation of the output.

The strategy of self-containment shifts the basis of the authority structure from one based on input, resource, skill, or occupational categories to one based on output or geographical categories. The shift reduces the amount of information processing through several mechanisms. First, it reduces the amount of output diversity faced by a single collection of resources. For example, a professional organization with multiple skill specialties providing service to three different client groups must schedule the use of these specialties across three demands for their services and determine priorities when conflicts occur. But, if the organization changed to three groups, one for each client category, each with its own full complement of specialties, the schedule conflicts across client groups disappears and there is no need to process information to determine priorities.

The second source of information reduction occurs through a reduced division of labor. The functional or resource specialized structure pools the demand for skills across all output categories. In the example above each client generates approximately one-third of the demand for each skill. Since the division of labor is limited by the extent of the market, the division of labor must decrease as the demand decreases. In the professional organization, each client group may have generated a need for one-third of a computer programmer. The functional organization would have hired one programmer and shared him across the groups. In the self-contained structure there is insufficient demand in each group for a programmer so the professionals must do their own programming. Specialization is reduced but there is no problem of scheduling the programmer's time across the three possible uses for it.

The cost of the self-containment strategy is the loss of resource specialization. In the example, the organization foregoes the benefit of a specialist in computer programming. If there is physical equipment, there is a loss of economies of scale. The professional organization would require three machines in the self-contained form but only a large time-shared machine in the functional form. But those resources which have large economies of scale or for which specialization is necessary may remain centralized. Thus, it is the degree of self-containment that is the variable. The greater the degree of uncertainty, other things equal, the greater the degree of self-containment.

The design choices are the basis for the self-contained structure and the number of resources to be contained in the groups. No groups are completely self-contained or they would not be part of the same organization. But one product divisionalized firm may have eight of fifteen functions in the division while another may have twelve of fifteen in the division. Usually accounting, finance, and legal services are centralized and shared. Those functions which have economies of scale, require specialization, or are necessary for control remain centralized and not part of the self-contained group.

The first two strategies reduced the amount of information by lower performance standards and creating small autonomous groups to provide the output. Information is reduced because an exception is less likely to occur and fewer factors need to be considered when an exception does occur. The next two strategies accept the performance standards and division of labor as given and adapt the organization so as to process the new information which is created during task performance.

3. *Investment in Vertical Information Systems*

The organization can invest in mechanisms which allow it to process information acquired during task performance without overloading the hierarchical communication channels. The investment occurs according to the following logic. After the organization has created its plan or set of targets for inventories, labor utilization, budgets, and schedules, unanticipated events occur which generate exceptions requiring adjustments to the original plan. At some point when the number of exceptions becomes substantial, it is preferable to generate a new plan rather than make incremental changes with each exception. The issue is then how frequently should plans be revised--yearly, quarterly, or monthly? The greater the frequency of replanning the greater the resources, such as clerks, computer time, input-output devices, etc., required to process information about relevant factors.

The cost of information processing resources can be minimized if the language is formalized. Formalization of a decision-making language simply means that more information is transmitted with the same number of symbols. It is assumed that information processing resources are consumed in proportion to the number of symbols transmitted. The accounting system is an example of a formalized language.

Providing more information, more often, may simply overload the decision maker. Investment may be required to increase the capacity of the decision maker by employing computers, various man-machine combinations, assistants-to, etc. The cost of this strategy is the cost of the information processing resources consumed in transmitting and processing the data.

The design variables of this strategy are the decision frequency, the degree of formalization of language, and the type of decision mechanism which will make the choice. This strategy is usually operationalized by creating redundant information channels which transmit data from the point of origination upward in the hierarchy where the point of decision rests. If data is formalized and quantifiable, this strategy is effective. If the relevant data are qualitative and ambiguous, then it may prove easier to bring the decisions down to where the information exists.

4. *Creation of Lateral Relationships*

The last strategy is to employ selectively joint decision processes which cut across lines of authority. This strategy moves the level of decision making down in the organization to where the information exists but does so without reorganizing around self-contained groups. There are several types of lateral decision processes. Some processes are usually referred to as the informal organization. However, these informal processes do not always arise spontaneously out of the needs of the task. This is particularly true in multi-national organizations in which participants are separated by physical barriers, language differences, and cultural differences. Under the circumstances lateral processes need to be designed. The lateral processes evolve as follows with increases in uncertainty.

4.1. *Direct Contact* between managers who share a problem. If a problem arises on the shop floor, the foreman can simply call the design engineer, and they can jointly agree upon a solution. From an information processing view, the joint decision prevents an upward referral and unlaods the hierarchy.

4.2 *Liaison Roles.* When the volume of contacts between any two departments grows, it becomes economical to set up a specialized role to handle this communication. Liaison men are typical examples of specialized roles designed to facilitate communication between two interdependent departments and to bypass the long lines of communication involved in upward referral. Liaison roles arise at lower and middle levels of management.

4.3 *Task Forces.* Direct contact and liaison roles, like the integration mechanisms before them, have a limited range of usefulness. They work when two managers or functions are involved. When problems arise involving seven or eight departments, the decision making capacity of direct contacts is exceeded. Then these problems must be referred upward. For uncertain, interdependent tasks such situations arise frequently. Task forces are a form of horizontal contact which is designed for problems of multiple departments.

The task force is made up of representatives from each of the affected departments. Some are full-time members, others may be part-time. The task force is a temporary group. It exists only as long as the problem remains. When a solution is reached, each participant returns to his normal tasks.

To the extent that they are successful, task forces remove problems from higher levels of the hierarchy. The decisions are made at lower levels in the organization. In order to guarantee integration, a group problem solving approach is taken. Each affected subunit contributes a member and therefore provides the information necessary to judge the impact on all units.

4.4. *Teams.* The next extension is to incorporate the group decision process into the permanent decision processes. That is, as certain decisions consistently arise, the task forces become permanent. These groups are labeled teams. There are many design issues concerned in team decision making such as at what level do they operate, who participates, etc. [Galbraith, 1973, Chapters 6 and 7]. One design decision is particularly critical. This is the choice of leadership. Sometimes a problem exists largely in one department so that the department manager is the leader. Sometimes the leadership passes from one manager to another. As a new product moves to the market place, the leader of the new product team is first the technical manager followed by the production and then the marketing manager. The result is that if the team cannot reach a consensus decision and the leader decides, the goals of the leader are consistent with the goals of the organization for the decision in question. But quite often obvious leaders cannot be found. Another mechanism must be introduced.

4.5 *Integrating Roles.* The leadership issue is solved by creating a new role--an integrating role [Lawrence and Lorsch, 1967, Chapter 3]. These roles carry the labels of product managers, program managers, project managers, unit managers (hospitals), materials managers, etc. After the role is created, the design problem is to create enough power in the role to influence the decision process. These roles have power even when no one reports directly to them. They have some power because they report to the general manager. But if they are seclected so as to be unbiased with respect to the groups they integrate and to have technical competence, they have expert power. They collect information and equalize power differences due to preferential access to knowledge and information. The power equalization increases trust and the quality of the joint decision process. But power equalization occurs only if the integrating role is staffed with someone who can exercise expert power in the form of persuasion and informal influences rather than exert the power of rank or authority.

    4.6   *Managerial Linking Roles.* As tasks become more uncertain, it is more difficult to exercise expert power. The role must get more power of the formal authority type in order to be effective at coordinating the joint decisions which occur at lower levels of the organization. This position power changes the nature of the role which for lack of a better name is labeled a managerial linking role. It is not like the integrating role because it possesses formal position power but is

FIGURE 2
A Pure Matrix Organization

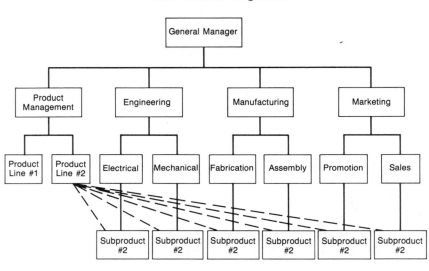

— — = Technical authority over the project
———— = Formal authority over the product (in product organization, these relationships may be reversed)

different from line managerial roles in that participants do not report to the linking manager. The power is added by the following successive changes:

    a)   The integrator receives approval power of budgets formulated in the departments to be integrated.

    b)   The planning and budgeting process starts with the integrator making his initiation in budgeting legitimate.

c)   Linking manager receives the budget for the area of responsibility and buys resources from the specialist groups.

These mechanisms permit the manager to exercise influence even though no one works directly for him. The role is concerned with integration but exercises power through the formal power of the position. If this power is insufficient to integrate the subtasks and creation of self-contained groups is not feasible, there is one last step.

4.7   *Matrix Organization.* The last step is to create the dual authority relationship and the matrix organization [Galbraith, 1971]. At some point in the organization some roles have two superiors. The design issue is to select the locus of these roles. The result is a balance of power between the managerial linking roles and the normal line organization roles. Figure 2 depicts the pure matrix design.

The work of Lawrence and Lorsch is highly consistent with the assertions concerning lateral relations [Lawrence and Lorsch, 1967; Lorsch and Lawrence, 1968]. They compared the types of lateral relations undertaken by the most successful firm in three different industries. Their data are summarized in Table 1. The plastics firm has the greatest rate of new product introduction (uncertainty) and the greatest utilization of lateral processes. The container firm was also very successful but utilized only standard practices because its information processing task is much less formidable. Thus, the greater the uncertainty the lower the level of decision making and the integration is maintained by lateral relations.

TABLE 1

	Plastics	Food	Container
% new products in last ten years	35%	20%	0%
Integrating Devices	Rules	Rules	Rules
	Hierarchy	Hierarchy	Hierarchy
	Planning	Planning	Planning
	Direct Contact	Direct Contact	Direct Contact
	Teams at 3 levels	Task forces	
	Integrating Dept.	Integrators	
% Integrators/Managers	22%	17%	0%

[Adopted from Lawrence and Lorsch, 1967, pp. 86-138 and Lorsch and Lawrence, 1968].

Table 1 points out the cost of using lateral relations. The plastics firm has 22% of its managers in integration roles. Thus, the greater the use of lateral relations the greater the managerial intensity. This cost must be balanced against the cost of slack resources, self-contained groups and information systems.

Choice of Strategy

Each of the four strategies has been briefly presented. The organization can follow one or some combination of several if it chooses. It will choose that strategy which has the least cost in its environmental context. [For an example, see Galbraith, 1970.] However, what may be lost in all of the explanations is that the four strategies are hypothesized to be an exhaustive set of alternatives. That is, if the organization is faced with greater uncertainty due to technological change, higher performance standards due to increased competition, or diversifies its product line to reduce dependence, the amount of information processing is increased. *The organization must adopt at least one of the four strategies when faced with greater uncertainty.* If it does not consciously choose one of the four, then the first, reduced performance standards, will happen automatically. The task information requirements and the capacity of the organization to process information are always matched. If the organization does not consciously match them, reduced performance through budget overruns, schedule overruns will occur in order to bring about equality. Thus the organization should be planned and designed simultaneously with the planning of the strategy and resource allocations. But if the strategy involves introducing new products, entering new markets, etc., then some provision for increased information must be made. Not to decide is to decide, and it is to decide upon slack resources as the strategy to remove hierarchical overload.

There is probably a fifth strategy which is not articulated here. Instead of changing the organization in response to task uncertainty, the organization can operate on its environment to reduce uncertainty. The organization through strategic decisions, long term contracts, coalitions, etc., can control its environment. But these maneuvers have costs also. They should be compared with costs of the four design strategies presented above.

Summary

The purpose of this paper has been to explain why task uncertainty is related to organizational form. In so doing the cognitive limits theory of Herbert Simon was the guiding influence. As the consequences of cognitive limits were traced through the framework various organization design strategies were articulated. The framework provides a basis for integrating organizational interventions, such as information systems and group problem solving, which have been treated separately before.

Bibliography

Cyert, Richard, and March, James, The Behavioral Theory of the Firm, Prentice-Hall, Englewood Cliffs, N.J., 1963.

Galbraith, Jay, "Environmental and Technological Determinants of Organization Design: A Case Study" in Lawrence and Lorsch (ed.) Studies in Organiztion Design, Richard D. Irwin Inc., Homewood, Ill., 1970.

Galbraith, Jay, "Designing Matrix Organizations," Business Horizons, (Feb. 1971), pp. 29-40.

Galbraith, Jay, Organization Design, Addison-Wesley Pub. Co., Reading, Mass., 1973.

Lawrence, Paul, and Lorsch, Jay, Organization and Environment, Division of Research, Harvard Business School, Boston, Mass., 1967.

Lorsch, Jay, and Lawrence, Paul, "Environmental Factors and Organization Integration," Paper read at the Annual Meeting of the American Sociological Association, August 27, 1968, Boston, Mass.

March, James, and Simon, Herbert, Organizations, John Wiley & Sons, New York, N.Y., 1958.

Pounds, William, "The Scheduling Environment" in Muth and Thompson (eds.) Industrial Scheduling, Prentice-Hall Inc., Englewood Cliffs, N.J., 1963.

Simon, Herbert, Models of Man, John Wiley & Sons, New York, N.Y., 1957.

DESIGNING MANAGERIAL AND PROFESSIONAL WORK FOR HIGH PERFORMANCE: A SOCIOTECHNICAL APPROACH

Calvin H. P. Pava

Improving the performance of managers and professionals is emerging as a cardinal concern for the eighties. Yet ideas about how to improve the performance of "knowledge work" are scanty, and there are few systematic methods by which to analyze or redesign the way managerial and professional work is organized. Against this paucity stands a rich heritage of work-design methods developed in the factory. Foremost among these is sociotechnical design, which, since its inception in the 1950s, has become a powerful means for designing high-performance organizations.[1]

This article formulates a new approach to the design of managerial and professional work. It is based upon the fundamental postulates of sociotechnical design but represents a significant departure from the traditional analytic techniques used in the factory. The result is a method by which managers and professionals can redesign their own unit for a higher level of performance. This technique renders organizations more productive for knowledge work and can guide the selection and deployment of new office technology.

An Emerging Challenge

The changing structure of our economy is creating a new priority on the agenda of organizational leaders. Approaching the turn of this century, we see the emergence of an "information economy" in which the creation and management of information is becoming the dominant sector of activity. This transformation is reflected in labor-force statistics, which show the proportion of U.S. workers employed in white-collar jobs as rising from 20 percent in 1978 to a projected 40 percent in 1988.[2] At the same time, existing data suggest that productivity improvement has remained virtually flat in the information sector. For example, analysis of data from 1972 to 1977 indicates that the rate of productivity for U.S. blue-collar workers rose 2 percent annually, while that for white-collar workers rose 0.4 percent annually.[3] A different analysis estimated that between 1960 and 1970, blue-collar productivity grew 83 percent, whereas white-collar productivity increased only 4 percent.[4] None of these studies is precise, but overall they indicate a major opportunity for faster improvement in the productivity of white-collar work. A major item of management's priorities through the 1980s will therefore be to build more productive office organizations.

Not all white-collar work affects the bottom line equally. Professional and managerial employees draw the greatest dollar volume of salary. In 1979, total compensation for U.S. secretarial, typist, and clerical personnel totaled $125 billion. At the same time, total compensation for professional, managerial, and administrative personnel totaled $400 billion.[5] From the standpoint of a cost-benefit ratio, enhancing the productivity of these latter workers offers exceptional opportunities for adding value.

Yet attempts to rationalize such labor as if it were a set of factory operations usually fail. To enhance the performance of such work, management will need to draw upon new concepts and methods that suit the texture of managerial and professional endeavors rather than prevailing models drawn from industrial factory work.

The emergence of new office technology further complicates the enhancement of managerial and professional work. The declining costs of microelectronics and accumulating experience with information-systems design are creating a pervasive shift in office tools. A proliferation of new office equipment is coming to market: smart typewriters, word processors, desk top work stations, smart public branch phone exchanges, integrated voice-data switches, local area networks, facsimile transmitters, cellular radio, and numerous software products. Foreseeable developments through the 1980s promise yet further remarkable offerings that include greater networking capabilities, limited voice input/output, and rudimentary inferential (artificial intelligence) software.

Advertising by equipment vendors aside, this flood of new technology will have mixed effects that both encourage and complicate the improvement of productivity for the manager and professional. New information technology will allow unprecedented augmentation of the capabilities of knowledge workers, but performance will not improve magically by simply installing new equipment. New operator skills, procedural developments, structural transformation, and cultural metamorphosis will be essential for the harvesting of real operational advantages from exotic new office technology.

In the past, new operator skills and procedural changes have been the primary domain for learning and change, with specialist staffs and vendors providing key impetus and support. More advanced office equipment, with still higher functionality and greater capacity for interconnection, makes changes in organizational structure and culture more important than before. These are realms that cannot be entrusted to staff specialists or vendors alone. Management must take an active role to shape how new technology reshapes the structure, ethos, and mission of knowledge work. Only inside this context of management prerogative can new equipment be selected with any real organizational validity.

An emerging information economy and a changing office tool stock thus present a double-edged challenge in the decade ahead. Extracting genuine operational improvements amidst a changing work force and enhanced technology requires that managers find new ways to organize work in the office.

The Heritage of Sociotechnical Design

Sociotechnical design is a way of designing high-performance organizations. It consists of both theory and procedure. Sociotechnical theory is general; it establishes a novel way of viewing work and its organization. Sociotechnical procedure is analytic; based upon the theory, it provides one means of searching for a way to organize work better. The analytic method is not imposed unilaterally by an outside expert. Rather, it entails self-design, whereby people can analyze their own operation and how to improve it.

Originated in England at the Tavistock Institute during the 1950s, a sociotechnical theory was the first approach that viewed work as a system of technical and social components. The technical subsystem is the tools and procedures used to create desired outputs, and the social subsystem is the division of labor and methods of coordination by which tools and procedures are managed.

The social and the technical represent dissimilar elements; each is a distinct realm that operates according to different laws. The technical subsystem is subject to the physical constraints that govern transformation of raw materials into finished products and to the procedural arrangements for structuring the orderly progression of labor. The social subsystem of work is shaped by psychological and social conditions that affect the patterns of interacting through which people operate the technical subsystem.

Sociotechnical theory maintains that high performance is obtained by coupling these dissimilar realms in mutually enhancing ways. Hence, the sociotechnical approach stresses finding a "best match" between social and technical subsystems. This emphasis goes beyond job enrichment for its own sake by insisting that better quality work be harnessed to the improvement of the technical production flow.

Beyond Taylorist Principles

This emphasis upon "best match" runs counter to prevailing tradition. Since the 1920s, American enterprise has applied principles based upon Frederick W. Taylor's "scientific management" to determine the organization of work. This approach led to emphasizing simplification of jobs and reliance upon mechanization as ways to organize work for better results. Job simplification is a tendency to divide work into the smallest possible units. The idea is that narrow, repetitive tasks maximize efficiency and minimize replacement costs. Reliance upon mechanization is an inclination to maximize the level of automation, thereby minimizing human toil and error. These postulates seemed helpful through the 1950s as America's production line became the quintessential model of efficient organization.

But times have changed since the principles of job simplification and maximum automation were developed. Our more affluent and better educated labor force brings a different set of expectations to the work place. High wages in exchange for simplistic work managed by unilateral decree is no longer sufficient to evoke high levels of performance. Meanwhile, the evolution of technology has changed the very texture of work itself. With the growing prevalence of integrated, automatic systems, narrow responsibility requiring less real initiative does not any longer yield a competitive edge. Rather, there is a need for workers to exercise broadly responsible initiative on a continuing basis if outstanding performance is to be achieved.

In the U.S., breakdown of the traditional approach to work design has been evident in some of our most essential industries. The auto industry is a case in point. Labor strife in 1972 at General Motors' Lordstown plant dramatically underscored the need for a fundamental transformation in how work is organized. At the time, Lordstown housed America's most technologically advanced automotive assembly line. In accord with the Taylorist principles of efficiency, automation was maximized and worker roles greatly simplified. Workers went on strike to protest the low quality of their jobs in this supposedly optimal system. Overoptimization of technology by itself and subpar development of the plant's social system led to a deterioration in the overall performance of the facility. The Lordstown episode marked a watershed in American management of human resources. It signified the need to obtain superior performance in ways that depart from traditional reliance upon simple work and purely technological optimization.

With an emphasis upon striking a best match between social and technical subsystems, sociotechnical design represents a genuine alternative to outmoded Taylorist principles. But sociotechnical design consists of more than general theory. It also entails specific analytic procedures by which people can design a better match between the social and technical aspects of work. This analytic method was for the most part developed in factory settings.

Sociotechnical Analysis

The method of sociotechnical analysis examines the technical subsystem, the social subsystem, and their overall mission. The technical subsystem is analyzed as a sequence of operations that converts inputs to outputs. Particular attention is given to variations, or errors, that can arise in any step of the conversion process and to the systematic interdependencies that run between upstream and downstream errors. The social subsystem is scrutinized in terms of each organizational role in order to examine the motivational factors for each job along with patterns of information and responsibility that designate how people manage the technical conversion process. In addition, the overall mission of the unit is revalidated by analyzing its environment, history, and purpose.

This analysis reveals information that permits alternative types of organization to be considered. Often, a sociotechnical analysis leads people to establish a work-group form of organization. In work-group organizations, a cluster of steps in the overall conversion process is assigned to a group of workers. The group is responsible for an interim product that results from these steps. Ideally, the group manages day-to-day operations itself. Individual workers are responsible for being effective group contributors, which often entails learning a variety of production, maintenance, and management skills. Supervision becomes less detailed and less authoritarian as coaching tends to replace decree, and there is greater worker involvement in long-range issues.

Designed through sociotechnical analysis, work-group organization can achieve better performance than can traditional forms of organization. This advantage has been demonstrated in a variety of industries such as refining, chemical processing, automotive fabrication and assembly, food production, semiconductor wafer fabrication, and light industrial production. Today, a

130

number of major firms depend upon the sociotechnical approach to systematically gain higher productivity and employee commitment.

Application of sociotechnical design to white-collar work has been limited. Most attempts have involved clerical or support-staff work in word processing, records management, and claims processing. Until recently there have been few attempts to design managerial and professional work from a sociotechnical perspective. But prior results indicate that sociotechnical design offers considerable promise for performance improvement. This history of success against the moving background of new information technology and a new economic order makes translation of sociotechnical design from the factory to the office a realm of substantial opportunity.

Applying Sociotechnical Design to Office Work

The term "office" is actually a misnomer. Office work denotes a wide assortment of operations that includes everything from ticket processing to strategic planning. People who work in offices do many different things. They hold different jobs, run different sorts of operations, and draw upon a variety of skills and equipment. Many forms of office work may have the same basic activities, such as filing, telephoning, and writing. But merely improving each of these component activities is not equivalent to substantive improvement in the guts of a particular office operation.

One useful way to categorize this variety of office work is in terms of *routine and nonroutine tasks*.[6] The relative balance of each type of work is different for various sorts of office jobs. Routine work primarily involves completing a structured problem. The tasks are characterized by accuracy of detail, short-term horizon, predominantly internal information, and narrow scope. the work usually proceeds through some kind of linear and sequential conversion process, a series of particular steps that yields a predefined output. Office jobs with a predominance of routine work have typically been the province of nonexempt clerical and staff-support workers (usually female) and to exempt staff administering fixed, repetitive procedures.

Nonroutine office work primarily involves managing unstructured or semistructured problems. Professional and managerial jobs are in this category. These jobs are characterized by plausible but general information inputs, variable detail, extended and unfixed time horizons, internal and external data, and diffuse or general scope. Such work rarely proceeds through a sequential conversion process. Instead, the less structured nature of problems may frequently require abandoning stepwise progression. Often, multiple objectives must be balanced through time, which further undermines strictly linear progression by diffusing the clarity of both initial problem and desired outcome. For example, changing the strategic posture of a firm almost never proceeds through explicitly orderly "corporate planning." Instead of advancing through discrete linear steps, the executive must orchestrate a disjointed, nonsequential, consensus-building process. Progression is nonlinear, with the start and finish of the process never totally clear.

Admittedly, this is a rough set of categories, but virtually any office job and be located along this routine-nonroutine continuum in relative proximity to other jobs.

The people who undertake routine and nonroutine office work are characteristically different in background and expectation. Most general managers and professionals are highly trained. Their education focuses upon individual practice, and by definition they expect to wield a degree of unilateral expertise and authority. Expectations about work activities, career advancement, and reward emphasize individual performance and ability. In contrast, those employed in routine office activities, where highly specialized training is less prevalent, are more likely to develop a group identification. Furthermore, managers and professionals cannot easily learn each others' skills, which is a usual requisite for work-group organization with its task rotation.

This range of work in an office requires modifications in the sociotechnical approach for white-collar settings. The existing form of analysis and design appears best suited to routine office work, which more closely resembles the factory settings where the initial analytic procedure was developed. Because of the sequential progression of activity in routine office work, the classic form of technical analysis, in terms of processing steps and their variances, remains applicable. The stability of work engenders clearly defined niches that are amenable to the standard form of social analysis with its emphasis upon work-quality factors for each specific role. Because they are less likely to emphasize individual performance, people engaged in routine office work may consider work groups as a viable alternative to current organizational patterns. Given the boredom that inherently creeps into routine office tasks, work-group organization may appear as a particularly welcome and enriching option that adds complexity to tasks.

Nonroutine office work appears less amenable to the conventional form of sociotechnical analysis. A strictly sequential chain of steps either simply does not exist or fails to capture the essence of such work. Also, the constellation of individuals needed to run nonroutine work is always shifting, depending upon changing circumstance, while social analysis emphasizes stable, discrete roles and their accumulation of satisfying features. Finally, work-group design runs against the more individualistic orientation of managers and professionals, making it a less viable alternative for nonroutine office work. Since the complexity of such work often is already overwhelming, work-group alternatives may actually generate excessive task variety in an indiscriminate fashion. Furthermore, the highly specialized training required for nonroutine work precludes the genuine rotation of skills and duties that is normally found in work-group organizations.

A Sociotechnical Approach for Nonroutine Work

For improving performance in the domain of nonroutine office work, the sociotechnical design approach--analysis of technical and social subsystems to design a best match between subsystems--still applies overall. But the specific units of analysis must be transformed, thereby rendering a new procedure for the analysis and design of high performance work.

One alternative method derived from recent work is based upon a revised concept of social and technical subsystems that applies to nonroutine office endeavors. This new approach discards notions of sequential conversion processes and fixed-role analysis that characterize the more traditional form of analysis.

Instead, the technical and social aspects of office work are seen respectively in terms of *deliberations* and *discretionary coalitions*.

Deliberations concerning a topic can be seen to occur in various forums. These forums are arenas in which a topic is deliberated either with one's self (tracing alternative projections on the back of an envelope) or with others (holding a meeting where the topic is discussed). Forums may be structured, semi-structured, or unstructured. Often, important topics are deliberated through more than one forum. For instance, the redirection of a division's strategy is a highly complex affair. As a topic it may be pursued through multiple forums, including ad hoc discussions, occasional individual reflection, special retreat meetings, key allocation or promotional processes, and formal strategic planning sessions.

In the traditional sociotechnical method, technical analysis hinges upon sequential operations and their variances, but in nonroutine office work, with the prevalence of multiple and nonlinear conversion processes, the technical analysis is better conducted in terms of deliberations with topics and forums. Apparently disordered and disarrayed, deliberations constitute the actual gist of "information work" for nonroutine tasks in the office.

As an uncommon category of analysis, deliberations are easily mistaken for limited but more familiar terms. For instance, deliberations are not decisions. Decisions are discrete choices where one alternative is pursued at the expense of others. Deliberations are a more continuous affair than decisions, but decisions may occasionally be rendered from deliberations. Deliberations are the context and subtext of decisions, rather than the act of decision making itself. Also, deliberations are not just meetings. Meetings are sessions where people gather. They can be one vital forum in a deliberation, but they are not the deliberation itself. Nor will more meetings necessarily improve the conduct of deliberation. Often the inverse is true. The concept of deliberations points to forums of encounter, exchange, and reflection other than meetings that also can help to resolve an ambiguous topic.

A new analytic concept of the social subsystem is also required, one that corresponds to the concept of deliberations in the technical subsystem. Discretionary coalitions provide one way to view the social subsystem of nonroutine office work. Discretionary coalitions are alliances struck of necessity in which intelligent trade-offs are made for the sake of general objectives.

Discretionary coalitions arise because of the continuing equivocality of nonroutine office issues. Since a definitive solution is unobtainable, a process of continuing trade-off becomes essential. In product design specification, for example, every function and speciality will tend to seek optimization of its own narrow subunit agenda. Research and development will want the most exotic design possible; manufacturing will insist on a design that is easily produced; and marketing may require total compatability with earlier products, perhaps at the cost of higher functionality or lower production costs. But commerical viability requires that no one function or speciality triumph completely. All sides are reciprocally interdependent; inherently they are divergent and yet necessary to each other. Under these circumstances, high performance becomes the ability to balance contention with informed trade-offs.

Discretionary coalitions are networks of people who must jointly render a continuing series of informed trade-offs on some equivocal topic of deliberation. A coalition's composition is driven by both parsimony (excluding extraneous persons) and necessity (including required persons); the chain of command is short-circuited, and to the coalition belong all the necessary players regardless of their formal rank or assignment.

Deliberations and discretionary coalitions together provide a new analytic framework for the redesign of nonroutine office work. High performance for truly knotty nonroutine office work requires building effective discretionary coalitions around key topics of deliberation.

Typically a dysfunctional arrangement takes hold. Deliberations become obscurely defined, losing their clear focus and priority. In their place administrative procedures, long since ossified, become an obsession for their own sake. A maze of red tape obscures the genuine realities of an enterprise. Coalitions go unacknowledged. By default there emerge narrow allegiances and uninformative, ceremonial patterns of involvement. The wrong patterns of people go chasing after the wrong issues. Everyone may appear busy, but effectiveness declines. This decline cannot be cured by pep talks, relations training, or a veneer of exotic new office technology. What is required is a fundamental reformation to bring viable coalitions into alignment with deliberations of genuine importance.

Reformulating Deliberations and Discretionary Coalitions

A new form of sociotechnical analysis is needed to reformulate deliberations and their attendant coalitions. A specific method outlined by the author enables members of a unit to better match the technical and social aspects of their work in terms of key deliberations and discretionary coalitions.[7] More effective organizations can thereby be designed for nonroutine office work on a systematic basis. Improved deliberations can be developed selectively, with explicit charters. Discretionary coalitions can be designated for each deliberation. Responsibilities should be specified for every party involved. Policies should be established for compensation, promotion, assignment, and symbolic parity that create within the coalition a balance of influence among the various informed perspectives represented.

This alternative form of sociotechnical design leads to a new format of organization--reticular organization--different from the work-group configuration that often results from the more traditional method. Reticular organization is characterized by constantly shifting networks of information and authority. There is very little of the cross-training or job switching that normally characterizes work-group organizations. Instead, the axis of reference and identification alters ceaselessly within an ever-changing complex of deliberation-coalition configurations. Within that complex, an ongoing balance among divergent interests is maintained across a set of deliberations in a fluid way that complements the purely formal chain of command. Coalitions become acknowledged, legitimate, and adaptable. Previously underground phenomena come to the surface. Emphasis is upon harnessing contention to engender understanding among various parties and intelligent trade-offs.

In and of itself, reticular organization may not alter the formal chart of organization as explicitly as a work-group design. Instead, the transformation is more subtle; it runs "between the lines." Everyday sequences of communication change. Ongoing dialogue between disparate functions grows more dynamic, and issues get taken full circle with greater care and frequency. Relations between managers may "click" as rigid lines of traditional demarcation become less absolute and confining. The result is improved performance as nonroutine tasks are undertaken with better deliberations and more effective coalitions.

Case Study: A Strategic Planning Group

An alternative sociotechnical design method for nonroutine office work, based upon new concepts like deliberations and coalitions, is exemplified by the Strategic Planning Group in a rapidly growing $180-million firm. A new integrated information system was proposed to help the group function better. Based on prior experience, the executive in charge of the unit suspected that enhanced technology alone would prove insufficient. Rather, the unit's overall function and specific operations needed thorough renewal.

An organization design project was therefore undertaken before design purchase or installation of the new computer system. Individuals representing the variety of people in the planning unit were asked to join a design team. Meeting weekly, the design team analyzed current operations and proposed a new organization design. Major staff and line executives became members of a steering committee. To guide the entire project and to help the design team and the steering committee, an outside consultant was retained.

Early steps of the analysis required the design team to research and identify major trends in the planning group, the company, and the company's environment. Some major developments became apparent. First, the company's major source of competitive advantage was shifting from cost to advanced technology and project features. Second, the firm's most promising opportunities lay in second- or third-generation projects rather than first-generation offerings obtained from acquisitions. Third, the nature of the planning function was changing from acquisitions development to internal coordination between functions and to adaptation to growing competition. The design team capped this phase of analysis with the formulation of a mission statement that emphasized the planning unit's role as corporate "glue" amid rising complexity. This statement was ratified, with some revision, by the steering committee.

Next, the design team analyzed the technical subsystem of work in the planning unit. Because of the highly ambiguous and nonlinear nature of the unit's work, the analysis was couched in terms of deliberation topics. The following were selected: elicit identification of recent market and competitor trends, evoke new product category designations, appraise and match dispersed development resources, broker new product applications, and collate joint agreement opportunities that may exist in-house. This portrait of the unit's work was counterintuitive. It revealed that the planning unit mostly addressed interactive processes rather than confining itself to just abstract analysis. The design team recognized that the unit's analytical prowess yielded advantage only if it led to the edification of other groups in the firm. Technical analysis proceeded, with the design team specifying key deliberations and the forums through which they were conducted.

Following the interim report to the steering committee, the design team proceeded to analyze the planning department's subsystem in terms of the discretionary coalitions needed to maintain the key deliberations of the unit. A coalition was traced for each deliberation, noting the parties involved, information required, characteristic bias, and relative status. The analysis permitted the design team to check for proper alignment between the micropolitical landscape of their unit and the major topics of deliberation, to see if there were any mismatches between the two. For example, it was discovered that R&D lacked a good channel through which to inquire about recent market trends, and that diametrically opposed biases caused all sides to leave this gap unacknowledged and unsolved.

Alternative Organization Outline

Finally, the design team proceeded to outline an alternative organization for the planning unit. This proved to be a difficult task, since the new design did not simply leap out of the data collected thus far. Rather than defining every detail, the design team outlined a number of minimum critical specifications for a more effective planning organization. Among these were:

1. Mission. A reason for the unit's existence in terms of greater coordination and liaison with a more complex environment.
2. Philosophy. An ethos for the way people should be managed in the planning unit, emphasizing clear understanding of goals, autonomy of methods, and more work in small teams.
3. Social System Changes. A set of proposals for changes in the unit's social subsystem, including:
   . Charters for deliberations including topics, desired outcomes, concerned parties, and respective contributions;
   . Greater recognition of direct involvement with parties outside the unit in planning processes;
   . Less complex job ratings with fewer levels and more flexible job descriptions; and
   . New recruitment strategies to attract a better mix of appropriate talent.
4. Technical System Changes. A set of proposals for changes in the unit's technical subsystem, including:
   . Establishment of new forums for deliberations--including reports, meetings, and reviews--elimination of many outmoded forums, and consolidation of splintered forums;
   . Changes in physical layout and distribution of resources, such as planning unit conference rooms in other areas of the firm; and
   . Proposals for enhanced information systems (data and telecommunications) that genuinely augment key deliberations with a blend of functions overlooked in the initial proposal for a new computer installation.

Together, these changes would shift the basic pattern of organization away from an overly formal structure. The design proposed movement toward a reticular organization in which a changing network of information exchange and authority arrangements grows to complement the rigid scaffold of a purely hierarchical structure.[8]

The proposed changes eventually won consent and were implemented with extensive consultation from the steering committee and a great measure of interaction with others in the unit and the firm. Preliminary indications show that the redesigned planning organization sustains a much greater level of contribution to the firm's conduct and that future planning needs will be met with a leaner staff. Meanwhile, turnover has declined and more planners are being accepted into line positions. Beyond any of these initial results, the process of sociotechnical design also created a group experienced in organizational analysis that is both able and willing to improve other aspects of the firm's operation with the same method.

Conclusion

The conventional method of sociotechnical design and the new variation suggested here together comprise a spectrum of analytic methods for the design of high-performance office organizations. Units with mostly routine tasks are best suited for the established analytic procedure and for the work-group format that may result. Managerial and professional units that do highly nonroutine information work are better served by the alternative method stressing deliberations, coalitions, and reticular organization. Between these lies a vast range of middle-ground applications for units doing mixed routine and nonroutine work. These operations should adopt a hybrid approach in which aspects of the two divergent methods of analysis are selectively blended.[9]

Overall, this spectrum of methods (routine, nonroutine, and hybrid) permits a contingency framework that gives sociotechnical design sufficient variety for widespread application in the office. The general principles at the core of a sociotechnical approach remain valid throughout all ranges of the spectrum. But these postulates are implemented through different kinds of analysis, contingent upon the level of routinization involved.

Sufficient cumulative experience with sociotechnical design makes it possible to speak today of a high-performance factory: a work-group facility designed to make people and technology enhance each other. Major firms now routinely depend upon this approach to gain superior commitment and performance in their operations. The realm of knowledge work has not yet attained such a consistent vision. The high-performance office as a general guide for exceptional performance of knowledge work remains embryonic. More experience with sociotechnical design in the office is needed before clear patterns emerge. With time, a general profile will appear that provides an outline of the high-performance office. Early exploration of this frontier today will afford substantial advantage later for those who seed to organize information-based work more effectively.

Notes

[1] E. L. Trist, The Evolution of Socio-Technical Systems (Toronto: Ontario Quality of Working Life Centre, Occasional Paper No. 2, 1981).
[2] R. P. Uhlig, D. J. Farber, and J. H. Bair, The Office of the Future (Amsterdam: North Holland, 1979).
[3] Diebold Group, People Impacts of Office Technology (New York: Automated Office Program Document 019, 1982).
[4] A. Purchase and C. F. Glover, "Office of the Future," SRI Long Range Planning Service, No. 1001.
[5] "Multiclient Study of Managerial/Professional Productivity," New York: Booz, Allen, and Hamilton, Inc., 1979.
[6] C. Pava, "Microelectronics and The Design of Organization," Working Paper 82-67, Harvard Business School Division of Research, 1982.
[7] C. Pava, Managing New Office Technology: An Organizational Strategy (New York: The Free Press, 1983).
[8] C. Pava, "Microelectronics and The Design of Organization," Working Paper 82-67, Harvard Business School Division of Research, 1982.
[9] C. Pava, Managing New Office Technology: An Organizational Strategy (New York: The Free Press, 1983).

INCREASING ORGANIZATIONAL EFFECTIVENESS
THROUGH BETTER HUMAN RESOURCE PLANNING
AND DEVELOPMENT

Edgar H. Schein
Massachusetts Institute of Technology

Planning for and managing human resources is emerging as an increasingly important determinant of organizational effectiveness. It is an area all too often ignored by line managers. As organizations evolve, the complexity of the environments within which they operate will cause increased dependence upon the very people making up the organization. This article focuses upon two key issues: the increasing importance of human resource planning and development in organizational effectiveness, and how the major components of a human resource planning and development system should be coordinated for maximum effectiveness. The author concludes that these multiple components must be managed by both line managers and staff specialists as part of a total system to be effective. Ed.

Introduction

In this article I would like to address two basic *questions*. *First*, why is human resource planning and development becoming increasingly important as a determinant of organizational effectiveness? *Second*, what are the major *components* of a human resource planning and career development system, and how should these components be *linked* for maximum organizational effectiveness?

The field of personnel management has for some time addressed issues such as these and much of the technology of planning for and managing human resources has been worked out to a considerable degree.[1] Nevertheless there continues to be in organizations a failure, particularly on the part of line managers and functional managers in areas other than personnel, to recognize the true importance of planning for and managing human resources. This paper is not intended to be a review of what is known but rather a kind of position paper for line managers to bring to their attention some important and all too often neglected issues. These issues are important for organizational *effectiveness*, quite apart from their relevance to the issue of humanizing work or improving the quality of working life.[2]

The observations and analyses made below are based on several kinds of information:

. Formal research on management development, career development, and human development through the adult life cycle conducted in the Sloan School and at other places for the past several decades.[3]

- Analysis of consulting relationships, field observations, and other involvements over the past several decades with all kinds of organizations dealing with the planning for and implementation of human resource development programs and organization development projects.[4]

Why Is Human Resource Planning and Development (HRPD) Increasingly Important?

The Changing Managerial Job

The first answer to the question is simple, though paradoxical. Organizations are becoming more dependent upon people because they are increasingly involved in more complex technologies and are attempting to function in more complex economic, political, and sociocultural environments. The more different technical skills there are involved in the design, manufacture, marketing, and sales of a product, the more vulnerable the organization will be to critical shortages of the right kinds of human resources. The more complex the process, the higher the interdependence among the various specialists. The higher the interdependence, the greater the need for effective integration of all the specialties because the entire process is only as strong as its weakest link.

In simpler technologies, managers could often compensate for the technical or communication failures of their subordinates. General managers today are much more dependent upon their technically trained subordinates because they usually do not understand the details of the engineering, marketing, financial, and other decisions which their subordinates are making. Even the general manager who grew up in finance may find that since his day the field of finance has outrun him and his subordinates are using models and methods which he cannot entirely understand.

What all this means for the general manager is that he cannot any longer safely make decisions by himself; he cannot get enough information digested within his own head to be the integrator and decision maker. Instead, he finds himself increasingly having to manage the *process* of decision making, bringing the right people together around the right questions or problems, stimulating open discussion, insuring that all relevant information surfaces and is critically assessed, managing the emotional ups and downs of his prima donnas, and insuring that out of all this human and interpersonal process, a good decision will result.

As I have watched processes like these in management groups, I am struck by the fact that *the decision emerges out of the interplay*. It is hard to pin down who had the idea and who made the decision. The general manager in this setting is *accountable* for the decision, but rarely would I describe the process as one where he or she actually makes the decision, except in the sense of recognizing when the right answer has been achieved, ratifying that answer, announcing it, and following up on its implementation.

If the managerial *job* is increasingly moving in the direction I have indicated, managers of the future will have to be much more skilled in how to:

1. Select and train their subordinates.
2. Design and run meetings and groups of all sorts.

3. Deal with all kinds of conflict between strong individuals and groups.
4. Influence and negotiate from a low power base, and
5. Integrate the efforts of very diverse technical specialists.

If the above image of what is happening to organizations has any generality, it will force the field of human resource management increasingly to center stage. The more complex organizations become, the more they will be vulnerable to human error. They will not necessarily employ more people, but they will employ more sophisticated highly trained people both in managerial and in individual contributor, staff roles. The price of low motivation, turnover, poor productivity, sabotage, and intraorganizational conflict will be higher in such an organization. Therefore it will become a matter of *economic necessity* to improve human resource planning and development systems.

Changing Social Values

A second reason why human resource planning and development will become more central and important is that changing social values regarding the role of work will make it *more complicated to manage people*. There are several kinds of research findings and observations which illustrate this point.

First, my own longitudinal research of a panel of Sloan School graduates of the 1960s strongly suggests that we have put much too much emphasis on the traditional success syndrome of "climbing the corporate ladder."[5] Some alumni indeed want to rise to high-level general manager positions, but many others want to exercise their particular technical or functional competence and only rise to levels of functional management or senior staff roles with minimal managerial responsibility. Some want security, others are seeking nonorganizational careers as teachers or consultants, while a few are becoming entrepreneurs. I have called these patterns of motivation, talent, and values "career anchors" and believe that they serve to stabilize and constrain the career in predictable ways. The implication is obvious--organizations must develop multiple ladders and multiple reward systems to deal with different types of people.[6]

Second, studies of young people entering organizations in the last several decades suggest that work and career are not as central a life preoccupation as was once the case. Perhaps because of a prolonged period of economic affluence, people see more options for themselves and are increasingly exercising those options. In particular, one sees more concern with a balanced life in which work, family, and self-development play a more equal role.[7]

Third, closely linked to the above trend is the increase in the number of women in organizations, which will have its major impact through the increase of dual career families. As opportunities for women open up, we will see more new life-styles in young couples which will affect the organization's options as to moving people geographically, joint employment, joint career management, family support, etc.[8]

Fourth, research evidence is beginning to accumulate that personal growth and development is a life-long process and that predictable issues and crises come up in every decade of our lives. Organizations will have to be much more aware of what these issues are, how work and family interact, and how to manage people at different ages. The current "hot button" is *mid-career crisis*, but the more research we do the more we find developmental crises at *all* ages and stages.[9]

An excellent summary of what is happening in the world of values, technology, and management is provided in a recent text by Elmer Burack:

> The leading edge of change in the future will include the new technologies of information, production, and management, interlaced with considerable social dislocation and shifts in manpower inputs. These developments are without precedent in our industrial history.

> Technological and social changes have created a need for more education, training, and skill at all managerial and support levels. The lowering of barriers to employment based on sex and race introduces new kinds of manpower problems for management officials. Seniority is coming to mean relatively less in relation to the comprehension of problems, processes, and approaches. The newer manpower elements and work technologies have shifted institutional arrangements: the locus of decision making is altered, role relationship among workers and supervisors are changed (often becoming more collegial), and the need to respond to changing routines has become commonplace....

> These shifts have been supported by more demanding customer requirements, increasing government surveillance (from product quality to anti-pollution measures), and more widespread use of computers, shifting power bases to the holders of specialized knowledge skills.[10]

In order for HRPD systems to become more responsive and capable of handling such growing complexity they must contain all the necessary components, must be based on correct assumptions, and must be adequately integrated.

Components of a Human Resource Planning and Development System

The major problem with existing HRPD systems is that they are fragmented, incomplete, and sometimes built on faulty assumptions about human or organizational growth.

Human growth takes place through successive encounters with one's environment. As the person encounters a new situation, he or she is forced to try new responses to deal with that situation. Learning takes place as a function of how those responses work out and the results they achieve. If they are successful in coping with the situation, the person enlarges his repertory of responses; if they are not successful the person must try alternate responses until the situation has been dealt with. If none of the active coping responses work, the person sometimes falls back on retreating from the new situation, or denying that there is a problem to be solved. These responses are defensive and growth limiting.

The implication is that for growth to occur, people basically need two things: *new challenges* that are within the range of their coping responses, and *knowledge of results*, information on how their responses to the challenge have worked out. If the tasks and challenges are too easy or too hard, the person will be demotivated and cease to grow. If the information is not available on how well the person's responses are working, the person cannot grow in a systematic, valid direction but is forced into guessing or trying to infer information from ambiguous signals.

Organizational growth similarly takes place through successful coping with the internal and external environment.[11] But since the organization is a complex system of human, material, financial, and informational resources, one must consider how each of those areas can be properly managed toward organizational effectiveness. In this article I will only deal with the human resources.

In order for the organization to have the capacity to perform effectively over a period of time it must be able to plan for, recruit, manage, develop, measure, dispose of, and replace human resources as warranted by the tasks to be done. The most important of these functions is the *planning* function, since task requirements are likely to change as the complexity and turbulence of the organization's environment increase. In other words, a key assumption underlying organizational growth is that the nature of jobs will change over time, which means that such changes must be continuously monitored in order to insure that the right kinds of human resources can be recruited or developed to do those jobs. Many of the activities such as recruitment, selection, performance appraisal, and so on presume that some planning process has occurred which makes it possible to assess whether or not those activities are meeting *organizational needs*, quite apart from whether they are facilitating the individual's growth.

In an ideal HRPD system one would seek to match the organization's needs for human resources with the individual's needs for personal career growth and development. One can then depict the basic system as involving both individual and organizational planning, and a series of matching activities which are designed to facilitate mutual need satisfaction. If we further assume that both individual and organizational needs change over time, we can depict this process as a developmental one as in Figure 1.

In the right-hand column we show the basic stages of the individual career through the life cycle. While not everyone will go through these stages in the manner depicted, there is growing evidence that for organizational careers in particular, these stages reasonably depict the movement of people through their adult lives.[12]

Given those developmental assumptions, the left-hand side of the diagram shows the organizational planning activities which must occur if human resources are to be managed in an optimal way, and if changing job requirements are to be properly assessed and continuously monitored. The middle column shows the various matching activities which have to occur at various career stages.

The components of an effective HRPD system now can be derived from the diagram. *First*, there have to be in the organization the overall planning components shown on the left-hand side of Figure 1. *Second*, there have to be components which insure an adequate process of staffing the organization. *Third*, there have to be components which plan for and monitor growth and development. *Fourth*, there have to be components which facilitate the actual process of the growth and development of the people who are brought into the organization; this growth and development must be organized to meet *both* the needs of the organization and the needs of the individuals within it. *Fifth*, there have to be

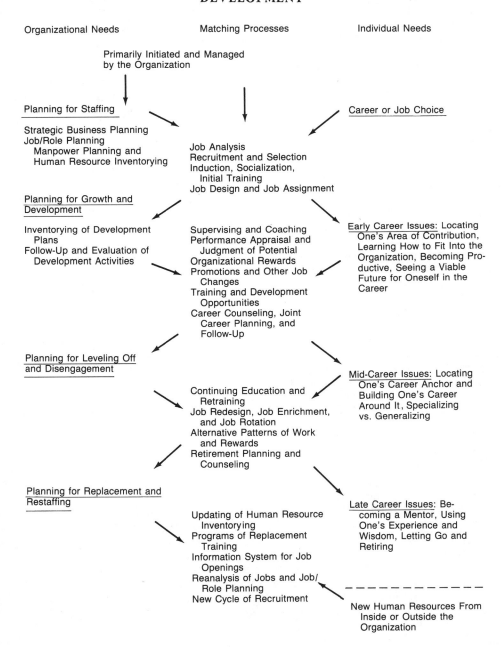

FIGURE 1
A DEVELOPMENTAL MODEL OF HUMAN RESOURCE PLANNING AND DEVELOPMENT

Organizational Needs   Matching Processes   Individual Needs

Primarily Initiated and Managed
by the Organization

Planning for Staffing

Strategic Business Planning
Job/Role Planning
  Manpower Planning and
  Human Resource Inventorying

Career or Job Choice

Job Analysis
Recruitment and Selection
Induction, Socialization,
  Initial Training
Job Design and Job Assignment

Planning for Growth and
Development

Inventorying of Development
  Plans
Follow-Up and Evaluation of
  Development Activities

Supervising and Coaching
Performance Appraisal and
  Judgment of Potential
Organizational Rewards
Promotions and Other Job
  Changes
Training and Development
  Opportunities
Career Counseling, Joint
  Career Planning, and
  Follow-Up

Early Career Issues: Locating
  One's Area of Contribution,
  Learning How to Fit Into the
  Organization, Becoming Pro-
  ductive, Seeing a Viable
  Future for Oneself in the
  Career

Planning for Leveling Off
and Disengagement

Continuing Education and
  Retraining
Job Redesign, Job Enrichment,
  and Job Rotation
Alternative Patterns of Work
  and Rewards
Retirement Planning and
  Counseling

Mid-Career Issues: Locating
  One's Career Anchor and
  Building One's Career
  Around It, Specializing
  vs. Generalizing

Planning for Replacement and
Restaffing

Updating of Human Resource
  Inventorying
Programs of Replacement
  Training
Information System for Job
  Openings
Reanalysis of Jobs and Job/
  Role Planning
New Cycle of Recruitment

Late Career Issues: Be-
  coming a Mentor, Using
  One's Experience and
  Wisdom, Letting Go and
  Retiring

New Human Resources From
  Inside or Outside the
  Organization

143

components which deal with decreasing effectiveness, leveling off, obsolescence of skills, turnover, retirement, and other phenomena which reflect the need for either a new growth direction or a process of disengagement of the person from his or her job. *Finally,* there have to be components which insure that as some people move out of jobs, others are available to fill those jobs, and as new jobs arise that people are available with the requisite skills to fill them.

In the remainder of this article I would like to comment on each of these six sets of components and indicate where and how they should be linked to each other.

Overall Planning Components

The function of these components is to insure that the organization has an adequate basis for selecting its human resources and developing them toward the fulfillment of organizational goals.
 • *Strategic Business Planning.* These activities are designed to determine the organization's goals, priorities, future directions, products, markets growth rate, geographical location, and organization structure or design. This process should lead logically into the next two planning activities but is often disconnected from them because it is located in a different part of the organization or is staffed by people with different orientations and backgrounds.
 • *Job/Role Planning.* These activities are designed to determine what actually needs to be done at every level of the organization (up through top management) to fulfill the organization's goals and tasks. This activity can be thought of as a dynamic kind of job analysis where a continual review is made of the skills, knowledge, values, etc. which are presently needed in the organization *and will be needed in the future.* The focus is on the predictable consequences of the strategic planning for managerial roles, specialist roles, and skill mixes which may be needed to get the mission accomplished. If the organization already has a satisfactory system of job descriptions, this activity would concern itself with how those jobs will evolve and change, and what new jobs or roles will evolve in the future.[13]
 This component is often missing completely in organizations or is carried out only for lower level jobs. From a planning point of view it is probably most important for the highest level jobs--how the nature of general and functional management will change as the organization faces new technologies, new social values, and new environmental conditions.
 • *"Manpower Planning" and Human Resource Inventorying.* These activities draw on the job/role descriptions generated in job/role planning and assess the capabilities of the present human resources against those plans or requirements. These activities may be focused on the numbers of people in given categories and are often designed to insure that under given assumptions of growth there will be an adequate supply of people in those categories. Or the process may focus more on how to insure that certain scarce skills which will be needed will in fact be available, leading to more sophisticated programs of recruitment or human resource development. For example, the inventorying process at high levels may reveal the need for a new type of general manager with broad integrative capacities which

may further reveal the need to start a development program that will insure that such managers will be available five to ten years down the road.

These first three component activities are all geared to identifying the *organization's* needs in the human resource area. They are difficult to do and tools are only now beginning to be developed for job/role planning.[14] In most organizations I have dealt with, the three areas, if they exist at all, are not linked to each other organizationally. Strategic planning is likely to exist in the Office of the President. Job/role planning is likely to be an offshoot of some management development activities in Personnel. And human resource inventorying is likely to be a specialized subsection within Personnel. Typically, no one is accountable for bringing these activities together even on an ad hoc basis.

This situation reflects an erroneous assumption about growth and development which I want to mention at this time. The assumption is that if the organization develops its *present* human resources, it will be able to fill whatever job demands may arise in the future. Thus we do find in organizations elaborate human resource planning systems, but they plan for the present people in the organization, not for the organization per se. If there are no major changes in job requirements as the organization grows and develops, this system will work. But if jobs themselves change, it is no longer safe to assume that today's human resources, with development plans based on *today's* job requirements, will produce the people needed in some future situation. Therefore, I am asserting that more job/role planning must be done, independent of the present people in the organization.

The subsequent components to be discussed which focus on the matching of individual and organizational needs all assume that some sort of basic planning activities such as those described have been carried out. They may not be very formal, or they may be highly decentralized (e.g. every supervisor who has an open slot might make his own decision of what sort of person to hire based on his private assumptions about strategic business planning and job/role planning). Obviously, the more turbulent the environment, the greater the vulnerability of the organization if it does not centralize and coordinate its various planning activities, and generate its HRPD system from those plans.

Staffing Processes

The function of these processes is to insure that the organization acquires the human resources necessary to fulfill its goals.

 • *Job Analysis.* If the organizational planning has been done adequately, the next component of the HRPD system is to actually specify what jobs need to be filled and what skills, etc. are needed to do those jobs. Some organizations go through this process very formally, others do it in an informal unprogrammed manner, but in some form it must occur in order to specify what kind of recruitment to do and how to select people from among the recruits.

 • *Recruitment and Selection.* This activity involves the actual process of going out to find people to fulfill jobs and developing systems for deciding which of those people to hire. These components may be very formal including testing, assessment, and other aids to the selection process. If this component is seen as part of a total HRPD system, it will alert management to the fact that the recruitment selection system communicates to future employees something about the nature of the organization and its approach to people. All too often this

145

component sends incorrect messages or turns off future employees or builds incorrect stereotypes which make subsequent supervision more difficult.[15]

. *Induction, Socialization, and Initial Training.* Once the employee has been hired, there ensues a period during which he or she learns the ropes, learns how to get along in the organization, how to work, how to fit in, how to master the particulars of the job, and so on. Once again, it is important that the activities which make up this component are seen as part of a total process with long-range consequences for the attitudes of the employee.[16] The goal of these processes should be to facilitate the employees becoming productive and useful members of the organization both in the short run and in terms of long-range potential.

. *Job Design and Job Assignment.* One of the most crucial components of staffing is the actual design of the job which is given to the new employee and the manner in which the assignment is actually made. The issue is how to provide *optimal challenge*, a set of activities which will be neither too hard nor too easy for the new employee, and which will be neither too meaningless nor too risky from the point of view of the organization. If the job is too easy or too meaningless, the employee may become demotivated; if the job is too hard and/or involves too much responsibility and risk from the point of view of the organization, the employee will become too anxious, frustrated, or angry to perform at an optimal level. Some organizations have set up training programs for supervisors to help them to design optimally challenging work assignments.[17]

These four components are geared to insuring that the work of the organization will be performed. They tend to be processes that have to be performed by line managers and personnel staff specialists together. Line managers have the basic information about jobs and skill requirements; personnel specialists have the interviewing, recruiting, and assessment skills to aid in the selection process. In an optimal system these functions will be closely coordinated, particularly to insure that the recruiting process provides to the employee accurate information about the nature of the organization and the actual work that he or she will be doing in it. Recruiters also need good information on the long-range human resource plans so that these can be taken into account in the selection of new employees.

Development Planning

It is not enough to get good human resources in the door. Some planning activities have to concern themselves with how employees who may be spending thirty to forty years of their total life in a given organization will make a contribution for all of that time, will remain motivated and productive, and will maintain a reasonable level of job satisfaction.

. *Inventorying of Development Plans.* Whether or not the process is highly formalized, there is in most organizations some effort to plan for the growth and development of all employees. The planning component that is often missing is some kind of pulling together of this information into a centralized inventory that permits coordination and evaluation of the development activities. Individual supervisors may have clear ideas of what they will do with and for their subordinates, but this information may never be collected, making it impossible to determine whether the individual plans of supervisors are connected in any way. Whether it is done by department, division, or total company, some effort to collect such information and to think through its implications would be of great value to furthering the total development of employees at all levels.

   •   *Follow-up and Evaluation of Development Activities.* I have observed two symptoms of insufficient planning in this area--one, development plans are made for individual employees, are written down, but are never implemented, and two, if they are implemented they are never evaluated either in relation to the individual's own needs for growth or in relation to the organization's needs for new skills. Some system should exist to insure that plans are implemented and that activities are evaluated against both individual and organizational goals.

Career Development Processes

   This label is deliberately broad to cover all of the major processes of managing human resources during their period of growth and peak productivity, a period which may be several decades in length. These processes must match the organization's needs for work with the individual's needs for a productive and satisfying work career. The system must provide for some kind of forward movement for the employee through some succession of jobs, whether these involve promotion, lateral movement to new functions, or simply new assignments within a given area.[18] The system must be based both on the organization's need to fill jobs as they open up and on employees' needs to have some sense of progress in their working lives.

   •   *Supervision and Coaching.* By far the most important component in this area is the actual process of supervising, guiding, coaching, and monitoring. It is in this context that the work assignment and feedback processes which make learning possible occur, and it is the boss who plays the key role in molding the employee to the organization. There is considerable evidence that the first boss is especially crucial in giving new employees a good start in their careers,[19] and that training of supervisors in how to handle new employees is a valuable organizational investment.

   •   *Performance Appraisal and Judgment of Potential.* This component is part of the general process of supervision but stands out as such an important part of the general process that it must be treated separately. In most organizations there is some effort to standardize and formalize a process of appraisal above and beyond the normal performance feedback which is expected on a day-to-day basis. Such systems serve a number of functions--to justify salary increases, promotions, and other formal organizational actions with respect to the employee; to provide information for human resource inventories or at least written records of past accomplishments for the employee's personnel folder; and to provide a basis for annual or semiannual formal reviews between boss and subordinate to supplement day-to-day feedback and to facilitate information exchange for career planning and counseling. In some organizations so little day-to-day feedback occurs that the *formal* system bears the burden of providing the employees with knowledge of how they are doing and what they can look forward to. Since knowledge of results, of how one is doing, is a crucial component of any developmental process, it is important for organizations to monitor how well and how frequently feedback is actually given.

   One of the major dilemmas in this area is whether to have a single system which provides both feedback for the growth and development of the employee and information for the organization's planning systems. The dilemma arises because the information which the planning system requires (e.g. "how much potential does this employee have to rise in the organization?") may be the kind of information which neither the boss nor the planner wants to share with the employee. The more potent and more accurate the information, the less likely it is to be fed back to the employee in anything other than very vague terms.

On the other hand, the detailed work-oriented, day-to-day feedback which the employee needs for growth and development may be too cumbersome to record as part of a selection-oriented appraisal system. If hundreds of employees are to be compared, there is strong pressure in the system toward more general kinds of judgments, traits, rankings, numerical estimates of ultimate personnel, and the like. One way of resolving this dilemma which some companies have found successful is to develop two separate systems--one oriented toward performance improvement and the growth of the employee, and the other one oriented toward a more global assessment of the employee for future planning purposes involving judgments which may not be shared with the employee except in general terms.

A second dilemma arises around the identification of the employee's "development needs" and how that information is linked to other development activities. If the development needs are stated in relation to the planning system, the employee may never get the feedback of what his needs may have been perceived to be, and, worse, no one may implement any program to deal with those needs if the planning system is not well linked with line management.

Two further problems arise from this potential lack of linkage. One, if the individual does not get good feedback around developmental needs, he or she remains uninvolved in their own development and potentially becomes complacent. We pay lip service to the statement that only the individual can develop himself or herself, but then deprive the individual of the very information that would make sensible self-development possible. Two, the development needs as stated for the various employees in the organization may have nothing to do with the organization's needs for certain kinds of human resources in the future. All too often there is complete lack of linkage between the strategic or business planning function and the human resource development function resulting in potentially willy-nilly individual development based on today's needs and individual managers' stereotypes of what will be needed in the future.

    . *Organizational Rewards--Pay, Benefits, Perquisites, Promotion, and Recognition.* Entire books have been written about all the problems and subtleties of how to link organizational rewards to the other components of a HRPD system to insure both short-run and long-run human effectiveness. For purposes of this short paper I wish to point out only one major issue--how to insure that organizational rewards are linked *both* to the needs of the individual and to the needs of the organization for effective performance and development of potential. All too often the reward system is neither responsive to the individual employee nor to the organization, being driven more by criteria of elegance, consistency, and what other organizations are doing. If the linkage is to be established, line managers must actively work with compensation experts to develop a joint philosophy and set of goals based on an understanding of both what the organization is trying to reward and what employee needs actually are. As organizational careers become more varied and as social values surrounding work change, reward systems will probably have to become much more flexible both in time (people at different career stages may need different things) and by type of career (functional specialists may need different things than general managers).

• *Promotions and Other Job Changes.* There is ample evidence that what keeps human growth and effectiveness going is continuing optimal challenge.[20] Such challenge can be provided for some members of the organization through promotion to higher levels where more responsible jobs are available. For most members of the organization the promotion opportunities are limited, however, because the pyramid narrows at the top. An effective HRPD system will, therefore, concentrate on developing career paths, systems of job rotation, changing assignments, temporary assignments, and other lateral job moves which insure continuing growth of all human resources.

One of the key characteristics of an optimally challenging job is that it both draws on the person's abilities and skills and that it has opportunities for "closure." The employee must be in the job long enough to get involved and to see the results of his or her efforts. Systems of rotation which move the person too rapidly either prevent initial involvement (as in the rotational training program), or prevent closure by transferring the person to a new job before the effects of his or her decisions can be assessed. I have heard many "fast track" executives complain that their self-confidence was low because they never really could see the results of their efforts. Too often we move people too fast in order to "fill slots" and thereby undermine their development.

Organizational planning systems which generate "slots" to be filled must be coordinated with development planning systems which concern themselves with the optimal growth of the human resources. Sometimes it is better for the organization in the long run not to fill an empty slot in order to keep a manager in another job where he or she is just beginning to develop. One way of insuring such linkage is to monitor these processes by means of a "development committee" which is composed of both line managers and personnel specialists. In such a group the needs of the organization and the needs of the people can be balanced against each other in the context of the long-range goals of the organization.

• *Training and Development Opportunities.* Most organizations recognize that periods of formal training, sabbaticals, executive development programs outside of the company, and other educational activities are necessary in the total process of human growth and development. The important point about these activities is that they should be carefully linked both to the needs of the individual and to the needs of the organization. The individual should want to go to the program because he or she can see how the educational activity fits into the total career. The organization should send the person because the training fits into some concept of future career development. It should not be undertaken simply as a generalized "good thing," or because other companies are doing it. As much as possible the training and educational activities should be tied to job/role planning. For example, many companies began to use university executive development programs because of an explicit recognition that future managers would require a broader perspective on various problems and that such "broadening" could best be achieved in the university programs.

• *Career Counseling, Joint Career Planning, Follow-up, and Evaluation.* Inasmuch as the growth and development which may be desired can only come from within the individual himself or herself, it is important that the organization provide some means for individual employees at all levels to become more proactive about their careers and some mechanisms for joint dialogue, counseling, and career planning.[21] This process should ideally be linked to performance appraisal, because it is in that context that the boss can review with the subordinate the future potential, development needs, strengths, weaknesses, career options, etc. The boss is often not trained in counseling but does possess some of the key information which the employee needs to initiate any kind of career planning. More formal counseling could then be supplied by the personnel development staff or outside the organization altogether.

The important point to recognize is that employees cannot manage their own growth development without information on how their own needs, talents, values, and plans mesh with the opportunity structure of the organization. Even though the organization may only have imperfect, uncertain information about the future, the individual is better off to know that than to make erroneous assumptions about the future based on no information at all. It is true that the organization cannot make commitments, nor should it unless required by legislation or contract. But the sharing of information if properly done is not the same as making commitments or setting up false expectations.

If the organization can open up the communication channel between employees, their bosses, and whoever is managing the human resource system, the groundwork is laid for realistic individual development planning. Whatever is decided about training, next steps, special assignments, rotation, etc. should be jointly decided by the individual and the appropriate organizational resource (probably the supervisor and someone from personnel specializing in career development). Each step must fit into the employee's life plan and must be tied into *organizational needs*. The organization should be neither a humanistic charity nor an indoctrination center. Instead, it should be a vehicle for meeting both the needs of society and of individuals.

Whatever is decided should not merely be written down but executed. If there are implementation problems, the development plan should be renegotiated. Whatever developmental actions are taken, it is essential that they be followed up and evaluated both by the person and by the organization to determine what, if anything, was achieved. It is shocking to discover how many companies invest in major activities such as university executive development programs and never determine for themselves what was accomplished. In some instances, they make no plans to talk to the individual before or after the program so that it is not even possible to determine what the activity meant to the participant, or what might be an appropriate next assignment for him or her following the program.

I can summarize the above analysis best by emphasizing the two places where I feel there is the most fragmentation and violation of growth assumptions. First, too many of the activities occur without the involvement of the person who is "being developed" and therefore may well end up being self-defeating. This is particularly true of job assignments and performance appraisal where too little involvement and feedback occur. Second, too much of the human resource system functions as a personnel *selection* system unconnected to either the needs of the organization or the needs of the individual. All too often it is only a system for short-run replacement of people in standard type jobs. The key planning functions are not linked in solidly and hence do not influence the system to the degree they should.

The planning and management processes which will be briefly reviewed here are counterparts of ones that have already been discussed but are focused on a different problem--the problem of the late career, loss of motivation, obsolescence, and ultimately retirement. Organizations must recognize that there are various options available to deal with this range of problems beyond the obvious ones of either terminating the employee or engaging in elaborate measures to "remotivate" people who may have lost work involvement.[22]

　　． *Continuing Education and Retraining.* These activities have their greatest potential if the employee is motivated and if there is some clear connection between what is to be learned and what the employee's current or future job assignments require in the way of skills. More and more organizations are finding out that it is better to provide challenging work first and only then the training to perform that work once the employee sees the need for it. Obviously for this linkage to work well continuous dialogue is needed between employees and their managers. For those employees who have leveled off, have lost work involvement, but are still doing high quality work other solutions such as those described below are more applicable.

　　． *Job Redesign, Job Enrichment, and Job Rotation.* This section is an extension of the arguments made earlier on job changes in general applied to the particular problems of leveled off employees. In some recent research, it has been suggested that job enrichment and other efforts to redesign work to increase motivation and performance may only work during the first few years on a job.[23] Beyond that the employee becomes "unresponsive" to the job characteristics themselves and pays more attention to surrounding factors such as the nature of supervision, relationships with co-workers, pay, and other extrinsic characteristics. In other words, before organizations attempt to "cure" leveled off employees by remotivating them through job redesign or rotation, they should examine whether those employees are still in a responsive mode or not. On the other hand. one can argue that there is nothing wrong with less motivated, less involved employees so long as the quality of what they are doing meets the organizational standards.[24]

　　． *Alternative Patterns of Work and Rewards.* Because of the changing needs and values of employees in recent decades, more and more organizations have begun to experiment with alternative work patterns such as flexible working hours, part-time work, sabbaticals or other longer periods of time off, several people filling one job, dual employment of spouses with more extensive childcare programs, etc. Along with these experiments have come others on flexible reward systems in which employees can choose between a raise, some time off, special retirement, medical, or insurance benefits, and other efforts to make multiple career ladders a viable reality. These programs apply to employees at all career stages but are especially relevant to people in mid and late career stages where their own perception of their career and life goals may be undergoing important changes.

None of those innovations should be attempted without first clearly establishing a HRPD system which takes care of the organization's needs as well as the needs of the employees and links them to each other. There can be little growth and development for employees at any level in an *organization* which is sick and stagnant. It is in the best interests of both the individual and the organization to have a healthy organization which can provide opportunities for growth.

. *Retirement Planning and Counseling.* As part of any effective HRPD system, there must be a clear planning function which forecasts who will retire, and which feeds this information into both the replacement staffing system and the counseling functions so that the employees who will be retiring can be prepared for this often traumatic career stage. Employees need counseling not only with the mechanical and financial aspects of retirement, but also to prepare them psychologically for the time when they will no longer have a clear organizational base or job as part of their identity. For some people it may make sense to spread the period of retirement over a number of years by using part-time work or special assignments to help both the individual and the organization to get benefits from this period.

The counseling function here as in other parts of the career probably involves special skills and must be provided by specialists. However, the line manager continues to play a key role as a provider of job challenge, feedback, and information about what is ahead for any given employee. Seminars for line managers on how to handle the special problems of pre-retirement employees would probably be of great value as part of their managerial training.

Planning for and Managing Replacement and Restaffing

With this step the HRPD cycle closes back upon itself. This function must be concerned with such issues as:

1. Updating the human resource inventory as retirements or terminations occur;

2. Instituting special programs of orientation or training for new incumbents to specific jobs as those jobs open up;

3. Managing the information system on what jobs are available and determining how to match this information to the human resources available in order to determine whether to replace from within the organization or to go outside with a new recruiting program.

4. Continuously reanalyzing jobs to insure that the new incumbent is properly prepared for what the job *now* requires and *will* require in the future.

How these processes are managed links to the other parts of the system through the implicit messages that are sent to employees. For example, a company which decides to publicly post all of its unfilled jobs is clearly sending a message that it expects internal recruitment and supports self-development activities. A company which manages restaffing in a very secret manner may well get across a message that employees might as well be complacent and passive about their careers because they cannot influence them anyway.

Summary and Conclusions

I have tried to argue in this article that human resource planning and development is becoming an increasingly important function in organizations, that this function consists of multiple components, and that these components must be managed *both* by line managers and staff specialists. I have tried to show that the various planning activities are closely linked to the actual processes of supervision, job assignment, training, etc. and that those processes must be designed to match the needs of the organization with the needs of the employees throughout their evolving careers, whether or not those careers involve hierarchical promotions. I have also argued that the various components are linked to each other and must be seen as a total system if it is to be effective. The total system must be managed as a system to insure coordination between the planning functions and the implementation functions.

I hope it is clear from what has been said above that an effective human resource planning and development system is integral to the functioning of the organization and must, therefore, be a central concern of line management. Many of the activities require specialist help, but the accountabilities must rest squarely with line supervisors and top management. It is they who control the opportunities and the rewards. It is the job assignment system and the feedback which employees get that is the ultimate raw material for growth and development. Whoever designs and manages the system, it will not help the organization to become more effective unless that system is *owned* by line management.

References

1. Alfred, T. "Checkers or Choice in Manpower Management." Harvard Business Review, January-February 1967, pp. 157-169.

2. Bailyn, L. "Involvement and Accommodation in Technical Careers." In Organizational Careers: Some New Perspectives, edited by J. Van Maanen. New York: John Wiley & Sons, 1977.

3. Bailyn, L. "Career and Family Orientations of Husbands and Wives in Relation to Marital Happiness." Human Relations (1970): 97-113.

4. Bailyn, L. and Schein, E. H. "Life Career Considerations as Indicators of Quality of Employment." In Measuring Work Quality for Social Reporting, edited by A. D. Biderman and T. F. Drury. New York: Sage Publications, 1976.

5. Beckhard, R. D. Organization Development: Strategies and Models. Reading, MA: Addison-Wesley, 1969.

6. Bennis, W. G. Changing Organizations. New York: McGraw-Hill, 1966.

7. Bennis, W. G. Organization Development: Its Nature, Origins, and Prospects. Reading, MA: Addison-Wesley, 1969.

8. Berlew, D., and Hall, D. T. "The Socialization of Managers." Administrative Science Quarterly, 11 (1966): 207-223.

9. Bray, D. W., Campbell, R. J., and Grant, D. E. Formative Years in Business. New York: John Wiley & Sons, 1974.

10. Burack, E. Organization Analysis. Hinsdale, IL: Dryden, 1975.

11. Dalton, G. W., and Thompson P. H. "Are R&D Organizations Obsolete?" Harvard Business Review, November-December 1976, pp. 105-116.

12. Galbraith, J. Designing Complex Organizations. Reading, MA: Addison-Wesley, 1973.

13. Hackman, J. R. and Suttle, J. L. Improving Life at Work. Los Angeles: Goodyear, 1977.

14. Hall, D. T. Careers in Organizations. Los Angeles: Goodyear, 1976.

15. Heidke, R. Career Pro-Activity of Middle Managers. Master's Thesis, Massachusetts Institute of Technology, 1977.

16. Kalish, R. A. Late Adulthood: Perspectives on Aging. Monterey, CA: Brooks-Cole, 1975.

17. Kanter, R. M. Work and Family in the United States. New York: Russell Sage, 1977.

18. Katz, R. "Job Enrichment: Some Career Considerations." In Organizational Careers: Some New Perspectives, edited by J. Van Maanen. New York: John Wiley & Sons, 1977.

19. Lesieur, F. G. The Scanlon Plan. New York: John Wiley & Sons, 1958.

20. McGregor, D. The Human Side of Enterprise. New York: McGraw-Hill, 1960.

21. Meltzer, H., and Wickert, F. R. *Humanizing Organizational Behavior*. Springfield, IL: Charles C. Thomas, 1976.

22. Myers, C. A. "Management and the Employee." In *Social Responsibility and the Business Predicament*, edited by J. W. McKie. Washington, D.C.: Brookings, 1974.

23. Pearse, R. F., and Pelzer, B. P. *Self-directed Change for the Mid-Career Manager*. New York: AMACOM, 1975.

24. Pigors, P., and Myers, C. A. *Personnel Administration*, 8th ed. New York: McGraw-Hill, 1977.

25. Roeber, R. J. C. *The Organization in a Changing Environment*. Reading, MA: Addison-Wesley, 1973.

26. Schein, E. H. "How to Break in the College Graduate." *Harvard Business Review*, 1964, pp. 68-76.

27. Schein, E. H. "Organizational Socialization and the Profession of Management." *Industrial Management Review*, Winter 1968, pp. 1-16.

28. Schein, E. H. *Process Consultation: Its Role in Organization Development*. Reading, MA: Addison-Wesley, 1969.

29. Schein, E. H. *Organizational Psychology*. Englewood Cliffs, NJ: Prentice-Hall, 1970.

30. Schein, E. H. "The Individual, the Organization, and the Career: A Conceptual Scheme." *Journal of Applied Behavioral Science* 7 (1971): 401-426.

31. Schein, E. H. How "Career Anchors" Hold Executives to Their Career Paths. *Personnel* 52, no. 3 (1975): 11-24.

32. Schein, E. H. *The Individual, the Organization and the Career: Toward Greater Human Effectiveness*. Reading, MA: Addison-Wesley, forthcoming.

33. Sheehy, G. "Catch 30 and Other Predictable Crises of Growing Up Adult." *New York Magazine*, February 1974, pp. 30-44.

34. Super, D. E., and Bohn, M. J. *Occupational Psychology*. Belmont, CA: Wadsworth, 1970.

35. Troll, L. E. *Early and Middle Adulthood*. Monterey, CA: Brooks-Cole, 1975.

36. Van Maanen, J. "Breaking In: Socialization to Work." In *Handbook of Work, Organization, and Society*, edited by R. Dubin. Chicago: Rand McNally, 1976.

37. Van Maanen, J., ed. *Organizational Careers: Some New Perspectives*. New York: John Wiley & Sons, 1977.

38. Van Maanen, J., Bailyn, L., and Schein, E. H. "The Shape of Things to Come: A New Look at Organizational Careers." In *Perspectives on Behavior in Organizations*, edited by J. R. Hackman, E. E. Lawler, and L. W. Porter. New York: McGraw-Hill, 1977.

39. Van Maanen, J., and Schein, E. H. "Improving the Quality of Work Life: Career Development." In *Improving Life at Work*, edited by J. R. Hackman and J. L. Suttle. Los Angeles: Goodyear, 1977.

Footnotes

Much of the research on which this paper is based was done under the sponsorship of the Group Psychology branch of the Office of Naval Research. Their generous support has made continuing work in this area possible. I want to thank my colleagues Lotte Bailyn and John Van Maaren for many of the ideas expressed in this paper.

1 See Pigors and Myers [24], and Burack [10].

2 See Hackman and Suttle [13], and Meltzer and Wickert [21].

3 See McGregor [20], Bennis [6], Pigors and Myers [24], Schein [29], Van Maanen [36], Bailyn and Schein [4], and Katz [18].

4 See Beckhard [5], Bennis [6], Schein [28], Galbraith [12], Lesieur [19], and Alfred [1].

5 See Schein [31].

6 See Schein [32].

7 See Bailyn and Schein [4], Myers [22], Van Maanen, Bailyn, and Schein [38], and Roeber [25].

8 See Van Maanen and Schein [39], Bailyn [3] and [2], and Kanter [17].

9 See Sheehy [33], Troll [35], Kalish [16], and Pearse and Pelzer [23].

10 See Burack [10], pp. 402-403.

11 See Schein [29].

12 See Dalton and Thompson [11], Super and Bohn, [34], Hall [14], and Schein [32].

13 See Schein [32].
14 See Schein [32].
15 See Schein [26] and [32].
16 See Schein [27], and Van Maanen [36].
17 See Schein [26].
18 See Schein [30] and [32].
19 See Schein [26], Bray, Campbell, and Grant [9], Berlew and Hall [8], and Hall [14].
20 See Dalton and Thompson [11], and Katz [18].
21 See Heidke [15].
22 See Bailyn [2].
23 See Katz [18].
24 See Bailyn [2].

A CRITICAL REEVALUATION OF MOTIVATION, MANAGEMENT, AND PRODUCTIVITY

Erwin S. Stanton, President
E. S. Stanton & Associates, Inc.
New York, New York

We Must Take a More Realistic Look at How Employees Are Managed

The problem of declining productivity and work performance started slowly several years ago--perhaps almost imperceptibly--and many thought that it was only temporary and would soon disappear. However, the problem did not vanish and, if anything, it worsened to the point that it is currently causing ever-increasing concern to companies, the government, and to most responsible Americans.

Indeed, the long-standing belief and assumption that U.S. business and industry was invincible and that no other country could ever approach us--much less surpass our technological superiority and leadership--was virtually taken for granted. It was assumed that the nation's industrial machine would continue just as it had in the past, making periodic improvements as it went along and, in so doing, advance our ever-rising standard of living. As such, a pattern of expectations was established in the minds of most people that better things--for many, even affluence--lay ahead.

But something has drastically gone wrong and it has been long in the making. The American industrial machine is currently ailing and clearly is not the vaunted and unchallenged mechanism that it has been for such a long time. Furthermore, our traditional technological superiority is being increasingly challenged by overseas competitors. In addition, our national productivity is declining, while our labor costs keep on rising. Over the course of the past years, American employees have demanded--and generally received--higher wages and benefits that have unquestionably enhanced their standard of living. At the same time, however, productivity has failed to keep pace with rising labor costs, causing

155

business and industry to lose much of its traditional and long-standing competitive advantage. During the past decade, wages have increased at an annual rate of 8.2%, while productivity growth has been limited to only 1.3%. The end result is that many American products are being outpriced, both at home and abroad.

The Japanese Challenge

The effects of this disastrous slippage in our industrial vitality is evident all around us. By now most Americans are clearly aware of the powerful challenge that has been posed by the Japanese auto industry, which is competing very successfully against U.S.-built cars, not only in our own country but also in the international market. But the nation's competitive decline is hardly limited to the automobile market, although it probably has received the greatest amount of publicity and attention. Actually, the list of industries in which foreign competition has become a formidable and threatening factor is ever growing, and now includes industries in which the U.S. has long been the leader, such as steel, textiles, footwear, and consumer electronics.

Business Week estimates that the loss of competitiveness by American industry in recent years equals $125 billion in lost production and some two million lost jobs. As a result, not only is the nation's standard of living being threatened, but also the profitability, viability, and even the very survival of numerous U.S. companies is likely to be in future jeopardy. In addition, the decline of the U.S. industrial machine could have serious implications for America's standing, power, and world role in these turbulent times.

Why Has Productivity Declined?

It is much easier to document the decline in productivity growth than to offer a truly satisfactory explanation as to why it is occurring in the first place. While there is no universal agreement as to the cause of the decline in productivity growth, most observers concur that the reasons are numerous, complex, and interrelated. However, a recently emerged consensus agrees that the following factors bear major responsibility:
- a decline in the rate of investment in new capital equipment
- a decline in research and development expenditures
- an increase in the cost and burden of government regulations
- the effects of inflation
- a rise in energy costs
- a decline in employee motivation and a commitment to high quality work performance

Motivation and Productivity

I fully recognize and respect the widely held belief that the drop in productivity growth unquestionably is the result of multiple factors and causes. Nevertheless, I believe that the decline in employee motivation and a commitment to work are two of the major causes of the slowdown in productivity.

To be sure, many employees *are* motivated to work productively, they take hold of the job, and they do contribute to their organization. However, every manager has encountered employees who, despite the company's best efforts, do not really care about either the company or the job. Such employees are a drain on their department and they simply do not earn their keep. Similarly, as consumers, we have all encountered personnel whose work is shoddy and of poor quality and whose application and interest appears to be almost totally lacking.

On the other hand, some people take a drastically different view in assessing the relationship between employee motivation and productivity. These individuals, who may be referred to as the Motivational School, seriously challenge the above explanation of the decline in business productivity. Armed with numerous research studies, they contend that most people want to work and are both interested in and capable of making a significant contribution to their company.

Furthermore, they argue, people seek personal fulfillment and self-actualization through their work. If employee productivity is unsatisfactory, they contend, then the fault likes with management and its failure to pay proper heed to these research findings and to appropriately implement the recommendations suggested by the behavioral scientists.

Which is the correct answer? Do people *really* want to work? Are they, in fact, self-motivated and self-directed? Or is the opposite more typically the case? Which factors, conditions, and situations affect the relationship between employee behavior and productivity? What specific recommendations can help managers direct the activities of their employees and achieve the goals and objectives of their companies?

Theories of Work Motivation

For the past 20 years, numerous studies, research reports, and well-formulated theories have attempted to explain the complex behavior of people at work and, more importantly, to gain the practicing manager some rather specific prescriptions as to the best way to manage employees for optimized productivity. Indeed, the influence of such applied psychologists as Maslow, McGregor, Herzberg, Likert, and Argyris on the management of human resources has been quite formidable. It is most unlikely that there is a manager today who, at one time or another, has not been exposed to some of the ideas and people management suggestions offered by these behavioral scientists.

The 1960s--when these theories were first proposed--were fruitful years for the formulation and development of psychological concepts designed to make a contribution to the world of work. In order to more clearly understand these theories, one must consider the time frame during which their formulations were developed, as well as some of the more significant economic, political, and sociological factors which influenced their thinking.

Essentially, the conceptual underpinnings of the various motivational principles put forth by the psychologists were predicated on the fact that America had a powerful, impressive, and magnificent industrial machine that offered the prospect of considerable prosperity for all of its citizens. At the same time, these psychologists believed that people had within them the ability, talent, and latent potential to enable the industrial machine to function in the best possible manner, and to, consequently, virtually guarantee economic prosperity and an ever-higher national standard of living.

157

In this context, the vast majority of employees have an almost inherent desire and motivation to work productively and to contribute substantially to the progress of their companies. Furthermore, the motivational psychologists asserted, most people want to and indeed are capable of participating actively with management in decision-making as it affects their jobs. As a result, if management wants to fully utilize its human resources, a participative leadership approach should contribute substantially to reach this objective.

How Well Have These Theories Held Up?

Many seasoned managers--including those who have been exposed to the popular work motivation theories in the course of their training and development sessions--become quite uncomfortable whenever they hear these principles so enthusiastically and universally proclaimed by ardent supporters. To seasoned managers, the concepts sound very good in theory, but their own experiences tell them that the principles do not always work as well as they have been heralded-- and frequently they do not work at all.

Many managers see a paradoxical inconsistency between the theories and recommendations so convincingly put forth by the motivationalists and the stark reality of the practical world of work in which the managers function every day. Indeed, on numerous occasions these managers have personally encountered many employees who simply are not committed to high quality work and who consistently fail to perform at a satisfactory level--despite management's best efforts to implement the motivationalists' recommendations.

In the final analysis, then, how valid, realistic, and practical are these highly acclaimed motivational theories? Do they really hold up under critical scrutiny? Or are we merely dealing with the utopian and ultrahumanistic theories of idealists, rather than looking at reality as it actually exists?

An Equivocal Answer

In my opinion, the answer is an equivocal one. Yes, at times the motivational theories do work--and they work quite well with interested and committed employees deriving considerable satisfaction from their work while contributing to the effectiveness of their companies. And no, at times the motivational principles do not hold up in practice and, as a result, many managers who have attempted to implement the theories have become disappointed and sadly disillusioned. Why, then, the paradox and the dramatic inconsistency in the results?

I would suggest that the many discrepancies are the result of the motivationalists' virtual claim of universality of their findings and the general applicability of their recommendations for the management of human resources. The motivationalists appear to have minimized the complexity and diversity of the motivational process and the influence and effects of numerous situational and contingency factors and circumstances in the workplace.

Essentially, three factors explain why some employees are indeed motivated to work, while others are not:

1) The motivation to work varies widely with people.

2) In the past decade, there has been a significant change in many employees' attitudes toward work.

3) The increase in various government social support programs has contributed significantly to the decline in work motivation in many people.

Different Work Ethics

It is true that many people are strongly motivated toward work and that they seek to fulfill themselves through the job. Frequently, work serves as the main focus of a person's life. However, to be motivated toward work is not a universal human phenomenon inherent in every individual. Actually, the importance of work varies tremendously and, for many, work is simply not the most essential part of their lives. In fact, it may not even be all that important in the first place.

To some people, since work provides income, it serves predominantly as a means to an end--that end frequently being off-the-job, leisure, and family activities. Of course, this does not mean that a person does not want a pleasant, interesting, and generally agreeable job--these are subjective qualifications that will vary with each individual. However, many people do not seek, or even expect to find, self-fulfillment through work, but rather seek it through nonwork activities. Nor does this mean that these individuals are dissatisfied with their work, as many behavioral scientists and journalists would have us believe. Essentially, people want different things from life.

Similarly, the motivationalists have stressed that most people have a strong need to plan, organize, and control their work, and to have more of a participative input in matters that directly affect them on the job. (Note, for example, the current fascination with quality circles, an idea imported from Japan.) However, as many managers have learned from first-hand experience, not everyone has the ability, intelligence, or experience--or, for that matter, the desire--to engage in such functions.

To categorically expect all employees to engage in participative management is completely unrealistic and may even invite chaos in the workplace. While many employees do want to participate--and indeed may come up with some useful ideas that can be implemented--others require a more structured, clearly defined, and nonambiguous work environment in which management provides precise instructions on how the job is to be done and what is expected of them. Indeed, many employees find such a work atmosphere most supportive psychologically, and report that they perform at their best under these very conditions.

Changing Attitudes Toward Work

One of the major factors contributing to the decline in productivity is a very profound change in the attitude toward work. Historically, Americans have been taught to work hard and to put their shoulder firmly to the wheel. Indeed, the work ethic has long been an integral part of the American way of life and of our cultural heritage.

In recent years, however, disturbing evidence has indicated that many people simply do not want to work too hard any longer. Indeed, it would seem that the relative affluence that our country has enjoyed for many years has given rise to a preoccupation with the self, a dramatic rise in self-indulgence, and an

FIGURE 1

Factors Suggesting a More Directive
Management Style

The employee tends to be more leisure-oriented, rather than seeking fulfillment through work.

The employee's job experience is such that he or she lacks the requisite qualifications to take on greater responsibilities.

The employee's educational or skill level is relatively modest.

The employee has a personal reluctance to take on additional job responsibilities.

The employee requires a relatively structured, clearly defined, and essentially nonambiguous work environment in order to perform most effectively.

The employee needs fairly close and supportive supervision.

The employee does not express a personal interest in becoming involved in decision-making activities.

The employee fails to identify sufficiently with the goals and objectives of the organization.

increased emphasis on instant gratification and the pursuit of pleasure-seeking activities--accompanied by a decline in commitment to work.

Some observers have linked this change in work attitude to the rising phenomenon currently referred to as the "psychology of entitlement." Succinctly put, this attitude is the widespread expectation that everyone deserves certain benefits, privileges, and rights without necessarily having to expend a whole lot of effort--not because they have earned them, but rather because they are entitled to them by virtue of living in today's world. Put another way, they feel that society basically "owes" them certain privileges--a good, comfortable job and a high income, for starters.

FIGURE 2

Factors Suggesting a More Participative
Management Style

The employee seeks to fulfill many of his or her ego and psychological needs through expression at work.

The employee has the necessary intelligence, education, and experience to take on additional responsibilities.

The employee is interested in having more of a say in matters that affect him or her on the job, and wants to participate in decision-making with management.

The employee does not feel anxious, uncomfortable, or insecure when faced with relatively unstructured and ill-defined work situations.

The employee is sufficiently self-reliant and self-confident to not need close and supportive supervision from his or her superior.

Undoubtedly, the vast number of government social support programs currently available has encouraged the changing attitude toward work. At one time, being unemployed was a personal catastrophe. Today, losing one's job may still be a major problem, but the event is considerably cushioned by liberal unemployment benefits, which are often supplemented by food stamps and other forms of government assistance. While ordinarily these programs serve a most useful purpose, in many cases they have been abused by people and have resulted in a weakening of employee motivation and a lessening of the will to work.

160

In short, I believe that many people have become fat, lazy, and complacent. And, while I would not go so far as to declare the work ethic dead, it would certainly seem that it is currently ailing and needs a good dose of revitalization.

Reality-Centered Management

In my opinion, if we are to get productivity growth moving again, we must take a fresh and more realistic look at how we manage employees. In any organization, one will find many very different kinds of jobs being carried out. These jobs call for a wide range of abilities, interests, and talents, and accordingly make very different demands on the people holding them.

At the same time, a wide diversity exists among employees. For example, a given person may be well suited to one job, but clearly unsatisfactory in another. Effective management calls for a more realistic evaluation of the type of individual who is right for a given assignment, as well as the most appropriate leadership style. Consequently, there is no one correct management style that will fit all employees and all situations.

Reality-Centered Management recognizes that some employees will want to express themselves and will seek maximum self-fulfillment through their work, and will, as a result, be quite eager to participate with management in decision-making activities. At the same time, however, other employees in the very same department will not attach such meaning to work and will, consequently, look to management for clear and explicit direction and supportive supervision.

Flexible Leadership

To be effective, therefore, managers need a more flexible leadership style that will allow them to be more participative with certain employees, while taking on a much more directive and supportive posture in their approach with other employees.

Reality-Centered Management advocates a leadership style that ranges anywhere from being highly directive to notably participative. As such, it should not be viewed as a dichotomous model. It is most unlikely that any manager will fall at either extreme end of the scale. Rather, a manager's customary leadership style and manner of directing employees tends to gravitate toward either the directive or the participative side. However, I wish to emphasize that effective managers need to be flexible in their approach to managing employees.

How does the manager know which is the correct or most appropriate leadership style to use in any specific situation? To respond to this very strategic question, let's take a look at some of the factors that would suggest that a manager's style should lean either toward the directive or the participative end of the continuum. Figures 1 and 2 will offer some appropriate guidelines.

Get Back to Basics

In addition to managing employees in a more realistic manner, organizations should get back to some of the management basics that seem to have been neglected in recent years. Specifically, we need to revitalize the following essentials of sound management:

in recent years. Specifically, we need to revitalize the following essentials of sound management:

Recruitment and selection. Extra attention should be given to initial personnel recruitment and selection so that truly qualified individuals who are inherently more motivated and capable of contributing to the company will be hired.

Training and development. Appropriate training and development should be given to employees so that they will become more productive on the job. In part, such training should instill a positive attitude in employees and an acceptance of the concept of mutual obligation. Unquestionably the company has certain obligations to the employee, but the employee also has a reciprocal responsibility to the company, which includes a high level of excellence in work performance.

Performance appraisals. A fair, objective, and accurate employee performance appraisal program should be developed which will provide factual information with respect to a person's current work and which will clearly indicate the specific areas where future improvement is required.

Supervision. Effective, ongoing supervision and direction of employees by qualified and properly trained managers is necessary if a satisfactory degree of productivity is to be attained. As part of such a strategy, managers should set high standards of work performance that stress excellence and insist that these standards be met.

Compensation. An organization must have an equitable and attractive reward and compensation system that clearly and tangibly recognizes the achievements and contributions of employees.

The above five strategies may not constitute a true breakthrough in management practice. Indeed, these strategies have been around for some time, but inadequate attention has been given to them. It is time to return to proven management basics if we are to regain our competitive edge. Fortunately, American business and industry is still strong and powerful--in fact, it remains as the undisputed world leader. In addition, our potential for yet greater growth is exceedingly promising. Clearly, the hour is late, but there is still time if vigorous and decisive steps are taken promptly.

References

Argyris, Chris. Integrating the Individual and the Organization (New York: John Wiley & Sons, 1964).

Herzberg, Frederick. Work and the Nature of Man (Cleveland: World Publishing Company, 1966).

Likert, Rensis. The Human Organization (New York: McGraw-Hill, 1967).

Maslow, A. H. Motivation and Personality 2nd ed. (New York: Harper & Row, 1970).

McGregor, Douglas. The Human Side of Enterprise (New York: McGraw-Hill, 1960).

"The Reindustrialization of America," Business Week (June 30, 1980), pp. 56-142.

Yankelovich, Daniel. We Need New Motivational Tools," Industry Week (August 6, 1979), pp. 61-68.

ON THE FOLLY OF REWARDING A,
WHILE HOPING FOR B

Steven Kerr
Ohio State University

Illustrations are presented from society in general, and from organizations in particular, of reward systems that "pay off" for one behavior even though the rewarder hopes dearly for another. Portions of the reward systems of a manufacturing company and an insurance firm are examined and the consequences discussed.

Whether dealing with monkeys, rats, or human beings, it is hardly controversial to state that most organisms seek information concerning what activities are rewarded, and then seek to do (or at least pretend to do) those things, often to the virtual exclusion of activities not rewarded. The extent to which this occurs of course will depend on the perceived attractiveness of the rewards offered, but neither operant nor expectancy theorists would quarrel with the essence of this notion.

Nevertheless, numerous examples exist of reward systems that are fouled up in that behaviors which are rewarded are those which the rewarder is trying to *discourage*, while the behavior he desires is not being rewarded at all.

In an effort to understand and explain this phenomenon, this paper presents examples from society, from organizations in general, and from profit making firms in particular. Data from a manufacturing company and information from an insurance firm are examined to demonstrate the consequences of such reward systems for the organizations involved, and possible reasons why such reward systems continue to exist are considered.

Societal Examples

Politics

Official goals are "purposely vague and general and do not indicate ... the host of decisions that must be made among alternative ways of achieving official goals and the priority of multiple goals ..." (8, p. 66). They usually may be relied on to offend absolutely no one, and in this sense can be considered high acceptance, low quality goals. An example might be "build better schools." Operative goals are higher in quality but lower in acceptance, since they specify where the money will come from, what alternative goals will be ignored, etc.

The American citizenry supposedly wants its candidates for public office to set forth operative goals, making their proposed programs "perfectly clear," specifying sources and uses of funds, etc. However, since operative goals are lower in acceptance, and since aspirants to public office need acceptance (from at least 50.1 percent of the people), most politicians prefer to speak only of official goals, at least until after the election. They of course would agree to speak at the

Reprinted from <u>Academy of Management Journal</u>, 1975, Vol. 18, No. 4, pp. 769-83, by permission of the author and publisher.

operative level if "punished" for not doing so. The electorate could do this by refusing to support candidates who do not speak at the operative level.

Instead, however, the American voter typically punishes (withholds support from) candidates who frankly discuss where the money will come from, rewards politicians who speak only of official goals, but hopes that candidates (despite the reward system) will discuss the issues operatively. It is academic whether it was moral for Nixon, for example, to refuse to discuss his 1968 "secret plan" to end the Vietnam war, his 1972 operative goals concerning the lifting of price controls, the reshuffling of his cabinet, etc. The point is that the reward system made such refusal rational.

It seems worth mentioning that no manuscript can adequately define what is "moral" and what is not. However, examination of costs and benefits, combined with knowledge of what motivates a particular individual, often will suffice to determine what for him is "rational."[1] If the reward system is so designed that it is irrational to be moral, this does not necessarily mean that immorality will result. But is this not asking for trouble?

War

If some oversimplification may be permitted, let it be assumed that the primary goal of the organization (Pentagon, Luftwaffe, or whatever) is to win. Let it be assumed further that the primary goal of most individuals on the front lines is to get home alive. Then there appears to be an important conflict in goals-- personally rational behavior by those at the bottom will endanger goal attainment by those at the top.

But not necessarily! It depends on how the reward system is set up. The Vietnam war was indeed a study of disobedience and rebellion, with terms such as "fragging" (killing one's own commanding officer) and "search and evade" becoming part of the military vocabulary. The difference in subordinates' acceptance of authority between World War II and Vietnam is reported to be considerable, and veterans of the Second World War often have been quoted as being outraged at the mutinous actions of many American soldiers in Vietnam.

Consider, however, some critical differences in the reward system in use during the two conflicts. What did the GI in World War II want? To go home. And when did he get to go home? When the war was won! If he disobeyed the orders to clean out the trenches and take the hills, the war would not be won and he would not go home. Furthermore, what were his chances of attaining his goal (getting home alive) if he obeyed the orders compared to his chances if he did not? What is being suggested is that the rational soldier in World War II, *whether patriotic or not*, probably found it expedient to obey.

Consider the reward system used in Vietnam. What did the man at the bottom want? To go home. And when did he get to go home? When his tour of duty was over! This was the case *whether or not* the war was won. Furthermore, concerning the relative chance of getting home alive by obeying orders compared to the chance if they were disobeyed, it is worth noting that a mutineer in Vietnam was far more likely to be assigned rest and rehabilitation (on the assumption that fatigue was the cause) than he was to suffer any negative consequences.

In his description of the "zone of indifference," Barnard stated that "a person can and will accept a communication as authoritative only when ... at the

164

time of his decision, he believes it to be compatible with his personal interests as a whole" (1, p. 165). In light of the reward system used in Vietnam, would it not have been personally irrational for some orders to have been obeyed? Was not the military implementing a system which *rewarded* disobedience, while *hoping* that soldiers (despite the reward system) would obey orders?

Medicine

Theoretically, a physician can make either of two types of error, and intuitively one seems as bad as the other. A doctor can pronounce a patient sick when he is actually well, thus causing him needles anxiety and expense, curtailment of enjoyable foods and activities, and even physical danger by subjecting him to needless medication and surgery. Alternately, a doctor can label a sick person well, and thus avoid treating what may be a serious, even fatal ailment. It might be natural to conclude that physicians seek to minimize both types of error.

Such a conclusion would be wrong.[2] It is estimated that numerous Americans are presently afflicted with iatrogenic (physician *caused*) illnesses (9). This occurs when the doctor is approached by someone complaining of a few stray symptoms. The doctor classifies and organizes these symptoms, gives them a name, and obligingly tells the patient what further symptoms may be expected. This information often acts as self-fulfilling prophecy, with the result that from that day on the patient for all practical purposes is sick.

Why does this happen? Why are physicians so reluctant to sustain a type 2 error (pronouncing a sick person well) that they will tolerate many type 1 errors? Again, a look at the reward system is needed. The punishments for a type 2 error are real: guilt, embarrassment, and the threat of lawsuit and scandal. On the other hand, a type 1 error (labeling a well person sick) "is sometimes seen as sound clinical practice, indicating a healthy conservative approach to medicine" (9, p. 69). Type 1 errors also are likely to generate increased income and a stream of steady customers who, being well in a limited physiological sense, will not embarrass the doctor by dying abruptly.

Fellow physicians and the general public therefore are really *rewarding* type 1 errors and at the same time *hoping* fervently that doctors will try not to make them.

General Organizational Examples

Rehabilitation Centers and Orphanages

In terms of the prime beneficiary classification (2, p. 42) organizations such as these are supposed to exist for the "public-in-contact," that is, clients. The orphanage therefore theoretically is interested in placing as many children as possible in good homes. However, often orphanages surround themselves with so many rules concerning adoption that it is nearly impossible to pry a child out of the place. Orphanages may deny adoptions unless the applicants are a married couple, both of the same religion as the child, without history of emotional or vocational instability, with a specified minimum income and a private room for the child, etc.

165

If the primary goal is to place children in good homes, then the rules ought to constitute means toward that goal. Goal displacement results when these "means become ends-in-themselves that displace the original goals" (2, p. 229).

To some extent these rules are required by law. But the influence of the reward system on the orphanage's management should not be ignored. Consider, for example, that the:

1. Number of children enrolled often is the most important determinant of the size of the allocated budget.
2. Number of children under the director's care also will affect the size of his staff.
3. Total organizational size will determine largely the director's prestige at the annual conventions, in the community, etc.

Therefore, to the extent that staff size, total budget, and personal prestige are valued by the orphanage's executive personnel, it becomes rational for them to make it difficult for children to be adopted. After all, who wants to be the director of the smallest orphanage in the state?

If the reward system errs in the opposite direction, paying off only for placements, extensive goal displacement again is likely to result. A common example of vocational rehabilitation in many states, for example, consists of placing someone in a job for which he has little interest and few qualifications, for two months or so, and then "rehabilitating" him again in another position. Such behavior is quite consistent with the prevailing reward system, which pays off for the number of individuals placed in any position for 60 days or more. Rehabilitation counselors also confess to competing with one another to place relatively skilled clients, sometimes ignoring persons with few skills who would be harder to place. Extensively disabled clients find that counselors often prefer to work with those whose disabilities are less severe.[3]

Universities

Society *hopes* that teachers will not neglect their teaching responsibilities but *rewards* them almost entirely for research and publications. This is most true at the large and prestigious universities. Cliches such as "good research and good teaching go together" notwithstanding, professors often find that they must choose between teaching and research oriented activities when allocating their time. Rewards for good teaching usually are limited to outstanding teacher awards, which are given to only a small percentage of good teachers and which usually bestow little money and fleeting prestige. Punishments for poor teaching also are rare.

Rewards for research and publications, on the other hand, and punishments for failure to accomplish these, are commonly administered by universities at which teachers are employed. Furthermore, publication oriented resumes usually will be well received at other universities, whereas teaching credentials, harder to document and quantify, are much less transferable. Consequently it is rational for university teachers to concentrate on research, even if to the detriment of teaching and at the expense of their students.

By the same token, it is rational for students to act based upon the goal displacement which has occurred within universities concerning what they are rewarded for. If it is assumed that a primary goal of a university is to transfer

166

knowledge from teacher to student, then grades become identifiable as a means toward that goal, serving as motivational, control, and feedback devices to expedite the knowledge transfer. Instead, however, the grades themselves have become much more important for entrance to graduate school, successful employment, tuition refunds, parental respect, etc., than the knowledge or lack of knowledge they are supposed to signify.

It therefore should come as no surprise that information has surfaced in recent years concerning fraternity files for examinations, term paper writing services, organized cheating at the service academies, and the like. Such activities constitute a personally rational response to a reward system which pays off for grades rather than knowledge.

Business Related Examples

Ecology

Assume that the president of XYZ Corporation is confronted with the following alternatives:
1. Spend $11 million for antipollution equipment to keep from poisoning fish in the river adjacent to the plant; or
2. Do nothing, in violation of the law, and assume a one in ten chance of being caught, with a resultant $1 million fine plus the necessity of buying the equipment.

Under this not unrealistic set of choices it requires no linear program to determine that XYZ Corporation can maximize its probabilities by flouting the law. Add the fact that XYZ's president is probably being rewarded (by creditors, stockholders, and other salient parts of his task environment) according to criteria totally unrelated to the number of fish poisoned, and his probable course of action becomes clear.

Evaluation of Training

It is axiomatic that those who care about a firm's well-being should insist that the organization get fair value for its expenditures. Yet it is commonly known that firms seldom bother to evaluate a new GRID, MBO, job enrichment program, or whatever, to see if the company is getting its money's worth. Why? Certainly it is not because people have not pointed out that this situation exists; numerous practitioner oriented articles are written each year to just this point.

The individuals (whether in personnel, manpower planning, or wherever) who normally would be responsible for conducting such evaluations are the same ones often charged with introducing the change effort in the first place. Having convinced top management to spend the money, they usually are quite animated afterwards in collecting arigorous vignettes and anecdotes about how successful the program was. The last thing many desire is a formal, systematic, and revealing evaluation. Although members of top management may actually *hope* for such systematic evaluation, their reward systems continue to *reward* ignorance in this area. And if the personnel department abdicates its responsibility, who is to step into the breach? The change agent himself? Hardly! He is likely to be too busy collecting anecdotal "evidence" of his own, for use with his next client.

Many additional examples could be cited of systems which in fact are rewarding behaviors other than those supposedly desired by the rewarder. A few of these are described briefly below.

Most coaches disdain to discuss individual accomplishments, preferring to speak of teamwork, proper attitude, and a one-for-all spirit. Usually, however, rewards are distributed according to individual performance. The college basketball player who feeds his teammates instead of shooting will not compile impressive scoring statistics and is less likely to be drafted by the pros. The ballplayer who hits to right field to advance the runners will win neither the batting nor home run titles, and will be offered smaller raises. It therefore is rational for players to think of themselves first, and the team second.

In business organizations where rewards are dispensed for unit performance or for individual goals achieved, without regard for overall effectiveness, similar attitudes often are observed. Under most Management by Objectives (MBO) systems, goals in areas where quantification is difficult often go unspecified. The organization therefore often is in a position where it *hopes* for employee effort in the areas of team building, interpersonal relations, creativity, etc., but it formally *rewards* none of these. In cases where promotions and raises are formally tied to MBO, the system itself contains a paradox in that it "asks employees to set challenging, risky goals, only to face smaller paychecks and possibly damaged careers if these goals are not accomplished" (5, p. 40).

It is *hoped* that administrators will pay attention to long run costs and opportunities and will institute programs which will bear fruit later on. However, many organizational reward systems pay off for short run sales and earnings only. Under such circumstances, it is personally rational for officials to sacrifice long term growth and profit (by selling off equipment and property, or by stifling research and development) for short term advantages. This probably is most pertinent in the public sector, with the result that many public officials are unwilling to implement programs which will not show benefits by election time.

As a final, clear-cut example of a fouled-up reward system, consider the cost-plus contract or its next of kin, the allocation of next year's budget as a direct function of this year's expenditures. It probably is conceivable that those who award such budgets and contracts really hope for economy and prudence in spending. It is obvious, however, that adopting the proverb "to him who spends shall more be given," rewards not economy, but spending itself.

Two Companies' Experiences

A Manufacturing Organization

A midwest manufacturer of industrial goods had been troubled for some time by aspects of its organizational climate it believed dysfunctional. For research purposes, interviews were conducted with many employees and a questionnaire was administered on a companywide basis, including plants and offices in several American and Canadian locations. The company strongly encouraged employee participation in the survey, and made available time and space during the workday for completion of the instrument. All employees in attendance during the day of the survey completed the questionnaire. All instruments were collected directly by the researcher, who personally administered each session. Since no one employed by the firm handled the questionnaires, and since respondent names were not asked for, it seems likely that the pledge of anonymity given was believed.

A modified version of the Expect Approval scale (7) was included as part of the questionnaire. The instrument asked respondents to indicate the degree of approval or disapproval they could expect if they performed each of the described actions. A seven point Likert scale was used, with one indicating that the action would probably bring strong disapproval and seven signifying likely strong approval.

Although normative data for this scale from studies of other organizations are unavailable, it is possible to examine fruitfully the data obtained from this survey in several ways. First, it may be worth noting that the questionnaire data corresponded closely to information gathered through interviews. Furthermore, as can be seen from the results summarized in Table 1, sizable differences between various work units, and between employees at different job levels within the same work unit, were obtained. This suggests that response bias effects (social desirability in particular loomed as a potential concern) are not likely to be severe.

TABLE 1

Summary of Two Divisions' Data Relevant to
Conforming and Risk-Avoidance Behaviors
(Extent to Which Subjects Expect Approval)

Dimension	Item	Division and Sample	Total Responses	Percentage of Workers Responding		
				1,2, or 3 Disapproval	4	5,6, or 7 Approval
Risk Avoidance	Making a risky decision based on the best information available at the time, but which turns out wrong.	A, levels 1-4 (lowest)	127	61	25	14
		A, levels 5-8	172	46	31	23
		A, levels 9 and above	17	41	30	30
		B, levels 1-4 (lowest)	31	58	26	16
		B, levels 5-8	19	42	42	16
		B, levels 9 and above	10	50	20	30
	Setting extremely high and challenging standards and goals, and then narrowly failing to make them.	A, levels 1-4	122	47	28	25
		A, levels 5-8	168	33	26	41
		A, levels 9+	17	24	6	70
		B, levels 1-4	31	48	23	29
		B, levels 5-8	18	17	33	50
		B, levels 9+	10	30	0	70

169

TABLE 1 (Continued)

Dimension	Item	Division and Sample	Total Responses	Percentage of Workers Responding		
				1,2, or 3 Disapproval	4	5,6, or 7 Approval
Risk Avoidance (Continued)	Setting goals which are extremely easy to make and then making them.	A, levels 1-4	124	35	30	35
		A, levels 5-8	171	47	27	26
		A, levels 9+	17	70	24	6
		B, levels 1-4	31	58	26	16
		B, levels 5-8	19	63	16	21
		B, levels 9+	10	80	0	20
Conformity	Being a "yes man" and always agreeing with the boss.	A, levels 1-4	126	46	17	37
		A, levels 5-8	180	54	14	31
		A, levels 9+	17	88	12	0
		B, levels 1-4	32	53	28	19
		B, levels 5-8	19	68	21	11
		B, levels 9+	10	80	10	10
	Always going along with the majority	A, levels 1-4	125	40	25	35
		A, levels 5-8	173	47	21	32
		A, levels 9+	17	70	12	18
		B, levels 1-4	31	61	23	16
		B, levels 5-8	19	68	11	21
		B, levels 9+	10	80	10	10
	Being careful to stay on the good side of everyone, so that everyone agrees that you are a great guy.	A, levels 1-4	124	45	18	37
		A, levels 5-8	173	45	22	33
		A, levels 9+	17	64	6	30
		B, levels 1-4	31	54	23	23
		B, levels 5-8	19	73	11	16
		B, levels 9+	10	80	10	10

Most importantly, comparisons between scores obtained on the Expect Approval scale and a statement of problems which were the reason for the survey revealed that the same behaviors which managers in each division thought dysfunctional were those which lower level employees claimed were rewarded. As compared to job levels 1 to 8 in Division B (see Table 1), those in Division A claimed a much higher acceptance by management of "conforming" activities. Between 31 and 37 percent of Division A employees at levels 1-8 stated that going along with the majority, agreeing with the boss, and staying on everyone's good side brought approval; only once (level 5-8 responses to one of the three items) did a majority suggest that such actions would generate disapproval.

Furthermore, responses from Division A workers at levels 1-4 indicate that behaviors geared toward risk avoidance were as likely to be rewarded as to be punished. Only at job levels 9 and above was it apparent that the reward system was positively reinforcing behaviors desired by top management. Overall, the same "tendencies toward conservatism and apple-polishing at the lower levels" which divisional management had complained about during the interviews were those claimed by subordinates to be the most rational course of action in light of the existing reward system. Management apparently was not getting the behaviors it was *hoping* for, but it certainly was getting the behaviors it was perceived by subordinates to be *rewarding*.

An Insurance Firm

The Group Health Claims Division of a large eastern insurance company provides another rich illustration of a reward system which reinforces behaviors not desired by top management.

Attempting to measure and reward accuracy in paying surgical claims, the firm systematically keeps track of the number of returned checks and letters of complaint received from policyholders. However, underpayments are likely to provoke cries of outrage from the insured, while overpayments often are accepted in courteous silence. Since it often is impossible to tell from the physician's statement which of surgical procedures, with different allowable benefits, was performed, and since writing for clarifications will interfere with other standards used by the firm concerning "percentage of claims paid within two days of receipt," the new hire in more than one claims section is soon acquainted with the informal norm: "When in doubt, pay it out!"

The situation would be even worse were it not for the fact that other features of the firm's reward system tend to neutralize those described. For example, annual "merit" increases are given to all employees, in one of the following three amounts:

1. If the worker is "outstanding" (a select category, into which no more than two employees per section may be placed): 5 percent
2. If the worker is "above average" (normally all workers not "outstanding" are so rated): 4 percent
3. If the worker commits gross acts of negligence and irresponsibility for which he might be discharged in many other companies: 3 percent

Now, since (a) the difference between the 5 percent theoretically attainable through hard work and the 4 percent attainable merely by living until the review date is small and (b) since insurance firms seldom dispense much of a salary increase in cash (rather, the worker's insurance benefits increase, causing him to be further overinsured), many employees are rather indifferent to the possibility of

171

obtaining the extra one percent reward and therefore tend to ignore the norm concerning indiscriminant payments.

However, most employees are not indifferent to the rule which states that, should absences or latenesses total three or more in any six-month period, the entire 4 or 5 percent due at the next "merit" review must be forfeited. In this sense the firm may be described as *hoping* for performance, while *rewarding* attendance. What it gets, of course, is attendance. (If the absence-lateness rule appears to the reader to be stringent, it really is not. The company counts "times" rather than "days" absent, and a ten-day absence therefore counts the same as one lasting two days. A worker in danger of accumulating a third absence within six months merely has to remain ill (away from work) during his second absence until his first absence is more than six months old. The limiting factor is that at some point his salary ceases, and his sickness benefits take over. This usually is sufficient to get the younger workers to return, but for those with 20 or more years' service, the company provides sickness benefits of 90 percent of normal salary, tax-free! Therefore . . . .)

Causes

Extremely diverse instances of systems which reward behavior A although the rewarder apparently hopes for behavior B have been given. These are useful to illustrate the breadth and magnitude of the phenomenon, but the diversity increases the difficulty of determining commonalities and establishing causes. However, four general factors may be pertinent to an explanation of why fouled up reward systems seem to be so prevalent.

Fascination with an "Objective" Criterion

It has been mentioned elsewhere that:

> Most "objective" measures of productivity are objective only in that their subjective elements are a) determined in advance, rather than coming into play at the time of the formal evaluation, and b) well concealed on the rating instrument itself. Thus industrial firms seeking to devise objective rating systems first decide, in an arbitrary manner, what dimensions are to be rated, ... usually including some items having little to do with organizational effectiveness while excluding others that do. Only then does Personnel Division churn out official-looking documents on which all dimensions chosen to be rated are assigned point values, categories, or whatever (6, p. 92).

Nonetheless, many individuals seek to establish simple, quantifiable standards against which to measure and reward performance. Such efforts may be successful in highly predictable areas within an organization, but are likely to cause goal displacement when applied anywhere else. Overconcern with attendance and lateness in the insurance firm and with number of people placed in the vocational rehabilitation division may have been largely responsible for the problems described in those organizations.

Overemphasis on Highly Visible Behaviors

Difficulties often stem from the fact that some parts of the task are highly visible while other parts are not. For example, publications are easier to demonstrate than teaching, and scoring baskets and hitting home runs are more readily observable than feeding teammates and advancing base runners. Similarly,

172

the adverse consequences of pronouncing a sick person well are more visible than those sustained by labeling a well person sick. Team-building and creativity are other examples of behaviors which may not be rewarded simply because they are hard to observe.

Hypocrisy

In some of the instances described the rewarder may have been getting the desired behavior, notwithstanding claims that the behavior was not desired. This may be true, for example, of management's attitude toward apple-polishing in the manufacturing firm (a behavior which subordinates felt was rewarded, despite management's avowed dislike of the practice). This also may explain politicians' unwillingness to revise the penalties for disobedience of ecology laws, and the failure of top management to devise reward systems which would cause systematic evaluation of training and development programs.

Emphasis on Morality or Equity Rather than Efficiency

Sometimes consideration of other factors prevents the establishment of a system which rewards behaviors desired by the rewarder. The felt obligation of many Americans to vote for one candidate or another, for example, may impair their ability to withhold support from politicians who refuse to discuss the issues. Similarly, the concern for spreading the risks and costs of wartime military service may outweigh the advantage to be obtained by committing personnel to combat until the war is over.

It should be noted that only with respect to the first two causes are reward systems really paying off for other than desired behaviors. In the case of the third and fourth causes the system *is* rewarding behaviors desired by the rewarder, and the systems are fouled up only from the standpoints of those who believe the rewarder's public statements (cause 3), or those who seek to maximize efficiency rather than other outcomes (cause 4).

Conclusions

Modern organization theory requires a recognition that the members of organizations and society possess divergent goals and motives. It therefore is unlikely that managers and their subordinates will seek the same outcomes. Three possible remedies for this potential problem are suggested.

Selection

It is theoretically possible for organizations to employ only those individuals whose goals and motives are wholly consonant with those of management. In such cases the same behaviors judged by subordinates to be rational would be perceived by management as desirable. State-of-the-art reviews of selection techniques, however, provide scant grounds for hope that such an approach would be successful (for example, see 12).

Training

Another theoretical alternative is for the organization to admit those employees whose goals are not consonant with those of management and then, through training, socialization, or whatever, alter employee goals to make them consonant. However, research on the effectiveness of such training programs, though limited, provides further grounds for pessimism (for example, see 3).

Altering the Reward System

What would have been the result if:

1. Nixon had been assured by his advisors that he could not win reelection except by discussing issues in detail?
2. Physicians' conduct was subjected to regular examination by review boards for type 1 errors (calling healthy people ill) and to penalties (fines, censure, etc.) for errors of either type?
3. The President of XYZ Corporation had to choose between (a) spending $11 million dollars for antipollution equipment, and (b) incurring a fifty-fifty chance of going to jail for five years.

Managers who complain that their workers are not motivated might do well to consider the possibility that they have installed reward systems which are paying off for behaviors other than those they are seeking. This, in part, is what happened in Vietnam, and this is what regularly frustrates societal efforts to bring about honest politicians, civic-minded managers, etc. This certainly is what happened in both the manufacturing and the insurance companies.

A first step for such managers might be to find out what behaviors currently are being rewarded. Perhaps an instrument similar to that used in the manufacturing firm could be useful for this purpose. Chances are excellent that these managers will be surprised by what they find--that their firms are not rewarding what they assume they are. In fact, such undesirable behavior by organizational members as they have observed may be explained largely by the reward systems in use.

This is not to say that all organizational behavior is determined by formal rewards and punishments. Certainly it is true that in the absence of formal reinforcement some soldiers will be patriotic, some presidents will be ecology minded, and some orphanage directors will care about children. The point, however, is that in such cases the rewarder is not *causing* the behaviors desired but is only a fortunate bystander. For an organization to *act* upon its members, the formal reward system should positively reinforce desired behaviors, not constitute an obstacle to be overcome.

It might be wise to underscore the obvious fact that there is nothing really new in what has been said. In both theory and practice these matters have been mentioned before. Thus in many states Good Samaritan laws have been installed to protect doctors who stop to assist a stricken motorist. In states without such laws it is commonplace for doctors to refuse to stop, for fear of involvement in a subsequent lawsuit. In college basketball additional penalties have been instituted against players who foul their opponents deliberately. It has long been argued by Milton Friedman and others that penalties should be altered so as to make it irrational to disobey the ecology laws, and so on.

By altering the reward system the organization escapes the necessity of selecting only desirable people or of trying to alter undesirable ones. In Skinnerian terms (as described in 11, p. 704), "As for responsibility and goodness--as commonly defined--no one ... would want or need them. They refer to a man's behaving well despite the absence of positive reinforcement that is obviously sufficient to explain it. Where such reinforcement exists, 'no one needs goodness.'"

References

1. Barnard, Chester I. The Functions of the Executive (Cambridge, Mass.: Harvard University Press, 1964).

2. Blau, Peter M., and W. Richard Scott. Formal Organizations (San Francisco: Chandler, 1962).

3. Fiedler, Fred E. "Predicting the Effects of Leadership Training and Experience from the Contingency Model," Journal of Applied Psychology, Vol. 56 (1972), 114-119.

4. Garland, L. H. "Studies of the Accuracy of Diagnostic Procedures," American Journal Roentgenological, Radium Therapy Nuclear Medicine, Vol. 82 (1959), 25-38.

5. Kerr, Steven. "Some Modifications in MBO as an OD Strategy," Academy of Management Proceedings, 1973, pp. 39-42.

6. Kerr, Steven, "What Price Objectivity?" American Sociologist, Vol. 8 (1973), 92-93.

7. Litwin, G. H., and R. A. Stringer, Jr. Motivation and Organizational Climate (Boston: Harvard University Press, 1968).

8. Perrow, Charles. "The Analysis of Goals in Complex Organizations," in A. Etzioni (Ed.), Readings on Modern Organizations (Englewood Cliffs, N.J.: Prentice-Hall, 1969).

9. Scheff, Thomas J. "Decision Rules, Types of Error, and Their Consequences in Medical Diagnosis," in F. Massarik and P. Ratoosh (Eds.), Mathematical Explorations in Behavioral Science (Homewood, Ill.: Irwin, 1965).

10. Simon, Herbert A. Administrative Behavior (New York: Free Press, 1957).

11. Swanson, G. E. "Review Symposium: Beyond Freedom and Dignity," American Journal of Sociology, Vol. 78 (1972), 702-705.

12. Webster, E. Decision Making in the Employment Interview (Montreal: Industrial Relations Center, McGill University, 1964).

Footnotes

[1] In Simon's (10, pp. 76-77) terms, a decision is "subjectively rational" if it maximizes an individual's valued outcomes so far as his knowledge permits. A decision is "personally rational" if it is oriented toward the individual's goals.

[2] In one study (4) of 14,867 films for signs of tuberculosis, 1,216 positive readings turned out to be clinically negative; only 24 negative readings proved clinically active, a ratio of 50 to 1.

[3] Personal interviews conducted during 1972-1973.

LEADERSHIP THEORY:
SOME IMPLICATIONS FOR MANAGERS

Chester A. Schriesheim
James M. Tolliver
Orlando C. Behling

In the past seventy years more than 3,000 leadership studies have been conducted and dozens of leadership models and theories have been proposed.[1] Yet, a practicing manager who reads this literature seeking an effective solution to supervisory problems will rapidly become disenchanted. Although we have access to an overwhelming volume of leadership theory and research, few guidelines exist which are of use to a practitioner. Nevertheless, interest in leadership--and in those qualities which separate a successful leader from an unsuccessful one-- remains unabated. In almost any book dealing with management one will find some discussion of leadership. In any company library there are numerous volumes entitled "Increasing Leadership Effectiveness," "Successful Leadership," or "How to Lead." Typical management development programs conducted within work organizations and universities usually deal with some aspect of leadership. This intensity and duration of writing on the subject and the sums spent annually on leadership training indicate that practicing managers and academicians consider good leadership essential to organizational success.

What is meant by leadership, let alone *good* leadership? Many definitions have been proposed, and it seems that most are careful to separate management from leadership. This distinction sometimes becomes blurred in everyday conversations. The first term, *management,* includes those processes, both mental and physical, which result in other people executing prescribed formal duties for organizational goal attainment. It deals mainly with planning, organizing, and controlling the work of other people to achieve organizational goals.[2] This definition usually includes those aspects of managers' jobs, such as monitoring and controlling resources, which are sometimes ignored in current conceptualizations of leadership. *Leadership*, on the other hand, is a more restricted type of managerial activity, focusing on the interpersonal interactions between a leader and one or more subordinates, with the purpose of increasing organizational effectiveness.[3] In this view, leadership is a social influence process in which the leader seeks the voluntary participation of subordinates in an effort to reach organizational objectives. The key idea highlighted by a number of authors is that the subordinate's participation is voluntary.[4] This implies that the leader has brought about some change in the way subordinates want to behave. Leadership, consequently, is not only a specific process (more so than management), but also is undoubtedly political in nature. The political aspect of leadership has been discussed elsewhere, so at this point it suffices to note that a major implication of leadership's political nature is that such attempts at wielding influence will not necessarily succeed.[5] In fact, other types of managerial tasks may have a stronger influence on organizational effectiveness than those interpersonal tasks usually labeled leadership.[6]

Chester A. Schriesheim, James M. Tolliver, Orlando C. Behling, "Leadership Theory: Some Implications for Managers," MSU Business Topics, Summer 1978, pp. 34-40.

Despite this shortcoming, the examination of leadership as it relates to interpersonal interactions is still worthwhile simply because managers may, in many cases, have more control over how they and their subordinates behave than over nonhuman aspects of their jobs (such as the amount and types of resources they are given). In addition, some information does exist concerning which leadership tactics are of use under various conditions. For this information to be of greatest use, however, practicing managers should have some concept of the direction leadership research has taken. Thus, before attempting to provide guidelines for practitioners, we shall briefly review major approaches to the subject of leadership and point out their weaknesses and limitations.

Basic Approaches to Leadership

Thinking concerning leadership has moved through three distinct periods or phases.

The trait phase. Early approaches to leadership from the pre-Christian era to the late 1940s, emphasized the examination of leader characteristics (such as age and degree of gregariousness) in an attempt to identify a set of universal characteristics which would allow a leader to be effective in all situations. At first a few traits seemed to be universally important for successful leaders, but subsequent research yielded inconsistent results concerning these traits; in addition, research investigating a large number of other traits (about one hundred) was generally discouraging. As a result of this accumulation of negative findings and of reviews of this evidence, such as that conducted by R. M. Stogdill, the tide of opinion about the importance of traits for leadership effectiveness began to change.[7] In the late 1940s, leadership researchers began to move away from trait research. Contemporary opinion holds the trait approach in considerable disrepute and views the likelihood of uncovering a set of universal leadership effectiveness traits as essentially impossible.

The behavioral phase. With the fall of the trait approach, researchers considered alternative concepts, eventually settling on the examination of relationships between leader behaviors and subordinate satisfaction and performance.[8] During the height of the behavioral phase, dating roughly from the late 1940s to the early 1960s, several large research programs were conducted, including the Ohio State University leadership studies, a program of research which has received considerable publicity over the years.

The Ohio State studies started shortly after World War II and initially concentrated on leadership in military organizations. In one of these studies, a lengthy questionnaire was administered to B-52 bomber crews, and their answers were statistically analyzed to identify the common dimensions underlying the answers.[9] This analysis discovered two dimensions which seemed more important in summarizing the nature of the crews' perceptions about their airplane commanders' behavior toward them.

Consideration was the stronger of the two factors, and it involved leader behaviors indicative of friendship, mutual trust, respect, and warmth.

The second factor was Initiation of Structure, a concept involving leader behaviors indicating that the leader organizes and defines the relationship between self and subordinates.[10]

In subsequent studies using modified versions of the original questionnaire, Consideration and Structure were found to be prime dimensions of leader behavior in situations ranging from combat flights over Korea to assembly line work.[11] In addition, studies were undertaken at Ohio State and elsewhere to compare the effects of these leader behaviors on subordinate performance and satisfaction. A high Consideration-high Structure leadership style was, in many cases, found to lead to high performance and satisfaction. However, in a number of studies dysfunctional consequences, such as high turnover and absenteeism, accompanied these positive outcomes. In yet other situations, different combinations of Consideration and Structure (for example, low Consideration-high Structure) were found to be more effective.[12]

Similar behaviors were identified and similar results obtained in a large number of studies, such as those conducted at the University of Michigan.[13] Although the display of highly Considerate-highly Structuring behavior was sometimes found to result in positive organizational outcomes, this was not true in all of the cases or even in most of them.[14] The research, therefore, clearly indicated that no single leadership style was universally effective, as the relationship of supervisory behavior to organizational performance and employee satisfaction changed from situation to situation. By the early 1960s this had become apparent to even the most ardent supporters of the behavioral approach, and the orientation of leadership researchers began to change toward a situational treatment.

The situational phase. Current leadership research is almost entirely situational. This approach examines the interrelationships among leader and subordinate behaviors or characteristics and the situations in which the parties find themselves. This can clearly be seen in the work of researchers such as F. E. Fiedler, who outlined one of the first situational models.[15]

Fiedler claims that leaders are motivated primarily by satisfactions derived from interpersonal relations and task-goal accomplishment. Relationship-motivated leaders display task-oriented behaviors (such as Initiating Structure) in situations which are favorable for them to exert influence over their work group, and they display relationship-oriented behaviors (such as Consideration) in situations which are either moderately favorable or unfavorable. Task-motivated leaders display relationship-oriented behaviors in favorable situations and task-oriented behaviors in both moderately favorable and unfavorable situations. Fiedler's model specifies that relationship-motivated leaders will be more effective in situations which are moderately favorable for the leader to exert influence, and that they will be less effective in favorable or unfavorable situations; the exact opposite is the case for task-motivated leaders. (They are most effective in favorable or unfavorable situations and least effective in moderately favorable ones.) According to Fiedler, the favorableness of the situation for the leader to exert influence over the work group is determined by (1) the quality of leader-group member relations (the warmer and friendlier, the more favorable the situation); (2) the structure of the tasks performed by the leader's subordinates (the more structured, the more favorable); and (3) the power of the leader (the more power, the more favorable the situation).[16]

A number of other authors propose similar types of interactions among the leader, the led, and the situation. We will not review all these other models but the situational model of Victor Vroom and Phillip Yetton deserves mention.[17] Their model suggests the conditions under which the leader should share decision-making power. Five basic leadership styles are recommended. These range from unilateral decisions by the leader to situations in which the leader gives a great deal of decision power to subordinates and serves as a discussion coordinator who does not attempt to influence the group. Which style is recommended depends upon the leader's "yes" or "no" response to seven quality and acceptability questions which are asked sequentially. In those cases where more than a single style is suggested, the leader is expected to choose between recommendations on the basis of the amount of time to be invested. While this model, as is the case with most of the situational models, has not been fully tested, the literature supports the basic notion that a situational view is necessary to portray accurately the complexities of leadership processes.

Organizational Implications

What does this discussion of leadership theory and research have to do with the practice of management?

Selection does not seem to be the primary answer to the organization's need to increase the pool of effective leaders. The results of the numerous trait studies summarized by Stogdill and others indicate that the search for universal personality characteristics of effective leaders is doomed.[18] This statement requires qualification, however. It should be recognized that the assertion concerns leadership effectiveness, which is only one aspect of managerial effectiveness. A manager may contribute to organizational effectiveness in many ways other than by being an effective leader. The role of selection in picking effective managers, as distinguished from effective leaders, consequently may be much greater. Furthermore, present disappointment with attempts at leader selection is derived from research which has sought to identify universal characteristics of effective leaders in all situations. Summaries such as Stogdill's demonstrate that leadership effectiveness is highly dependent upon the relationship between leader characteristics and the demands of particular situations, and thus universal approaches will not work. Exploration of leader traits as they relate to performance in particular situations may reveal that careful selection has some potential. Unfortunately, given the many situational factors which appear to influence leadership effectiveness, it seems unlikely that selection procedures will be able to follow typical actuarial (statistical) selection procedures.[19] (It appears almost impossible to gather enough individuals in identical jobs to do this.) However, this does not preclude the use of clinical (judgmental) techniques for the selection of leaders.

A further limitation on selection procedures as ways of increasing the pool of effective managers and/or leaders within organizations is the dynamic nature of managerial jobs and managers' careers. If, as research seems to indicate, leadership success is situation-specific, then the continual and inevitable shifts in the nature of a manager's assignment and his or her movement from one assignment to another may make the initial selection invalid.

Another implication is that existing forms of leadership training appear to be inappropriate, based on the evidence outlined here. There are two reasons for this. First, the majority of such training programs are based upon the assumption that there exists one best way to manage. Great emphasis usually is placed on an employee-centered (Considerate) approach or one which combines a concern for employees with a concern for high output (Initiating Structure). For example, the Managerial Grid and its associated Grid Organizational Development Program are popular approaches to management and organizational development.[20] Both are based on the premise that a managerial style which shows high concern for people and high concern for production is the soundest way to achieve excellence, and both attempt to develop this style of behavior on the part of all managers.[21] Rensis Likert's "System-Four" approach to managerial and organizational development, although different from the Grid approach, also assumes that one best way to manage exists (employee-centered leadership).[22] Clearly, these ideas are in conflict with the evidence and with contemporary opinion.

The other limitation of leadership training is that it seems ineffective in changing the behavior of participants. Leadership training aimed not directly at leadership behavior itself, but at providing diagnostic skills for the identification of the nature of the situation and the behaviors appropriate to it, appears to offer considerable potential for the improvement of leadership effectiveness. Obviously, however, additional research is needed to identify the dimensions of situations crucial to leadership performance and the styles effective under various circumstances.

Fiedler's suggestion that organizations engineer the job to fit the manager also has potential.[23] However, the idea is impractical, if not utopian. Application of this approach is limited because we have not identified the crucial dimensions of situations which affect leadership performance. Also, while the overall approach may offer theoretical advantages when leadership is treated in isolation, it ignores dysfunctional effects on other aspects of the organization's operations. Leadership effectiveness cannot be the only concern of administrators as they make decisions about job assignments. They must consider other aspects of the organization's operations which may conflict with their attempts to make good use of leadership talent. Some characteristics of the job, task, or organization simply may not be subject to change, at least in the short run. Thus, engineering the job to fit the manager may increase leadership effectiveness, but this approach seems risky, at least for the forseeable future.

It should also be noted that it is not unusual for work organizations to use traits and trait descriptions in their evaluations of both leadership and managerial performance. A quick glance at a typical performance rating form usually reveals the presence of terms such as *personality* and *attitude* as factors for individual evaluation. Clearly, these terms represent a modern-day version of the traits investigated thirty years ago, and they may or may not be related to actual job performance, depending upon the specifics of the situation involved. Thus, some explicit rationale and, it is hoped, evidence that such traits do affect managerial performance should be provided before they are included in performance evaluations. Just feeling that they are important is not sufficient justification.

Individual Implications

The implications of our discussion of leadership theory and research for individual managers are intertwined with those for the total organization. The fact that leadership effectiveness does not depend on a single set of personal characteristics with which an individual is born or which the individual acquires at an early age should provide a sense of relief to many managers and potential managers. Success in leadership is not limited to an elite, but can be attained by almost any individual, assuming that the situation is proper and that the manager can adjust his or her behavior to fit the situation. The process leading to effective leadership, in other words, is not so much one of changing the characteristics of the individual as it is one of assuring that he or she is placed in an appropriate situation or of teaching the individual how to act to fit the situation.

Thus, a manger's effectiveness can be improved through the development of skills in analyzing the nature of organizational situations--both task and political demands. Although it is difficult to provide guidelines, some recent research points to tentative prescriptions.[24]

Generally speaking, a high Consideration-high Structure style often works best. However, this approach cannot be used in all instances because dysfunctional consequences can result from such behaviors. For example, upper management sometimes gives highly considerate managers poor performance ratings, while in other instances high Structure has been related to employee dissatisfaction, grievances, and turnover. It sometimes will be necessary for a manager to choose between high Consideration and High Structure, and in these cases an individual's diagnostic ability becomes important.

If the diagnostician (manager) has little information, it is probably safe to exhibit high Consideration. Although it does not guarantee subordinate performance, its positive effects on frustration-instigated behavior--such as aggression--are probably enough to warrant its recommendation as a general style. However, in some situations Structure probably should be emphasized, although it may mean a decrease in subordinate perceptions of Consideration. Although the following is not an exhaustive list of these exceptions, it does include those which are known and appear important. The individual manager, from a careful analysis of the situation, must add any additional factors that can be identified.

Emergencies or high-pressure situations. When the work involves physical danger, when time is limited, or when little tolerance for error exists, emphasis on Initiating Structure seems desirable. Research has demonstrated that subordinates often expect and prefer high Structure in such instances.

Situations in which the manager is the only source of information. When the leader is the only person knowledgeable about the task, subordinates often expect him or her to make specific job assignments, set deadlines, and generally engage in structuring their behavior. This does not mean that the leader cannot be considerate if this is appropriate.

Subordinate preferences. There is limited evidence that some subordinates prefer high Structure and expect it, while others expect low Consideration and are suspicious of leaders who display high Consideration. Other preference patterns undoubtedly exist, and managers should attempt to tailor their behavior to each individual employee, as the situation dictates.

Preferences of higher management. In some instances, higher management has definite preferences for certain leadership styles. Higher management sometimes prefers and expects high Structure and low Consideration, and rewards managers for displaying this behavioral style. The manager should be sensitive to the desires of superiors, in addition to those of subordinates. While it is not possible to specify how these expectations may be reconciled if they diverge, compromise or direct persuasion might be useful.[25] Once again, the success of these methods probably will depend both upon the situation and the manager's skill. This leads to the last point--adaptability.

Leader ability to adjust. Some managers will be able to adjust their behavior to fit the situation. For others, attempts to modify behavior may look false and manipulative to subordinates. In these instances, the manager probably would be better off keeping the style with which he or she is most comfortable.

Limitations and Conclusion

The situational approach avoids the major shortcomings of both the trait and behavioral approaches to leadership. However, the implicit assumption that hierarchical leadership is always important has recently come into question. Steven Kerr, for example, points out that many factors may limit the ability of a hierarchical superior to act as a leader for subordinates.[26] Factors such as technology (for example, the assembly line), training, clear job descriptions, and the like, may provide subordinates with enough guidance so that supervisor Structure may be unnecessary to ensure task performance. Also, jobs which are intrinsically satisfying may negate the need for supervisor Consideration, since Consideration is not needed to offset job dullness.

Another problem with the situational approach, and with leadership as a major emphasis in general, is that effective leadership may account for only 10 to 15 percent of the variability in unit performance.[27] While this percentage is certainly not trivial, it is clear that much of what affects performance in organizations is not accounted for by leadership. While studying and emphasizing leadership certainly has its merits, it could be argued that there is much to be gained by treating leadership effectiveness as but one component of managerial effectiveness. As an earlier publication emphasized:

> It is necessary to note that leadership is only one way in which the manager contributes to organizational effectiveness. The manager also performs duties which are *externally oriented* so far as his unit is concerned. For example, he may spend part of his time coordinating the work of his unit with other units. Similarly, not all of the manager's *internally oriented* activities can be labeled leadership acts. Some of them concern the physical and organizational conditions under which the work unit operates. For example, the manager spends part of his time obtaining resources (materials, equipment, manpower, and so on) necessary for unit operations. This is an essential internally oriented activity but hardly constitutes leadership. Clearly, the manager must perform a mix of internal and external activities if his unit is to perform well. Leadership is only one of the internal activities performed by managers.[28]

Thus, the manager should not overemphasize the importance of leadership activities, especially if this causes other functions to be neglected.

For managers to be effective as leaders, they must attempt to be politically astute and to tailor their behaviors, taking into account differences in subordinates, superiors, and situations. Leadership should be kept in perspective. Clearly, it is important, but it cannot be treated in isolation; the importance of leadership depends upon the situation, and the practicing manager must take this into account.

Footnotes

[1] R. M. Stogdill, Handbook of Leadership (New York: The Free Press, 1974).

[2] A. C. Filley, R. J. House, and Steven Kerr, Managerial Process and Organizational Behavior, 2nd ed. (Glenview, Ill.: Scott, Foresman, 1976). See also R. C. Davis, Industrial Organization and Management (New York: Harper, 1957).

[3] C. A. Gibb, "Leadership," in Gardner Lindzey and Elliot Aronson, eds. The Handbook of Social Psychology (Reading, Mass.: Addison-Wesley, 1969), vol. 4.

[4] See, for example, R. H. Hall, Organizations: Structure and Process (Englewood Cliffs, N.J.: Prentice-Hall, 1972).

[5] C. A. Schriesheim, J. M. Tolliver, and L. D. Dodge, "The Political Nature of the Leadership Process," unpublished paper, 1978.

[6] For examples of other types of managerial tasks which may have more of an impact on organizations, see J. P. Campbell, M. D. Dunnette, E. E. Lawler, and K. E. Weick, Managerial Behavior, Performance, and Effectiveness (New York: McGraw-Hill, 1970).

[7] R. M. Stogdill, "Personal Factors Associated with Leadership: A Survey of the Literature," Journal of Psychology 25 (January 1948): 35-71.

[8] T. O. Jacobs, Leadership and Exchange in Formal Organizations (Alexandria, Va.: Human Resources Research Organization, 1970).

[9] A. W. Halpin and B. J. Winer, "A Factorial Study of the Leader Behavior Descriptions," in R. M. Stogdill and A. E. Coons, eds., Leader Behavior: Its Description and Measurement (Columbus: Bureau of Business Research, The Ohio State University, 1957).

[10] Ibid., p. 42.

[11] Stogdill and Coons, Leader Behavior.

[12] Steven Kerr, C. A. Schriesheim, C. J. Murphy, and R. M. Stogdill, "Toward a Contingency Theory of Leadership Based upon the Consideration and Initiation Structure Literature," Organizational Behavior and Human Performance 12 (August 1974): 62-82.

[13] See, for example, Daniel Katz, Nathan Maccoby, and Nancy Morse, Productivity, Supervision and Morale in an Office Situation (Ann Arbor: Survey Research Center, University of Michigan, 1951).

[14] Kerr et al., "Contingency Theory."

[15] See F. E Fiedler, "Engineer the Job to Fit the Manager," Harvard Business Review 43 (September-October 1965); 115-22.

[16] F. E. Fiedler, A Theory of Leadership Effectiveness (New York: McGraw-Hill, 1967).

[17] V. H. Vroom and P. W. Yetton, Leadership and Decision-Making (Pittsburgh, Pa.: University of Pittsburgh Press, 1973).

[18] R. M. Stogdill, "Personal Factors."

[19] Kerr et al., "Contingency Theory."

[20] R. R. Blake and J. S. Mouton, The Managerial Grid (Houston, Texas: Gulf, 1964), and Building a Dynamic Corporation Through Grid Organizational Development (Reading, Mass.: Addison-Wesley, 1969).

[21] Ibid., p. 63.

[22] Rensis Likert, New Patterns of Management (New York: McGraw-Hill, 1961), and The Human Organization: Its Management and Value (New York: McGraw-Hill, 1967).

[23] Fiedler, "Engineer the Job."

[24] Kerr et al., "Contingency Theory."

[25] See Filley, House, and Kerr, Managerial Process, especially pp. 162-80; and George Strauss, "Tactics of Lateral Relations," in H. J. Leavitt and L. R. Pondy, eds., Readings in Managerial Psychology, 1st ed. (Chicago: University of Chicago Press, 1964), pp. 226-48.

[26] Steven Kerr, "Substitutes for Leadership: Their Definition and Measurement," unpublished paper, 1978.

[27] O. C. Behling and C. A. Schriesheim, Organizational Behavior: Theory, Research and Application (Boston: Allyn and Bacon, 1976).

[28] Ibid., p. 294.

ACTIVE LISTENING

Carl R. Rogers
Richard E. Farson

The Meaning of Active Listening

One basic responsibility of the supervisor or manager is the development, adjustment, and integration of individual employees. He tries to develop employee potential, delegate responsibility, and achieve cooperation. To do so, he must have, among other abilities, the ability to listen intelligently and carefully to those with whom he works.

There are, however, many kinds of listening skills. The lawyer, for example, when questioning a witness, listens for contradictions, irrelevancies, errors, and weaknesses. But this is not the kind of listening skill we are concerned with. The lawyer usually is not listening in order to help the witness adjust, cooperate, or produce. Our emphasis will be on listening skills of the supervisor and manager that will help employees gain a clearer understanding of their situations, take responsibility, and cooperate with each other.

Two Examples

The kind of listening we have in mind is called "active listening." It is called "active" because the listener has a very definite responsibility. He does not passively absorb words which are spoken to him. He actively tries to grasp the facts and the feelings in what he hears, and he tries, by his listening, to help the speaker work out his own problems.

To get a clearer picture of what active listening means, let us consider two different approaches to the same work problem. The example is set in the printing industry, but the behavior of the men could surface in any organization.

Example No. 1:

Foreman: Hey, Al, I don't get this rush order. We can't handle any 50,000 run today. What do they think we are?

Supervisor: But that's the order. So get it out as soon as you can. We're under terrific pressure this week.

F: Don't they know we're behind schedule already because of that press breakdown?

S: Look, Kelly, I don't decide what goes on upstairs. I just have to see that the work gets out and that's what I'm gonna do.

F: The guys aren't gonna like this.

S: That's something you'll have to work out with them, not me.

Reprinted by special permission of the University of Chicago.

184

Example No. 2:

F: Hey, Ross, I don't get this rush order. We can't handle any run of 50,000 today. What do they think we are?

S: They're pushing you pretty hard aren't they Kelly?

F: They sure are and I'm getting sore. We were just about back to schedule after the press breakdown. Now this comes along.

S: As if you didn't have enough work to do, huh?

F: Yeah. I don't know how I'm going to tell the pressman about this.

S: Hate to face him with a rush order now, is that it?

F: I really do. Joe is under a real strain today. Seems like everything we do around here is rush, rush, rush!

S: I guess you feel it's unfair to load anything more on him today.

F: Well, yeah. I know there must be plenty of pressure on everybody to get the work out, but--well, Joe doesn't deserve all the rush orders. But, if that's the way it is--I guess I'd better get the word to him and see how I can rearrange the work flow.

There are obviously many differences between these two examples. The main one, however, is that Ross, the supervisor in the second example is using the active-listening approach. He is listening and responding in a way that makes it clear that he appreciates both the meaning and the feeling behind what Kelly is saying.

Active listening does not necessarily mean long sessions spent listening to grievances, personal or otherwise. It is simply a way of approaching those problems which arise out of the usual day-to-day events of any job.

To be effective, active listening must be firmly grounded in the basic attitudes of the user. We cannot employ it as a technique if our fundamental attitudes are in conflict with its basic concepts. If we try, our behavior will be empty and sterile, and our associates will be quick to recognize such behavior. Until we can demonstrate a spirit which genuinely respects the potential worth of the individual, which considers his rights and trusts his capacity for self-direction, we cannot begin to be effective listeners.

What We Achieve by Listening

Active listening is an important way to bring about changes in people. Despite the popular notion that listening is a passive approach, clinical and research evidence clearly shows that sensitive listening is a most effective agent for individual personality change and group development. Listening brings about changes in people's attitudes toward themselves and others, and also brings about changes in their basic values and personal philosophy. People who have been listened to in this new and special way become more emotionally mature, more open to their experiences, less defensive, more democratic, and less authoritarian.

When people are listened to sensitively, they tend to listen to themselves with more care and make clear exactly what they are feeling and thinking. Group

185

members tend to listen more to each other, become less argumentative, more ready to incorporate other points of view. Because listening reduces the threat of having one's ideas criticized, the person is better able to see them for what they are and is more likely to feel that his contributions are worthwhile.

Not the least important result of listening is the change that takes place within the listener himself. Besides the fact that listening provides more information about people than any other activity, it builds deep, positive relationships and tends to alter constructively the attitudes of the listener. Listening is a growth experience.

How to Listen

The goal of active listening is to bring about changes in people. To achieve this end, it relies upon definite techniques--things to do and things to avoid doing. Before discussing these techniques, however, we should first understand why they are effective. To do so, we must understand how the individual personality develops.

The Growth of the Individual

Through all of our lives, from early childhood on, we have learned to think of ourselves in certain, very definite ways. We have built up pictures of ourselves. Sometimes these self-pictures are pretty realistic but at other times they are not. For example, an average, overweight lady may fancy herself a youthful, ravishing siren, or an awkward teenager regard himself as a star athlete.

All of us have experiences which fit the way we need to think about ourselves. These we accept. But it is much harder to accept experiences which don't fit. And sometimes, if it is very important for us to hang on to this self-picture, we don't accept or admit these experiences at all.

These self-pictures are not necessarily attractive. A man, for example, may regard himself as incompetent and worthless. He may feel that he is doing his job poorly in spite of favorable appraisals by the organization. As long as he has these feelings about himself he must deny any experiences which would seem not to fit this self-picture, in this case any that might indicate to him that he is competent. It is so necessary for him to maintain this self-picture that he is threatened by anything which would tend to change it. Thus, when the organization raises his salary, it may seem to him only additional proof that he is a fraud. He must hold onto this self-picture, because, bad or good, it's the only thing he has by which he can identify himself.

This is why direct attempts to change this individual or change his self-picture are particularly threatening. He is forced to defend himself or to completely deny the experience. This denial of experience and defense of the self-picture tend to bring on rigidity of behavior and create difficulties in personal adjustment.

The active-listening approach, on the other hand, does not present a threat to the individual's self-picture. He does not have to defend it. He is able to explore it, see it for what it is, and make his own decision as to how realistic it is. He is then in a position to change.

186

If I want to help a man or woman reduce defensiveness and become more adaptive, I must try to remove the threat of myself as a potential changer. As long as the atmosphere is threatening, there can be no effective communication. So I must create a climate which is neither critical, evaluative, nor moralizing. The climate must foster equality and freedom, trust and understanding, acceptance and warmth. In this climate and in this climate only does the individual feel safe enough to incorporate new experiences and new values into his concept of himself. Active listening helps to create this climate.

What to Avoid

When we encounter a person with a problem, our usual response is to try to change his way of looking at things--to get him to see his situation in the way we see it, or would like him to see it. We plead, reason, scold, encourage, insult, prod-- anything to bring about a change in the desired direction, that is, in the direction we want him to travel. What we seldom realize, however, is that under these circumstances we are usually responding to *our own* needs to see the world in certain ways. It is always difficult for us to tolerate and understand actions which are different from the ways in which we believe *we* should act. If, however, we can free ourselves from the need to influence and direct others in our own paths, we enable ourselves to listen with understanding, and thereby employ the most potent available agent of change.

One problem the listener faces is that of responding to demands for decisions. judgments, and evaluations. He is constantly called upon to agree or disagree with someone or something. Yet, as he well knows, the question or challenge frequently is a masked expression of feelings or needs which the speaker is far more anxious to communicate than he is to have the surface questions answered. Because he cannot speak these feelings openly, the speaker must disguise them to himself and to others in an acceptable form. To illustrate, let us examine some typical questions and the type of answers that might best elicit the feeling beneath it.

Employee's Question	Listener's Answer
Just who is responsible for getting this job done?	Do you feel that you don't have enough authority?
Don't you think talent should count more than seniority in promotions?	What do you think are the reasons for your opinion?
What does the boss expect us to do about those broken-down machines?	You're tired of working with worn-out equipment, aren't you?
Don't you think my performance has improved since the last review?	Sounds as if you feel your work has picked up over these last few months?

These responses recognize the questions but leave the way open for the employee to say what is really bothering him. They allow the listener to participate in the problem or situation without shouldering all responsibility for decision-making or actions. This is a process of thinking *with* people instead of *for* or *about* them.

Passing judgment, whether critical or favorable, makes free expression difficult. Similarly, advice and information are almost always seen as efforts to change a person and thus serve as barriers to his self-expression and the development of a creative relationship. Moreover, advice is seldom taken and information hardly ever utilized. The eager young trainee probably will not become patient just because he is advised that, "The road to success is a long, difficult one, and you must be patient." And it is no more helpful for him to learn that "only one out of a hundred trainees reach top management positions."

Interestingly, it is a difficult lesson to learn that *positive evaluations* are sometimes as blocking as negative ones. It is almost as destructive to the freedom of a relationship to tell a person that he is good or capable or right, as to tell him otherwise. To evaluate him positively may make it more difficult for him to tell of the faults that distress him or the ways in which he believes he is not competent.

Encouragement also may be seen as an attempt to motivate the speaker in certain directions or hold him off rather than as support. "I'm sure everything will work out O.K." is not a helpful response to the person who is deeply discouraged about a problem.

In other words, most of the techniques and devices common to human relationships are found to be of little use in establishing the type of relationship we are seeking here.

What to Do

Just what does active listening entail, then? Basically, it requires that we get inside the speaker, that we grasp, *from his point of view*, just what it is he is communicating to us. More than that, we must convey to the speaker that we are seeing things from his point of view. To listen actively, then, means that there are several things we must do.

Listen for Total Meaning. Any message a person tries to get across usually has two components: the *content* of the message and the *feeling* or attitude underlying this content. Both are important, both give the message *meaning*. It is this total meaning of the message that we must try to understand. For example, a secretary comes to her boss and says: "I've finished that report." This message has obvious factual content and perhaps calls upon the boss for another work assignment. Suppose, on the other hand, that the secretary says, "Well! I'm finally finished with your damned report!" The factual content is the same, but the total meaning of the message has changed--and changed in an important way for both supervisor and worker. Here sensitive listening can facilitate the work relationship in this office. If the boss were to respond by simply giving his secretary some letters to type, would the secretary feel that she had gotten her total message across? Would she feel free to talk to her boss about the difficulty of her work? Would she feel better about the job, more anxious to do good work on her next assignment?

Now, on the other hand, suppose the supervisor were to respond, "Glad to get that over with, huh?" or "That was a rough one, wasn't it?" or "Guess you don't want another one like that again," or anything that tells the worker that he heard and understands. It doesn't necessarily mean that her next work assignment need be changed or that he must spend an hour listening to the worker complain about the problems she encountered. He may do a number of things differently in the light of the new information he has from the worker--but not necessarily. It's just that extra sensitivity on the part of the supervisor that can transform an average working climate into a good one.

Respond to Feelings. In some instances the content is far less important than the feeling which underlies it. To catch the full flavor or meaning of the message one must respond particularly to the feeling component. If, for instance, our secretary had said, "I'd like to pile up all those carbons and make a bonfire out of them!" responding to content would be obviously absurd. But to respond to her disgust or anger in trying to work with the report recognizes the meaning of this message. There are various shadings of these components in the meaning of any message. Each time the listener must try to remain sensitive to the total meaning the message has to the speaker. What is she trying to tell me? What does this mean to her? How does she see this situation?

Note All Cues. Not all communication is verbal. The speaker's words alone don't tell us everything he is communicating. And hence, truly sensitive listening requires that we become aware of several kinds of communication besides verbal. The way in which a speaker hesitates in his speech can tell us much about his feelings. So too can the inflection of his voice. He may stress certain points loudly and clearly, and he may mumble others. We should also note such things as the person's facial expressions, body posture, hand movements, eye movements, and breathing. All of these help to convey his total message.

What We Communicate by Listening

The first reaction of most people when they consider listening as a possible method for dealing with human beings is that listening cannot be sufficient in itself. Because it is passive, they feel, listening does not communicate anything to the speaker. Actually, nothing could be farther from the truth.

By consistently listening to a speaker you are conveying the idea that: "I'm interested in you as a person, and I think that what you feel is important. I respect your thoughts, and even if I don't agree with them, I know that they are valid for you. I feel sure that you have a contribution to make. I'm not trying to change you or evaluate you. I just want to understand you. I think you're worth listening to, and I want you to know that I'm the kind of person you can talk to."

The subtle but most important aspect of this is that it is the *demonstration* of the message that works. Although it is most difficult to convince someone that you respect him by *telling* him so, you are much more likely to get this message across by really *behaving* that way--by actually *having* and *demonstrating* respect for this person. Listening does this most effectively.

Like other behavior, listening behavior is contagious. This has implications for all communications problems, whether between two people, or within a large organization. To insure good communication between associates up and down the line, one must first take the responsibility for setting a pattern of listening. Just as one learns that anger is usually met with anger, argument with argument, and deception with deception, one can learn that listening can be met with listening. Every person who feels responsibility in a situation can set the tone of the interaction, and the important lesson in this is that any behavior exhibited by one person will eventually be responded to with similar behavior in the other person.

It is far more difficult to stimulate constructive behavior in another person but far more valuable. Listening is one of these constructive behaviors, but if one's attitude is to "wait out" the speaker rather than really listen to him, it will fail. The one who consistently listens with understanding, however, is the one who eventually is most likely to be listened to. If you really want to be heard and understood by another, you can develop him as a potential listener, ready for new ideas, provided you can first develop yourself in these ways and sincerely listen with understanding and respect.

Testing for Understanding

Because understanding another person is actually far more difficult than it at first seems, it is important to test constantly your ability to see the world in the way the speaker sees it. You can do this by reflecting in your own words what the speaker seems to mean by his words and actions. His response to this will tell you whether or not he feels understood. A good rule of thumb is to assume that one never really understands until he can communicate this understanding to the other's satisfaction.

Here is an experiment to test your skill in listening. The next time you become involved in a lively or controversial discussion with another person, stop for a moment and suggest that you adopt this ground rule for continued discussion. Before either participant in the discussion can make a point or express an opinion of his own, he must first restate aloud the previous point or position of the other person. This restatement must be in his own words (merely parroting the words of another does not prove that one has understood, but only that he has heard the words). The restatement must be accurate enough to satisfy the speaker before the listener can be allowed to speak for himself.

You might find this procedure useful in a meeting where feelings run high and people express themselves on topics of emotional concern to the group. Before another member of the group expresses his own feelings and thought, he must rephrase the *meaning* expressed by the previous speaker to that person's satisfaction. All the members in the group should be alert to the changes in the emotional climate and the quality of the discussion when this approach is used.

Problems in Active Listening

Active listening is not an easy skill to acquire. It demands practice. Perhaps more important, it may require changes in our own basic attitudes. These changes come slowly and sometimes with considerable difficulty. Let us look at some of the major problems in active listening and what can be done to overcome them.

The Personal Risk

To be effective in active listening, one must have a sincere interest in the speaker. We all live in glass houses as far as our attitudes are concerned. They always show through. And if we are only making a pretense of interest in the speaker, he will quickly pick this up, either consciously or subconsciously. And once he does, he will no longer express himself freely.

Active listening carries a strong element of personal risk. If we manage to accomplish what we are describing here--to sense the feelings of another person, to understand the meaning his experiences have for him, to see the world as he sees it we risk being changed ourselves. For example, if we permit ourselves to listen our way into the life of a person we do not know or approve of--to get the meaning that life has for him we risk coming to see the world as he sees it. We are threatened when we give up, even momentarily, what we believe and start thinking in someone else's terms. It takes a great deal of inner security and courage to be able to risk one's self in understanding another.

For the manager, the courage to take another's point of view generally means that he must see *himself* through another's eyes--he must be able to see himself as others see him. To do this may sometimes be unpleasant, but it is far more *difficult* than unpleasant. We are so accustomed to viewing ourselves in certain ways--to seeing and hearing only what we want to see and hear--that it is extremely difficult for a person to free himself from the need to see things his way.

Developing an attitude of sincere interest in the speaker is thus no easy task. It can be developed only by being willing to risk seeing the world from the speaker's point of view. If we have a number of such experiences, however, they will shape an attitude which will allow us to be truly genuine in our interest in the speaker.

Hostile Expressions

The listener will often hear negative, hostile expressions directed at himself. Such expressions are always hard to listen to. No one likes to hear hostile words or experience hostility which is directed against them. And it is not easy to get to the point where one is strong enough to permit these attacks without finding it necessary to defend himself or retaliate.

Because we all fear that people will crumble under the attack of genuine negative feelings, we tend to perpetuate an attitude of pseudo-peace. It is as if we cannot tolerate conflict at all for fear of the damage it could do to us, to the situation, to the others involved. But of course the real damage is done by the denial and suppression of negative feelings.

Out-of-Place Expressions

Expressions dealing with behavior that is not usually acceptable in our society also pose problems for the listener. These out-of-place expressions can take the extreme forms that psychotherapists hear--such as homicidal fantasies or expressions of sexual perversity. The listener often blocks out such expressions because of their obvious threatening quality. At less extreme levels, we all find

191

unnatural or inappropriate behavior difficult to handle. Behavior that brings on a problem situation may be anything from telling an "off-color" story in mixed company to seeing a man cry.

In any face-to-face situation, we will find instances of this type which will momentarily, if not permanently, block any communication. In any organization, expressions of weakness or incompetency will generally be regarded as unacceptable and therefore will block good two-way communication. For example, it is difficult to listen to a manager tell of his feelings of failure in being able to "take charge" of a situation in his department because *all* administrators are supposed to be able to "take charge."

Accepting Positive Feelings

It is both interesting and perplexing to note that negative or hostile feelings or expressions are much easier to deal with in any face-to-face relationship than are positive feelings. This is especially true for the manager because the culture expects him to be independent, bold, clever, and aggressive and manifest no feelings of warmth, gentleness, and intimacy. He therefore comes to regard these feelings as soft and inappropriate. But no matter how they are regarded, they remain a human need. The denial of these feelings in himself and his associates does not get the manager out of the problem of dealing with them. The feelings simply become veiled and confused. If recognized they would work for the total effort; unrecognized, they work against it.

Emotional Danger Signals

The listener's own emotions are sometimes a barrier to active listening. When emotions are at their height, when listening is most necessary, it is most difficult to set aside one's own concerns and be understanding. Our emotions are often our own worst enemies when we try to become listeners. The more involved and invested we are in a particular situation or problem, the less we are likely to be willing or able to listen to the feelings and attitudes of others. That is, the more we find it necessary to respond to our own needs, the less we are able to respond to the needs of another. Let us look at some of the main danger signals that warn us that our emotions may be interfering with our listening.

Defensiveness. The points about which one is most vocal and dogmatic, the points which one is most anxious to impose on others--these are always the points one is trying to talk oneself into believing. So one danger signal becomes apparent when you find yourself stressing a point or trying to convince another. It is at these times that you are likely to be less secure and consequently less able to listen.

Resentment of Opposition. It is always easier to listen to an idea which is similar to one of your own than to an opposing view. Sometimes, in order to clear the air, it is helpful to pause for a moment when you feel your ideas and position being challenged, reflect on the situation, and express your concern to the speaker.

Clash of Personalities. Here again, our experience has consistently shown us that the genuine expression of feelings on the part of the listener will be more

192

helpful in developing a sound relationship than the suppression of them. This is so whether the feelings be resentment, hostility, threat, or admiration. A basically honest relationship, whatever the nature of it, is the most productive of all. The other party becomes secure when he learns that the listener can express his feelings honestly and openly to him. We should keep this in mind when we begin to fear a clash of personalities in the listening relationship. Otherwise, fear of our own emotions will choke off full expression of feelings.

Listening to Ourselves

To listen to oneself is a prerequisite to listening to others. And it is often an effective means of dealing with the problems we have outlined above. When we are most aroused, excited, and demanding, we are least able to understand our own feelings and attitudes. Yet, in dealing with the problems of others, it becomes most important to be sure of one's own position, values, and needs.

The ability to recognize and understand the meaning which a particular episode has for you, with all the feelings which it stimulates in you, and the ability to express this meaning when you find it getting in the way of active listening, will clear the air and enable you once again to be free to listen. That is, if some person or situation touches off feelings within you which tend to block your attempts to listen with understanding, begin listening to yourself. It is much more helpful in developing effective relationships to avoid suppressing these feelings. Speak them out as clearly as you can, and try to enlist the other person as a listener to your feelings. A person's listening ability is limited by his ability to listen to himself.

Active Listening and Organization Goals

"How can listening improve productivity?"

"We're in business, and it is a rugged, fast, competitive affair. How are we going to find time to counsel our employees?"

"We have to concern ourselves with organizational problems first."

"We can't afford to spend all day listening when there is work to do."

"What's morale got to do with service to the public?"

"Sometimes we have to sacrifice an individual for the good of the rest of the people in the organization."

Those of us who are trying to advance the listening approach in organizations hear these comments frequently. And because they are so honest and legitimate, they post a real problem. Unfortunately, the answers are not so clear-cut as the questions.

Individual Importance

One answer is based on an assumption that is central to the listening approach. That assumption is: the kind of behavior which helps the individual will eventually be the best thing that could be done for the work group. Or saying it another way: the things that are best for the individual are best for the organization. This is a conviction of ours, based on our experience in psychology and education. The research evidence from organizations is still coming in. We

193

find that putting the group first, at the expense of the individual, besides being an uncomfortable individual experience, does *not* unify the group. In fact, it tends to make the group less a group. The members become anxious and suspicious.

We are not at all sure in just what ways the group does benefit from a concern demonstrated for an individual, but we have several strong leads. One is that the group feels more secure when an individual member is being listened to and provided for with concern and sensitivity. And we assume that a secure group will ultimately be a better group. When each individual feels that he need not fear exposing himself to the group, he is likely to contribute more freely and spontaneously. When the leader of a group responds to the individual, puts the individual first, the other members of the group will follow suit, and the group comes to act as a unit in recognizing and responding to the needs of a particular member. This positive, constructive action seems to be a much more satisfying experience for a group than the experience of dispensing with a member.

Listening and Productivity

As to whether or not listening or any other activity designed to better human relations in an organization actually makes the organization more productive--whether morale has a definite relationship to performance is not known for sure. There are some who frankly hold that there is no relationship to be expected between morale and productivity--that productivity often depends upon the social misfit, the eccentric, or the isolate. And there are some who simply choose to work in a climate of cooperation and harmony, in a high-morale group, quite aside from the question of achievement or productivity.

A report from the Survey Research Center at the University of Michigan on research conducted at the Prudential Life Insurance Company lists seven findings related to production and morale. First-line supervisors in high-production work groups were found to differ from those in low-production groups in that they:

1. Are under less close supervision from their own supervisors.

2. Place less direct emphasis upon production as the goal.

3. Encourage employee participation in the making of decisions.

4. Are more employee-centered.

5. Spend more of their time in supervision and less in straight production work.

6. Have a greater feeling of confidence in their supervisor roles.

7. Feel that they know where they stand with the company.

After mentioning that other dimensions of morale, such as identification with the company, intrinsic job satisfaction, and satisfaction with job status, were not found significantly related to productivity, the report goes on to suggest the following psychological interpretations:

People are more effectively motivated when they are given some degree of freedom in the way in which they do their work than when every action is prescribed in advance. They do better when some degree of decision-

194

making about their jobs is possible than when all decisions are made for them. They respond more adequately when they are treated as personalities than as cogs in a machine. In short if the ego motivations of self-determination, of self-expression, of a sense of personal worth can be tapped, the individual can be more effectively energized. The use of external sanctions, or pressuring for production may work to some degree, but not to the extent that the more internalized motives do. When the individual comes to identify himself with his job and with the work of his group, human resources are much more fully utilized in the production process.

The Survey Research Center has also conducted studies among workers in other industries. In discussing the results of these studies, Robert L. Kahn writes:

> In the studies of clerical workers, railroad workers, and workers in heavy industry, the supervisors with the better production records gave a larger proportion of their time to supervisory functions, especially to the interpersonal aspects of their jobs. The supervisors of the lower-producing sections were more likely to spend their time in tasks which the men themselves were performing, or in the paper-work aspects of their jobs.

Maximum Creativeness

There may never be enough research evidence to satisfy everyone on this question. But speaking from an organizational point of view, in terms of the problem of developing resources for productivity, the maximum creativeness and productive effort of the human beings in the organization are the richest untapped source of power available. The difference between the maximum productive capacity of people and that output which the organization is now realizing is immense. We simply suggest that this maximum capacity might be closer to realization if we sought to release the motivation that already exists within people rather than try to stimulate them externally.

This releasing of the individual is made possible first of all by listening, with respect and understanding. Listening is a beginning toward making the individual feel himself worthy of making contributions, and this could result in a very dynamic and productive organization. Profit making organizations are never too rugged or too busy to take time to procure the most efficient technological advances or to develop rich sources of raw materials. But technology and materials are but paltry resources in comparison with the resources that are already within the people in the organization.

G. L. Clements, of Jewel Tea Co., Inc., in talking about the collaborative approach to management says:

> We feel that this type of approach recognizes that there is a secret ballot going on at all times among the people in any business. They vote for or against their supervisors. A favorable vote for the supervisor shows up in the cooperation, teamwork, understanding, and production of the group. To win this secret ballot, each supervisor must share the problems of his group and work for them.

195

The decision to spend time listening to employees is a decision each supervisor or manager has to make for himself. Managers increasingly must deal with people and their relationships rather than turning out goods and services. The minute we take a man from work and make him a supervisor he is removed from the basic production of goods or services and now must begin relating to men and women instead of nuts and bolts. People are different from things, and our supervisor is called upon for a different line of skills completely. These new tasks call for a special kind of person. The development of the supervisor as a listener is a first step in becoming this special person.

REFORMING THE U.S. SYSTEM OF
COLLECTIVE BARGAINING

D. Quinn Mills

Can collective bargaining in the United States meet the challenge of the 1980's by tempering traditional confrontation with new cooperative approaches? Can management and labor modify their adversarial, rulemaking relationship by exploring and recognizing mutual needs? This article examines some recent events that suggest affirmative answers to both of these questions.

Labor unions developed in the United States within a generally hostile business and legal environment. As early as 1806, unions in major eastern cities were being prosecuted in court as "combinations in restraint of trade." During the economically turbulent 1870's, industrial workers seeking better pay and conditions of work attempted strikes and public protests, only to be dispersed by police. In 1877, railway strikers throughout the country were repulsed by Federal troops. During the depression of the 1890's, martial law was declared to break strikes in the western mines. And the Federal Government intervened at the railroads' request to defeat the 1894 strike by the American Railway Union against the Pullman Co.; to further assist the company, a Federal court enjoined the railway workers from interfering with interstate commerce.

Following World War I, strong opposition by employer associations and further unfavorable court decisions contributed to a dramatic decline in the labor movement. Revitalization of the unions occurred during the 1930's, but only after lengthy strikes, and the enactment of Federal legislation--the Norris-Laguardia Act (1932) and the Wagner Act (1935)--favorable to the organizing rights of workers.[1]

Born in turmoil, and victorious over adamant employer oppositions, U.S. unions view themselves essentially as adversaries to management, a role which their legislative successes during the 1930's appeared to legitimize. And during organizing campaigns in recent decades, employers have tended to force unions

Reprinted from The Monthly Labor Review, March 1983, pp. 18-22.

ever more strongly into an overall anti-management posture. The turbulence of labor relations in the construction and textile industries exemplifies this phenomenon.

Ambiguous National Labor Policy

Some have argued that the purpose of our system of collective bargaining no longer commands a national consensus. When the Wagner Act was passed, it included a statement endorsing collective bargaining and the right of workers to join unions as being in the national interest. It appeared that the United States was committed to incorporating unions among the institutions of its pluralist democracy and to making its economic system work by and through their addition. But with passage of the Taft-Hartley Act in 1947, the mood of the Congress and of the public seems to have shifted somewhat: the right of employees not to join unions in effect became enshrined with their right to join unions. When, by decisions of the courts in subsequent years, employers were permitted to attempt to persuade employees not to join unions, the national policy had come full circle. For all practical and legal purposes, government has ceased to favor a specific industrial relations policy, and seeks rather to serve as an unbiased umpire in the choice which employees make as to union affiliation.

The result of this apparent shift in public policy is, as might be expected, that labor relations in the United States is now best described as a series of disconnected events. There is no overall pattern or purpose. The national policy is one of free choice for individual employees, and the choices vary considerably among individuals and over time. The energies of business and labor are channeled into the struggle over union recognition rather than into making collective bargaining an institution which contributes to national economic objectives. Within this environment, which might best be termed "benign neglect" by government, collective bargaining has stagnated.

In practice, then, collective bargaining in the United States involves open economic conflict over the rights of employees, unions, and management in the workplace. Under U.S. law, employees who strike for better wages and benefits, or to preserve existing levels of wages and benefits, are gambling with their jobs. Managers are free to replace the strikers either on a temporary or permanent basis. Thus it is that economic strikes by long-established unions in our country often quickly become struggles over the continued existence of the union.

The Result: A Law of the Shop

Some management and union representatives have described collective bargaining in our country in terms of a fistfight: the question is which side will be knocked down, or out, first. Given such a relationship, it is not surprising that there is little trust between the two sides. Where there is little trust, conflicts over the terms of the employment relationship are resolved not through mutual understanding but with specific, written contractual arrangements which the Congress has chosen to make legally enforceable.

The American collective bargaining agreement consequently reflects the importation of much of the adversarial system of U.S. law into the workplace. The agreement sets forth rules which are legally binding on the parties and establishes

197

a grievance procedure as the mechanism by which the rules are enforced. The union and management take the roles of contending parties, as in a lawsuit, whenever there is a dispute in the plant. And increasingly, the parties bring attorneys into the grievance procedure to conduct what is virtually, though not yet entirely, a formal court proceeding to resolve their differences.

Many of the requirements of due process in our legal system have been incorporated directly into the contract grievance procedure. (The major exception is that the strict rules of evidence do not apply.) Thus, the grievance procedure involves several steps with appeals to higher levels, ending in a quasi-judicial proceeding before an arbitrator. To ensure that a disciplinary action will survive the oversight of an arbitrator, the employer must have established clear rules of conduct in the workplace; have communicated them to employees; and have documented transgressions. At some plants, for example, groups of managers (for arbitrators insist that there be more than one witness of an employee's infraction of a company rule) assemble to watch workers punch out at the timeclock at the end of the workday. Employees seen punching out early or punching more than one card are subject to disciplinary action by management.

Due process is a treasured right of U.S. citizens and is not to be disparaged. But its incorporation in the industrial relations world has given us a "law of the shop" that has become more and more burdensome to our economic enterprises. For, like U.S. law generally, collective bargaining agreements have grown increasingly complex. What began as one-page documents establishing that the union and the company would deal with each other have become contracts, hundreds of pages long, specifying in minute detail rules for the operation of economic enterprises. In some agreements, for example, many pages of rules are devoted solely to the question of how management is to make temporary assignments of employees to cover for other workers who are absent. But, because neither managers nor union officials really know what all the rules mean in certain instances, each noncustomary assignment made by the company tends to find its way into the grievance procedure.

Rules as a Productivity Drain

Rules alone cannot ensure that an organization will perform well. They may keep it from dissolving into self-defeating open warfare, but often do not permit it to achieve its potential. An organization which depends upon adherence to a myriad of rules will always be vulnerable to competition from other organizations which operate in a more consensual and cooperative fashion, even when the latter have fewer resources. And, although an organization of rules may sometimes pull itself together to respond to an emergency, this need not necessarily occur.

It follows, then, that primary dependence on establishing and enforcing rules is a very poor way to run an economic enterprise. The existence of a multitude of rules, many of which attempt to "stretch the work" to maintain jobs in ways reminiscent of depression-era tactics, constrains productivity and raises costs. For example, maintenance classifications may prohibit an employee from doing incidental work outside the strict limits of his or her trade; multiple job classifications may exist even where a person in a single combined classification could do the work effectively, without undue effort and stress; and, job classifications may be perpetuated although technological change has rendered the incumbents' work trivial. Other restrictions may limit the amount of work a person may be assigned, such as permitting a mechanic to open only two flanges. The location of materials and inventory may be restricted by contract or past practice to retain jobs in now-inefficient areas of the plant. In some cases, rules may prohibit employees being assigned work during breaks, and simultaneously prohibit supervisors from doing the employees' work, so that emergencies occurring at coffee breaks or lunchtime cannot be legally handled under the agreement.

Over time, rules tend to become increasingly costly and constraining as technology, materials, products, and other aspects of production change. Even rules which made great sense at first become out-of-date under changing conditions. But the rules are difficult to change, and particular employees may be further benefited the more outdated the rules become. Sometimes a company can pay a high price and "buy the rules out," or a union can persuade some workers to give up favored positions for the good of the membership as a group. But often, change cannot be accomplished without a bitter struggle between management and labor.

Furthermore, the rulemaking process promotes a set of attitudes which are inimical to successful enterprise. The existence of the rulebook encourages both management and labor to assert their rights under the contract, rather than to attempt to work out problems. It gives rise to "shop-floor lawyers," rather than problemsolvers. It fosters conflict and controversy. It undermines trust.

To a large degree, it seems that unions have become captives of their origins. Born in adversity and conflict, they continued to act as opponents of management even when their strength had become much greater. In some instances, unions have created thickets of rules in which to immobilize management, just as spiders build webs to ensnare prey. But when the thickets of rules have crippled productivity, the unions have discovered themselves to be caught alongside management in the trap. Plants have declined in competitiveness, and jobs have been lost. The unions have discovered too late that a snare is no less a snare because they have set it themselves.

A Prescription for Change

In a recent survey conducted by the Harris organization, a majority of the general public professed the belief that unions contribute less than they once did to the growth and efficiency of business. Not surprisingly, only 15 percent of union leaders agreed with this judgment.[2] The need for unions to assist companies in the light of increased foreign competition is apparent to the public. To the inhabitants of the Snow Belt, it is similarly evident that unions should cooperate with local business to stem the outflow of industry and jobs to the South and West. Public perceptions of a productivity problem are supported by Bureau of Labor Statistics estimates, which show particularly sluggish growth in output per labor hour after 1973.[3]

Collective bargaining practiced primarily as rule-making has become self-defeating for both unions and management. It interferes with management's efficient operation of the enterprise, and ensnares employees with legitimate grievances in a web of red tape. It also contributes to the vehemence of employer attempts to resist union organization drives. Study after study of U.S. managers have shown that managers fear the imposition of restrictive work practices far more than the higher wages and benefits which unionization may bring. Companies' efforts to make competitive operations out of older plants often fail because changes in current work rules take the form of additional complex rules which do not provide the flexibility needed to turn a facility around. What management really needs is fewer rules altogether, and willing cooperation from the work force. The union, for its side, needs a management sensitive to the needs of people. Both are very difficult to obtain in the U.S. labor relations environment.

There are, of course, many reasons for this. The unions cite a long list of management actions and inactions which they feel justify an emphasis on protected rules and challenges to management action. Among the accusations frequently leveled at management are its failure to update the equipment in union plants; its location of new and more profitable products in nonunion facilities; and its burdening of unionized facilities with unfairly heavy overhead charges. Such actions call into question the good faith that management would show in any more cooperative relationship.

Managers have also helped to shore up the archaic labor relations system. American management has often proved unsympathetic to the problems of workers. For example, U.S. firms are quick to turn to layoffs during business downturns in an effort to maintain profit levels. (In contrast, many first abroad and some few U.S. firms attempt to preserve employment at the cost of short-term fluctuations in profits.) It should be acknowledged, however, that U.S. unions often contribute to the problem by insisting upon layoffs by seniority in preference to worksharing among employees during business declines, and that the U.S. unemployment insurance system encourages this preference by generally denying benefits to workers on short workweeks due to economic conditions.

Because of the substantial inefficiencies created by outdated rules, and the risk of resulting job losses, managers and union officials should always have at the top of their agenda the minimizing of rulemaking and the broadening of cooperation and consensus. This is the only method by which the flexibility needed to meet changing conditions and the ability to call forth the full potential of people can be obtained. In some instances, the relaxation of restrictive rules will cause employees to lose jobs, or to be assigned to less desirable jobs. But it is an illusion in most situations to think that jobs can be preserved in the long term by restrictive practices. Instead of preserving the few jobs at risk, high costs imperil the jobs of all persons in a plant.

Collective bargaining should be more than a fistfight, more than rulemaking. It must be more than merely adversarial. And there is ample evidence that it can be.

A great irony of history may serve as an example. At the end of World War II, the U.S. occupation authorities, under General Douglas MacArthur, reorganized the Japanese economy. The great trading companies, or *zaibatsu*, were broken up. Trade unions were established to add a dimension of social responsibility to Japanese political life. But the occupation authorities did not simply copy the U.S. industrial relations system. Instead, they imposed what they thought would be a better system, of which company-specific unions were to be the building blocks. And in West Germany, British occupation authorities with similar purposes in mind reorganized German industrial relations. In the British zone of occupation they introduced three major reforms: elected work councils, union representation on the boards of directors of companies (initially in the coal and steel industries only), and a few national industrial unions to bargain at the industry level with companies on behalf of the workers. In later years, a reunited Western Germany adopted the British innovations on a nationwide basis. In Japan, MacArthur avoided the adversarial and rulemaking obsession of U.S. labor relations. In Germany, the British avoided the multiplicity of trade union organizations that contributes to decentralized and disorderly industrial relations in Great Britain.

The reforms in Germany and Japan were largely a dramatic break with prewar institutions in both countries. Such substantial change was made possible be the virtually total devastation which war had imposed on the industrial and social fabric of both nations. But over the years since the war, managers and unions in Japan and Germany have, by and large, built successfully upon the reforms instituted by occupation authorities. Many observers believe that these reforms in industrial relations have had as much to do with the economic success of the two nations as did any material assistance they were given in the postwar period.

The irony is that neither the United States nor Britain has been able to implement domestically the sorts of reforms in industrial relations practices that were imposed on the defeated powers. The result is that both Germany and Japan today have systems of collective bargaining which are much better suited to the needs of a competitive international economy than that of Britain or the United States. We in the United States apparently have known for many years the direction in which we should move, but we do not know how to get there from here.

Of course, there is no "clean slate" in this country as there was in the defeated powers at the end of World War II. We are not in a position to abandon collective bargaining as rulemaking, or simply to dispense with the adversarial element of our collective bargaining process. But we must move beyond these obsessions in substantial ways if a major new contribution to U.S. economic performance is to be made. Rulemaking may be replaced by a greater degree of employee participation and commitment in the workplace, but unless the adversarial posture also changes, increased participation may be of no use. Instead of resolving production problems, participatory schemes may simply add delays to management decisionmaking. And if the parties insist on treating earlier participatory decisions as precedents for further matters, the problemsolving mechanism may itself become yet another source of conflict and rigidity in the bargaining relationship.

Fortunately, a concept of collective bargaining that goes beyond rulemaking has deep roots in the U.S. labor movement. Before the 1930's, unions ordinarily envisioned themselves becoming involved in a broad range of problems associated not only with the difficulties of employees on the job, but also with the performance of the business enterprise. In union meetings, skilled trade workers debated what we would today call management issues. The dividing line between prerogatives of management and those of labor was far less well-defined than it is now.

It is time to draw on this older tradition of the U.S. labor movement, and leave behind the concept of collective bargaining as primarily a rulemaking process. This should be accomplished by putting far more flexibility into the collective bargaining agreement--making provisions less detailed, reorganizing work arrangements, and designing different incentives for both management and labor. Some rulemaking and the legal enforceability of contracts are not to be abandoned. But they must take a back seat to attempts to move the collective bargaining process beyond continual confrontation and into a more constructive mode.

A commitment to enhancing productivity is not easily made by the U.S. unionist. Too often, past attempts to boost productivity have simply meant speeding up the pace at which managers require employees to work. But there is far more to improving productivity than speed-ups; and the failure to seek productivity improvement in a company threatens the continued existence of jobs that the company provides. Unions must become more sophisticated in their response to management efforts to improve productivity. Some efforts, perhaps, should be opposed, but others must be supported. And the goal of improving productivity should be accepted.

Today, the United States is full of experimental efforts to extend collective bargaining beyond the concepts of the 1930's--to increase the participation of the worker in his or her job and to help preserve jobs by keeping business viable. These efforts extend across many industries and various sectors of the economy, and take many forms, including quality circles, Scanlon plans, and job enrichment programs. They cannot yet be described as successes, although many have shown promise. These endeavors are of great significance for the future--they are steps that are being taken today to meet tomorrow's needs. If successful, these innovations may provide the basis for a new system of collective bargaining which will help preserve jobs, increase the number of U.S. businesses that successfully meet the challenge of foreign competitors, and enhance the contribution and satisfaction of employees in the American workplace.

The economic revitalization of the United States in the 1980's is getting off to a start, though slow and uneven. With recent tax legislation, the Government has provided certain economic incentives which may help to restore the U.S. goods-producing sector to long-term viability, although much remains to be done in the important area of job creation for the next decade.

Within this broad economic context, both business and labor have their separate obligations. Business should be prepared to assist our work force in adjusting to the substantial production and employment changes which the 1980's are going to bring, both by providing workers with more advance notice of planned innovations, and by implementing changes in ways that minimize adverse effects on employees. The unions, for their part, should be ready to work with management toward a broader concept of collective bargaining than has been common in recent decades--one which is based on the participation of employees and union officials in the business process and which includes their commitment to the success of the individual enterprise.

The transition to a new cooperative mode of collective bargaining will be a difficult one, given the traditionally antagonistic atmosphere of U.S. labor-management relations and the fact that the change will probably have to be accomplished within a generally unfavorable business environment. But the alternative is a degree of economic and social unrest which cannot be in the best interests of management, workers, or, indeed, of the Nation as a whole.

WHAT JAPANESE MANAGERS KNOW THAT AMERICAN MANAGERS DON'T

William H. Franklin, Jr.

Why is this worth reading? After all, hardly a newspaper or business magazine can be picked up that doesn't include some reference to the Japanese industrial mystique. Books and articles evangelize the gospel of Theory Z, quality circles, and consensual decision making, lionizing the Japanese manager as something of a giant-killer in the international marketplace, one whose economy is growing faster than any other Free World economy, and whose products--once repudiated as cheap junk--are now recognized as fine quality.

This article takes nothing away from Japan's industrial accomplishments since World War II. Their commercial success is rooted in the application to Japanese firms of universally sound business and management concepts, most of which were originally learned from us. But we should not lose sight of the fact that every organization is a reflection of the culture in which it exists. A slavish copying of current Japanese management practice by American firms would fail--as it has when the Japanese themselves tried it. Our cultures are very different. They are a consensual society; we are very confrontive. To the Japanese employee, the firm stands in locus parentis; but individualistic American employees suspect, if not resent, corporate paternalism.

There is however, much that we can transplant in what the Japanese do well. No longer the undisputed industrial kingpins of the world, American managers must admit that good ideas are not a U.S. invention. As humbling as it may be, a nation that our resourcefulness and industrial clout totally destroyed 35 years ago is now in a position to teach us a few things about how to run a business. While the implementation of Japanese management techniques alone will obviously not herald the beginning of a new millennium for this country, a number of American firms acquired or managed by the Japanese have enjoyed renewed vigor and productivity growth. This article describes management practices that work for the Japanese and will work for us also.

A recent national poll revealed that for the first time American workers believe that we have a productivity problem, and that the solution of that problem is crucial to our further success as an industrial nation. Prior to this time, "productivity" was a term that had somehow come to mean methods whereby management gets more out of the worker without paying for it. Nothing could be less true. Increased individual productivity is the only way we can *all* have more. Otherwise, the only way to solve the problem of some having too little is redistribution of existing wealth--the anathema of every industrial society that has flirted with it.

Yet, the U.S. productivity record of the last few decades is a poor one. Between 1948 and 1979, the output per labor hour grew at an average annual rate of just over 3 percent. Between 1965 and the present, the productivity growth rate was just above 2 percent, and the growth of the last five years has barely exceeded 1 percent. But in the ten years from 1969 to 1979, Japan's average annual productivity growth was over 9 percent. Our productivity growth is exceeded even by that of Great Britain.

Clearly, we have a problem. Given the present trend, we will become a zero growth economy in a few years, something all other Free World economies have avoided, and unless we reverse the trend, the 1990s will witness negative productivity growth: a shrinking pie and smaller slices for us all. In a nutshell, this is the central issue which confronts us as an ongoing industrial society.

It is tempting to place blame for our sagging productivity on a number of factors: big government and four decades of big spending by it, tax policies that discourage capital formation, scarce resources, dependence on foreign oil, rising expectations and a decline in the work ethic, and a shrinking manufacturing sector. While all of these have contributed to our productivity problems, they are not a sufficient explanation in themselves. Japan has some of these same pressures and others that we don't.

It is becoming increasingly clear that there are also problems on the American work scene. The average annual turnover rate in the U.S. is over 25 percent, meaning the entire work force is replaced every four years. In Europe, the rate is half our rate, and in Japan, it is about 5 percent. Twenty-seven percent of Americans in a recent poll had changed jobs four times compared with 12 percent in the United Kingdom, 2 percent in Germany, and 1 percent in Japan. A mobile society? Possibly. But Americans also have the highest rate of work stoppages in the Free World and the highest absenteeism rate, 8 percent.

In a study of 175,000 workers in 159 American companies, it was found that most believed they were not respected as individuals and their jobs lacked challenge and satisfaction. Salary level, however, was not a source of discontent. In another study of male union workers, job attitudes were expressed in the most negative terms and it was said would not change even with more money, shorter hours, or longer vacations.

These facts are not new. Similar information appears in print so often it becomes wearisome, but it always says the same thing: something is wrong with the work climate created in most of our organizations. We may complain that people "ain't what they used to be," which is probably true. But we must come to grips with the fact that organizations don't change people. Organizations reflect people. Ours seem to have gotten out of sync with where the people are right now.

Yet, the Japanese have evidently succeeded in developing an organizational setting that more accurately reflects the culture and needs of their people. It is safe to say, then, that successful, highly productive organizations are a cultural phenomenon: they give form and expression to what motivates the people and groups that work in them. In Japan's management boom of the '50s and '60s, their

204

managers toured our plants and studied our management practices and theories--
then adapted them to the cultural and social needs of their people. During the
intervening years, as they closed the industrial gap between their country and ours,
many improvements in management practice have been made. Given the problems
we see in our own organizations, we should do what they did: study the success of
Japanese management techniques to identify what can be adapted to give form and
expression to the needs of our workers.

Opposites

The Japanese and American value systems occupy philosophically opposite
positions in many respects. Over a thousand years are behind the development of
Japanese culture; they are holistic people, seeing a natural harmony in all of the
dimensions of life, which serves to integrate social and economic needs.
Relationships between individuals are quite intimate by our standards and more
open and trustful. They tend to view themselves as a national family with duties
and loyalties to each other. Naturally this submerges the importance of the
individual and gives rise to a strong cooperative group orientation. Economic
employment is an extension, not a separate activity, in this value spectrum.

Americans, on the other hand, are the product of a relatively recent culture.
We emphasize individuality, personal freedom, and competitiveness as a means to
get ahead. Unlike the Japanese, we are ethnically and racially a diverse
population of values. Economic activity is a much more separate and detached life
pursuit; we engage in competition and conflict to achieve self-worth and
distinction.

Some would argue that Japan is an immature industrial economy whose
people will change, becoming more like Americans as industrialism takes hold. No
doubt this is true. There is evidence that the Japanese are becoming more mobile
and more acquisitive. But it is also true that American society is changing. We
were once a nation of immigrants, barely literate, fiercely independent. Now
highly educated and talented, enjoying a substantial and established standard of
living, work is no longer engaged in for economic survival but rather to express
what we are and what we need. Work is taking on more of a social role, to fulfill
life--as it does in the Japanese culture.

Much of what the Japanese businessman does and the way he does it will
remain uniquely Japanese, but there are five qualities in Japanese management
practice that can be imported to our organizational setting if we are to cope with
declining labor productivity and satisfy the needs of the people who work in them.
The are:

- A longer-term view to business practice.
- A partnership in the needs of firm and employee.
- Openness in organizational structure and interactive communications.
- Sharing of organizational power.
- An ongoing search for improving productivity.

American management practice suffers from a strong emphasis on short-
term goals and achievement. Most incentive systems, for example, focus a
manager's attention on immediate results, usually a fiscal year, and the amount of
the reward paid is a function of what has happened in the year, quarter, or period
just ended. We are only now beginning to see the consequences of this perspective.

Any decision that has a dysfunctional effect on short-term performance and, therefore, management bonuses, is avoided or delayed.

Because of the life-long employment ethic in Japan, their managers are discouraged from power plays and short-term razzle-dazzle tactics. Any problem they create for the future they must cope with themselves. While Japanese managers are concerned with short-term profitability, this is not the primary measure of achievement. Rather they must give attention to the long-term consequences of their actions, the growth and well-being of their companies, the development and welfare of employees, and many non-economic issues.

Given a long-term perspective, there is no incentive to avoid or delay the immediate and effective use of new technology or the systematic rejection of old equipment or practices when necessary. Resources are stripped from slower growing markets when markets offering greater long-run growth emerge, even though short-term profits may suffer.

In such a schema, all people are naturally viewed as an investment. Considerable money is spent on training them throughout their careers to keep the productive in the long run, something American firms don't do as well (see "Why Training Fails," *Administrative Management*, July, 1981). As part of this training, Japanese employees will make many non-promotional job changes during their careers in order to give them a non-specialized, global view of business life, not to mention more exciting careers, as they move up the organization.

While the Japanese propensity to take the long view in business is facilitated by the culture of lifetime employment, it is not caused by it. There is no reason why the American business culture will not accommodate the ethic that the economic and non-economic interest of both the company and all its employees can coincide for a lifetime. Indeed, American firms do offer life-long employment in the sense that people are not terminated spuriously, and considerable inducements are offered to keep good workers. It is, in fact, turnover that firms bewail. The problem seems to be that employees themselves are not willing in many cases to remain with one firm for life.

Americans are characteristically a mobile society not at all reluctant to leave a job to go with a better offer. In a 1976 study, when asked if one would stay with a firm during a prolonged period of decline, even if a job in a more prosperous firm was available, only 5 percent of Japanese workers polled said they would leave while 36 percent of American workers answered affirmatively when asked the same question.

This is where the challenge to American management practice lies. When we can admit to the exhorbitant costs of turnover--the cost of replacement, the loss of continuity and stabilization, and the reluctance to invest heavily in the education of people we may lose in a few years--and when we begin to believe that the interests of employees and their firms can converge for long periods, perhaps careers, we will have broken through the principal obstacle blocking development of the benefits in a long-term perspective to business management.

As a consequence of the Japanese long-range view of every aspect of business, it is understandable that they would have a substantial commitment to the well-being of all employees. The well-known Japanese paternalism encompasses employee housing, if necessary, health care for life, gifts for births and marriages, recreational facilities, even allowances for holiday expenses. In modern Japanese society, the firm comfortably assumes the role of family to its employees, providing their lifetime needs for employment, recognition, security, and leisure. In return, the employee gives considerable loyalty and commitment to his employer.

Underlying the commitment to provide an employee a job for life is the fact that a substantial part of every employee's compensation is made in the form of a bonus, usually paid twice a year. Figured as a percentage of a person's salary, the bonus is not determined by the employee's performance during the period, but rather the firm's performance in the preceding period. Without laying anyone off, therefore, the Japanese firm can make a significant reduction in its payroll costs during bad years that virtually guarantees permanent employment to all workers. When good years occur, employees receive a better than expected bonus, not only indemnifying them for the risks of reduced compensation in difficult times, but also allowing them to participate substantially in an unexpected windfall.

Would this system work in America? Maybe not. But millions of people in this country are employed under variable compensation methods. They gear their lifestyles to what they perceive to be their "permanent income" so that variations in income are not as disruptive as might be thought. Certainly a system that makes people feel a part of the firm by being *partners* in the perils and progress of their company makes more sense than one in which employees receive salary increases even when their company suffers an earnings decline. In fact, a compensation system that disconnects its employees from the realities of the firm's performance in the marketplace can hardly inspire commitment to that performance. It more likely encourages disinterest--after all, how many employees read (let alone understand) their company's financial statement?

Notice that the Japanese variable compensation scheme is not profit sharing, which in American is usually deferred to a trust and paid out at retirement or separation. Rather, it is a true bonus, paid in cash to the employee according to the firm's performance, usually during the preceding six months. It is designed to shift the risks *and* rewards from stockholders to employees, and since the rewards are substantial in good years, employees work hard for the company. (Individual incentive payments are rare in Japan, due to their group-oriented culture, but team performance incentives operate as they do in the U.S.)

While there may be many reasons preventing American firms from using the Japanese-style compensation scheme, we need to understand the principle it reflects. More creative thinking must be given to the way we compensate *all* employees so that they jointly identify their need for security and income with those of the firm. To accomplish this, four things must be present: (1) all employees must prosper *substantially* when the firm fares better than average, (2) they must have confidence in the abilities of their leaders and co-workers, (3) there must be inherent equity in the systems, and, (4) during the transitional period from the present method of compensation, employees must be provided options.

In addition to the job security and stability afforded by their compensation method, the Japanese firm uses a large temporary work force. These are mostly women who even today are rarely promoted into professional ranks. When times are slack the temporaries are cut back in·time worked or laid off until they can be rehired. To accommodate the responsibilities the women have to their families or otherwise, there is a considerable amount of flexibility in timing their work shifts. Nevertheless, they serve as a cushion to protect the job security of the permanent work force.

Of course, part-time employment is not new in this country, although it usually is relegated to menial work and minimum wages. However, there are millions of professionally trained men and women in America who cannot or will not make a full-time career commitment to an organization. Though it has yet to enjoy widespread acceptance, the concept of "job sharing" has provided some answer to this problem, i.e., a "whole" job is shared by two or more people who likewise share the income and benefits. Job sharing has not yet caught on because firms fear the potential coordination and scheduling problems, and they suspect that loyalty would suffer for people employed under these circumstances.

Openness

Trappings of rank abound in a typical U.S. firm. They are designed to set people apart in levels of status and house them in insulated cubicles, which reflect how and where one functions in the hierarchy. This industrial caste system creates distinction and separation from one's associates, and it is the antithesis of the setting in a Japanese firm.

The Japanese put great emphasis on communication as the mainspring of cooperation and collective effort and abhor any physical or psychological separation that might interfere with that end, such as status distinction and private offices. Privacy is rarely desirable, since every interaction is intentionally public to avoid breakdowns and retransmissions of information. The Japanese believe that people of good faith, if they know what is going on and how to help, will do so without being told.

The typical Japanese "office" is a large room with desks and tables arranged in much the same way as the people are arranged in the organization chart. This layout is essentially a decision-making factory designed to provide widespread communication and promote consensus. Superiors, subordinates, assistants, and secretaries sit side by side. Superiors are highly accessible and do little that their associates do not see and hear.

Understandably, such a setting discourages political and conflict gameship or any other activities that require secrecy to transact. Since there are usually several departments in one room, a manager need only turn in his chair to communicate a problem that arises. In such a highly verbal environment, many important messages are spoken rather than written. Subordinates are thus kept up to date not only on the workings of their own department, but also related departments. Consequently, if a manager or any other employee is incapacitated, the work is able to continue without interruption or temporary patchwork.

Japanese managers demand far more responsible participation of all workers than we do, believing that all employees are capable of thinking a problem through, and those in management don't necessarily think best. Active participation by everyone tends to close status gaps and facilitates considerably more creative output in the workplace.

The Japanese decision-by-consensus technique is well known and often exasperating to an American manager exposed to it. This participatory decision process is called *ringi*, from the words *ri*, meaning "ask from below," and *gi*, meaning "deliberate." The ritual of *ringi* begins when a problem is identified or defined and assigned to a group for a proposal--usually the group most impacted by the decision outcome. The group then engages in much debate and argument until the essence of a solution is committed to a memorandum, or *ring-sho*, *sho* meaning "form" or "sheet of paper."

Picture again the office layout previously described. The *ringi-sho* is shuttled from position to position, desk to desk, where it is further debated, modified, and confirmed by each manager who fixes his seal of approval to the document when he agrees with it. The *ringi* process is essentially an authorization-confirmation process designed to spread, not individually pinpoint, the responsibility for a decision--the opposite of the American decision ethic. Therefore, the more seals of approval, the more confident is a senior manager that sufficient bargaining, discussion, and compromise have occurred to permit successful and rapid implementation of a decision. At the end of the process, a *ringi-sho* may have 60 to 80 stamps of approval.

Clearly, the major weakness of the *ringi* process is the time it takes. Its strength, however, is that commitment to the outcome is created as the process proceeds, allowing rapid and cooperative implementation. Possibly a less conservative decision is reached jointly than would be made by an individual who alone had to stand behind the outcome.

The essence rather than the form of power sharing is what should be important to American management. At all levels of an organization there are employed people who, outside of the workplace, make major decisions and plans regarding their own lives. They plan their own personal finances, enter into long-term obligations, work out ways to send their children to college; yet in their jobs we treat them as if they are incapable of responsible and thoughtful action.

People are a power source, and the job of management is neither to tend nor to tame but rather to release the power in people. The Japanese manager insists that his people think and participate responsibly in business affairs; the primary role is not giving orders but facilitating action, bringing about the cooperation and consensus among dissident viewpoints, and providing people with the information and resources they need to do their jobs. There is no limit to what American industry could accomplish if the creative thinking people demonstrate in every other area of their lives could be given full expression in their jobs.

Ongoing Improvement

The guiding ethos of Japanese industry is the ongoing search for quality and productivity improvement. When an idea is implemented that results in better productivity or product quality, the search begins anew for a successor idea. This process never ends. And Japanese work teams are rewarded handsomely for good ideas--particularly those that eliminate jobs. Such ideas are not withheld, because the worker knows that while his job may be eliminated *he* will not be eliminated. This devotion to improvement has allowed Japanese marketers to shift from price competition to strategies that focus on quality and value, service, and distribution effectiveness.

Quality awareness began early in post-war industrial Japan when an American, W. Edwards Deeming, was invited to Japan to teach statistically-based methods of problem solving that would reduce job-related quality problems and increase productivity through *elimination* of scrap, rework, and downtime. Notice the work delineation. The heart of the Deeming philosophy is that quality improvement does not come from inspection and elimination of bad product;

improvement comes from making the product right in the first place. The quality is built in by the workers who do most of their own inspection and quality control using statistical methods.

The heart of the Japanese quality consciousness is the Quality Control Circle, a fundamental work group which not only critiques and improves the quality of its output, but also concerns itself with plant safety, cost efficiency, automation opportunities, marketing ideas, and general suggestions for management. The QC Circle is a basic organizational change agent conceived as *jishu kanri*, which translates "worker's voluntary control." A QC Circle consists of a small group of people, usually ten workers and a foreman or senior worker, centered around a particular task. The lesson for American management is this: inspection does not build quality; *workers* build quality. Work must be organized and equipped so that people are *able* to take responsibility for its quality.

Declining American labor productivity is a both social and economic issue that will affect the lives of every one of us. If we do not reverse the trend, the next generation will be the first generation of Americans to have a standard of living which is lower than that of their parents. Yet, our productivity is not a problem in itself as much as an expression that a problem exists. If statistics regarding work attitudes and behavior are an indication, our needs as individuals are remarkably at odds with our needs as organizational collectives.

The practice of management in Japan is a subset of life in Japanese society. It does not have that meaning in this country, and it is unlikely that it can in the future. They are a holistic society. Still, it is possible to manage our organization in a style that captures the essence rather than the form of Japan's industrial success.

As managers, we must be committed to the psychological success of individuals in organizations, believing that a partnership of interest can be forged that merges the qualities of American society with the realities of the marketplace.

THE CONTROL FUNCTION OF MANAGEMENT

Kenneth A. Merchant
Harvard University

After strategies are set and plans are made, management's primary task is to take steps to ensure that these plans are carried out, or, if conditions warrant, that the plans are modified. This is the critical control function of management. And since management involves directing the activities of others, a major part of the control function is making sure other people do what should be done.

The management literature is filled with advice on how to achieve better control. This advice usually includes a description of some type of measurement and feedback process:

> The basic control process, wherever it is found and whatever it controls, involves three steps: (1) establishing standards, (2) measuring performance against these standards, and (3) correcting deviations from standards and plans.[1]

> A good management control system *stimulates action* by spotting the *significant* variations from the original plan and highlighting them *for the people who can set things right.*[2]

> Controls need to focus on results.[3]

This focus on measurement and feedback, however, can be seriously misleading. In many circumstances, a control system built around measurement and feedback is not feasible. And even when feasibility is not a limitation, use of a feedback-oriented control system is often an inferior solution. Yet, good controls can be established and maintained using other techniques.

What is needed is a broader perspective on control as a management function: this article addresses such a perspective. The first part summarizes the general control problem by discussing the underlying reasons for implementing controls and by describing what can realistically be achieved. In the second part, the various types of controls available are identified. The last part discusses why the appropriate choice of controls is and should be different in different settings.

Why Are Controls Needed?

If all personnel always did what was best for the organization, control--and even management--would not be needed. But, obviously individuals are sometimes unable or unwilling to act in the organization's best interest, and a set of controls must be implemented to guard against undesirable behavior and to encourage desirable actions.

One important class of problems against which control systems guard may be called *personal limitations*. Please do not always understand what is expected of them nor how they can best perform their jobs, as they may lack some requisite ability, training, or information. In addition, human beings have a number of innate perceptual and cognitive biases, such as an inability to process new information optimally or to make consistent decisions, and these biases can reduce organizational effectiveness.[4] Some of these personal limitations are correctable or avoidable, but for others, controls are required to guard against their deleterious effects.

Even if employees are properly equipped to perform a job well, some choose not to do so, because individual goals and organizational goals may not coincide perfectly. In other words, there is a *lack of goal congruence*. Steps must often be taken either to increase goal congruence or to prevent employees from acting in their own interest where goal incongruence exists.

If nothing is done to protect the organization against the possible occurrence of undesirable behavior or the omission of desirable behavior caused by these personal limitations and motivational problems, severe repercussions may result. At a minimum, inadequate control can result in lower performance or higher risk of poor performance. At the extreme, if performance is not controlled on one or more critical performance dimensions, the outcome could be organizational failure.

What Is Good Control?

Perfect control, meaning complete assurance that actual accomplishment will proceed according to plan, is never possible because of the likely occurrence of unforeseen events. However, *good* control should mean that an informed person could be reasonably confident that no major unpleasant surprises will occur. A high probability of forthcoming poor performance, despite a reasonable operating plan, sometimes is given the label "out of control."

Some important characteristics of this desirable state of good control should be highlighted. First, control is future-oriented: the goal is to have no unpleasant surprises in the future. The past is not relevant except as a guide to the future. Second, control is multidimensional, and good control cannot be established over an activity with multiple objectives unless performance on all significant dimensions has been considered. Thus, for example, control of a production department cannot be considered good unless all the major performance dimensions, including quality, efficiency, and asset management, are well controlled. Third, the assessment of whether good performance assurance has been achieved is difficult and subjective. An informed expert might judge that the control system in place is adequate because no major bad surprises are likely, but this judgment is subject to error because adequacy must be measured against a future that can be very difficult to assess. Fourth, better control is not always economically desirable. Like any other economic good, the control tools are costly and should be implemented only if the expected benefits exceed the costs.

How Can Good Control Be Achieved?

Good control can be achieved by avoiding some behavioral problems and/or by implementing one or more types of control to protect against the remaining problems. The following sections discuss the major control options.

Control-Problem Avoidance

In most situations, managers can avoid some control problems by allowing no opportunities for improper behavior. One possibility is *automation.* Computers and other means of automation reduce the organization's exposure to control problems because they can be set to perform appropriately (that is, as the organization desires), and they will perform more consistently than do human beings. Consequently, control is improved.

Another avoidance possibility is *centralization,* such as that which takes place with very critical decisions at most organization levels. If a manager makes all the decisions in certain areas, those areas cease to be control problems in a managerial sense because no other persons are involved.

A third avoidance possibility is *risk-sharing* with an outside body, such as an insurance company. Many companies bond employees in sensitive positions, and in so doing, they reduce the probability that the employees' behavior will cause significant harm to the firm.

Finally, some control problems can and should be avoided by *elimination* of a business or an operation entirely. Managers without the means to control certain activities, perhaps because they do not understand the processes well, can eliminate the associated control problems by turning over their potential profits and the associated risk to a third party, for example by subcontracting or divesting.

If management cannot, or chooses not to, avoid the control problems caused by relying on other individuals, they must address the problems by implementing one or more control tactics. The large number of tactics that are available to help achieve good control can be classified usefully into three main categories, according to the *object* of control; that is, whether control is exercised over *specific actions, results,* or *personnel.* Table 1 shows many common controls classified according to their control object; these controls are described in the following sections.

TABLE 1

A Control Tool Classification Framework

OBJECT OF CONTROL

SPECIFIC ACTIONS	RESULTS	PERSONNEL
Behavioral Constraint: --Physical (e.g., locks, security guards) --Administrative (e.g., separation of duties)	Results Accountability: --Standards --Budgets --Management by Objective (MBO)	Upgrade Capabilities: --Selection --Training --Assignment
Action Accountability: --Work Rules --Policies and Procedures --Codes of Conduct		Improve Communication: --Clarify Expectations --Provide Information for coordination
Preaction Review: --Direct Supervision --Approval Limits --Budget Reviews		Encourage Peer Control: --Work Groups --Shared Goals

Control of Specific Actions

One type of control, specific-action control, attempts to ensure that individuals perform (or do not perform) certain actions that are known to be desirable (or undesirable). Management can limit the incidence of some types of obviously undesirable activity by using *behavioral constraints* that render the occurrence impossible, or at least unlikely. These constraints include physical devices, such as locks and key-personnel identification systems, and administrative constraints, such as segregation of duties, which make it very difficult for one person to carry out an improper act.

A second type of specific-action control is *action accountability*--a type of feedback control system by which employees are held accountable for their actions. The implementation of action-accountability control systems requires (1) defining the limits of acceptable behavior, as is done in procedures manuals; (2) tracking the behaviors that employees are actually engaged in; and (3) rewarding or punishing deviations from the defined limits. Although action-accountability systems involve the tracking and reporting of actual behaviors, their objective is to motivate employees to behave appropriately in the future. These systems are effective only if employees understand what is required of them, and they feel that their individual actions will be noticed and rewarded or punished in some significant way.

A third type of specific-action control is *preaction review*. This involves observing the work of others before the activity is complete, for example, through direct supervision, formal planning reviews, and approvals on proposals for expenditures. Reviews can provide effective control in several ways by: correcting potentially harmful behavior before the full damaging effects are felt; or influencing behavior just by the threat of an impending review, such as causing extra care in the preparation of an expenditure proposal. One advantage of reviews is that they can be used even when it is not possible to define exactly what is expected prior to the review.

Control of Results

Control can also be accomplished by focusing on results: this type of control comes in only one basic form, results accountability, which involves holding employees responsible for certain results. Use of results-accountability control systems requires: (1) defining the dimensions along which results are desired, such as efficiency, quality, and service; (2) measuring performance on these dimensions; and (3) providing rewards (punishments) to encourage (discourage) behavior that will lead (not lead) to those results. As with action-accountability systems, results-accountability systems are future-oriented; they attempt to motivate people to behave appropriately. But they are effective only if employees feel that their individual efforts will be noticed and rewarded in some significant way.

Control of Personnel

A third type of control can be called *personnel control* because it emphasizes a reliance on the personnel involved to do what is best for the organization, and it provides assistance for them as necessary. Personnel controls can be very effective by themselves in some situations, such as in a small family business or in a professional partnership, because the underlying causes of the needs for controls (personal limitations and lack of goal congruence) are minimal. However, even when control problems are present, they can be reduced to some extent by: (1) upgrading the capabilities of personnel in key positions, such as tightening hiring policies, implementing training programs, or improving job assignments; (2) improving communications to help individuals know and understand their roles better and how they can best coordinate their efforts with those of other groups in the organization; and (3) encouraging peer (or subordinate) control by establishing cohesive work groups with shared goals.

Feasibility Constraints on the Choice of Controls

The design of a control system often depends partly on the feasibility of the various types of controls: not all of these tools can be used in every situation. Personnel controls are the most adaptable to a broad range of situations. To some extent, all organizations rely on their employees to guide and motivate themselves, and this self-control can be increased with some care in hiring, screening, and training. Even in a prison, where administrators are faced with a sharp lack of goal congruence and where few control options are available other than physical constraints, inmates are screened so that dangerous ones are not assigned to high-risk positions, such as in a machine shop.

Most situations, however, require reinforcing personnel controls by placing controls over specific actions, results, or a combination of the two. This is where feasibility becomes a limiting factor.

For control over specific actions, management must have some knowledge of which actions are desirable. While it may be easy to define precisely the required behavior on the production line, the definition of preferred behavior for a research engineer cannot be as precise. Being able to keep track of specific actions is also necessary to enforce actions accountability; however, this is usually not a limiting factor, except in rare situations such as a remote outpost, because actions can be observed directly or assessed indirectly through action reports, such as hours worked, sales calls made, or procedural violations.

For control over results, the most serious constraint is the ability to measure the desired results effectively. (Management usually knows what results are desirable.) Ideally, measurements should: (1) assess the *correct* performance areas--the ones for which results are truly desired; (2) be *precise*--not determined by only crude estimations; (3) be *timely* and (4) be *objective*--not subject to manipulation. While perfect measures are rarely available, reasonable surrogates can often be found or developed. For example, "complaints received" might be a good (negative) indicator of the performance of hotel staff personnel along the customer-service dimension. Significant difficulty in achieving any of these four measurement qualities, however, can lead to failure of a results-oriented control system.

Figure 1 shows how the two factors most limiting control feasibility--knowledge of desirable actions and the ability to measure results on the important performance dimensions--can influence the choice of controls used.[5] The most difficult control situation, shown in box 4 of Figure 1, is one in which the desirable actions are not known and the important result areas cannot be measured well. Only personnel controls (or problem avoidance) are available options. In a research laboratory, for example, success might be difficult to assess for years, yet prescription of specific actions could be counter-productive. Fortunately, in this specific setting, control is not a serious problem because research scientists tend to be professional--well trained and responsible to the standards of their profession. They tend to control themselves, and consequently, control of research laboratories tends to be dominated by controls over personnel.

FIGURE 1

Key Control Object Feasibility Determinants

Ability to Measure Results on
Important Performance
Dimension

		High	Low
Knowledge of Which Specific Actions Are Desirable	Excellent	1. Specific Action and/or Results Control	2. Specific Action Control (e.g., Real-Estate Venture)
	Poor	3. Results Control (e.g., Movie Director)	4. Personnel Control (e.g., Research Laboratory)

In box 3 of Figure 1, where knowledge of desirable specific actions is poor but good results measurements are available, control is best accomplished by controlling results. Movie production is a good example. It is probably impossible to dictate what a movie director should do or even to observe his or her behavior and predict whether the finished product will be good. It is, however, a relatively easy task to measure the economic performance of the movie and the artistic merit, if that is a concern. In this situation, the best control system would seem to be a results-accountability system that defines to the director the results expected, holds him or her responsible for achieving them, and provides some reinforcement in the form of compensation and/or recognition.

For similar reasons, results controls tend to be dominant at most upper-management levels. It is usually not possible to prescribe and keep track of the specific actions each manager should be performing, but it is relatively easy to define the results desired, in terms similar to those desired by shareholders.

Specific-action controls should dominate where there is knowledge about which actions are desirable but where results measurement is impossible or difficult, as indicated in box 2 of Figure 1. Consider, for example, control over a real-estate development business where large capital investment decisions are made frequently. Results of these decisions are difficult to measure in a timely, accurate fashion because of their long-term nature; they tend to be inseparable from the results of other actions and are confounded by changes in the environment. However, the techniques of investment analysis are well developed (e.g., net present value analysis with tests of the sensitivity of assumptions), and control may be accomplished by formally reviewing the techniques used and the assumptions made.

How to Choose among the Feasible Options

Often managers cannot rely completely on the people involved in a given area and cannot employ one or more of the avoidance strategies mentioned earlier. When this is the case, the best situation is one in which either specific-action or results controls, or both, can be chosen, as is shown in box 1 of Figure 1. In general, the choice of one or more tools should involve consideration of: (1) the total need for control; (2) the amount of control that can be designed into each of the control devices; and (3) the costs of each, both in terms of money spent and unintended behavioral effects, if any. These decision parameters will be described more fully.

Need for Controls

The need for controls over any particular behavior or operation within an organization depends very simply on the impact of that area on overall organizational performance. Thus, more control should be exercised over a strategically important behavior rather than over a minor one, regardless of how easy it is to control each. For example, controlling the new-product-development activity is far more important in many companies than making sure that the production of existing products is accomplished as efficiently as possible. Consequently, more resources should be devoted to controlling the new-product activity, even though it is a far more difficult area to control.

Amount of Control Provided by Feasible Options

The amount of control provided by each of the control tools depends both on their design and on how well they fit the situation in which they are used. Personnel controls should usually provide some degree of control. But although they may be totally effective in some situations, such as in a small business, they provide little or no warning of failure. They can break down very quickly if demands, opportunities, or needs change.

Specific-action and results controls can provide widely varying amounts of control. In general, reasonably certain (or tight) control requires: (1) detailed specification of what is expected of *each individual*; (2) prevention of undesired actions, or effective and frequent monitoring of actions or results; and (3) administration of penalties or rewards that are significant to the individuals involved.

For example, with specific-action-accountability systems, the amount of control can be affected by changing one or more the elements of the system. First, tighter control can be effected by making the definitions of acceptability more specific. This might take the form of work rules (e.g., no smoking) or specific policies (e.g., a purchasing policy to secure three competing bids before releasing the purchase order), as opposed to general guidelines or vague codes of conduct (e.g., act professionally). Second, control can be made tighter by improving the effectiveness of the action-tracking system. Personnel who are certain that their actions will be noticed relatively quickly will be affected more strongly by an action-accountability system than will those who feel that the chance of their being observed is small. Thus, constant direct supervision should provide tighter control than would an audit sampling of a small number of action reports some time later. Third, control can be made tighter by making the rewards or punishments more significant to the individuals involved. In general, this impact should vary directly with the size of the reward (or the severity of the

217

punishment), although different individuals may react differently to identical rewards or punishments.

Results-accountability systems can be varied along similar lines. Expected performance can be defined broadly, for instance, with a goal for annual net income. Alternatively, expected performance can be defined in more detailed form by prescribing goals for specific result areas (for example, sales growth, efficiency, quality) and by using line items with short time horizons (e.g., month or quarter). Control is tighter when the performance dimensions for which results are desired are defined explicitly and, of course, correctly; this type of control is particularly effective if well-established results standards are available, perhaps in the form of output from an engineering study, industry survey, or historical analysis. Results-accountability control can also be tightened by improving the measurement of results. This can be accomplished by making the measures more precise, more timely, and/or less subject to manipulation.

In addition, reviews can be used to provide either tight or loose assurance. Tight assurance is more likely if the reviews are detailed, comprehensive, and frequent.

Of course, managers do not have to rely exclusively on a single type of control in a control system. Use of more than one type of control--in effect, overlapping controls--will often provide reinforcement. For example, most organizations rely on selecting good people, establishing some set procedures, implementing some accountability for results, and reviewing some key decisions before they are made.

Costs: Outlay and Behavioral

The cost of control depends on two factors: the incremental dollar cost of the tool and the cost of any unintended behavioral effects. The actual dollar cost of a control might be considerably less than it first appears because some devices that provide control may already be in place for other reasons. For example, a budgeting process for a small firm does not have to justify its cost on the basis of control reasons alone. Creditors probably already require *pro forma* financial statements, so the incremental cost might involve only additional detail. (e.g., down to the operations level) and involvement of a greater number of participants.

The costs of any unintended negative effects must also be considered, and these can be very significant. It is beyond the scope of this article to provide an exhaustive enumeration of the many negative side effects possible. Indeed, they come in many different forms, but it is nevertheless useful to mention a few examples.

A common problem with specific-action controls is that they cause operating delays. These can be relatively minor, such as delays caused by limiting access to a stockroom, but they can also be major. For example, after the executives of Harley-Davidson Motor Company bought the firm from AMF, Inc., they found that they were able to implement a rebate program in ten days, rather than the six to eight weeks it would have taken with all the reviews required in the multilayered AMF organization.[6] Obviously, where timely action is important, delays caused by control processes can be very harmful.

Another problem with specific-action controls is that they can cause rigid, bureaucratic behavior. Individuals who become accustomed to following a set routine are not as apt to sense a changing environment, nor are they likely to search for better ways of doing the tasks at hand in a stable environment.

Results controls can create severe, unintended negative effects when all the measurement criteria are not met satisfactorily. Perhaps the most serious common problem is a failure to define the results areas correctly. This causes "goal displacement," a situation where individuals are encouraged to generate the wrong results--in response to the goals defined in the control system--rather than those results truly needed by the organization. For example, a department store introduced an incentive compensation plan to pay employees on the basis of sales volume. The immediate impact was indeed an increase in sales volume, but the increase was accomplished in ways that were inconsistent with long-term organizational goals. The employees competed among themselves for customers and neglected important but unmeasured and unrewarded activities such as stocking and merchandising.[7] Another common example of goal displacement is caused by the practice of rewarding managers of the oft criticized return-on-investment criterion.[8]

Data distortion is another dangerous potential side effect of results controls. If the measurement methods are not objective, then the employees whose performances are being measured might falsify the data or change the measurement methods, and, in so doing undermine the whole organization's information system.

Many of the ramifications of these unintended effects of control systems are not well understood, and their costs are very difficult to quantify. However, consideration of these effects is an important control-system design factor: they cannot be ignored.

FIGURE 2

A Simple Feedback Control Model

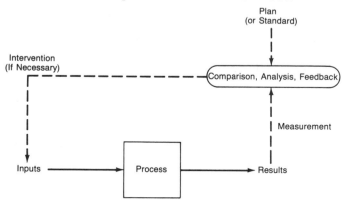

Where Does Feedback Fit In?

Because feedback does not appear prominently in the preceding discussion, it is useful for clarification purposes to consider where feedback fits in. Control is necessarily future-oriented, as past performance cannot be changed, but analysis of results and feedback of variances can often provide a particularly strong addition to a control system. A prerequisite, of course, is the ability to measure results, so feedback can only be useful in the situations presented in boxes 1 and 3 of Figure 1.

There are three reasons why feedback of past results is an important part of many control systems. First, feedback is necessary as reinforcement for a results-accountability system. Even if the feedback is not used to make input adjustments, it signals that results are being monitored. This can heighten employee awareness of what is expected of them and should help stimulate better performance.

Second, in repetitive situations, measurement of results can provide indications of failure in time to make useful interventions. This is shown in the simple feedback control model presented in Figure 2. When the results achieved are not satisfactory, the inputs, which include the specific actions and types of persons involved, can be changed to provide different results. Obviously, these input adjustments are more likely to improve results when there is a good understanding of how inputs relate to results; otherwise, the interventions are essentially experiments.

Third, analysis of how the results vary with different combinations of inputs might improve understanding of how the inputs relate to results. This process is depicted in loop A of Figure 3, a slightly more complicated feedback control model. As this input/results understanding improves, it provides the opportunity to shift the control system from a results-oriented to a specific-action-oriented focus. If managers discover that certain specific actions produce consistently superior results, then it might be beneficial to inform employees of the specific actions that are expected of them, for example, by publishing these desired actions in a procedures manual. The greater the knowledge about how actions bring about results, the greater the possibilities of using a tight, specific-action-oriented control system.

Note that these latter two reasons for analyzing feedback--for making interventions and for learning--are only useful in situations that at least partially repeat themselves. If a situation is truly a one-time occurrence, such as a major divestiture or a unique capital investment, management has little use for feedback information. In these cases, by the time the results are available, it is too late to intervene, and a greater understanding of how results are related to inputs is not immediately useful.

There are other circumstances where feedback need not, and perhaps should not, be a part of a good control system. In many cases, although feedback control systems are not really feasible, they are used anyway. This occurs because of the consistent tendency "to concentrate on matters that are concrete and quantifiable, rather than intangible concepts," which may be equally or more important.[9] Invariably, this will lead to dysfunctional effects, as will all other failures to satisfy the measurement criteria or to define results appropriately.

Cost considerations also commonly lead to decisions not to include feedback in a control system. The design, implementation, and maintenance of results-tracking information systems can often be very expensive. Thus, it is not feasible to have feedback as part of every control system, nor is it necessarily desirable even when feasibility constraints are not present.

The Design Process

As discussed at the beginning of this article, management control is a problem of human behavior. The challenge is to have each individual acting properly as often as possible. Thus, it seems logical to start the control-system design process by considering the personnel component of the organization by itself. In some situations, well-trained, highly motivated personnel can be expected, with a high degree of certainty, to perform their jobs satisfactorily without any additional control steps being taken. A confident reliance on personnel controls is a very desirable situation because additional controls cost money and may have undesirable side effects.

If however, management determines that personnel controls should be supplemented, the first step should be to examine the feasibility of the various control options. To do this, management must assess two factors: how much is known about which specific actions are desirable, and how well measurement can be accomplished in the important performance areas. This feasibility test might immediately determine whether the controls that can be added should be oriented toward specific actions or results. Control can be made tighter by strengthening the controls in place, along the lines discussed earlier, or by implementing overlapping controls, such as controls over results and specific actions.

In most cases, management has some, but less than complete, knowledge of which specific actions are desirable and some, but not perfect, ability to measure the important result areas. This situation usually calls for implementation of both specific-action and results controls, with feedback loops to improve understanding of the relevant processes.

FIGURE 3

A Feedback Control Model with Learning

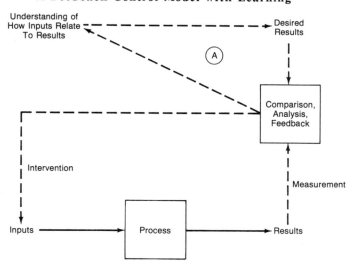

An Example: Control of a Sales Force

The above observations about control can be illustrated by describing how control of a sales force might work. Generally, personnel controls are some part of every sales force control system. Consider, for example, this statement by a sales and marketing consultant:

> I think I can tell a good salesman just by being around him. If the guy is experienced, confident, well-prepared, speaks well, maintains control of situations, and seems to have his time planned, I assume I have a good salesman.

If a sales manager feels confident about all of the salespeople employed, he or she might wish to allow personnel controls to dominate the control system. This is likely, for example, in a small business with a sales force comprised solely of relatives and close friends. But most sales managers are not willing to rely exclusively on hiring and training good people.

What controls should be added? The answer, of course, depends on the type of sales involved. In a single-product, high-volume operation, the volume of sales generated is probably a good simple factor on which to base a results-oriented control system. It provides a reasonable, although not perfect, surrogate for long-range profitability, and the measurements are very inexpensive because the data are already gathered as a necessary input to the financial reporting system. The results-accountability system can then be completed by providing reinforcement in the form of sales commissions. This simple solution will also work where multiple products with varying profitabilities are involved, if the commission schedules are varied so that rewards are assigned in proportion to the profitability of the sales generated.

Consider, however, a situation where salespeople sell large-scale construction equipment and where sales come in very large but infrequent chunks. A commission-type, results-accountability system is still feasible. Measurement of results is not difficult and can be accurate to the penny. The amount of control provided, however, is not high because the measurement fail on the timeliness dimension. Because sales are infrequent, zero sales is not an unusual situation in any given month. Therefore, a salesperson could be drawing advances on hypothetical future commissions for many months without performing any of the desired promotional activities.

Two solutions are possible. One is to augment the commission system with some specific-action controls, such as activity reports. Some activities are probably known to be desirable, such as the number of hours worked and the quantity of calls made. If the product mix and market environment are fairly stable, then requiring and monitoring activity reports is not as costly as it might seem, because it could provide an important side benefit--an activity-oriented data base. The patters in this data base can be analyzed and compared with results over time to add to knowledge about which activities yield the best results.

An alternate solution is to improve the results-accountability system. It might be possible to define some factors that are strong predictors of sales success, such as customer satisfaction with the salesperson or customer familiarity with the company's product. Measurement of these intangibles, of course, would have to be

FIGURE 4

Questions to Determine Feasibility of Control

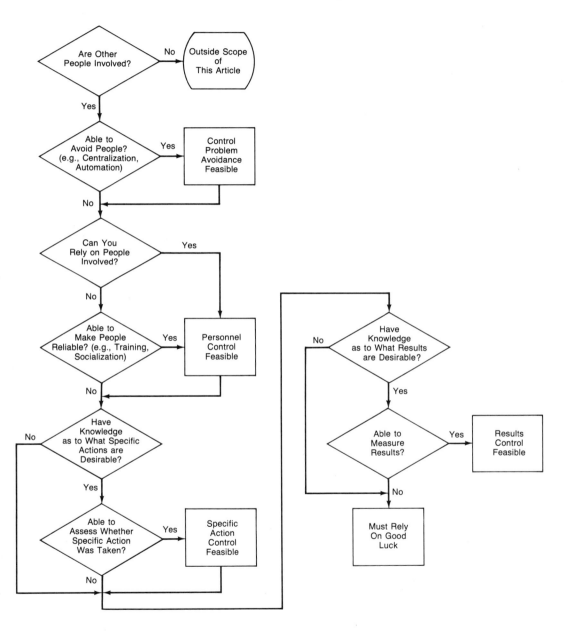

done by surveying customers. Even though these measures do not directly assess the desired results area (long-range profitability), and measurement is imprecise, they could provide a better focus for a results-oriented control system than a sales-generated measure because of the improvement in timeliness. Over time, it is likely that the choice of measures and measurement methodologies could be improved. The advantage of this results-oriented solution over an action-oriented system is that it is more flexible and less constraining to the salespeople; they can continue to use styles best suited to their personalities.

Conclusions

This article has taken a new look at the most basic organizational control problem--how to get employees to live up to the plans that have been established. In the course of discussion, the following major points were made:

1. Management control is a behavioral problem. The various control tools are only effective to the extent that they influence behavior in desirable directions.

2. Good control can often be achieved in several different ways. In some circumstances, the control problems can be avoided, for example, by centralizing or automating certain decisions. If problems cannot be avoided, one or more types of controls are usually desirable or necessary. The options can be classified according to the object of control, labeled in this article as specific actions, results, and personnel.

3. Not all types of controls are feasible in all situations. Figure 4 presents the questions to ask when assessing the feasibility of control types. If none of the controls is feasible, the probability of undesirable results occurring is high.

4. Control can be strengthened either by employing a tighter version of a single type of control or by implementing more than one type of control. However, tighter control is not always desirable because of additional system costs and the potential of undesirable side effects, such as destruction of morale, reduction of initiative, or displacement of employee focus toward measurable result areas only. Some of the qualities, benefits, and costs of each of the major control types are listed in Table 2.

5. The basic management control problems and alternatives are the same in all functional areas and at all levels in the organization, from the lowest supervisory levels to the very top levels of management. The best solutions, however, vary between situations.

An understanding of control can be an important input into many management decisions. For example, control problems should be considered in making some types of investments. An investment in an operation in which control is very difficult--such as a highly specialized and technical area where control must depend heavily on personnel controls--is, by definition, risky. Thus, investments in such areas should promise high returns to compensate for this risk.

Similarly, control considerations should affect the design of the other parts of the management system. Consider, for example, the organizational structure. If independent areas of *responsibility* cannot be carved out as part of the organizational structure, results-accountability control systems will not work well because employees will not feel that their individual actions have a noticeable effect on results. (It should be noted that many of the prescriptions calling for "responsibility accounting" only provide the illusion of results independence because of the many allocations of the costs and/or benefits of shared resources.) If independent areas of *authority* are not established, specific-action-accountability control systems cannot work. This principle underlies the internal control principle of "separation of duties." In addition, if tighter reviews of specific actions are necessary for adequate performance assurance, it is likely that the supervisory spans of control will have to be reduced. Similar observations can be made about other management functions, but they are beyond the scope of this article.

TABLE 2

Qualities of Control Tools

Object of Control:	SPECIFIC ACTIONS			RESULTS	PERSONNEL
	Constraint	Accountability	Review	Accountability	
Amount of Control Provided (tight or loose)	Tight	Tight if Specific; Loose if Vague	Tight if Detailed And Frequent	Tight if Expectations Are Specific And Detailed	Loose
Out-of-Pocket-Cost (relative)	Low	Low	High	High	Varies
Possible Unintended Effects (examples)	Slight Operating Delays	Rigid, Bureaucratic Behavior	Operating Delays	Goal Displacement, Data Distortion	

This article has attempted to provide a new look at this basic, but often overlooked, management problem. The control area is decidedly complex, and there is much that is not known about how controls work and how employees respond to different types of controls. For example, it would be worthwhile to know more about how controls can be designed to maximize the amount of control provided while minimizing the cost in the form of employee feelings of lost autonomy. However, an increased awareness of the control problem, of what can be accomplished, and of the options available should provide a new perspective that will suggest ways to improve control systems and overall organizational performance.

References

1.   See H. Koontz, C. O'Donnell, and H. Weihrich, Management, 7th ed. (New York: McGraw-Hill 1980), p. 722.

2.   See W.D. Brinckloe and M.T. Coughlin, Managing Organizations (Encino, CA: Glencoe Press, 1977), p. 298.

3.   See P.F. Drucker, Management: Tasks, Responsibilities, Practices (New York: Harper & Row, 1974), p. 497.

4.   A recent summary of many of the findings in this area (illustrating such cognitive limitations as conservative revision of prior subject probabilities when new information is provided, and the use of simplifying decision-making heuristics when faced with complex problems) is provided by W.F. Wright, "Cognitive Information Processing Biases: Implications for Producers and Users of Financial Information," Decision Sciences (April 1980): 284-298.

5.   A similar scheme is presented in W.G. Ouchi, "A Conceptual Framework for the Design of Organizational Control Mechanisms," Management Science (September 1979): 833-848.

6.   See H. Klein, "At Harley-Davidson, Life without AMF Is Upbeat but Full of Financial Problems," Wall Street Journal, 13 April 1982, p. 37.

7.   See N. Babchuk and W.J. Goode, "Work Incentives in a Self-Determined Group," American Sociological Review (1951): 679-687.

8.   For a summary of criticisms of return-on-investment (ROI) measures of performance, see J. Dearden, "The Case against ROI Control," Harvard Business Review, May-June 1969, pp. 124-135.

9.   See D. Mitchell, Control without Bureaucracy (London: McGraw-Hill Book Company Limited, 1979), p. 6.

SQC AND JIT:
PARTNERSHIP IN QUALITY

Sarah Priestman

Many companies today are approaching quality as a way of changing their employees' perception of the manufacturing process. If a company teaches quality in this broad way, it can combine complementary quality-related programs to achieve much greater improvement than individual programs could produce by themselves.

Hewlett-Packard's Computer Systems Division has taken this approach.[1] In 1982, it introduced a statistical quality control program; in March 1984, it launched just-in-time manufacturing. Having already established statistical control of its manufacturing processes, the company found that the transition to JIT was less a problem-solving exercise than a solution-oriented project.

Rick Walleigh, production manager for the Division, saw the results of the synergy between SQC and JIT. First, the cycle time in the printed circuit assembly area dropped from 17 days in July 1982, to six days by March 1984, through the use of SQC. Then, upon implementation of JIT, cycle time dropped to 1.6 days after two months and remained at that level. Says Walleigh, "Going into JIT was simplified by the data available through SQC. We were able to target problems and establish quality before moving into a new system. Getting the quality right before introducing JIT is the key to a successful JIT program."

The practice of JIT reflects its title: produce and deliver products just in time to be assembled into finished goods, fabricated parts just in time to go into

Sarah Priestman, "SQC and JIT: Partnership in Quality," Quality Progress, May 1985, pp. 31-34.

subassemblies, and materials just in time to be transferred into fabricated parts. According to Richard Schonberger,[2] inventory is the root of much manufacturing evil. Walleigh agrees. "We traditionally thought of inventory as a good thing because it provides a buffer against a lot of problems and isolates one department from things occurring in other areas, so that departments can concentrate on their own areas. But it also covers up problems, which then go unsolved. Inventory hides late delivery, bad parts from vendors, procedures that constantly break down because of poor maintenance, and processes that operate inconsistently."

JIT exposes these problems because of its hand-to-mouth mode of operation. Traditionally, most manufacturing systems operate in a batch-oriented mode, which recognizes a set-up time and cost. The formula used to calculate these costs is known as the economic order quantity. It is figured by balancing the expense of setting up a batch against the cost of covering materials in order to determine the economic lot size. Batches are large to amortize costs. JIT, on the other hand, fixes the lot size, and then determines the set-up cost. Rather than accepting the set-up cost as a fixed number, JIT works on lowering it. This requires a shift from a batch mode to a mode more like an assembly line.

Ingrained in the batch-oriented mode is the "push" method of manufacturing. Each operation has a schedule and produces a batch of material according to this schedule whether the next operation needs it or not. JIT introduces the concept of demand "pull," where the schedule is created by the final operation. When one station has completed all available work, it signals the next station to give it more; or, if an area of production is full, the operation that feeds it doesn't produce until receiving an indication--through a card or an empty space-- that there is a need to produce. In practice, an operation takes lead time into account in preparing work for the next station.

This system immediately uncovers equipment breakdowns. In a push system, by contrast, material waits in piles around the malfunctioning equipment while operators continue work, processing other material according to the original batch schedule, at individual stations. They do work put aside for late material delivery; they rework nonconformities; they do work they have hidden in preparation for these down times. In a push system, the problems that caused the machine breakdown, the late material delivery, or the nonconformities would not be recognized as contributing to the quality (or the lack thereof) of the manufacturing process.

Let us look at what happens in a JIT system when equipment breaks down. When one station does not receive work from the preceding station because of breakdowns, not only is the machine not working, but the operators are also not working. Addressing the source of equipment malfunction is now critical.

If an operator does run out of work, he or she may help solve the problem causing the stoppage, or may be assigned to work in another area.

Because JIT removes the buffer of inventory accrued by traditional stocking methods, it is vital to know what the true needs of production are to order accurately. Developing an understanding of those exact needs is the function of SQC. SQC and JIT offer complementary means of reaching quality objectives; used together, both programs are more successful.

In general terms, SQC can be broken down into three major elements:[3]

. Process analysis to understand the system.
. Inductive reasoning to measure the system.

.   Leadership to change the system.

SQC allows a company to understand its operations as a set of processes. The natural behavior of each process is defined and monitored by means of control charts. Process variations are recognized and evaluated. Nonconformities and errors can often be reduced by making changes in a process. When declines in productivity and quality appear, SQC exposes the patterns and locations of problems in processes and provides the tools to control those areas. By controlling errors, a company may also simplify its processes.

An example of SQC simplifying procedures and smoothing the introduction of JIT comes from the materials management function. For Chuck Cheshire, materials manager at the Computer Systems Division, the JIT program meant bringing materials to the back door, just in time. "JIT only works if there are no back orders," explains Cheshire. "When we were initially considering JIT, we assumed that if we had more material, back orders would decrease. However, by using SQC, we discovered that this assumption was false. We had several months of inventory, yet our back orders were running at over a hundred. That told us we had the wrong inventory. We focused on the problem, did a Pareto analysis, and asked ourselves, 'What are the real processes? What are the technologies, the commodities, the vendors?'

"We worked on these problems one at a time, and discovered a number of causes. Most were easy to fix, once the data was available. Our inventory dropped from two-and-one-half months to one month, including raw material, work in progress, and other finished goods. Our back orders are now down to two or three."

This means improved relations with vendors as well. Continues Cheshire, "In developing a single source, you must help your supplier be successful by providing information on the product before establishing JIT. That's were SQC comes into play. We were able to provide our supplier with specific feedback on what our incoming quality inspection found compared to the quality they defined when they sent us the parts. We also collected data on the production floor and provided the supplier with this information. Without SQC, we could only say, 'Here's the part, it's broken.' Now we can focus our efforts and the supplier's efforts to pinpoint material problems."

According to Walleigh, SQC and JIT work well together because they share four common action principles:

.   Simplicity
.   Waste elimination
.   Exposing problems
.   A climate for continuous improvement.[4]

Simplicity. Both JIT and SQC simplify the manufacturing process. In SQC, obtaining accurate evaluations of data to determine the source of nonconformities requires that operations be performed consistently. A major enemy of consistency is complexity, such as nonconforming raw materials, late deliveries of components, erratically functioning equipment, and poorly documented procedures. By using SQC analysis to expose and eliminate these complexities, a company can make its process consistent, reliable, and simple.

JIT simplifies the manufacturing process through material movement. Complex production scheduling of multiple levels of product subassemblies is eliminated, because when material is needed it is pulled from the preceding production operation. There is no need to track progress against schedule for the production of subassemblies because nothing is built until it is needed. An obvious signal or card displays the need. Only final production complexities need to be tracked. Employes do not have to guess at what they should work on next: the next action to be taken becomes obvious, and priorities are set automatically.

Waste elimination. As nonconformities are minimized through SQC, less scrap is produced, and labor is saved through a reduction in rework. Labor is also no longer wasted on improvised procedures with which workers previously adapted to the problems of a complex environment.

Says Perry Gluckman, SQC consultant, "Workers develop informal ways to get their work done no matter what the formal system is. But this is not the worst thing that can happen. It is far worse when the workers follow policy and build something to specification even though--because of a lack of understanding about the processes--the specification is wrong. Unfortunately, the worker is often blamed for the lack of quality in these situations."

With SQC and JIT, the workers' creativity is channeled to more productive projects. Bob Tellez, the section manager for Printed Circuit Assembly, is working with line operators to improve job satisfaction. "We've given a group of people full responsibility and ownership for major areas," he explains. "One group on day shift has responsibility for hand-loaded components on boards; they also oversee the wave-solder process. Ten people work within these two processes, but within that system, they rotate from one station to the next. When one station slows down, they can go help another. This is what the operators chose to do when we installed the JIT system, as the need for variety became evident. SQC offered the operators visible recognition for their abilities. Operators are now given opportunities to work together to make changes that will yield improvements."

JIT approaches waste from another perspective. Waste is primarily eliminated in inventory. Because products are not assembled until needed, inventory is lower throughout the manufacturing process. The obvious and direct benefit is increased asset productivity. However, the indirect benefits prove even more valuable. With less inventory separating different production operations, the cycle time is shortened and manufacturing is consequently more responsive. Another benefit is the elimination of wasted space previously used to store the unnecessary work-in-process inventory.

Because JIT requires that material be produced and moved in small amounts rather than in large batches, machine setup times are reduced, which also eliminates waste of labor and capital equipment.

Exposing problems. SQC distinguishes between variations in a process as a result of outside causes, and variations that are the result of inconsistencies within the process itself. Once this distinction is understood, appropriate resources can be committed to eliminate the source of the problem.

JIT exposes problems in a less direct but often more compelling way. It strips away the mask of inventory that hides the problems of late deliveries, nonconforming raw material, processes that produce scrap, processes with unbalanced capacities, and poor production planning. Without the buffer of back-up inventory, JIT forces managers to recognize and address these problems.

A climate for continuous improvement. Once SQC and JIT become a part of the manufacturing routine, continuous improvement becomes everyone's objective.

SQC and JIT have produced impressive results at the Computer Systems Division. The production process has been simplified, dropping from 26 steps to 14. Employe responsibilities are clearer, and communication has improved. According to Tellez, "SQC offers everyone a sense of ownership and allows worker participation at all levels of process improvement. Implementing JIT is a simpler transition than it would be without that sense of involvement in place."

Waste and problem visibility have been targeted in a number of areas. Since the July 1982 implementation of SQC, direct labor dropped from 62 hours per product to 52 by the first quarter of 1984. Seven months after JIT was introduced in March 1984, labor hours dropped to 39. Nonconformities in pretest IC insertion products, already monitored by SQC, plummeted from 1,950 ppm in January 1984 to 600 ppm three months later. After JIT, nonconformities fell to 210 ppm by October. Hand-loading nonconformities dropped from 120 ppm in January to 90 ppm in March to 48 ppm in October.

Solder nonconformities in the wave-solder process have demonstrated the most dramatic decline. Upon installation of SQC, nonconformities were recorded at 5,200 ppm. Five months later, documentation shows 100 ppm in the same wave-solder process. Though fluctuations occurred during 1983 and early 1984, nonconformities were lowered to under 100 within two months of JIT installation, and have remained under control ever since.

In the wave-solder section of Printed Circuit Assembly, functional nonconformities fell from 14 ppm in January to 11 ppm in March to five ppm in October 1984. PC Assembly final assembly nonformities started at 145 ppm in January, fell to 97 ppm by March, and were down to ten ppm in October.

These reductions were immediately felt in the working environment. Says Tellez, "When we eliminated a lot of the wasteful conditions that existed in the batch-oriented material flow system, people were relieved. They now know that the material they will be working on is just getting finished, and as soon as it arrives, they'll be ready for it. In the old system, people didn't feel comfortable unless they had a rack of work behind them. People would hide work so they'd have it to keep them busy for an entire week. We reduced floorspace by 32% when we eliminated this backlog."

Implementing both SQC and JIT requires the commitment of management and the direct involvement of operators. In making the decision to establish quality programs, warns Cheshire, "Management commitment is not just a matter of saying, 'you'll implement SQC, thank you.' Management commitment means allowing workers to try and, if they fail, to learn from these failures. Ten years ago, standard engineers might be on the floor, watching how much time each assembly would take. Now, through SQC, production workers know if they're out of statistical control they know they can stop and ask for assistance from engineering.

"SQC and JIT allows managers to listen to the operators, tap in their insights, and make the system more effective while making the operators' jobs more interesting. Quality commitment supports individual initiative. If people have pride in their jobs, and are trained to control their jobs, they do well, and the company does well."

References

1.   This article is based on interviews with employes of Hewlett-Packard's Computer System Division.

2.   Richard Schonberger, Japanese Manufacturing Techniques: Nine Hidden Lessons in Simplicity, The Free Press.

3.   For more detailed information about statistical quality control, see such books as <u>Statistical Quality Control</u>, Fifth Edition, by Eugene L. Grant and Richard S. Leavenworth, or <u>Guide to Quality Control</u>, by Kaoru Ishikawa.

4.   The material for this section is based on an internal Hewlett-Packard report, "Synergy in TQC and JIT" by Rick Walleigh.

IMPORTANT CONSIDERATIONS IN THE BUDGETING PROCESS

Steven D. Grossman
Richard Lindhe

The firm is a system; i.e. a series of interrelated elements working together to achieve a purpose. The well-managed firm has a sense of that interrelationship; management plans with that understanding and the budget reflects it.

Good management involves planning for both the long-term and the short-term. Planning of this sort builds upon the resources of the firm within the environment. If we can gain a reasonable feel for the possibilities of future conditions which could affect a firm, we can establish a long-term plan and a set of short-term plans within that plan for the firm. This process is called strategic planning, and it is the foundation of proper budgets.

The primary functions of the budget are to communicate expectations and to aid in the allocation of resources. There are certain steps that should be followed in the budgeting process. These steps involve goals and objectives, the environment, the availability of resources, and the establishment and implementation of strategy.

Budgets involve people. Therefore, motivation, participation, and communication are vital factors in the success of the budgeting process. A budget that is established without regard to these considerations is bound to fail.

The Long-Term Plan

The firm's management should decide what it wishes the organization to be like at some time in the future. The elements of the firm at that time are set in general terms: size, industry, products, etc. Of course, these elements must be feasible. The long-term strategy, then, is an action plan that is designed to achieve long-term objectives.

The long-term plan necessarily is general in nature and provides fairly broad guidelines rather than specific activities. Two aspects of this plan are of major concern to us. The first has to do with those actions which are specifically linked to long-term strategy. The second aspect of the long-term plan relates to the short-term activities which are necessary to carry out the long-term strategy as we face the near future.

As we picture the long-term strategy, we can see that it is composed of a series of short-term plans or strategies. Each of these short-term plans builds upon

Reprinted with permission from <u>Managerial Planning</u>, "Important Considerations in the Budgeting Process," Steven D. Grossman and Richard Lindhe, September-October 1982, pp. 24-29.

the one before it. Adjustments are made as needed to respond to changes in the environment, available resources, or even basic goals and objectives. Each of these short-term plans prepares the firm for the next short-term plan. (see Figure 1)

FIGURE 1

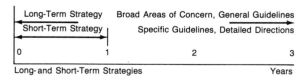

It is important to remember that these short-term strategies are subsets of the long-term strategy. When conditions cause changes to be necessary in the long-term, those changes should be reflected in the short-term as well. It is equally important to remember that these short-term strategies are individual steps which necessarily must be achieved in order to gain the larger goal. If each short-term plan is optimized separately, the long-term plan may not be achieved. The key to proper planning is to reach the end of one period in the best possible condition to implement the next short-term strategy. These short-term strategies are manifested in the operating budgets of the firm. The operating budget is often referred to as, simply, the budget.

We shall think of the long-term strategy as a continuous process which is constantly being upgraded and fit to the nuances of the forecasted future. In this sense, the long-term plan or strategy has no end. The budget, too, is an unending process which shifts and changes with the strategy that it represents.

The Budget

Both capital and operating budgets are meant to be reflections of their related strategies. Their primary functions, in this regard, are (1) to communicate expectations and, (2) to help allocate resources. These functions result in a series of highly complex actions, reactions, and interactions taking place.

The steps inherent in strategic development are as follows:

1. Establishment of goals and objectives.
2. Scanning of the environment.
3. Assessment of available resources
4. Establishment of the strategy.
5. Implementation of the strategy.

These steps do not have to be carried out in this particular order. In fact, there may be considerable movement back and forth between steps as viability of purpose is tested. Moreover, this is not really a periodic event, although major emphasis may be given at specific points of time; rather it is a continuous process. Let us examine each of these briefly.

Establishment of Goals and Objectives

An organization comes into being for a reason and stays in existence either for that reason or for some other. Accountants sometimes ascribe a particular objective to a firm--for example, maximization of profits or wealth--but, in fact, a firm may have a wide variety of objectives. The function of the accountant is not to set the goals and objectives for an organization, but to help in their achievement. Accountants also can help in the assessment of the viability and appropriateness of goals and objectives by supplying management with appropriate information.

Goals and objectives should be the focus for the firm, and the accountant must know and understand them. It is important that goals and objectives be enunciated, be communicated, and be reasonably well accepted. Otherwise, there can be no meaningful focus for the firm, and productive efforts may be dissipated.

The Environment

The environment will be defined as the composite of all those factors which can affect the organization but over which the organization's management has little or no control. To add clarity to this description, we can divide the environment into four categories: (1) economic, (2) technical, (3) legal, and (4) social.

The economic environment is composed of such elements as general business activity, the activities of the industry or industries in which the organization functions, and the activities of governments. These are the factors that are embodied in the forecasts of firms.

Technical activity in the environment relates mainly to scientific development. New machines, new processes, and new products can have profound impacts upon the firm's future and, therefore, it is imperative that the firm be aware of all such developments.

Legal aspects of the environment relate to all legislation which can affect the organization. Legislation for our purposes refers to the three phases of laws: (1) the enactment of legislation, (2) the administration of legislation, and (3) the interpretation of legislation by the courts. The fact is that laws are administered differently in different places and at different times; in addition, a law may be expanded, diminished, or even abolished by the courts.

The social aspect of environment refers to the changing lifestyle of society. Changes in attitude, perspective, or moral sense may lead to changes in the other aspects of environment and have strong implications to the firm. In a sense, the social aspect may be considered to be the early warning part of the environment.

The environment may also be classified according to its predominant condition as: (1) stable, (2) dynamic, or (3) turbulent. A stable environment is relatively unchanging; firms concentrate upon the improvement of existing products and processes. A dynamic environment is a changing one in which forecasts are considered to be appropriate and can be made reasonably accurately. Most writers in business activities assume that a dynamic environment exists. A turbulent environment is so unstable that managers tend to have little faith in forecasts. Their natural tendency toward short-term planning and decision making is increased dramatically. The time of the oil embargo was such a time for many firms.

The environment contains both constraints and opportunities. The successful firm understands them and is able to operate within the constraints and take advantage of the opportunities.

233

Available Resources

A resource may be defined as anything which can help the firm achieve its objectives within the existing or future environment. Resources must be seen within a particular focus; their values are set by the environment and change as it does.

Notice the difference between resources as we have just defined them and assets as defined in accounting. An accounting asset may or may not be a resource: a resource may or may not be an accounting asset. A resource may be money, a building, or a machine. In addition, it may be executive ability, marketing experience, or a good reputation.

Accounting assets are measured in terms of their costs. Resources should be measured in terms of their ability to aid in goal achievement.

Establishment of Strategy

Goals and objectives, the environment, and the available resources may be considered to be the building blocks of strategy, because the implementation of strategy must relate to them. Strategy is always tenuous--subject to change in the environment or, even, the purpose for which the firm exists. Thus, strategic development is always an ongoing process, and the budgets which reflect the strategy also must be in a continuous state.

In long-term strategy, the organization perceives a desired state of condition for that organization at some time (typically 5 to 10 years) in the future. Broad guidelines are established at this time for the functional areas such as marketing and finance.

Within this long-term plan, management sets desired conditions along the way--for example, at the end of each year. Obviously, these should not be rigid objectives, because the environment is likely to change in some way. The plan must be flexible so that it can be changed not simply in dimension but, if necessary, in its very basics.

It is clear that direction must be provided for all functions, for all divisions and for all departments. Although the ultimate focus of the firm must be long-term, this focus may be very difficult to maintain in the press of daily operations.

The short-term budget or operating budget is, then, a stage of the longer term. Operating budgets are typically for periods of one year with monthly updates. A number of firms follow the practice of setting a twelve month budget each month by adding a new month and dropping the past month.

Implementing the Strategy

The budget is the manifestation of the strategy and the most common way of implementing it. We shall see that the process of this implementation may be as important as the budget itself.

All of the essentials pertaining to measurement and behavior that are so crucial to the success of the plan are included in this process. If the costs that are measured are not the costs that are incurred, if the pattern of behavior that is assumed is not the actual pattern, if the way in which the measurements are used does not lead to appropriate behavior, then the plan must surely fail. Machines have behavior patterns; people have behavior patterns. The budget must reflect an understanding of these patterns and also the wide spectrum of human behavior which will do much to determine the success or failure of the budget.

The strategy and, hence, the budget which lead to the greatest profit for a particular period may not be the best choice for the firm. If that is so, then profit for the period may not be the best measure of success. Indeed, we need to measure success in terms of how well the firm moved along its strategic path. Each segment of the firm must perform its own unique function as intended, and its success must be measured in terms of that functional performance.

Human Behavior and the Budget

When a machine has a cutting edge, it is normal for that cutting edge to become progressively more dull with use until it must be replaced. The variation in efficiency is normal to that machine. In this sense a human being, like the machine, has a normal variation in efficiency. We know that Monday mornings and Friday afternoons are usually less productive than other days. We also know that people are physically incapable of maintaining the same level of efficiency, and budgets need to reflect that normality.

There is, however, another side to human behavior. We have come to see that motivation is an important factor in performance, but we seldom explore the broader implications of human behavior in budgets. Just as there is a normal physical behavior pattern for a person, there is also a normal behavior which relates to that person's cultural and psychological side.

Our codes of behavior are set to a large extent by our cultures; that is, in fact, a distinguishing feature of a culture. Indeed, cultural impact is well recognized as a factor in behavior We often overlook the fact that any large organization can be composed of a variety of disparate cultures.

Certainly, research scientists see a different role for themselves than finance people see either for themselves or for research scientists. Each group has its own culture; each sees a special set of rules for behavior; each has a set of normal behavior which is different than the other's.

We all "see" what we are conditioned to see. Accountants, marketing people, finance people, and others are each trained to look for certain things within an organization, and they will tend to "see" in terms of those things.

For example, assume that an engineer, an artist, and a psychologist all witness the same automobile accident. The odds are--and experience will verify-- that each will see some things the others do not and, of course, miss something the others see.

The engineer is more likely to note the condition and performance of the automobiles, the psychologist is more likely to be aware of the behavior of the participants, and the artist is more likely to be attuned to the general scene. What they see will be partly determined by their perceptions--what they have been conditioned to see.

Suppose that the witnesses saw the event from different places--street level, fifth floor, front, back, etc. Now we can say that each witness had a different perspective and, therefore, was likely to see something different. This is why eye witnesses sometimes report an incident in totally different ways.

235

Each group within the organization is likely to see the organization in terms of its own perceptions and from its own perspective. These perceptions and prospectives help to create normal behavior; they also create unique feelings about and reactions to the budget.

Motivation

Budgets motivate people, although we have a lot to learn about how they do so. Since people relate to things as they perceive them, we must understand motivation within the unique worlds of varying cultures.

A simplistic way of describing motivation is to say that we can positively motivate people when we provide them with a climate in which they can meet their needs while they are meeting our needs. A firm can positively motivate people when they can work to meet their own needs by working to achieve the firm's goals and objectives.

Virtually every phase of the budget and its processes has the potential for impacting motivation by shaping the perceptions of the participants. If we can learn to "see" a bit from others' eyes, we might be able to understand better the psychology of budgets.

Participation

While the traditional view of organizational behavior is that workers are motivated primarily by money, the more modern view is that workers are motivated by a wide variety of needs. An individual joins a firm and works for it as long as such action enables him to achieve his personal goals.

There seems to be relationship between the amount of participation and the quality of performance. Sometimes the relationship is positive due to the increased satisfaction by the members of the firm in utilizing their capabilities and achieving their objectives. However, the relationship may be negative if the members of the firm are reluctant to accept the risk of not achieving their own standards.

Although many people seem to accept the idea that participation in the budget process leads to better budget performance, it is not necessarily so. There are people who either cannot or do not wish to participate in the budget process. There are people who refuse to let a job be anything more than a means to other ends. They will do what they are told to do--and do it well--but they do not want any more involvement in the firm.

Some people may have difficulty understanding what is needed, others may not be able to communicate effectively, and still others may not have sufficient time available for meaningful participation. Meaningful participation can be very demanding.

In any case, if participation in the process is planned, it should be recognized that extensive preparation is necessary. New perceptions and new perspectives must be created for all parties if the process is to work.

Above all, there must be some minimum level of trust at all levels, and that trust must be deserved. Pseudo-participation can be very unproductive. Unless people believe that their actions have meaning, they will not provide meaningful input, and negative motivation is likely.

Budget Communication

We said earlier that one of the purposes of the budget is to communicate expectations. The budget as a communication device plays a significant role in establishing the climate of the firm.

The effect that the message that is communicated by the budget has upon the members of the firm is established by their mental condition or mental set. This set will be established by:

1.   Instruction--formal and informal.
2.   Environment:
      a.   The person's.
      b.   The firm's.
3.   The form of the message.
4.   The budget system.
5.   Knowledge about those in charge of the budget.

We shall look briefly at each of these elements in turn to see if we can gain some insights into the whole process.

Instructions   People will react to the budget, at least partly, in terms of the instructions that they have received about it. This instruction can be both formal and informal; it can be intentional and unintentional.

Although formal instruction is an imperative for a good budget, it is important that instructions be clear and complete. Too often, the instruction is, at best, cursory. Training tends to be informal. On-the-job training can be effective, however, if it is done properly.

Unintentional training is oftentimes both very effective and counter productive. Actions that are taken by budget managers or the inferences of such actions can have a strong impact in both the short-term and the long-term. Activities at this level can create misperceptions which can be very damaging. Time must be spent with operating managers so that they are not only clear in their understandings of budget operations but also are aware of the impact of their actions upon others.

Environment   People react to all sorts of stimuli--stimuli of the present or out of the past. The environment that has been created in the firm and individual perceptions are likely to be at least somewhat different for each person.

Although we cannot learn everything about each individual's background, we can gain a sense of the environment of the firm as perceived by the members of the firm in general and the key people in particular. Although the environment of the firm is difficult to articulate, it can be a significant part of the preparation of a successful budget.

Knowledge about the environment typically is determined by interviews and observations. Interviews must be carefully conducted and reinforced by observations. It is important to realize that the environment that we see may not be the environment that others see.

The attitude of managers at all levels will become incorporated into the budget. If managers tend to be uncommunicative, important questions about the budget may not only be unanswered, they may not even be asked. If managers generally are open and understanding, this attitude is likely to carry over into the budget.

The budget is part of the total environment of the firm, rather than separate and apart from it. The general feeling about the environment of the firm will transmit itself through the budget. Conversely, the spirit generated by the budget will be a tangible part of the environment of the firm.

The Form of the Message Whether the budget process is communicating expectation or results, it is sending messages. Interestingly enough, we find that the way we send those messages can have a significant effect. The form of the message can be important. We know that people react differently to reports issued directly from a computer or apparently issued from a computer as compared to reports which are issued in other ways. Indeed, there is ample evidence that the form of the message affects behavior. The phenomena of primacy and recent effects in messages have been well documented and deserve attention.

The color and bordering of the report paper can affect the receiver. The size of the type, the order of presentation, the headings of the reports, the language and the symbols chosen all can create particular patterns of behavior.

Since the purpose of the budget is to create positive behavior, every aspect which can impact upon behavior in the budget process is important. Those who are in charge of the budget have a responsibility to see that the budget process is effective by doing whatever is necessary to ensure its success.

The use of accounting terminology, accounting titles, and accounting type reports should not be used when dealing with nonaccountants. Some remarkable improvements in the use of budgets and related materials can be achieved by fitting the form and format of the messages to those who will use them. These improvements have been especially significant with regards to engineers, who like charts and graphs rather than accounting reports.

The Budget System The more we study the budget as a system that is part of an information system, the more we learn about the complexities of a process that is used to measure, judge performance, and communicate results. We find that the final judgment on the efficacy of the budget system must be made on the basis of the total impact of the total process.

Time can be a significant factor in budget communication. Just as Friday afternoons and Monday mornings are bad production periods, they are poor periods for communications as well. People are not as likely to be alert or responsive as they might be at other times.

If reports are regularly processed at particular times, deviations from the schedule can connote special significance. Obviously, if action is expected as a result of the budget report, it must be received in time for a meaningful response. If reports are received after action on a problem has already been taken, dysfunctional behavior could result.

Studies have shown that delays in reporting can cause persons to be negative about the potential results and also to translate the report when it is received more negatively than would have been the case earlier. This suggests that every effort should be made to avoid delay in the reports and, if delay is unavoidable, the reason for the delay should be communicated early.

Positive reinforcement has been shown to improve both attitudes and efficiency, while negative reinforcements produce a deterioration of morale and productivity. In practice, the now traditional "management by exception" tends to concentrate on those things which are perceived as unfavorable. Since this is clearly negative reinforcement, we need to be concerned about the results. In fact, there are a lot of defensive actions under such conditions--actions which certainly do not add to either effectiveness or efficiency.

There is a tendency for budgets to cause a narrowing of perspective by highlighting only segmental concerns. The best way to counteract this might be to base budget analysis upon the interrelated factors of the budget. To be more specific, we need to provide measurements which relate to total impact and focus on that which relates to the total system.

Knowledge of the Source   Knowledge of the other party to communication can affect the impact of a message. Teachers with low expectations for the performance of their students actually tend to induce poor performance. If managers have low expectations for performance in a budget situation, these expectations are likely to be inadvertently communicated and thereby help to induce the expected behavior.

Historically, certain segments of an organization have held certain other segments in low regard. This attitude is prevalent among many engineers and research scientists about accountants, budgets, budget processes, and budget directors. Whether or not this attitude is justified, it can be detrimental to performance. In some cases, it may be necessary to use nonaccountants as sources for certain budget messages. In the long run, it is far better to work on the basic relationship to ensure a more productive condition.

Summary

This article discussed three important aspects of the budgeting process. Each of these aspects should be considered carefully.

The long-term strategy is composed of a series of short-term strategies. Conditions which cause changes in the long-term strategy should be reflected in the short-term strategies also. Each short-term plan is a step along the path of the long-term plan. The important consideration is whether the long-term strategy is achieved.

There are five steps that are inherent in the development of a firm's strategy. These steps include the establishment of goals and objectives, the scanning of the environment, the assessment of available resources, the establishment of the strategy, and the implementation of the strategy. These steps are interrelated and there is considerable movement back and forth between steps.

Human behavior is a vital consideration in the budgeting process. Almost every part of the budget process impacts motivation by shaping the perceptions of the personnel in the firm. Participation in the budgeting process may or may not be helpful. If participation is to be used, extensive preparation will be necessary.

The budget is an important communication device. A budget sends a message to the members of the firm. The effect of that message is established by the mental set of the members.

MANAGING THE HUMAN SIDE OF CHANGE

Rosabeth Moss Kanter

This is a time of historically unprecendented change for most corporations. The auto and steel industries are in turmoil because of the effects of foreign competition. Financial services are undergoing a revolution. Telecommunications companies are facing profound and dramatic changes because of the breakup of AT&T and greater competition from newly organized long-distance carriers. Health care organizations are under pressure to cut costs and improve services in the face of government regulation and the growth of for-profit hospital chains.

Change, and the need to manage it well, has always been with us. Business life is punctuated by necessary and expected changes: the introduction of new toothpastes, regular store remodelings, changes in information systems, reorganizations of the office staff announcements of new benefits programs, radical rethinking of the fall product line, or a progression of new senior vice-presidents.

But as common as change is, the people who work in an organization may still not like it. Each of those "routine" changes can be accompanied by tension, stress, squabbling, sabotage, turnover, subtle undermining, behind-the-scenes footdragging, work slowdowns, needless political battles, and a drain on money and time--in short, symptoms of that ever-present bugaboo, resistance to change.

If even small and expected changes can be the occasion for decrease in organizational effectiveness, imagine the potential for disaster when organizations try to make big changes, such as developing a new corporate culture, restructuring the business to become more competitive, divesting losing operations and closing facilities, reshuffling product divisions to give them a market orientation, or moving into new sales channels.

Because the pace of change has speeded up, mastering change is increasingly a part of every manager's job. All managers need to know how to guide people through change so that they emerge at the other end with an effective organization. One important key is being able to analyze the reasons people resist change. Pinpointing the source of the resistance makes it possible to see what needs to be done to avoid resistance, or convert it into commitment to change.

As a consulting firm, Goodmeasure has worked with the change-related problems of over a hundred major organizations. We have distilled a list of the ten most common reasons managers encounter resistance to change, and tactics for dealing with each.

1. *Loss of Control*

How people greet a change has to do with whether they feel in control of it or not. Change is exciting when it is done *by us*.

Most people want and need to feel in control of the events around them. Indeed, behind the rise of participative management today is the notion that "ownership" counts in getting commitment to actions, that if people have a chance to participate in decisions, they feel better about them. Even involvement in details is better than noninvolvement. And the more choices that are left to people, the better they feel about the changes. If all actions are imposed upon them from outside, however, they are more likely to resist.

Thus, the more choices we can give people the better they'll feel about the change. But when they feel out of control and powerless, they are likely not only to feel stress, but also to behave in defensive, territorial ways. I proposed in my 1977 *Men and Women of the Corporation* that, in organizations at least, it is *powerlessness* that "corrupts," not power. When people feel powerless, they behave in petty, territorial ways. They become rules-minded, and they are over-controlling, because they're trying to grab hold of some little piece of the world they *do* control and then overmanage it to death. (One way to reassert control is to resist everyone else's new ideas.) People do funny things when they feel out of control, but giving people chances for involvement can help them feel more committed to the change in question.

2. *Excess Uncertainty*

A second reason people resist change is what I call the "Walking Off A Cliff Blindfolded Problem"--too much uncertainty. Simply not knowing enough about what the next step is going to be or feel like makes comfort impossible. If people don't know where the next step is going to take them, whether it is the organizational equivalent of off a cliff or under a train, change seems dangerous. Then they resist change, because they reason, "It's safer to stay with the devil you know than to commit yourself to the devil you don't."

Managers who do not share enough information with their employees about exactly what is happening at every step of a change process, and about what they anticipate happening next, and about when more information will be coming, make a mistake, because they're likely to meet with a great deal of resistance. Information counts in building commitment to a change, especially step-by-step scenarios with timetables and milestones. Dividing a big change into a number of small steps can help make it seem less risky and threatening. People can focus on one step at a time, but not a leap off the cliff; they know what to do next.

Change requires faith that the new way will indeed be the right way. If the leaders themselves do not appear convinced, then the rest of the people will not budge. Another key to resolving the discomfort of uncertainty is for leaders to demonstrate their commitment to change. Leaders have to be the first over the cliff if they want the people they manage to follow suit. Information, coupled with the leaders' actions to make change seem safer, can convert resistance to commitment.

3. *Surprise, Surprise!*

A third reason people resist change is the surprise factor. People are easily shocked by decisions or requests suddenly sprung on them without groundwork or preparation. Their first response to something totally new and unexpected, that they have not had time to prepare for mentally, is resistance.

Companies frequently make this mistake when introducing organizational changes. They wait until all decisions are made, and then spring them on an unsuspecting population. One chemical company that has had to reorganize and frequently lay people off is particularly prone to this error. A manager might come into work one day to find on her desk a list of people she is supposed to inform, immediately, that their jobs are changing or being eliminated. Consequently, that manager starts to wonder whether she is on somebody *else's* list, and she feels so upset by the surprise that her commitment to the organization is reduced. The question, "Why couldn't they trust me enough to even hint that this might happen?" is a legitimate one.

Decisions for change can be such a shock that there is no time to assimilate or absorb them, or see what might be good about those changes. All we can do is feel threatened and resist--defend against the new way or undermine it.

Thus, it is important to not only provide employees with information to build a commitment to change, but also to arrange the *timing* of the information's release. Give people advance notice, a warning, and a chance to adjust their thinking.

4. *The "Difference" Effect*

A fourth reason people resist change is the effect of "difference"--the fact that change requires people to become conscious of, and to question, familiar routines and habits.

A great deal of work in organizations is simply habitual. In fact, most of us could not function very well in life if we were not engaged in a high proportion of "mindless" habitual activities--like turning right when you walk down the corridor to work, or handling certain forms, or attending certain meetings. Imagine what it would be like if, every day you went to work, your office was in an entirely different place and the future was rearranged. You would stumble around, have trouble finding things, feel uncomfortable, and need to expend an additional amount of physical and emotional energy. This would be exhausting and fatiguing. Indeed, rapidly, growing high-technology companies often present people with an approximation of this new-office-every-day nightmare, because the addition of new people and new tasks is ubiquitous, while established routines and habitual procedures are minimal. The overwork syndrome and "burn-out" phenomenon are accordingly common in the industry.

One analogy comes from my work on the introduction of a person who is "different" (an "O") in a group formerly made up of only one kind of person (the "X's"), the theme of Goodmeasure's production, *A Tale of "O."* When a group of X's has been accustomed to doing things a certain way, to having habits and modes of conversation and jokes that are unquestioned, they are threatened by the presence of a person who seems to require operating in a different way. The X's are likely to resist the introduction of the O, because the difference effect makes them start feeling self-conscious, requires that they question even the habitual things that they do, and demands that they think about behavior that used to be taken for granted. The extra effort required to "reprogram" the routines is what causes resistance to the change.

Thus, an important goal in managing change is to minimize or reduce the number of "differences" introduced by the change, leaving as many habits and routines as possible in place. Sometimes managers think they should be doing just the opposite--changing everything else they can think of to symbolize that the core change is really happening. But commitment to change is more likely to occur when the change is not presented as a wild difference but rather as continuous with tradition. Roger Smith, the chairman of General Motors, launched what I considered one of the most revolutionary periods of change in the company's history by invoking not revolution, but tradition: "I'm going to take this company back to the way Alfred Sloan intended it to be managed."

Not only do many people need or prefer familiar routines, they also like familiar surroundings. Maintaining some familiar sights and sounds, the things that make people feel comfortable and at home, is very important in getting employees' commitment to a change.

5. *Loss of Face*

If accepting a change means admitting that the way things were done in the past was wrong, people are certain to resist. Nobody likes losing face or feeling embarrassed in front of their peers. But sometimes making a commitment to a new procedure, product, or prgram carries with it the implicit assumption that the "old ways" must have been wrong, thereby putting all the adherents of the "old ways" in the uncomfortable position of either looking stupid for their past actions or being forced to defend them--and thereby arguing against any change.

The great sociologist Erving Goffman showed that people would go to great lengths to save face, even engaging in actions contrary to their long-term interest to avoid embarassment.

I have seen a number of new chief executives introduce future strategies in ways that "put down" the preceding strategies, thus making automatic enemies of the members of the group that had formulated and executed them. The rhetoric of their speeches implies that the new way gains strength only in contrast to the failures and flaws of the old way--a kind of Maoist "cultural revolution" mentality in business. "The way we've been managing is terrible," one CEO says routinely. He thus makes it hard for people who lived the old ways to shed them for the new, because to do so is to admit they must have been "terrible" before. While Mao got such confessions, businesses do not.

Instead, commitment to change is ensured when past actions are put in perspective--as the apparently right thing to do then, but now times are different. This way people do not lose face for changing; just the opposite. They look strong and flexible. They have been honored for what they accomplished under the old conditions, even if it is now time to change.

6. *Concerns About Future Competence*

Sometimes people resist change because of personal concerns about their future ability to be effective after the change: Can I do it? How will I do it? Will I make it under the new conditions? Do I have the skills to operate in a new way? These concerns may not be expressed out loud, but they can result in finding many reasons why change should be avoided.

In local telephone companies, employees have been told for years that they would be promoted for one set of reasons, and the workers had developed one set of skills and competencies. It is very threatening for many employees to be told that, all of a sudden, the new world demands a new set of competencies, a new set of more market-oriented entrepreneurial skills. Nobody likes to look inadequate.

And nobody, especially people who have been around a long time, wants to feel that he or she has to "start over again" in order to feel competent in the organization.

It is essential, when managing a change, to make sure that people *do* feel competent, that there is sufficient education and training available so that people understand what is happening and know that they can master it--that they *can* indeed do what is needed. Positive reinforcement is even more important in managing change than it is in managing routine situations.

In addition to education and training, people also need a chance to practice the new skills or actions without feeling that they are being judged or that they are going to look foolish to their colleagues and peers. They need a chance to get comfortable with new routines or new ways of operating without feeling stupid because they have questions to ask. Unfortunately, many corporation I know have spent a lot of time making executives and managers feel stupid if they have questions; they're the ones that are supposed to have the *answers*.

We have to be sensitive enough in the management of change to make sure that nobody feels stupid, that everyone can ask questions, and that everybody has a chance to be a learner, to come to feel competent in the new ways.

7.   *Ripple Effects*

People may resist change for reasons connected to their own activities. Change does sometimes disrupt other kinds of plans or projects, or even personal and family activities that have nothing to do with the job, and anticipation of those disruptions causes resistance to change.

Changes inevitably send ripples beyond their intended impact. The ripples may also negate promises the organization has made. Plans or activities seemingly unrelated to the core of the change can be very important to people. Effective "change masters" are sensitive to the ripples changes cause. They look for the ripples and introduce the change with *flexibility* so that, for example, people who have children can finish out the school year before relocating, or managers who want to finish a pet project can do so, or departments can go through a transition period rather than facing an abrupt change. That kind of sensitivity helps get people on board and makes them feel committed, rather than resistant, to the change.

8.   *More Work*

One reasonable source of resistance to change is that change is simply *more work*. The effort it takes to manage things under routine circumstances needs to be multiplied when things are changing. Change requires more energy, more time, and greater mental preoccupation.

Members of project teams creating innovation put in a great deal of overtime on their own, because of the demands--and the lure--of creating something new. During the breakup of the Bell System, many managers worked 60 or 70 hour weeks during the process, not seeing their families, simply because of the work involved in moving such a large system from one state to another. And the pattern is repeated in corporation after corporation.

Change does require above-and-beyond effort. It cannot be done automatically, it cannot be done without extra effort, and it takes time. There is ample reason to resist change, if people do not want to put in the effort. They need support and compensation for the extra work of change in order to move from resistance to commitment.

Managers have options for providing that support. They can make sure that families are informed and understanding about the period of extra effort. They can make sure that people are given credit for the effort they are putting in and rewarded for the fact that they are working harder than ever before--rewards ranging from cash bonuses to special trips or celebrations. They can recognize that the extra effort is voluntary and not take it for granted, but thank people by providing recognition, as well as the additional support or facilities or comfort they need. While an employee is working harder, it certainly helps to know that your boss is acknowledging that extra effort and time.

9. *Past Resentments*

The ninth reason people resist change in negative, but it is a reality of organizational life--those cobwebs of the past that get in the way of the future. Anyone who has ever had a gripe against the organization is likely to resist the organization telling them that they now have to do something new.

The conspiracy of silence, that uneasy truce possible as long as everything remains the same and people can avoid confrontations, is broken when you ask for change. Unresolved grievances from the past rise up to entangle and hamper the change effort. One new plant manager at Honeywell was surprised by resistance to a quality-of-work-life program, which he though the workers would like because of the direct benefits to them. Then he discovered that the workers were still angry at management for failing to get them a quiet air-conditioning system despite years of complaints about summer noise levels in the factory. Until he listened to them and responded to their grievance, he could not get their commitment to his change plans.

Sweeping away the cobwebs of the past is sometimes a necessity for overcoming resistance to change. As long as they remain aggrieved, people will not want to go along with something *we* want. Going forward can thus mean first going back--listening to past resentments and repairing past rifts.

10. *Sometimes The Threat Is Real*

The last reason people resist change, is, in many ways, the most reasonable of all: *Sometimes the threat posed by the change is a real one.*

Sometimes a change does create winners and losers. Sometimes people do lose status, clout, or comfort because of the change. It would be naive to imagine otherwise. In fact, managing change well means recognizing its political realities.

The important thing here is to avoid pretense and false promises. If some people *are* going to lose something, they should hear about it early, rather than worrying about it constantly and infecting others with their anxiety or antagonism. And if some people are going to be let go or moved elsewhere, it is more humane to do it fast.

We all know the relief that people feel, even people who are being told the worst, at finally knowing that the thing they have feared is true. Now they can go ahead and plan their life. Thus, if some people are threatened by change because of the realities of their situations, managers should not pretend this is not so. Instead, they should make a clean break or a clean cut--as the first step in change, rather than leaving it to the end.

Of course, we all lose something in change, even the winners. Even those of us who are exhilarated about the opportunity it represents, or who are choosing to participate in a new era that we think is going to be better for our careers, more productive and technologically exciting, as many of the changes in American corporations promise to be.

Change is never entirely negative; it is also a tremendous opportunity. But even in that opportunity there is some small loss. It can be a loss of the past, a loss of routines, comforts, and traditions that were important, maybe a loss of relationships that became very close over time. Things will not, in fact, be the same any more.

Thus, we all need a chance to let go of the past, to "mourn" it. Rituals of parting help us say goodbye to the people we have been close to, rather than just letting those relationships slip away. "Memorial services," "eulogies," or events to honor the past help us let go. Unfortunately, those kind of ceremonies and rituals are not legitimate in some companies. Instead, people are in one state, and the next day they have to move to another state without any acknowledgment of the loss that is involved. But things like goodbye parties or file-burning ceremonies or tacking up the company's history on bulletin boards are not just frills or luxuries; they are rituals that make it easier for people to move into the future because their loss is acknowledged and dealt with.

Resistance to change is not irrational; it stems from good and understandable concerns. Managers who can analyze the sources of resistance are in the best position to invent the solution to it--and to manage change smoothly and effectively.

There may be no skills more important for the challenging times ahead.

Building Commitment To Change

- Allow room for participation in the planning of the change.
- Leave choices within the overall decision to change.
- Provide a clear picture of the change, a "vision" with details about the new state.
- Share information about change plans to the fullest extent possible.
- Divide a big change into more manageable and familiar steps; let people take a small step first.
- Minimize surprises; give people advance warning about new requirements.
- Allow for digestion of change requests--a chance to become accustomed to the idea of change before making a commitment.
- Repeatedly demonstrate your own commitment to the change.
- Make standards and requirements clear--tell exactly what is expected of people in the change.
- Offer positive reinforcement for competence; let people know they can do it.
- Look for and reward pioneers, innovators, and early successes to serve as models.
- Help people find or feel compensated for the extra time and energy change requires.

246

- Avoid creating obvious "losers" from the change. (But if there are some, be honest with them--early on.)
- Allow expressions of nostalgia and grief for the past--then create excitement about the future.

"CONFLICT MANAGEMENT" AND "CONFLICT RESOLUTION" ARE NOT SYNONYMOUS TERMS

Steven P. Robbins

The early evidence suggests that the 1970s may be remembered in the annals of management history as the decade that conflict management came to the forefront as a major interest of both practicing managers and academic researchers. And, if a recent study of middle- and top-level executives by the American Management Association can be generalized from, managers spend approximately 20 percent of their time dealing with conflict.[1] This would suggest that the recent interest in conflict management is well founded.

Of course, the study of organization conflict is not new. Economists, psychologists, sociologists, and political scientists have been researching the subject for many decades. Only in recent years, however, have we begun to study conflict from a management perspective, attempting to take the theoretical approaches developed by social scientists and modifying them to give some practical value to managers.

I would like to believe that we have come a long way since the days when conflict was believed to be universally destructive. Unfortunately, with the exception of some lip service given in recent years to the value of conflict in organizations, both practicing managers and management scholars continue to treat "conflict management" and "conflict resolution" as synonymous. In the following pages I will argue that not only are there some positive consequences to be gained from conflict, but also that (1) organizations require functional conflict if they are to survive; (2) there will be situations in which conflict levels are too low; and (3) as a result, we should not ignore the other side of the conflict management coin-- conflict stimulation! In developing this argument, I will focus on the value of conflict, differentiate between functional and dysfunctional conflicts, suggest some guidelines on when and how to stimulate conflict, and conclude by proposing the importance of viewing conflict management from a contingency perspective.

What Is Conflict?

Conflict is defined here as any kind of opposition or antagonistic interaction between two or more parties. It can be conceptualized as existing along a continuous range. At one extreme, there is no conflict. At the other extreme is conflict's highest state, described behaviorally as the act of destroying or annihilating the opposing party. All intensities of interpersonal, intragroup and intergroup conflicts would fall somewhere along this continuum. Inherent in this definition is the requirement that conflict must be perceived by the involved parties. In other words, if there is opposition but the parties fail to perceive it, then it does not exist. Similarly, if a conflict is perceived, it exists whether or not that perception is accurate.

FIGURE 1
Conflict Philosophies and Managerial Actions

Philosophy	States	Managerial Actions
Traditionalist	A=D, where D=0	Do nothing
	A>D, where D=0	Resolve conflict
Behavioralist	A=D, where D≥0	Do nothing
	A>D, where D≥0	Resolve conflict
Interactionist	A=D, where D>0	Do nothing
	A>D, where D>0	Resolve conflict
	A<D, where D>0	Stimulate conflict

Key: A = actual level of conflict; D = desired level of conflict.

Transitions in Conflict Thought

The development of conflict thought, as professed by academics, has gone through three distinct stages. I have arbitrarily labeled the stages or philosophical views as traditional, behavioral, and interactionist.[2]

The prescription of the early management theories, the traditionalists, toward conflict was simple. It should be eliminated. All conflicts were seen as destructive and it was management's role to rid the organization of them. This philosophy dominated during the nineteenth century and continued to the middle 1940s.

The traditional view was replaced in the late 1940s and early 1950s with a behavioral approach. Those who studied organizations began to recognize that all organizations, by their very nature, had built-in conflicts. Since conflict was inevitable, the behavioralists prescribed "acceptance" of conflict. They rationalized its existence. However, as with the traditionalists, the behavioralist approach to managing conflict was to resolve it.

If we look at the behavior of managers, it seems clear that the traditional philosophy is still the most prevalent in organizations. We live in a society that has been built upon anticonflict values. Since our earliest years we have been indoctrinated in the belief that it was important to get along with others and to avoid conflict. Parents in the home, teachers and administrators in school, teachings of the church, and authority figures in social groups all have historically reinforced the belief that disagreement bred discontent, which acted to dissolve common ties and could eventually lead to destruction of the system. Certainly we should not be surprised to find that children raised to view all conflict as destructive would mature into adult managers who would maintain and encourage the same values. In addition, the senior managers in most organizations praise and reward managers who maintain peace, harmony, and tranquility in their units, while disequilibrium, confrontation, and dissatisfaction are appraised negatively. Given that managers seek to "look good" on the criteria by which they are evaluated, and since the absence of conflict is frequently used at evaluation time as a proxy for managerial effectiveness, it should not be surprising to find that most managers are concerned with eliminating or suppressing *all* conflicts.

FIGURE 2
Conflict-Survival Model

Conflict ----> Change ----> Adaptation ----> Survival

Source: Stephen P. Robbins, Managing Organizational Conflict: A Nontraditional Approach (Englewood Cliffs, N.J.: Prentice-Hall, 1974), p. 20.

Practitioners are not alone in their enamoration with the traditional philosophy. Most current academics, in spite of their explicit recognition that conflict can have positive value, direct their efforts singularly to the topic of conflict resolution.[3]

It only seems natural that if conflict truly has value to an organization, and I will present evidence in the next section to support this position, then at least theoretically there is the possibility that conflict levels could be too low. If the desired level of conflict is something greater than zero, there are *three* possible outcomes: actual level of conflict equals the desired level; actual is greater than desired; and *actual is less than desired*. As Figure 1 demonstrates, this third state has been completely overlooked by both the traditionalists and behavioralists. I argued several years ago that there is a need for a third philosophy--the interactionist, which:

1.   recognizes the absolute necessity of functional conflict;
2.   explicitly encourages functional opposition;
3.   defines conflict management to include stimulation as well as resolution techniques;
4.   considers the management of conflict as a major responsibility of all managers.[4]

The Value of Conflict

The interactionist philosophy does not propose that *all* conflicts are good for an organization. Excessive levels of conflict can and do hinder organizational effectiveness. It shows itself in reduced job satisfaction by employees, increased absence and turnover rates, and eventually in lower productivity. What the interactionist approach says is that managers should continue to resolve those conflicts that hinder the organization, but stimulate conflict intensity when the level is below that which is necessary to maintain a responsive and innovative unit. Without some level of constructive conflict, an organization's survival will be in jeopardy. Survival can result only when an organization is able to adapt to constant changes in the environment. Adaptation is possible only through change, and change is stimulated by conflict. As Figure 2 demonstrates, conflict stimulates change, which brings about adaptation, and only through adapting can the organization survive.

The model shown in Figure 2 acknowledges that change develops from dissatisfaction, from a desire for improvement, and from creative development of alternatives. In other words, changes do not just happen; they are inspired by conflict. Conflict is the catalyst of change. If we do not adapt our products and services to the changing needs of our customers, actions of our competitors, and new technological developments, our organization will become sick and eventually die. Is it not possible that more organizations fail because of too little conflict, rather than too much?

Without change, no organization can survive, and conflict spurs change. Opposition to others' ideas, dissatisfaction with the status quo, concern about doing things better, and the desire to improve inadequacies are all seeds of change. Therefore, the factor that differentiates the interactionist philosophy most from its predecessors is the belief that just as the level of conflict may be too high, requiring resolution, it may also be too low and in need of stimulation.

There is a growing body of literature that supports my contention that organizations that have levels of conflict above zero are more effective; that is, functional levels of conflict are conducive to innovation and higher quality decisions. For example, a review of the relationship between bureaucracy and innovation found that conflict encourages innovative solutions.[5] This relationship was more recently confirmed in a comparison of six major decisions during the administrations of four U.S. presidents.[6] The comparison demonstrated that conformity among presidential advisers was related to poor decisions, while an atmosphere of constructive conflict and critical thinking surrounded the well-developed decisions.

The bankruptcy of the Penn Central Railroad has been generally attributed to mismanagement and a failure of the company's board of directors to question actions taken by management.[7] The board was composed of outside directors who met monthly to oversee the railroad's operations. Few questioned the decisions made by the operating management, though there was evidence that several board members were uncomfortable with many major decisions made by the management. Apathy and a desire to avoid conflict allowed poor decisions to stand unquestioned. It can only be postulated how differently things might have turned out for the Penn Central had it had an inquiring board which demanded that the company's management discuss and justify key decisions.

In addition to better and more innovative decisions in situations where there is some conflict, there is evidence that indicates that conflict can be positively related to productivity. It was demonstrated that among established groups, performance tended to improve more when there was conflict among members than when there was fairly close agreement.[8] The investigators observed that when groups analyzed decisions that had been made by the individual members of that group, the average group improvement among the high-conflict groups was 73 percent greater than that of those groups characterized by low-conflict conditions.

Similarly, an investigation of twenty-two teams of systems analysts, in which the researcher sought to assess the relationship between interpersonal compatibility and productivity, achieved results consistent with the previous studies.[9] The findings strongly suggested that the more incompatible groups were likely to be more productive.

Functional Versus Dysfunctional Conflicts

It is one thing to argue that conflict can be valuable for an organization, but how does one tell if a conflict is good or bad? What differentiates functional and dysfunctional conflicts?

The belief in the value of conflict cannot be interpreted in blanket fashion. I do not and cannot advocate all types of intensities of conflict. Some support the goals of the organization and improve performance; these are functional, constructive forms of conflict. They benefit or support the main purposes of the organization. Additionally, there are those types of conflict that hinder organizational performance; these are dysfunctional or destructive forms. They are undesirable and the manager should seek their eradication.

The demarcation between functional and dysfunctional is neither clear nor precise. No level of conflict can be adopted at face value as acceptable or unacceptable. The level that creates healthy and positive involvement towards one group's goals may, in another group or in the same group at another time, be highly dysfunctional, requiring immediate conciliatory attention by the manager.

It is important to note that my differentiation between functional and dysfunctional is in terms of organizational performance. This appears, for example, to be in contrast to Professor Filley's emphases. Filley appears to consider the welfare of the individual ahead of the organization; and here lies an important value difference between my view and several other academics who would agree with Filley. I believe that organizations exist to attain a set of goals which are developed and validated by senior management. It is my position that it is the impact that conflict has on the organization, not the individual, that defines functionality.

Conflict's impacts on the individual and the organization are, of course, not mutually exclusive. The ways in which individuals perceive a conflict may have an important impact on its effect on the organization. However, this need not be the case and when it is not, the relevant issue is the effect on the organization. This position is defended on the belief that organizations exist primarily to achieve goals, not to placate individual members. As a result, in my definitional form, functional or dysfunctional is determined by the conflict's impact on the organization, not on any individual or small group of individuals. Importantly, from a definitional standpoint, it is irrelevant how the participants perceive the conflict. The participants may perceive an action as dysfunctional, in that the outcome is personally dissatisfying to them. However, it would be functional within my framework if it furthers the objectives of the organization.

When Do You Stimulate Conflict?

Are there any signals that the practicing manager can look for to suggest that conflict levels may be too low? The answer to this question is a qualified "yes." While there is no definitive method for universally assessing the need for more conflict, affirmative answers to one or more of the following questions suggests

there may be a need for conflict simulation:[10]
1. Are you surrounded by "yes" men"?
2. Are subordinates afraid to admit ignorance and uncertainties to you?
3. Is there so much concentration by decision makers on reaching a compromise that they may lose sight of values, long-term objectives, or the company welfare?
4. Do managers believe that it is in their best interest to maintain the impression of peace and cooperation in their unit, regardless of the price?
5. Is there an excessive concern by decision makers in not hurting the feelings of others?
6. Do managers believe that popularity is more important for the obtaining of organizational rewards than competence and high performance?
7. Are managers unduly enamored with obtaining consensus for their decisions?
8. Do employees show unusually high resistance to change?
9. Is there a lack of new ideas forthcoming?
10. Is there an unusually low level of employee turnover?

How Do You Stimulate Conflict?

Our knowledge of stimulation techniques is primitive relative to our understanding of methods for resolving conflicts. Table 1 offers some ideas for increasing conflict between individuals and between groups; however, I make no claim that these suggestions comprehensively cover the available stimulation techniques. I have organized my suggestions into three categories--methods that manipulate the communication channel, those that alter the structure, and techniques that deal with modifying value and personality variables.

Two particularly strong *communication* stimulators are repression of information and the communication of ambiguous or threatening information. Each is rapidly implemented and easily controlled. By holding back data we can quickly stimulate greater conflict. It can work as an excellent fine-tuning device because the decision on the data repressed will influence the degree of increased hostility. Most important, it has an easily available escape valve should the intensity become too great and thus dysfunctional. A release of information should immediately initiate a reduction in conflict intensity.

Ambiguous information is very similar to repression. Ambiguity initiates discord, but the release of further information that can clarify the vague data will immediately set in action resolving forces. Threatening communications can successfully stimulate conflict as rapidly as any of the techniques that we will discuss. When an individual's or group's survival is at stake, especially under win-lose criteria, conflict will rapidly accelerate. In contrast to ambiguity or repression, threatening information does not offer the easy safety valve. Perception is the key. When individuals are threatened, the actual removal of the threat may not reduce hostility. If one perceives an action to be threatening, even though it no longer is he will behave as if he is truly threatened. Therefore, the manager who uses threatening communications to increase conflict must recognize that should intensity become too great, not only will the threat need to be rescinded but the perception that the threat still exists must also be removed.

Finally, initiating changes in channels or overloading the channel with

TABLE 1
Stimulation Techniques

Manipulate communication channel
- -- Deviate messages from traditional channels
- -- Repress information
- -- Transmit too much information
- -- Transmit ambiguous or threatening information

Alter the organization's structure (redefine jobs, alter tasks, reform units or activities)
- -- Increase a unit's size
- -- Increase specialization and standardization
- -- Add, delete or transfer organizational members
- -- Increase interdependence between units

Alter personal behavior factors
- -- Change personality characteristics of leader
- -- Create role conflict
- -- Develop role incongruence

information offers opportunities for stimulating conflict. Deviating communication from previous formal channels and utilization of the informal grapevine are both effective, the latter being a frequently used method for disseminating threatening information. Through the transmission of too much information, channels can be overloaded, resulting in confusion and accelerated conflict levels. One weakness in utilizing channel overload would be the possibility of organizational members selectively filtering the information. The full impact may be reduced as individuals only absorb facts they view as relevant, receiving only the data they want to hear.

Table 1 indicates four methods for stimulating conflict that relate to altering variables within or about the *structure*: size, bureaucratic qualities, position changes, and interdependence.

By increasing the number of organizational entities, the total organization becomes more complex and opposition is stimulated. Such actions are costly; therefore the decision to increase size solely to spur conflict would probably occur only when conflict intensity had reached a long impasse at an obviously inadequately low level. As the size of the organization expands, bureaucratic tendencies will be reinforced. Additionally, increased specialization will stimulate conflict intensity. Transferring into a unit a "devil's advocate," who seeks to challenge the traditional views of others, would be included here. Additionally, efforts to infuse units with young individuals and to increase turnover should intensify conflict.

Finally, structural conflict can be accelerated by increasing the interdependency between individuals or organizational units. By organizing so as to create interpersonal or interunit dependency, especially one-way dependency, the manager will stimulate conflict.

The third area for stimulating conflict is *personal behavior factors*. Generally, these techniques lack the potency of methods previously mentioned. For example, by placing into leadership positions individuals who possess personality characteristics of high authoritarianism, dogmatism, and low self-esteem, conflict should be stimulated between themselves and their followers.

When a group member finds the positional role behavior expected of him disagreeable, it can stimulate intraunit conflict. Also, stimulation will develop if members perceive a significant disparity between the status they discern in their position and the status others attribute to it.

The Obvious Solution: A Contingency Approach

Given that conflict management is not merely the application of conflict resolution methods, it becomes obvious that the old principle, "If there is conflict, it must be resolved," is no longer valid. Whether you engage in resolving or stimulating activities depends on the situation. The actual method chosen to resolve or stimulate conflict must also be appropriate to the situation. As a result, conflict management requires a contingency approach.

The development of a contingency model is a long and complex process.[11] It must consider the various sources of conflict and then assess the advantages and disadvantages of each source. It is not my purpose in this article to elaborate on methods for resolving conflict, since Professor Filley covers this in his article. For brevity, I have summarized the major resolution techniques and my assessment of their individual strengths and weaknesses in Table 2. However, let me utilize the contingency approach to dramatize why, even for the resolution of conflict, there is no panacea--no technique that is appropriate in *all* instances. Specifically, I will show that even a resolution technique like problem solving, which has received more than its fair share of favorable press, has very clear and specific limitations.

The sources of conflict can be condensed into three general categories: communication, structure, and personal behavior factors. The communicative source represents those disputes arising from semantic difficulties, misunderstandings, and noise in the the communication channels. Structural conflict refers to opposition that develops from organizationally imposed roles and to barriers developed by management in their attempt to differentiate and coordinate activities. Personal behavior factors include individual idiosyncrasies and differing personal value systems.

If you want to reduce a conflict, basically you have to determine its source and then ascertain which technique(s) in Table 2 would be most effective. Professor Filley, for example, argues that problem solving may be underutilized in organizations. I agree that the use of problem solving tends to be low, but not because managers do not understand it. I believe its use is low because it has limited applications in organizations. Problem solving is generally most appropriate with communicative conflicts, and in complex organizations these are not the major sources of conflicts, in spite of the fact that managers express most interest in poor communication as a source of conflict.[12]

I would also agree with Professor Filley that there are positive consequences from problem solving that seem sufficiently documented to emphasize its use. Where conflicts have arisen as a result of ambiguity, distortion, the inadequate passage of information, or channel overflow, problem solving is a natural remedy. The difference between Professor Filley and myself probably lies in the percent of situations that require conflict resolution efforts, and that meet the requirements

Table 2. Resolution Techniques

Technique	Brief Definition	Strengths	Weaknesses
Problem-solving (also known as confrontations or collaboration)	Seeks resolution through face-to-face confrontation of the conflicting parties. Parties seek mutual problem definition, assessment, and solution.	Effective with conflicts stemming from semantic misunderstandings. Brings doubts and misperceptions to surface.	Can be time-consuming. Inappropriate for most noncommunicative conflicts, especially those based on different value systems.
Superordinate Goals	Common goals that two or more conflicting parties each desire and cannot be reached without cooperation of those involved. Goals must be highly valued, unattainable without the help of all parties involved in the conflict, and commonly sought.	When used cumulatively and reinforced, develops "peacemaking" potential, emphasizing interdependency and cooperation.	Difficult to devise.
Expansion of Resources	Make more of the scarce resource available.	Each conflicting party can be victorious.	Resources rarely exist in such quantities as to be easily expanded.
Avoidance	Includes withdrawal and suppression.	Easy to do. Natural reaction to conflict.	No effective resolution. Conflict not eliminated. Temporary.
Smoothing	Play down differences while emphasizing common interests.	All conflict situations have points of commonality within them. Cooperative efforts are reinforced.	Differences are not confronted and remain under the surface. Temporary.
Compromise	Each party is required to give up something of value. Includes external or third party interventions, negotiation, and voting.	No clear loser. Consistent with democratic values.	No clear winner. Power-oriented--influenced heavily by relative strength of parties. Temporary.
Authoritative Command	Solution imposed from a superior, holding formal positional authority.	Very effective in organizations since members recognize and accept authority of superiors.	Cause of conflict is not treated. Does not necessarily bring agreement. Temporary.
Altering the Human Variable	Changing the attitudes and behavior of one or more of the conflicting parties. Includes use of education, sensitivity and awareness training, and human relations training.	Results can be substantial and permanent. Has potential to alleviate the source of conflict.	Most difficult to achieve. Slow and costly.
Altering Structural Variables	Change structural variables. Includes transferring and exchanging, group members, creating coordinating positions, developing an appeals system, and expanding the group or organization's boundaries.	Can be permanent. Usually within the authority of a manager.	Often expensive. Forces organization to be designed for specific individuals and thus requires continual adjustment as people join or leave the organization.

255

for successful problem solving. While I have no empirical data to support this point, observation leads me to conclude that probably less than 10 percent of all situations where conflict levels are too high can be effectively resolved through collaboration. Problem solving should, therefore, be viewed for what it is--a single tool in the manager's tool chest. With communicative conflicts, problem solving is generally the preferred method. On the other hand, there are more effective methods for dealing with the resolution of structural and personal behavior conflicts.

For example, value differences are a major source of conflict in organizations, yet individuals rarely change their values through collaborative methods. A dispute over the merits of racial integration between two individuals with conflicting value systems demonstrates this point.

It would be naive to assume that Mr. Jones, raised to believe blacks and whites are unquestionably equal, and Mr. Smith, raised in an environment that fostered the belief in the inequality of blacks and whites, can resolve their differences through problem solving. Such an approach can get to the root of the conflict, which unfortunately in this case, is two *incompatible* value systems. The attempt to reduce differences through problem solving will probably result in Mr. Jones's recognition that Mr. Smith is a "prejudiced bigot" and Mr. Smith's belief that Mr. Jones is "an ignorant liberal who doesn't realize that the good Lord meant that they be separated." To use problem solving where conflicts are rooted in value differences only widens the differences and entrenches each of the participants deeper into his position--for all intents and purposes probably increasing, and certainly not lessening, the level of conflict. Conflicts based on value differences tend to be most pragmatically resolved by falling back on authoritative command.

The manager who uses a contingency approach brings to the job a tool kit holding, a full complement of resolution and stimulation techniques. The potential for success is significantly increased when one has the right tool for the right job.

References

[1] K.W. Thomas and W.H. Schmidt, "A Survey of Managerial Interests With Respect to Conflict," Academy of Management Journal (June 1976), pp. 315-318.

[2] S.P. Robbins, Managing Organizational Conflict: A Nontraditional Approach (Englewood Cliffs, N.J.: Prentice-Hall, 1974), p. 12.

[3] See, for example: P.A. Renwick, "Impact of Topic and Source of Disagreement on Conflict Management," Organizational Behavior and Human Performance (December 1975), pp. 416-425; T.T. Herbert, Dimensions of Organizational Behavior (New York: Macmillan, 1976), pp. 354-360; and J.D. Hunger and L.W. Stern, "An Assessment of the Functionality of the Superordinate Goal in Reducing Conflict," Academy of Management Journal (December 1976), pp. 591-605.

[4] Robbins, op. cit., pp. 13-14.

[5] V.A. Thompson, "Bureaucracy and Innovation," Administrative Science Quarterly (1965), pp. 1-20.

[6] I.L. Janis, Victims of Groupthink (Boston: Houghton Mifflin, 1972).

[7] P. Binzen and J.R. Daughen, Wreck of the Penn Central (Boston: Little, Brown & Co., 1971).

[8] J. Hall and M.S. Williams, "A Comparison of Decision-Making Performances in Established and Ad Hoc Groups," Journal of Personality and Social Psychology (February 1966), p. 217.

[9] R.E. Hill, "Interpersonal Compatibility and Work Group Performance Among Systems Analysts: An Empirical Study," Proceedings of the 17th Annual Midwest Academy of Management Conference (Kent, Ohio: April, 1974), pp. 97-110.

[10] Several of these questions were adapted from the scoring table of the "Thomas-Kilmann Conflict MODE Instrument," by K. Thomas and R.H. Kilmann (Tuxedo, N.Y.: XICOM, 1974).

[11] For example, in S.P. Robbins, <u>Managing Organizational Conflict</u>, it is argued that resolution and stimulation techniques should be contingent on the source of the conflict. The relationship of the resolution techniques used to the topics and sources of conflict was considered by Renwick in "Impact of Topic and Source of Disagreement on Conflict Management," op. cit.

[12] Thomas and Schmidt, op. cit.

THE STRESS OF EXCELLENCE

Siegfried Streufert

A new profile of the successful corporate leader seems to be emerging that is far deeper and psychologically subtler than any proposed in the past. As described in the best-selling book, *In Search of Excellence*, the effective leader is master of apparently contradictory multiple tasks. For example, the authors, Thomas J. Peters and Robert H. Waterman, Jr., describe such a person as capable of patient coalition building, of altering agendas so that new priorities get enough attention, of encouraging cabals that will shake up the organization. According to them, excellence in leadership means listening carefully much of the time, frequently speaking with the encouragement, and reinforcing words with believable action. On the one hand, it means being tough when necessary, the occasional use of naked power; on the other, it requires, as Henry Kissinger once put it, the "subtle accumulation of nuances, a hundred things done a little better."

A few more details might be added to fill in this portrait. Leadership excellence means strategic planning but not rigid overplanning. It implies the capacity to maintain a flow of information that is ample for decision-making but not overwhelming. It means being able to quickly grasp relationships among rapidly flowing events, both within the corporation and outside, that will affect the organization's long-term goals.

We psychologists say that such a person is cognitively complex. The startling news is that such a person's very competence may lead to illness: There is a growing amount of evidence that an executive with this style of decision-making faces a greater risk than others of heart attacks and other circulatory diseases.

In past decades, poor executive performance and ill health have often been blamed on pressures in the office environment, viewed as entirely outside the individual. True, some aspects of life in the executive suite can seriously affect health and performance. In general, however, the work world of the executive is not particularly unhealthy, and much of the stress the executive feels is not imposed by the office.

It is now generally agreed that the most disastrous stress effects grow out of the minds and personalities of the executives themselves: from the way they perceive their environment and process information, from their characteristic manner of dealing with others, and from their style of decision-making.

Much has been written about the highly competitive executive who has a strong sense of time-urgency and often seems hostile and driven. The Type-A

Siegfried Streufert, "The Stress of Excellence," <u>Across the Board</u>, a publication of The Conference Board, October 1983, Vol. 20, pp. 8-16.

behavioral style, discovered by Drs. Ray Rosenman and Meyer Friedman of Stanford, is now a well-known risk for heart disease. What recent studies show, however, is that such a person is not necessarily a good performer, and that such a style is not essential to the making of a successful corporate manager.

While the Type-A corporate manager is not at all aided by his or her particular style, cognitively complex executives will find that their specific style is a necessary ingredient for success. It is not at all surprising that cognitive complexity aids in success while Type A does not. The two styles are very different than the relaxed Type B. The only thing common between the two behavioral styles appears to be their effect on health: both of them can be precursors of heart disease. As such, both of them are a liability, yet complexity is also an asset. The cognitively complex executive whose decision-making style is often described as "more multidimensional" is a much better planner and, particularly at higher executive levels, a more successful manager.

What is the evidence that these executives are subject to an increased risk of heart disease? And, if they are, what does this mean to the corporation? Will effective leadership have to be compromised for the sake of preserving executive health? Or are there ways of distributing work loads to minimize the risk?

Before addressing these questions, we need to review how behavioral scientists' understanding of stress has changed.

What We Now Know About Stress

Twenty years ago, even after the publication of Hans Selye's seminal work on stress, we were still primarily guessing about its effects on the human organism and on behavior. Initially, we tended to think of stress as something which comes from outside of the person. Selye proposed that threatening forces in the environment triggered certain physiological mechanisms that caused the subjective feeling of stress. Calamitous events, serious threats to our well-being, and even daily hassles were seen to other researchers as setting off negative experiences of stress. Modern stress researchers call those external threats "stressors," whether they arise from events, from persons, or from inanimate objects.

As a person perceives one or more stressors, "out there," his or her body releases a family of biochemicals called catecholamines (for example, epinephrine and norepinephrine) into the bloodstream. These chemicals are designed to help, by getting us ready for fight or flight--a response to a stressor that is built into the genes. The presence of these catecholamines prepares us to engage in greater exertion: to attack or flee from the source of our frustration or fear. But it is of little use to the modern executive who may, for example, have to cope with a demanding and aggressive boss: Neither hitting the boss nor running away, after all, is very appropriate. Thus, the executive may have to do nothing, to keep his mouth shut and restrain his anger--in which case he suffers the unfortunate physiological consequences. For the physiological exertion of fight or flight has the effect of reducing the circulating catecholamines.

When catecholamines are not removed from the bloodstream, serious physiological damage may occur. A number of researchers, observing lab animals in some studies and humans in others, have found that blood-platelet aggregation, which leads to clots in vital coronary arteries, results from the presence of excessive amounts of catecholamines in the blood. Cardiologist Robert Eliot of the

University of Nebraska reported that catecholamines are responsible for contraction bands in the cardiac muscle that follow severe stress and leave the heart unable to function. Jacob Haft, Director of Cardiology at St. Michael's Medical Center in Newark, New Jersey, demonstrated that chronic elevations in circulating catecholamines may cause lesions in blood vessels of the heart. In other words, excessive or chronically circulating catecholamines can lead to heart disease and death.

Stress and Work Load

Must every exposure to potential stressors in the environment result in physiological strain (including serious elevation of catecholamine levels) and in psychological stress? Certainly not. Where threatening stressors occur as unpredictable and uncontrollable events, stress is just about unavoidable and damaging. In most cases, however, we will marshal our resources to remove the stressor or to cope with it. If we view the stressor as something with which we *can* cope, then we may not experience stress or strain. Quite the contrary, the stressor may appear as a welcome challenge.

However, sometimes challenges occur in rather massive and uncontrollable doses, resulting in a serious overload. In the 1970s, Swedish scientists at the University of Stockholm initiated an extensive research program which demonstrated that rapidly paced information flow and rapidly paced work is one kind of stressor that sharply increases catecholamines in the bloodstream. Data obtained by my own research group agree. We placed executives in complex simulations where they made decisions partly in response to incoming information. In some cases the simulation content was carefully matched to their corporate environment, in others the tasks were less similar to their day-today activities. All of the simulations were highly involving.

The results were strikingly similar no matter what the task, the characteristics of the executives, their nationality, or ethnic origins. Work loads above a certain level increased blood pressure and heart rate considerably. The same overload produced sharp decrements in performance on the more complex tasks. The subjects used strategy less frequently, took into account fewer elements of the environment, and their responses to information typically reflected short-term, isolated and simplistic solutions. However, the quality difference between the performance of more-multidimensional (cognitively complex) and less-multidimensional subjects was maintained until overload reached very extreme levels. Nonetheless, decreases in, for example, strategic thinking occurred for both groups with less-multidimensional persons showing complete absence of strategy, even when overload reached only moderately high levels.

Styles of Executive Decision-Making

The charts show the sequence of decisions made by two executives in a simulation of international-business situations. The experiment lasted for several hours at Pennsylvania State University, College of Medicine.

The two received information--in written form and via telephone, computer and videotape--about investments abroad, raw materials, currency values, the stability of foreign governments, and the like. They were instructed to make the

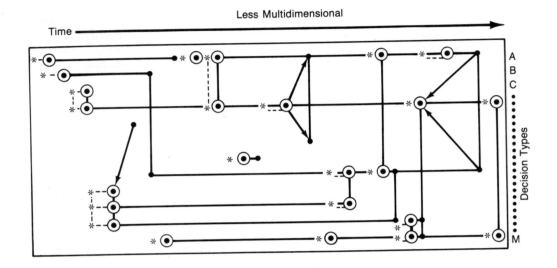

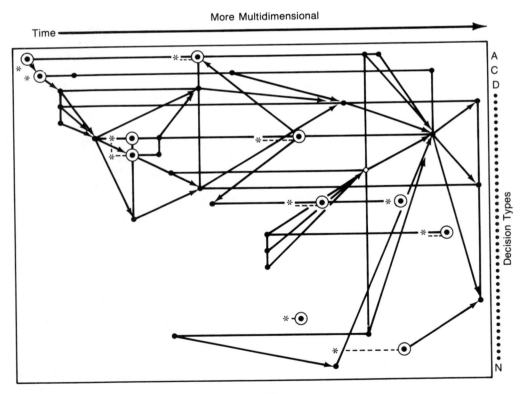

best decisions possible for their companies (but were not given specific goals, such as profit maximization), and could respond through any of the media available to them.

On each chart, various categories of decisions are listed along the vertical axis in the series A, B, C, etc. Time is plotted along the horizontal axis. The asterisks show points at which information was received, and the double circles represent decisions made in response to it. The single circles show decisions made without any such input.

Horizontal lines connect decisions of the same type. diagonal lines with arrows pointing forward connect earlier decisions that set the stage for planned later ones. Diagonal lines pointing backward indicate a later decision that makes use of the outcome of a previous decision, though it had not been planned that way.

The difference between the two executives who made the decisions shown here are readily apparent. The person in the lower chart planned extensively, was able to relate decisions to one another, and direct them toward achieving the goal-- the most crucial decision--near the end of the time sequence (the single circle with all the arrows pointing toward it). His performance was thus more multidimensional. In contrast, the executive whose decisions are represented in the upper chart tended to deal with information item-by-item and to establish few connections. His style was much less multidimensional.

Peer ratings of the two executives for on-the-job performance confirmed that the one in the lower chart was a much better planner and, generally, a more competent decision-maker than his counterpart. Recent studies suggest that the kind of executive who produced the second chart is much more susceptible to health-endangering stress.

The Swedish data as well as our own point to yet another interesting phenomenon: The same kind of physiological strain and a similar drop in some kinds of performance occur when work is understimulating and boring. In other words, both underload and overload are stressful. There is an *optimal* work load and level of information flow that is neither too high nor too low. That optimal level may well reflect limits on the processing capacity of the human brain: it is quite similar for various complex tasks, for different personalities and for persons from different cultures.

Understanding our limitations and the levels of work that produce optimal performance can be of considerable importance if we wish to reduce stress and improve performance. Where possible, that knowledge can aid us in designing better executive work environments. But other factors beyond work load can frequently cause stress--for example ambiguities or conflicts in responsibilities or a feeling of lack of control over one's own actions.

Too little control can lead to what psychologist Martin Seligman has termed "learned helplessness," associated with serious loss of self-confidence, performance decrements, and potential health problems. On the other hand, high levels of control can function as stress reducers. In a recent network television appearance, a group of CEOs were asked about their stress experiences. To the interviewer's surprise, these executives reported feeling very little stress: They clearly indicated that responsibility is not a stressor. As CEOs, these persons hardly suffered from lack of control.

261

Yet, even if we created optimal-load environments, even if we made sure that conflict and ambiguity were not part of the executive's experience, and even if we provided a sufficient level of control, our problem with executive health and performance would not yet be solved. We would still have to deal with the stress that the executive *personally* generates through his or her own style of dealing with environmental pressures.

We know that some persons cope well with stressors while others do not. Wherein lies the difference? Scientists have increasingly recognized that *psychological* variables are involved in stress and strain reactions. People don't respond only at the very moment when a stressor occurs: They anticipate a stressor, they react to it, and they continue to respond long after it is gone. All these reactions may be much more severe than the stressor would appear to justify. In many cases people respond to anticipated stressors that never happen. (A good example is Danny Thomas's famous story of a man with a flat tire who is tramping the streets in a rainstorm searching for a house where he can borrow a jack at 3 a.m. He gets madder and madder as he anticipates the anger of the person he will have to get out of bed. By the time he rings a doorbell, he is ready to punch whomever answers in the nose and tells the sleepy resident who comes to the door, "Keep your damn jack.") All in all, psychological stress may be much more severe and protracted that stress that occurs as a result of some real threatening event.

Of course, people differ in their overreaction to real stressors and in their reactions to imagined stressors. Many of these differences are evident in the *styles* of information processing that people develop over time. These styles have a major impact on how we deal with the environment, on what we perceive as stressful, on how healthy we are, and on how well we do our jobs. And most significant, these styles can have a considerable influence on how long we will live.

The Type-A Style

The psychological tendencies of the Type-A behavioral style emerge when the person is challenged by someone else or by his or her own thoughts. The jogger who has to finish another half mile, even when his body urgently tells him to give up (and who may collapse with a heart attack during that half mile) is a good example of the Type-A person. In contrast, the Type B is not as easily challenged and has a much lower risk of heart disease. Moreover, when the Type A smokes, has high blood pressure, or high levels of circulating cholesterol, he multiplies his risk of heart disease.

Type A is a conglomerate of stylistic characteristics. Which of them are most dangerous? Prof. Theodore Dembroski, director of the Stress and Cardiovascular Research Center at Eckerd College in Florida, has used laboratory simulations of the business world to challenge executives with various kinds of mental work. As the executives worked, he and his associates measured their blood pressure, heart rate, and other indicators of physiological strain. These studies demonstrated that it is not job involvement or striving for achievement that cause heart disease. Instead it is the intensity of hostility, particularly the tendency to hide one's anger, that can lead to severe coronary-artery disease and heart attacks.

Dr. Dembroski and his associates, including Dr. Robert Eliot, have used the term "hot reactor" to describe persons who respond to challenge with extreme physiological strain. Interestingly, the fact that an executive is a hot reactor may

FRIDAY

MAY 30 1980

APRIL 1980						
S	M	T	W	T	F	S
		1	2	3	4	5
6	7	8	9	10	11	12
13	14	15	16	17	18	19
20	21	22	23	24	25	26
27	28	29	30			

MAY 1980						
S	M	T	W	T	F	S
				1	2	3
4	5	6	7	8	9	10
11	12	13	14	15	16	17
18	19	20	21	22	23	24
25	26	27	28	29	30	31

JUNE 1980						
S	M	T	W	T	F	S
1	2	3	4	5	6	7
8	9	10	11	12	13	14
15	16	17	18	19	20	21
22	23	24	25	26	27	28
29	30					

151st Day

215 Days Left

Take the 5.24 in!

APPOINTMENTS	NOTES
7:00 A.M.	*Get Proposal ready BEFORE 8AM*
7:30	
8:00	
8:30	*See the boss — First thing !!*
9:00	
9:30	*Where is branch office report ?*
10:00	*GIVE 'EM HELL*
10:30	*Meet with Peterson*
11:00	*See Jacobs ← Squeeze in Paul W*
11:30	
12:00	*Lunch with ARB Don't let them know how mad we are*
12:30 P.M.	
1:00	*Time to call Walter?*
1:30	
2:00	*Negotiate with Union Steward*
2:30	
3:00	*DON'T GIVE UP BE NICE*
3:30	
4:00	*← Set up Sales Meeting*
4:30	*← Find out why the hell St. Louis hasn't sold their quota.*
5:00	
5:30	
6:00	
6:30	*Squash with P.M.J. MUST WIN !!*

Get home by 6:30 Jenkins coming.

The calendar of a Type-A executive. Type A's do risk heart attacks, but new evidence suggests they are *not* the top managerial performers.

not be apparent to the onlooker: not letting anger show to one's associates can be a wise strategic move. Expressing hostility to others in the office, even when one feels it, tends to have negative effects. But, holding one's anger under the surface may accelerate the dangers of approaching heart disease. The hot reactor is likely to be heading for a heart attack.

Research in our own laboratory at Penn State College of Medicine has focused on the relationship between Type-A characteristics and executive performance. Many executives credit their success in the business world to their Type-A style. Not surprisingly, since in our society we are told over and over again that the rewards go to the competitive, hard-driving executive who has little time to relax. Take, for example, the TV commercial for a prominent Wall Street firm that showed a broker getting up at dawn to obtain needed information from the London exchange so he would be ahead of the competition when trading opened in New York. The implication is clear: the driven, time-urgent, and competitive person is seen as more successful.

How correct is the belief in Type-A superiority? Our research with both simple and complex tasks shows that Type A's do not outperform their Type-B counterparts. Being Type A may sometimes be an asset during the early phases of one's career for getting things done quickly, and then some, to impress the boss. But it may turn into a liability as the executive advances toward more responsible positions. The Type A's characteristic rush to decision and their hostility are not longer effective when, for example, they must engage in more long-range planning and negotiation.

The best thing we could do for Type A's would be to change them into Type B's. However, so far intervention programs for this purpose have met with only limited success. For example, the time-urgent Type A may want to become a Type B, but he or she wants that goal to be achieved immediately! Type A's often go about becoming Type B's in typical Type-A fashion--and fail. They may even stop wearing a watch to demonstrate that they no longer feel time-urgent--only to keep looking at the wrists of their co-workers.

Dembroski's research suggests that the hostility of Type A's and their tendency to turn that hostility inward is the major culprit. With that in mind, attempts to modify Type-A behavior should concentrate on the reduction of hostility. Such methods as biofeedback and operant-conditioning have been used to change overall Type-A behavior, but programs aimed only at diminishing hostility have yet to be designed. An even more important target, however, may be the general attitude of Type A's: As long as they believe that Type-A behavior goes with success, they are not likely to want to change. Finally, when attempts to change their style fail, the reduction of other risk factors such as smoking, high blood pressure and cholesterol in the bloodstream must be taken even more seriously.

The Cognitively Complex Executive

The study of "cognitive complexity" analyzes how executives use knowledge and available information, how they apply past experiences to current problems, and how open and flexible they are when new experience challenges their beliefs, attitudes or methods. We have found that some executives use more dimensions

264

than others to process information and combine them and recombine more frequently as they reach new conclusions and make new decisions.

For the sake of brevity, let us make a somewhat oversimplified distinction between "more-multidimension" and "less-multidimensional" persons. The following descriptions of the two kinds of people would hold, no matter whether they fall into the Type-A or Type-B category. As a rule, less-multidimensional executives (and there are many of them) tend to view new problems and tasks in relative isolation from one another. They often have a single overriding goal into which all other actions must directly fit--for example, profit. They readily assimilate new information into existing thought patterns (but sometimes inaccurately). Typically they make decisions quickly and in response to a single specific task demand. In scientific terms, the less-multidimensional executives are often "respondent decision-makers."

The more multi-dimensional executives operate quite differently. They tend to see multiple implications even in single items of information. They consider various potential impacts of that information on a variety of future events and decisions. They are often strategists par excellence. They tend to plan long into the future, taking into account all possible events that can be anticipated, as well as the consequences of those events. Yet, their plans remain flexible and sensitive to developing changes in the task environment.

Decisions by these executives may come more slowly. They may be somewhat less "decisive." Yet their decisions are less likely to be upset by unforeseen events. Their flexible, sensitive and strategic style is the basis of a superiority which we have so often observed for these managers. On the other hand, the greater cognitive conflicts they experience, the larger number of contradictions they have to manage, may be the very basis of stress--and the heart disease that often follows.

Differences between the more-multidimensional and less-multidimensional executives becomes most evident at optimal load levels. In other words, optimizing load and task conditions allows the more-multidimensional executives to develop and apply their superior skills to the fullest extent.

Research results of other scientists have substantiated date obtained in our laboratory. Prof. Harold Schroder at the University of South Florida has demonstrated that more-multidimensional executives possess better analytical skills, are more flexible, tend to make better plans, and are better at making some kinds of decisions. Prof. Peter Suedfeld and his associates at the University of British Columbia studied the histories of a number of revolutionary leaders, from George Washington to Che Guevara, as well as the Japanese civil and military leadership prior to Pearl Harbor, and various United Nations representatives of Middle Eastern countries. They found that multidimensional information processing was required for success in dealing with the complex problems in the governments and organizations that were led by these individuals. In fact, a lack of multidimensional leadership could spell disaster: loss of power, failure at negotiations, even war.

Imagine a less-multidimensional decision-maker in a company that makes widgets. When he or she is informed that the competition has dropped their widget price by 25 percent, the reaction may be *respondent*: "We will drop our price by 25 percent also." In contrast, the more-multidimensional decision-maker would consider the potential reasons for the competitor's actions, the consequences for

265

that company and his own, and more. For example, he might think about various alternative actions and the possible consequences of each: Should the price be dropped? By how much? What will be the reaction of customers to a partial price reduction? Can one wait until the competition raises the price again? What about problems of cost vs. volume? Is it possible to persuade the customer that our more expensive product is of greater quality and longevity?

Effects of sequential actions in the price war between the two companies would be anticipated and included in strategic options. The executive's final decision may combine several actions: for example, reducing the price by 10 percent and advertising the quality and long life of the widget, along with other efforts designed to make it less attractive for the competition to maintain a 25 percent price cut. Finally, he may put in place contingency plans for dealing with potential future moves by the competition.

Improving Performance and Health

Without doubt, most corporations would wish to employ top-level executives that fit the mold of the more-multidimensional decision-maker. In complex tasks, that kind of person would have the edge over less-multidimensional counterparts, including those working for the competition. Unfortunately, more and more research strongly suggests that the health of the multidimensional executive is seriously endangered.

Let us examine the evidence. When compared with less-multidimensional executives, the multidimensionals show higher levels of physiological strain when challenged in work situations. For example, in our laboratory we measured blood pressure, heart rate, and other physiological indices of strain while representative samples of the two groups made decisions on typical management problems in competition with one another. On average, the more-multidimensional executive had elevations in blood pressure, heart rate and physiological arousal that were at times 83 percent higher than the increases for other executives.

Prof. Michael Driver and co-workers at the University of Southern California found evidence of considerable arousal in stressed multidimensional executives, including heartbeat irregularities (sinus arrhythmias), which frequently precede serious heart disease. Sinus arrhythmias did not occur in the less-multidimensional executives participating in Driver's studies. (Excessive physiological strain and arrhythmias are not quite heart attacks.)

To determine whether the multidimensional style is related to actual heart disease, we obtained medical histories from several hundred adults. We matched those who had experienced heart attacks with others who had not. The two groups were equivalent in age, sex, and socioeconomic status. The stylistic differences between the groups were striking: heart-attack victims were much more multidimensional.

Not all the evidence is yet in; studies on a large number of executives must be conducted over a period 10 to 20 years, as was done in research that clearly demonstrated the health risks in the Type-A style. However, current evidence is strong enough to call for immediate measures in support of executive health. We can comfortably argue for interventions against the Type-A style; after all, Type A does not improve performance. But, regarding the cognitively complex executive, we face a dilemma. We want our executives, particularly at senior levels, to be

266

more multidimensional. Yet we do not want to increase their risk of heart disease. What, then, can we do?

We might start with efforts to optimize work load. Unfortunately, work load is not always under our control: At times events outside of the organization hit the busy executive in bunches and require rapid responses. But at other times (and within the organization), load can be controlled or at least modified. One can train personnel to maintain information-flow levels that generate optimal loads. For that purpose, specific simulation systems can be developed that allow executives to learn to recognize optimal load levels.

We have designed experimental simulations for just that purpose. These management simulations must, of course, match the task environment which an executive normally experiences. Programmed information is provided; some of it relevant, some less relevant or even irrelevant to the task at hand. Of course, many managers believe that a maximum of information should be considered at all times. As a result, they overload themselves. They may even request additional information, although al necessary information is already available. As a consequence, the quality of their decision-making must suffer.

We measure the level of that decision quality with a computerized system. On the basis of a profile of measures, we easily demonstrate how the executive's decision quality has suffered from overload. By clearly showing that self-induced overload means loss of quality and, for example, by letting the executive try the simulation again, we can help the executive to learn how information flow can be restricted to more manageable levels. As a result of that learning, decision quality is likely to improve.

Organizational environments can be created that permit greater flexibility in dealing with the task environment. Some environments of this kind are described in the Peters and Waterman book, *In Search of Excellence*. We must realize that decision-makers do not have unlimited capacities. We must also recognize that the hierarchical rationality that mathematical-decision theorists have seen as an organizational panacea is not useful in many complex decision-making situations. Such planning strategies as "decision trees" and "utility theory" may not help executives suffering from overload. Enough time to process information is necessary to maintain an optimal load level: requiring an executive to "develop a plan for the next 10 years of corporate operations and present that plan at the meeting tomorrow morning at 9" may discourage quality planning and *may* contribute to long-range health problems.

With various task tests, we can easily identify more-multidimensional and less-multidimensional executives. We can match their specific dimensionality to the task demands of specific jobs; for example, people with the ability to consider a number of dimensions and to relate them to one another make good vice presidents for planning. Optimal personnel selection and placement can be achieved through the use of man-machine simulation, systems that closely approximate executive work environments, yet allow control over information flow and work load. With the use of such simulation, we can train executives to employ more-multidimensional styles when they are useful. We can measure an executive's physiological strain response to various task challenges in the simulation-- providing, in effect, a psychological stressor parallel to the treadmill now used to measure the effects of physical exercise on heart functioning.

Our research suggests that strain responses that can lead to heart disease are, in many cases, *not* the same for physical and psychological (work-related) exertion. Some people respond with the same kind and degree of arousal to both physical (treadmill) and psychological (work-related) stress. For others, however, the responses can be strikingly different. A good number of people, for example, will show lesser effects of physical stress on heart rate and blood pressure, yet drastic increases can be observed when they experience stress in their work environment.

As in the case of the Type-A style, not all features of the cognitively complex decision-maker's approach may be related to heart disease. Both Dr. Driver's research group and mine have begun to distinguish degrees of strain caused by the different components of multidimensionality. We need to learn more about how these various components function as they influence either performance or health or both. And we need to develop methods of training that will diminish the physiological responses of multidimensional executives to stressful environments while maintaining their high-quality performance.

HOW MULTINATIONAL ORGANIZATIONS EVOLVE

Christopher A. Bartlett

For most of this century, Westinghouse's international activities were managed through Westinghouse Electric International, a separate organization based in New York and maintaining only limited contact and interaction with the rest of the company.[1] In the 1960s, Westinghouse tried to build its overseas strength by acquiring strong national firms and linking them to the U.S. parent through its international division. Difficulties arose not only in obtaining suitable companies (de Gaulle personally vetoed one key acquisition), but also in integrating them into Westinghouse. Thus, in 1971 the separate international organization was disbanded and the company's 125 division managers were given worldwide responsibility for the businesses they had been managing in the domestic U.S. market.

By 1978, however, top management was concerned that the company was gaining a reputation abroad for being internally disorganized with a total lack of coordination between divisions. Several of its overseas companies were in difficulty and had to be sold off. Furthermore, foreign customers and governments were complaining that the company was difficult to do business with because of its insensitivity to local situations and its inability to coordinate various businesses in a given country.

In early 1979, the vice-chairman's response was to reorganize once again. He gave one of his key executives ninety days to analyze Westinghouse's international operations and make recommendations for the organizational change required. The report recommended that the company supplement its worldwide product organization with a network of geographic managers reporting to a strong international chief. By July 1979, Westinghouse had begun installing a formal global matrix organization structure by overlaying the existing product organization with the new geographic organization. Newly appointed country managers reported to four regional presidents who, in turn, reported to an international president with a seat on the powerful corporate management committee. This reorganization, the company believed, would help it achieve the global integration it needed to remain efficient and competitive and the sensitivity to national environments it required to be effective locally.

Westinghouse's situation provides a good illustration not only of the multiple strategic pressures that have confronted most companies as they have expanded abroad, but also of the typical structural responses in U.S.-based multinational corporations (MNCs).

Like Westinghouse, many MNCs found themselves confronted by multiple, and often conflicting, strategic demands as they grew internationally. Most became aware quite early of the need to develop an understanding of the diverse characteristics of the various national environments in which they operated. However, as foreign operations grew, they began to recognize the opportunity and the need to rationalize these diverse worldwide operations to capitalize on their

Reprinted with permission from Journal of Business Strategy, Summer 1982, Vol. 3, No. 1. Copyright 1982, Warren, Gorham & Lamont, Inc., 210 South Street, Boston, MA 02111. All rights reserved.

potential global efficiencies. As global competition intensified and, at the same time, pressures from host countries grew, managers of MNCs were confronted with the simultaneous need to be globally competitive and nationally responsive.[2] Responding consistently and appropriately to the variety of diverse, changing, and often conflicting demands has provided, for many companies, the major administrative challenge of the past decade. Their decision processes had to adapt to the challenge of becoming multidimensional--able to respond simultaneously to the global and the national strategic imperatives.

For many companies, the need for the decision-making process to respond to these diverse and growing pressures led to a series of reorganizations similar to those undertaken by Westinghouse. So familiar did the pattern become that various "stages theories" of organizational development became widely recognized.[3] Some academics, consultants, and managers began to think of this series of reorganizations in normative rather than descriptive terms, and for some MNCs it seemed that organizational structure followed fashion as much as it related to strategy.[4] Reorganizations from international divisions to global product or area organizations, or from global structures to matrix forms, became widespread. This, after all, was the classic organizational sequence described in the "stage theories."

Yet many companies that had expected such changes to provide them with the strategy-structure "fit" to meet the new pressures were disappointed. Developing a multidimensional decision-making process that was able to balance the conflicting global and national needs was a subtle and time-consuming process not necessarily achieved by redrawing the lines on a chart. Examples of failed or abandoned multinational organizations abound.[5]

While there were many companies, like Westinghouse, that appeared to concentrate largely on changes in the formal organizational structure as a means to achieve the desired changes in their administrative processes, there were others that appeared to have developed successful multidimensional decision-making processes without resorting to major changes in their formal organizations. Most notable was the substantial number of companies that had built large, complex, and successful foreign operations while retaining their supposedly embryonic international division structures.[6] If these companies had been successful in achieving a strategy-structure fit, they had done so without resorting to the sequence of traumatic reorganizations as described in the stages theories and as experienced by Westinghouse.

To understand why this substantial group of MNCs had not followed the stages model of organizational change, a detailed clinical study of nine of these companies was undertaken.[7] It was hypothesized that either the parameters of the generally accepted stages models were inappropriate or there were alternative means of structural response that were not revealed in a simple classification of formal organization.

The companies studied were selected from two industries with diverse strategic characteristics: four from the food processing industry and five from the health care industry. In trying to understand why these companies did not evolve through the series of reorganizations described in the stages models, two quite different explanations emerged.

The companies in the food processing industry had retained their international division structure for a very simple reason: the key strategic demands of their operations were perceived as being unidimensional. The nature of the business resulted in the key tasks being focused at the national level, with little long-term advantage to be gained by global operations. Product development, manufacturing, and marketing were all national rather than global tasks for a variety of cultural as well as economic reasons.[8] The conclusion reached was that increasing size and complexity did not cause these companies to abandon the "federal" organization structure needed to manage this business.

This article concentrates on the findings relating to the five companies in the health care industry (ethical and proprietary drugs, hospital supplies). The administrative challenges confronting managers in these companies were more interesting since they clearly did face the diversity of global and national demands and environmental conditions that had forced many other companies to follow the traditional stages of reorganization into global and then matrix forms of organization. The companies studied, however, seemed to achieve their state of strategy-structure fit by a different process. Rather than focusing on "anatomical" changes, these companies seemed to spend more time modifying the "physiological" and even the "psychological" characteristics of their organizations. They seemed to view the required change from unidimensional to multidimensional organization as an adaptive, evolutionary process rather than as a series of powerful, yet perhaps traumatic, reorganizations. In contrast to companies such as Westinghouse and others which followed the "strategic crisis-structural reorganization" route, these companies developed, adjusted, and integrated the required new skills, structures, and processes gradually but continuously. It is this alternative process of adaptation from unidimensional to multidimensional organization that will be described in the remainder of this article.

Strategic Demand: Handling Multidimensional Tasks

Before describing the structural and administrative changes made by the various companies, it may be helpful to have an understanding of the overall task demands that provoked the changes. What were the strategic issues facing companies in the health care industry that prevented them from retaining the simple unidimensional "federal" organization structure that proved adequate for the food processing companies?

The task complexity facing the health care companies could be described briefly along three dimensions: the need to be simultaneously responsive at the national level yet efficient globally; the need to develop multiple functional expertise at multiple organization levels; the need to be flexible in the way all of these demands were managed. Each will be described briefly.

. As they expanded abroad, these companies needed to understand and respond to the variety of local national demands that affected their success in each national market. They had to understand the structure and operation of national health delivery systems, the nature of government product registration processes, the formal and informal demands for local sourcing of critical products, and a variety of other such national pressures. However, they also had to recognize that if they were to be effective global competitors, their research efforts, manufacturing capacity, product policy, and a variety of other tasks had to be coordinated and perhaps integrated on a worldwide basis. In short, they were faced with the challenge of being simultaneously responsive and flexible at the national level while maintaining the competitive efficiency that comes from global coordination.

. Unlike the food processing industry where the marketing function was the dominant success factor, in the health care industry the marketing, research, and manufacturing functions were all regarded as key success factors. Furthermore, in the food industry all the key tasks were concentrated at the national level (e.g., products developed to meet national tastes, local manufacturing due to freshness and transportation limitations, etc.). Key tasks in the drug industry, however, needed to be managed at multiple organizational levels (e.g., for economic and quality-control reasons, active ingredients for most drugs were prepared centrally, while tablet and capsule plants could be operated efficiently on a regional or national basis; basic research obviously needed global coordination, yet product development was often handled on a regional basis, and local clinical trials were needed for national product registration).

. Unlike the food processing industry, where the markets, the technology, and the products were typically mature, the health care industry tended to present a much more dynamic operating environment. Particularly in the areas of new product development and government controls and regulations, changes were occurring at a very rapid rate in the 1960s and 1970s. Furthermore, the state of maturity and rate of change varied substantially by market.

The Multidimensional Organization: How Companies Responded

Clearly, companies could not hope to manage this set of complex, diverse, and changing demands through their simple, unidimensional "federal" organizational structures. They were faced with the major challenge of developing complex, multidimensional "global" organization. As stated previously, in the companies studied, such organizational structures were developed not through the series of reorganizations described by the stages theories, but through a more gradual evolutionary process. This process appeared to involve three distinct yet closely interrelated changes, and although there was considerable overlap, these changes tended to occur sequentially. First, new management skills and perspectives were gradually developed to reflect and respond to the growing range of task demands facing these companies; next, subtle modifications were made to the organizational structures and systems to allow better interaction between the newly developed range of management perspectives; finally, conscious efforts were made to change the organizational "climate" in an attempt to institutionalize the relationships required in an effective decision-making process in a complex and uncertain multidimensional organizational environment.

The purpose of these changes in the formal and informal structures and systems was to allow the organization's decision-making process to evolve from a unidimensional to a multidimensional focus. Associated with each stage of the structural development was a change in what can be termed the predominant "management mode." Substantive decision management by senior management in the first phase tended to evolve toward a temporary coalition management mode, which in turn gave way to decision context management in the final phase. Each will be explained and illustrated in the following sections.

The nature of these structural developments and the changes in the decision-making process that accompanied them will provide the focus for the remainder of this article. Only one additional note needs to be added at this stage. Although each company studied had made adaptations to skills, structure, and "climate," it was also clear that they were not all the same stage of development in creating their multidimensional organizational structures and management processes. One had concentrated mainly on developing the range of management skills and perspectives required to respond to the diversity of task demands it faced and continued to utilize the substantive decision management mode. Others had supplemented such changes with varying degrees of change in their structures, systems, and basic administrative processes and had broadened their repertoire of "management modes" in decision making. To illustrate the description of each of these modes, however, examples are provided from the companies that most closely correspond to the phase of multidimensional development being described. It should be recognized, however, that none of the companies fit neatly into such convenient categories: in effect, there were as many structural and administrative solutions as there were companies studied.

Developing New Management Perspectives:
Substantive Decision Management

Changing the Organization

In their early stages of overseas expansion, all five of the health care companies studied had developed networks of strong, independent country subsidiaries. The key strategic tasks were perceived as being, first, to develop an understanding of the various national operating environments and, second, to use that knowledge to build strong initial market positions. Thus, country subsidiary managers with local expertise were granted considerable autonomy and independence to perform these tasks.

The organizational structure that resulted could best be described as a "federal" structure in which the country managers' knowledge of their national operating environments gave them a dominant role in key decisions. Their power was formally recognized by the fact that geographic managers were line managers in organizations in which line authority was rarely challenged. Product and functional managers filled staff roles that were primarily defined as support functions for the country managers. Headquarters intervention into subsidiary operations was limited and infrequent, and the country managers' view dominated the strategic decision process.

As a consequence, even decisions with global implications were frequently made on the largely unchallenged recommendation of country subsidiary managers. For example, in each of the companies studied, this early period of development was marked by the proliferation of manufacturing operations worldwide as country managers argued that a local plant was essential for the success of the national subsidiary. There was little resistance to such demands for two reasons. First, nobody in the organization had sufficient knowledge of the various national environments to challenge country managers' claims of customer demands or

273

government pressures; second, little if any analysis was being done to determine the global costs and efficiency of this multiple plant "strategy."

Although this "federal system" proved adequate for the early stages of establishing foreign subsidiaries, it became clear that a company's global strategy could not be defined by the simple sum of its various national strategies. Geographically based demands had to be supplemented with product and functional views; national perspectives had to be counterbalanced by regional and global perspectives.

The major impediment to the goal of adding new perspectives to the decision process was that the product and functional managers who should have been able to provide such input were unable to do so. The dominance of the geographic perspective in the past had resulted in the development of product and functional managers whose major task was to service the needs of country subsidiary managers and act as headquarters links and information conduits. They had neither the expertise nor the organizational credibility to counter the country managers' proposals with arguments that took a more integrated global viewpoint. The first challenge in building a more multidimensional organization, therefore, was to develop managers who could represent these additional perspectives.

In all five health care companies, the process of developing the broader product and functional management skills and viewpoints followed a remarkably similar pattern. It began with the growth of a regional office and culminated with the establishment of management groups at the divisional level that had a substantial input to all major strategic decisions.

Ironically, it was the demands of the geographic line managers for more support at the regional level that gave product and functional managers an opportunity to develop their information access, their control role, and their coordination responsibilities. Through these changes their power and influence in the ongoing decision process increased substantially. In response to subsidiary criticism that the staff groups at division headquarters were too distant and often of too little experience to provide the required level of support, regional offices were established in all five companies studied. By working closer to the various markets, product and functional managers made important developmental advances as they gained greater understanding of and credibility in the subsidiary operations.

The next critical phase in the development of the product and functional managers occurred during the control period that tended to follow the initial rapid growth abroad. As foreign sales and overseas investment levels grew to a level of corporate importance, senior management began demanding better information about and control over the largely autonomous subsidiaries. The product and functional management groups, with their closer contact with operations, began to be seen as appropriate sources of information and means of control. Increasingly, their visits to subsidiaries were at the instruction of top management to report on a problem rather than at the request of the country manager to provide technical information or support.

With increased market knowledge, access to regular, current, reliable data, and power gained through their new control responsibility, it was inevitable that the product and functional managers eventually would move to the third important phase in their development within the organization. In each of the companies observed, these more sophisticated, more powerful management groups began to

274

recognize opportunities to coordinate and integrate activities being managed separately by the various country operations. While initial projects tended to concentrate on the provision of regional services to subsidiaries (e.g., EDP systems and facilities, intercompany payments netting), as soon as their credibility was established, these managers often began to take on major coordination and integration responsibilities such as regional manufacturing rationalization or regional product management coordination.

The increased credibility that grew out of their greater access to operations, the new influence that derived from their control role, and the upgraded power that flowed from their new coordination responsibilities all provided the regional product and functional managers with considerably greater impact on the decision process. Their increasing importance and power was symbolized by the growth of the regional office that took place during this period in each of the companies observed. Country managers were particularly conscious of this change in influence of product and functional managers, and in numerous instances tensions and even open conflict developed between staff and line.

Nevertheless, senior management found the additional information, services, and advice helpful in counterbalancing the previously unidimensional analyses and recommendations they had been receiving. To develop better global perspectives and to obtain improved access to the newly developed expertise, senior management typically began to build the product and functional management groups at the division headquarters level. Many of the stronger managers developed at the regional level were transferred to the division level as part of this process.

This development resulted in the power and influence of product and functional managers being developed even more. First, their proximity to senior management enhanced their access to and influence in key decision-making processes. Equally important, however, was the role these managers began to play in linking the international division to the rest of the corporation. Their product or functional expertise gave them credibility in other parts of the organization, while their greatly improved understanding of country-level operations made them knowledgeable spokesmen on international issues. Typically, these managers became international representatives to corporate bodies responsible for product policy, research priorities, capacity decisions, and other such global issues.

In all five health care companies studied, the development of strong, credible product and functional management groups appeared to be the first major step in supplementing the country-level, geographically dominated decision process. The pattern of building a strong regional office and then developing strong division-level management groups was remarkably consistent. This process seemed to provide a means to educate and legitimize the product and functional managers close to country-level questions before bringing them to headquarters where they could input more directly into major decisions.

Changing Management Process

Prior to the development of managers who could represent the global product and functional perspectives, country managers' analyses and proposals to senior managers went largely unchallenged. Even if a staff manager did question the country manager's views, his protests often went unheeded due to his low status and credibility in the organization. Clearly in these companies, decision influence was dominated by the geographic line managers.

As the new management skills and perspectives were developed, however, the decision process on key issues became more complex. Arguments for national responsiveness faced strong counterproposals for global integration, and the only means of resolving the inherent conflict was to elevate it to the senior management level. This mode of management can be termed "substantive decision management" because senior management's key role is as arbitrator on the merits of issues in dispute.

This process arose largely due to the lack of any other organizational means to resolve the inevitable differences in opinions and recommendations. However, it was also a process that seemed to suit senior management, at least temporarily. By retaining the integrator and arbitrator role, these managers were able to develop a fuller understanding of the global issues being raised by the newly developed product and functional groups and to appreciate the nature and extent of the trade-offs required between national and global perspectives.

All of the sample companies found the substantive decision management mode a convenient and simple way to integrate new perspectives into the management process in their early stages of multidimensional development. Not only did it provide a means for the newly developed global skills and perspectives to be integrated into the decision process, it also represented a process of education for senior management, allowing them to form judgments on the relative importance of the various perspectives on different issues. Eventually, however, most of them found it a cumbersome administrative system to maintain as the prime decision-making process.

There were three major classes of problems that these companies seemed to encounter after using this management process over a period of time. The first related to the reliability of the inputs to key decisions. By having advocacy groups take frequently opposing positions on issues, the analysis and recommendations being fed to senior management risked being less than objective. Analyses were often based on incomplete, conflicting, or even biased data and decisions frequently had to be made from the limited and sometimes extreme set of alternatives generated.

The second type of problem encountered in this decision mode related to top management overload. As the only source of integration and resolution, senior management soon became overburdened. The inevitable slowdown in the decision-making process that followed had the effect of dampening the generation of proposals from within the organization, or of leading middle managers to short-circuit the system by making decisions without referral to others.

The third problem area was related to implementation. Disputed issues resolved by senior management often had to be implemented by managers who had fought hard for an opposite outcome. Without the uncompromising support of those responsible, implementation effectiveness often suffered.

While these problems caused most companies eventually to abandon the substantive decision management mode, one of the sample group retained this as a key part of its decision-making process. Having developed extremely strong functional management to counterbalance its geographic line managers, Merck and Company had used a substantive decision management style for many years and continued to use it as its dominant decision process in 1979.

The main reason for the continued use of this management mode appeared to be that such a process was neither unfamiliar nor uncomfortable in a company with an historical origin rooted in the fine chemicals business. Since this industry was characterized by large-scale centralized manufacturing and research and a few big customers, centralized decision making was the norm, and Merck followed the pattern.

The acquisition of Sharp and Dohme took Merck into the international pharmaceutical business, and while its traditional management style did not appear to restrict the growth of foreign subsidiaries with substantial autonomy, senior management at Merck recognized very early the need to control its activities and counterbalance its strong national perspectives with more integrated global views. The division level functional staffs that were developed in this company were substantially larger than equivalent groups in similar companies studied. The international division marketing staff, for example, numbered over 100 and its manufacturing staff over seventy-four, ten times the size of other similar-sized drug companies studied.

These functionally organized division staff groups quickly established credibility with senior management and began to act as a filter and a control on subsidiary proposals, elevating those with which they did not agree for arbitration. A weekly international executive committee meeting, consisting of the division president and his geographic and functional vice-presidents, was the center of major decisions. From the different perspectives presented on key issues, senior management felt it was able to obtain a broader appreciation of implications than any of the middle managers alone. They felt this put them in a better position to resolve differences in opinions. The strength of their division staff groups allowed extensive analyses to be made at senior management's request to help reach final decisions.

Yet despite its strong tradition of centralized decision making, even Merck seemed to be moving away from the substantive decision management mode as its primary administrative process. The senior vice-president responsible for Europe said: "We centralize many more decisions than we should. Personally, I am trying to change this practice, primarily through my emphasis on grass roots profit planning." His expectations were that alternative structures and systems would be developed to allow more views to be integrated and trade-offs to be made below the senior management level. This certainly had been the path followed by the other companies in the sample.

Developing New Structures and Systems:
Temporary Coalition Management

More Organizational Change

The process of developing appropriate and credible new management skills and perspectives clearly had implications for and impact on existing organizational structures and systems. Regional offices were established, division level staff groups were strengthened in both quality and size, and management information and control systems became more sophisticated. These changes to the formal organizational structure and systems provided the means by which the newly developed staff groups could enter the existing strategy decision-making process.

277

The regional and division offices gave them the legitimate power base, and the new systems provided them with the information flow and the communication channels they required to exercise their new skills and perspectives.

While these changes in formal structure increased the new product and functional managers' access to and credibility with senior management, the existing organizational structure and decision processes ensured that "geographic" managers retained the power implicit in their line positions. This, although the new formal structures allowed the product and functional managers to influence the decision process, it required them to do so through the existing formal hierarchy. While most senior managements found this process helpful in educating themselves to the new perspectives being developed, in many situations the administrative burden of consolidating and resolving the conflicts generated by an evolving multidimensional organization created difficulties.

Most of the companies studied tried to alleviate some of these problems by developing additional structures and systems that would allow the required integration of divergent points of view to take place within the organization, rather than at the senior management level. Through the use of temporary structures and systems, many of them were able to bring together managers with different perspectives to review complex issues before automatically elevating any problems or conflicts for resolution.

As senior management became more familiar with the implications of the multiple management perspectives, they became more willing to delegate the responsibility of resolving the implicit conflict. Rather than asking a product manager to critique a subsidiary manager's proposal, for example, a product-subsidiary project team might be created to make a joint recommendation on the particular issue. Ongoing decisions that required continual balancing of input were often passed through a standing committee that incorporated managers representing the various relevant points of view.

In four of the companies observed, there was a proliferation of such temporary structures and ad hoc groups soon after the newly established management perspectives were in place in the organization. It was through such task forces, joint teams, and committees that the variety of management perspectives could be engaged selectively into various decision processes. The key attribute of all of the devices used was that they were flexible, allowing management to continually shift the composition of the inputs to various decisions and issues.

In the global recession of 1974/1975, Baxter Travenol used a series of task forces to reorient subsidiary managers from their traditional focus on the income statement (and particularly on sales volume) to a greater concern for the balance sheet. Corporate or regional finance managers worked with subsidiary managers to set targets for current asset levels, developed plans to achieve those targets, and often assisted in the implementation. The new status of these staff managers was reinforced by the power they derived by being appointed to this high-visibility task force by senior management. Their influence and achievements were very impressive, and senior management was, for example, relieved of the task of continually resolving arguments about the impact inventory reduction would have on budgeted sales levels.

Bristol-Myers' senior management found itself getting involved in product development disputes between country managers, with priorities and modifications

278

derived from their various market situations, and division product staff, whose priorities usually derived from existing corporate expertise and other constraints. A pharmaceutical council was formed with senior geographic line managers and business development staff managers as members. Debate in this forum allowed a jointly agreed set of priorities to be developed.

New-plant capacity decision were inevitably difficult ones in all companies, with various management perspectives justifying vastly different manufacturing configurations. For example, country managers typically promoted the need for local plants, finance managers argued to maximize the use of tax-sheltered operations, and manufacturing staff groups pushed for large specialized plants as regional or global sources. Warner-Lambert found that one useful solution was to create a joint task force of regional geographic managers, together with manufacturing, finance, materials, and marketing staff representatives to develop recommendations on worldwide capacity needs.

Forging Coalitions

Through the use of such teams, task forces, and committees, senior management was able to ensure that the diverse recommendations generated by the development of multiple management skills and perspectives were reconciled, or at least more focused, before being escalated. As such devices began to be used more extensively, managers with different perspectives on the same problem developed an ability to work together to find solutions. Senior management found itself having to intervene directly in the substance of key decisions far less frequently. Yet its control of the decision process remained strong. By being about to decide the agenda, the focus, the composition, the leadership, and the power of the particular overlaid structure, senior management could not only ensure that a particular issue was dealt with from a multidimensional perspective, but could also influence the direction of the resulting analysis, recommendations, or decisions. This mode of management can be termed "temporary coalition management."

The development of a variety of integrative structures and systems was a necessary phase for most of the sample companies in assimilating the new skills and perspectives that had been established. The use of such means of integration had an important impact on the interactions between managers with different perspectives and responsibilities. If the interventionist style of the "substantive decision management" phase served to raise senior management's awareness and understanding of key issues from a variety of viewpoints, the "temporary coalition management" phase tended to broaden the perspectives of the middle-management group. Not only was this phase important in exposing managers throughout the organization to the complex tradeoffs required in most decisions, but it also served to develop the interrelationships and communications necessary in a multidimensional decision-making process.

Of the sample companies, Bristol-Myers and Warner-Lambert seemed to have evolved to this stage. Not only had they developed managers with the skills and perspectives necessary to supplement and counterbalance the predominantly local national view, but they had supplemented the traditional structure with a variety of temporarily overlaid devices that allowed these new perspectives to be integrated into the decision process lower in the organization. In effect, these companies had increased their decision-making repertoire by supplementing the substantive resolution made with a coalition management approach.

In both companies, the increased use of task force teams and committees provided the vehicles by which product and functional managers could become involved in the decision process at an earlier stage. Yet as the use of those temporary structures increased, country managers felt that corporate level understanding of local needs was being increasingly threatened. Their concerns derived not only from the fact that product and functional groups were being upgraded in size and status, but also because they were positioned organizationally to leverage their point of view. On the latter point, two facts were important. First, they had the substantial advantage of physical proximity to senior management; second, they had strong well-established product and functional counterparts elsewhere in the organization with whom they could form powerful alliances. The country managers expressed the concern that because they were so distant from corporate headquarters and because they had no geographic counterparts there to defend their point of view, the proposals for global coordination and integration presented by the product and functional managers could easily swamp their arguments for local flexibility and responsiveness.

Senior management at both Bristol-Myers and Warner-Lambert were conscious that such concerns could be well founded. Therefore, while the product and functional managers were given greater access to the decision-making process through their appointment to task forces and committees, simultaneous efforts were made to reassert the role and power of the country manager and to ensure that his point of view was not overwhelmed by these changes.

Although the reality clearly was that there was a narrowing power and influence gap between product and functional staff managers and geographic line managers, in both companies a vigorous defense of the key role of the country manager was undertaken. At Bristol-Myers, management continually emphasized that the country manager was "king in his country" and that the growing product and functional staff influence was to help him supplement his entrepreneurial skills with technical and administrative capabilities. Warner-Lambert's senior management also talked about the increasing role of staff managers as being "to help build rounded managers at the country level."

In the two companies that were using the temporary coalition mode to supplement their substantive decision management process, senior management seemed to concentrate on two key tasks: maintaining the legitimacy of the groups and individuals representing each of the decision perspectives and ensuring the appropriate influence of each of these perspectives in key decisions. The achievement of the first objective led senior management in Bristol-Myers and Warner-Lambert to spend considerable time supporting and emphasizing the continuing key role of country managers, while simultaneously creating the temporary structures that allowed product and functional staff to input to important issues. In both companies, all groups of managers felt their influence and responsibility had increased--an impression that was probably well founded given their prior roles in a more "substantive decision management" process. It was this widespread sense of legitimacy and influence in the decision process that appeared to be a prerequisite for the successful operations of the temporary coalition mode of management. In the words of the Bristol-Myers International president, "As all managers began to be perceived as having legitimate points of

280

view and viable influence on decisions the absolute distinction that has historically been drawn between line and staff managers is starting to have less meaning."

The second prerequisite of this mode of management was to ensure that the various management perspectives were appropriately represented in each of the many key decisions. It was here that companies experienced the greatest difficulty.

Despite the clear advantages the "coalition management" process offered over the "substantive decision intervention" stage, demands on senior management were still substantial in forming, restructuring, and dissolving coalitions to manage the growing number of multidimensional problems. Furthermore, the mere creation of various coalitions did not ensure that the resulting decision process would be cooperative, and stress and divisiveness seemed an inevitable part of the operation of many teams and committees. In some cases the result was paralysis as opposing views became locked in impasse; in other instances decision making deteriorated to "horse trading" rather than the open interchange of views that was expected.

This, while task forces, teams, and committees often did provide useful means by which solutions to multidimensional issues could be found without continual intervention by senior management, they were limited when they degenerated into forced alliances between reluctant colleagues. Some companies that had perceived the coalition management mode as being the solution to the bottleneck problems of their earlier substantive decision management process began to recognize the need for further organizational adaptation. The open communication, cooperation, and understanding that is required between managers in multidimensional decisions could not be legislated by changes in the formal organization alone.

Developing a New Organizational "Climate": Decision Context Management

Just as they had recognized the difficulty of having senior management intervening in the content of key decisions, some companies began to recognize that to have them continually involved in structuring and controlling a large number of complex, variable decision-making processes was also very limiting. In the judgment of many managers, a process that often depended on forced alliances between reluctant colleagues, each protective of his turf, probably would not be effective in the long run.

Having developed the appropriate management perspectives and created viable structures and systems through which they could interact, the next major challenge for the developing multidimensional organization was to build an appropriate decision-making environment. The goal was to create an organizational climate in which flexible, constructive, and cooperative interaction between managers with different perspectives was institutionalized. Rather than having individual decisions being arbitrated or regulated from above, the objective was to achieve a more self-regulating decision process in which managers themselves could negotiate the appropriate balance of views in multidimensional decisions.

In order to achieve this kind of environment, the managers had to supplement their ability and willingness to represent a particular viewpoint with an overall understanding of the corporation's broad objectives and a willingness to adapt, cooperate, and compromise to achieve those larger goals. Such changes could not be achieved overnight and required top management to focus on three major tasks:

- To broaden managers' perspectives and open multiple channels of communication through the creative use and control of manager movement and interaction within the organization;
- To change formal systems so as to facilitate and reinforce the desired cooperative and flexible decision-making climate; and
- To create a value system that provided the organizational security required to encourage managers to take the risks involved in such flexible, broad-perspective decision making.

Of the companies studied, Eli Lilly and Baxter Travenol appeared to be the most conscious of creating this type of flexible, cooperative decision environment. Examples of the changes made will be drawn from these companies.

Management of both companies seemed to realize that flexible cooperative interactions would be difficult to develop solely through the limited channels and hierarchical relationships provided by the formal organization. Management's considerable control over individuals' movements and interactions in the organization gave it a powerful tool to impact two separate aspects of the decision environment. First, managers' understanding and appreciation of different organizational issues could be influenced; second, interpersonal relationships and informal communications channels could be developed. For example, a subsidiary marketing manager transferred to a headquarters staff is likely to develop a far greater appreciation for both the local and the global issues involved in key marketing decisions. Furthermore, the personal relationships he develops in each assignment facilitate communications and cooperation on issues involving national and global marketing input.

Eli Lilly had a well-established career development system in which managers were transferred throughout their careers from line positions to staff, from country operations to headquarters, from product to functional or geographic responsibility. Several managers attributed the good contacts and cooperative working relationships that were the norm at Lilly largely to this strongly institutionalized career development track. While less well developed Baxter had also consciously begun to engage in a similar use of temporary assignments and long-term transfers.

Both companies also created forums in which multidimensional issues could be explored openly, without the pressures or competitiveness that often existed in task forces. Baxter, for instance, modified its annual country general managers meeting to become a senior management conference to which staff and line managers were invited. For one week each year, common management problems were confronted by the entire group and joint recommendations and action plans agreed to. The president explained that his objectives were twofold: to broaden the identification of his top management from their parochial geographic or functional views to a companywide perspective, and to create an environment in which they could cooperate on key multidimensional problems.

By consciously focusing on transfers, assignments, career paths, forums, and meetings, senior management was shifting its means of influence from the formal to the informal organizational structures and systems.

This conscious subtle use of transfers, assignments, and meetings provided senior management with a means of influencing the organization's informal structure and systems rather than the formal channels that had previously been their main focus. Their ability to influence the informal structure was strengthened by the fact that in a multinational corporation there were considerable barriers of distance, language, and culture that tended to limit contacts and interactions between individuals. Management's control of the nature, frequency, and composition of interpersonal interactions therefore could have a very strong influence on the development of an informal structure.

In both Lilly and Baxter, senior management was conscious of this important influence and used it continuously. It also recognized that the behaviors and relationships that could be developed through the informal systems needed to be reinforced through the formal organization. Existing management systems had to be changed to recognize the need for cooperative flexible decision-making behavior.

In Eli Lilly, for example, the formal evaluation process was changed so that a manager would be evaluated not only by his immediate line superior, but also by managers in other parts of the company with whom he had regular working relationships. Baxter also began broadening its evaluation process to allow product and functional managers to input into the evaluation of country managers and vice versa.

At Lilly, career path management had become highly formalized. There were personnel directors for each major function, product, and geographic area who met frequently with senior management to review all actual and potential openings and all possible candidates. Managers were counseled on the importance of developing contacts and expertise in multiple responsibilities, and the broad career development histories of the senior management provided models for younger managers.

However, the process of influencing the informal system to develop cooperation and mutual understanding and realigning formal systems to reinforce such behavior could only be successful if undertaken in an operating environment that was extremely supportive. Asking a manager to abandon the simple certainty of defending his clear point of view from his defined position of organizational responsibility is asking him to take substantive personal and organizational risk. To foster the desired flexible compromising decision-making process, an organization needs a strong, well-established value system that provides the stability and security to allow an individual to take such risks.

Eli Lilly had an internal value system that not only had its roots in the founders' objectives, but also was continually reinforced by current management. In the words of the late Mr. Eli Lilly, "Values are, quite simply the core of both men and institutions. By combining our thoughts and helping one another, we are able to merge the parts of the corporation into a rational, workable management system." The values he spoke of were also referred to frequently in the organization, and included openness, honesty in dealings with others, and the need for mutual trust. With strongly held corporate values such as these, the development of the desired cooperative, flexible interaction between managers was more easily achieved.

Although Baxter's corporate value system had tended to be more competitive and less supportive, over a number of years the international division president had been working to modify some of the accepted organizational norms. At every gathering of managers, his speeches and private remarks emphasized the need for cooperation and joint action between managers. He tried to make his own behavior and management style a model for the organization. He publicly applauded appropriate cooperative problem solving and decision making among management groups with diverse interests and perspectives. Gradually the adversary relationship that existed between country managers and headquarters staff gave way to a cooperative mutual respect.

There was a noticeable cumulative effect of helping to build a network of cooperative informal relationships, reinforcing such cooperation through the formal systems, and institutionalizing the resulting decision-making behavior in a set of organizational values that strongly supported a flexible and cooperative management style. The companies that consciously worked on these changes began to develop an organizational climate in which managers recognized the broad corporate goals and worked cooperatively to help achieve them, even when this meant compromising some more parochial concerns. This management mode can be labeled "decision context management."

Senior management's role in this mode was two-fold: to support the organizational values, the informal structure, and the formal systems that created the cooperative flexible decision process, and to communicate clearly and frequently the broad corporate objectives toward which such decisions should be directed. This represented a subtle and a delicate task, but less all-consuming than an involvement with individual decision outcomes or even with coalition building and management.

In the decision context management mode, the middle-management level showed a much greater willingness to take a multidimensional approach on key issues. In Baxter, for example, when the general manager of the Brazilian subsidiary wanted to build a local plant, he first discussed the matter at length with both the manufacturing manager and the product marketing manager at division headquarters and with the corporate financial staff. When all views had been fully discussed, a mutually agreed-upon set of alternatives and a recommended approach were submitted to top management.

It should be noted again that decision making in companies that pursued the decision context management mode were not all so easily self-regulated. On sensitive issues, senior management still had to intervene either by defining the coalition that was to make the analysis, recommendation, or decision, or by actually resolving specific issues where resolution by cooperation and compromise had not been possible. Like the other modes, this one simply broadened the repertoire of decision processes available to help resolve complex multidimensional issues.

Conclusion

The strategic challenges faced by the five health care companies are typical of the situation confronting many MNCs. Increasing pressure from host governments and global competitors increasingly force companies to develop and integrate their management capabilities at the local and the global levels;

accelerating change in both arenas require that these multiple skills and perspectives interact flexibly.

While change in the formal organization has been thought of by many managers as the principal means of adapting the decision processes, the subtlety and complexity of a flexible multidimensional decision-making process appears difficult to achieve solely (or even primarily) through formal organizational change. By retaining their simple international division structures, the five companies observed maintained a stability in their formal organization that allowed gradual changes in people, relationships, and processes to be introduced through more informal and less traumatic means. Rather than focusing their attention on the structure per se, managers of these companies seemed to be more concerned with the nature of decision process that the change was designed to achieve.

While their formal organizational structures seemed to belie the fact, each of these companies had developed the flexible multidimensional decision process that its strategic environment demanded. Westinghouse's hope was that its newly installed matrix structure might take five years "to force product managers to interact with geographic specialists." Managers in the health care companies studied believed that their evolutionary approach achieved the same ends with less trauma.

Footnotes

[1] This account of Westinghouse's growth abroad is based largely on the article "Westinghouse Takes Aim at the World," Fortune, Jan. 14, 1980, pp. 48-53.

[2] Yves Doz has written extensively on the nature of these demands. See, e.g., "Strategic Management in Multinational Companies," Sloan Management Revue.

[3] Perhaps the best known of the "stages theories" of multinational organization development was developed by John Stopford. See, e.g., John M. Stopford and Louis T. Wells, Managing the Multinational Enterprise (New York: Basic Books, 1972). The first half of the book describes the patterns of organizational structure evolution based on a study of 170 companies. The typical "stages" evolution is described as follows: a structure in which autonomous foreign subsidiaries are loosely linked to the parent company is replaced by one in which subsidiaries are consolidated under an international division. Then a "global" product or area organization is typically installed, which, in turn, is replaced by a multidimensional (or "grid") organizational structure.

[4] Richard Rumelt noted a tendency for strategy to follow fashion in his study of Fortune 500 companies. See Richard P. Rumelt, Strategy, Structure, and Economic Performance (Boston: Division of Research, Harvard Business School, 1974), p. 149.

[5] Perhaps the two most widely cited examples of multidimensional matrix organizations apparently have pulled back from their original structure. Davis and Lawrence describe the demise of Dow Chemical's global matrix but point to the emergence of a more recent multinational matrix success: Citibank. Stanley M. Davis and Paul R. Lawrence, Matrix (Reading, Mass.: Addison Wesley, 1977), pp. 206-222. Recent reports indicate that Citibank has now abandoned its global matrix. See "It's a Stronger Bank That David Rockefeller Is Passing to His Successor," Fortune, Jan. 14, 1980, p. 44.

[6] A follow-up study of the original Stopford sample of companies is planned. A preliminary estimate indicates that well over 30 percent of the companies classified as having international divisions in 1967 retained them twelve years later despite their growth and the changing environmental demands.

[7] See Christopher A. Bartlett, Multinational Structural Evolution: The Changing Decision Environment in International Divisions, unpublished doctoral dissertation, Harvard University Graduate School of Business Administration, 1979.

[8] For a full exploration of the strategic demands in the food industry, see Ulrich E. Wiechmann, Marketing Management in Multinational Firms (New York: Praeger, 1976).

THE FOUR FACES OF SOCIAL RESPONSIBILITY

Dan R. Dalton
Richard A. Cosier

Imagine that your company is considering introducing a new plastic container to the market. Your company considers itself to be socially responsible; therefore, an extensive impact assessment program is undertaken. One of your environmentally-minded employees suggests that people might light the containers and then cook their meals over the fire. Although the idea sounds bizarre, you don't want to take any chances, so for over a month you cook hamburgers over a fire made from your plastic bottles. Rats are fed this hamburger, then carefully monitored for negative side effects. Tests indicate that these rats suffer no ill effects.

Of course you also perform an extensive series of tests involving energy usage, disposal, and recycling opportunities. Then you invite the public to carefully scheduled hearings across the country in order to encourage consumer inputs. Finally, you market the new product and land a major soft drink company as a customer.

Sound as if your company has fulfilled its responsibilities and forestalled any possible objections? In the mid-1970's Monsanto went through this very process in developing Cycle-Safe bottles and spent more than $47 million to market the product. But in 1977 the FDA banned the bottle because, when stored at 120 degrees for an extended period of time, molecules strayed from the plastic into the contents. Rats, fed with doses that were equivalent to consuming thousands of quarts of soft drink over a human lifetime, developed an above-normal number of tumors.

Monsanto felt that they were providing a product that did something for society--a plastic bottle that could be recycled. But social responsibility is unavoidably a matter of degree and interpretation. Forces outside of the business are liable to interpret a product to be socially unacceptable, even when the company has undertaken an extensive impact analysis.

A precise evaluation of what is socially responsible is difficult to establish and of course, many definitions have been suggested. Joseph McGuire, in *Business and Society*, provided a persuasive focus when he stated that the corporation "must act 'justly' as a proper citizen should." Large corporations have, not only legal obligations, but also certain responsibilities to society which extend beyond the parameters set by law. As the Monsanto case illustrates, the line between legality and responsibility is sometimes very fine.

Peter Drucker offers a useful way to distinguish between behaviors in organizations; the first is what an organization does *to* society, the other what an organization can do *for* society. This suggests that organizations can be evaluated on at least two dimensions with respect to their performance as "citizens": legality and responsibility. The accompanying Table illustrates the various combinations of legality and responsibility which may characterize an organization's performance.

These combinations are the *four faces of social responsibility*. Each cell of the table represents a strategy which could be adopted by an organization. It is unfortunate, but we think true, that no matter which strategy is chosen, the corporation is subject to some criticism.

The Four Faces of Social Responsibility

	Illegal	Legal
Irresponsible	A	C
Responsible	B	D

Illegal and Irresponsible

In modern society, this strategy, if not fatal, is certainly extremely high risk. In an age of social consciousness, it is difficult to imagine an organization that would regularly engage in illegal and irresponsible behavior. What, for example, would be the consequences of an organization's blatantly refusing to employ certain minority groups or deliberately and knowingly using a carcinogenic preservative in foodstuff? Besides the fact that such behavior is patently illegal, it is offensive and irresponsible.

There are, however, instances of illegal and irresponsible corporate conduct which are not so easily condemned.

You Can Hardly Blame Them

Most of us have value systems. They vary, to be sure, from individual to individual and from corporation to corporation. They do, however, have common elements: they are tempered by temptation, consequence, and risk. Sometimes when faced with high temptation, low consequence, and low risk, our value systems are not the constraining force they could be. This may be the human condition and insufficient justification for the excesses which often accompany individual and corporate decision making. Nonetheless, an appreciation of these factors often makes those decisions entirely understandable.

Suppose that the state in which you live invokes a regulation that all motor vehicles operated on a public thoroughfare must be equipped with an "X" type pollution-control device. This law, for the sake of discussion, is retroactive. All automobiles registered in the state must be refitted with such a device, which costs $500. All automobiles are subject to periodic inspection to assure compliance with the law. Assume that the maximum fine (consequence) for violating this statute is $50. Assume, furthermore, that there is one chance in one hundred that you will be inspected and found in violation. The analytical question is simply stated: Would you have the device installed? If you do, it will cost $500. If you do not, the cost will be $500 plus a $50 fine, but only *if* you are caught. Many, if not most, of us surely would not install the device. Strictly speaking, our behavior is both illegal and irresponsible. Our failure to comply exacerbates a societal problem--namely, polluting the air. Our reluctance under the described circumstances, however, is understandable: temptation along with low consequence and low risk.

Compare this situation with that of a large organization faced with the decision to install pollution abatement equipment in one of its plants. Suppose, in this case, the total cost of the installation is $500,000; the maximum fine for noncompliance is $10,000; the chance of being caught is one in one hundred. We ask the same question: Would you comply? We have actually been charitable with the balance of costs and probabilities in this example. The Occupational Safety and Health Administration (OSHA), which was given the charter for establishing and enforcing occupational safety and health standards, has a limited number of inspectors and approximately five million organizations subject to its mandate. It has been estimated that an organization could plan on being inspected about every seventy-seven years, or approximately as often as you could expect to see Halley's comet.[1] Furthermore, $10,000 is a very large fine by OSHA standards. The fundamental point, of course, is that the temptation to ignore the law ($500,000) is large, the fine ($10,000) low, and the risk (once every seventy-seven years) very small. You cannot be surprised when an organization does not comply any more than you would be surprised that the individual with the polluting car did not comply.

It can be argued that the organization has the greater responsibility. Certainly, a polluting smokestack is more visible, literally and figuratively, than an automobile's exhaust. However, we daresay that the marginal pollution attributable to automobiles far exceeds that of smokestacks in most (if not all) regions. Illegal? Yes. Irresponsible? Yes. Understandable?

Whether or not the behavior is "understandable," the result, at a minimum, is bad publicity. The observation that a corporation is likely to be criticized for operating in that "Illegal/Irresponsible" area is obvious. There has, however, been testimony and documentation that the weight of potential litigations in a classic cost/benefit analysis is far less than the cost of recalling or correcting the alleged deficiencies. While we have suggested that behavior in this area is high risk, there is precious little evidence that it is suicidal.

Illegal/Responsible

Being in this cell raises very interesting issues. Monsanto found itself in this cell in the Cycle-Safe incident. The FDA ruled their product "illegal," even though Monsanto felt socially responsible. Many times however, organizations find themselves in this area because of jurisdictional disputes. Suppose that prior to the Civil Rights Act of 1964 and attendant legislation, an organization chose to embark on a program to employ women in equal capacities as male employees. At the time, this would have been forward-looking and extremely responsible corporate behavior. Unfortunately, much of the behavior involved in implementing that strategy would have been unquestionably illegal. During that period, "protective legislation" was very common. This legislation, designed to "protect" women, restricted working hours, overtime, the amount of weight that could be lifted, and types of jobs (bartending, for example) available to women. These and similar matters were eventually adjudicated largely at the federal court level.

Grover Starling cites an interesting jurisdictional paradox. It seems that the

288

Federal Meat Inspection Service ordered an Armour meat-packing plant to create an aperture in a conveyor line so that inspectors could remove samples for testing. Accordingly, the company did so. The Occupational Safety and Health Administration soon arrived and demanded that the aperture be closed. It seems that an aperture on that line constituted a safety hazard. Predictably, each agency threatened to close down the plant if it refused to comply with its orders.[2] This example demonstrates how an organization could be operating in a fundamentally desirable manner (safely) and yet run afoul of legislation at some level. An organization might adopt a program to train underprivileged children, for example, and find itself in violation of a minimum wage law.

One potential strategy for dealing with problems in this cell is challenging the law. Laws can be, and are regularly, deliberately violated for no other reason than to challenge their application. You cannot get a hearing in a state or federal court on a "what if" basis. In order to get a hearing, someone must be in jeopardy. A classic example is the famous Gideon vs. Wainwright case where the Supreme Court ruled that a suspect has the right to counsel and that the state must provide such counsel if the accused could not afford it. This case could not have been decided without an issue--a man convicted without benefit of counsel. Gideon had to be in jeopardy. Courts do not rule on hypothetical cases.

The public is often critical of the corporate use of the courts. It is true that the courts, aside from their jurisprudential charter, are often used as a delay mechanism. There are, for example, legendary antitrust cases which have been in the courts for years. The courts have ruled against the acquisition, but organizations, through a series of legal maneuvers, have managed to stall the actual separations. In the meantime, presumably, the benefits of the acquisition continue to accrue. Interestingly, everyone's "pursuit of justice" is someone else's "delay." Even in Gideon vs. Wainwright, we have little doubt that the prosecuting attorney's office saw the several appeals as both a nuisance and a delay.

Again, organizations can find themselves in a dilemma. An organization in the "Illegal/Responsible" cell faces a paradox. It is likely to be criticized whether it lives within the law or, potentially, challenges it.

Irresponsible/Legal

Historically, there have been astonishing excesses in this area. Some of them would have been laughable if they had not been so serious. For example, prior to the Pure Food and Drug Act, the advertising for a diet pill promised that a person taking this pill could eat virtually anything at any time and still lose weight. Too good to be true? Actually, the claim was quite true; the product lived up to its billing with frightening efficacy. It seems that the primary active ingredient in this "diet supplement" was tapeworm larvae. These larvae would develop in the intestinal tract and, of course, be well fed; the pill taker would in time, quite literally, starve to death.

In another case, which can only be described as amazing, an "anti-alcoholic elixir" was guaranteed to prevent the person who received the "potion" from drinking to excess. It was *very* effective. The product contained such a large dose of codeine that the people taking it became essentially comatose. The good news, of course, is that they certainly did not drink very much. And at the time, this product was not illegal.

289

There are more current examples with which we are all familiar--black lung disease in miners and asbestos poisoning, among others. Certainly, it was not always illegal to have miners working in mines without sufficient safety equipment to forestall black lung; nor was it illegal to have employees regularly working with asbestos without adequate protection. It can be argued that these consequences were not anticipated and that these situations were not deliberately socially irresponsible. It is, however, less persuasive to make that argument with respect to the ages and and extended working hours of children in our industrial past.

But enough of the past. Do major organizations continue to engage in behaviors which, while not illegal, may be completely irresponsible? Among several examples that come to mind, one is, we think, appropriate for discussion but likely to be highly contentious--the manufacture and distribution of cigarettes. Obviously, cigarette manufacturing is not illegal. Is it irresponsible?

We noted earlier that knowledge of the effects of certain drugs may have been lacking in the past. We mentioned codeine-based elixirs. There are others. Some compounds contained as much as three grams of cocaine per base ounce. One asthma reliever was nearly pure cocaine. Even so, perhaps their effects were little understood and little harm was thought to have been done. Can the same be said of tobacco industry? Is there anyone who is not aware of the harmful effects of smoking? True, there are warning labels which imply that the purchaser knows what he or she is taking. But how many people would endorse the use of codeine or cocaine or any other harmful substance, even with an appropriate warning label. Comparing apples and oranges? Perhaps, but fifty years from now, writers may talk about the manufacture of tobacco products and use terms such as "astonishing," "amazing," and "laughable" as we have to describe other legal, but irresponsible, behaviors.

Certainly, issues other than health are contained in this category. Suppose an organization is faced with more demand for its product than it can meet. Naturally, the organization does not care to encourage competition and would prefer to meet the demand itself if possible. Unfortunately, their plants are already operating twenty-four hours a day, seven days a week. There is simply no further capacity. Management decides to build a new plant, which can be completed in no less than four years.

In the meantime, it is discovered that an existing, abandoned plant can be acquired and refitted in six months. Now, this plant will not be efficient, and will be only marginally profitable at best. It will, however, serve to meet the escalating demand until such time as the new plant is ready for full operation, some four years hence.

Juryrigging this abandoned plant, however, involves several problems. Foremost among them is the fact that the community does not have the infrastructure to serve the plant and the expected influx of employees. School systems will have to be expanded; housing will have to be built; recreational services improved. For the sake of this discussion, suppose that the temporary plant will employ 1,200 persons. It would be reasonable to estimate that this would mean the addition of 3,000 to 3,500 persons in the community. But, remember, this plant will be closed as soon as the new plant in another location is operational.

What is your decision? Do you authorize the refitting of this temporary plant? Certainly, if you notify the community that the plant is temporary, you will pay certain costs. The community would be understandably unlikely to make permanent improvements. Local banks would be somewhat less than enthusiastic about financing building projects, home mortgages, or consumer loans of any description. The simple solution is obvious--don't tell.

The point is that to deliberately use this plant as a stop-gap measure knowing full well that it will be temporary is not illegal. We are aware of no legislation which would prevent this action. There remain, however, some obvious social ramifications of this strategy. The ultimate closing of this plant is likely to reduce this community to a ghost town; there will be widespread unemployment; property values will fall precipitously; the tax base will be destroyed.

Once again, operating in this area is subject to criticism, underscoring our earlier point that being a "law-abiding" corporate citizen is not nearly enough; while organizations may not violate a single law, they may not be socially responsible. What of gambling casinos dealing, not only in games of chance but also offering endless free liquor and decolletage? How about the manufacturers of handguns? Automobiles with questionable, if not lethal, fuel systems? Can a society hold organizations to a standard higher than that demanded by law?

Legal/Responsible

It would seem that we have finally arrived at a strategy for which an organization cannot be criticized. An organization in this sector is a law-abiding corporate citizen and engages in behaviors which exceed those required by law-- voluntary socially oriented action. Alas, even this proactive strategy is subject to four severe criticisms.

• Such behavior amounts to a unilateral, involuntary redistribution of assets.

• These actions lead to inequitable, regressive redistribution of assets;

• An organization engaging in these behaviors clearly exceeds its province; and

• Social responsibility is entirely too expensive and rarely subjected to cost/benefit analysis.

Involuntary Redistribution

Probably the chief spokesperson of this position is Nobel laureate and economist, Milton Friedman. He points out that today, unlike one hundred years ago, managers do not "own" the business. They are employees, nothing more and nothing less. As such their primary responsibility is to the owner--the stockholder. Their relationship is essentially a fiduciary one. Friedman argues that the primary charter of the manager, therefore, is to conduct the business in accordance with the wishes of the employer, given that these wishes are within the limits embodied in the law and ethical custom. Any social actions beyond that amount to an involuntary redistribution of assets. To the extent that these actions reduce dividends, stockholders suffer; to the extent that these actions raise prices, consumers suffer; to the extent that such actions reduce potential wages and benefits, employees suffer. Should any or all of these interested parties care to make philanthropic contributions to fund socially desirable projects, they may do so. Without their consent, however, such redistributions are clearly unilateral and involuntary.

Inequitable, Regressive Redistributions

This tendency can be referred to as a reverse Robin Hood effect.[3] Mr. Hood and his band of merry men stole from the rich and gave to the poor, but many programs under the loose rubric of social responsibility have not followed this redistribution pattern. In fact, it can be argued that many programs actually rob the poor to serve the rich. Obviously, the more wealthy persons are, the more regressive this social responsibility "tax."

Many projects which are not commercially feasible are supported by the largest of organizations under the banner of social responsibility. Opera and dance companies, for example, may be subsidized by corporate contributions. Public television is heavily financed by corporate sponsors. The reason that these subsidies are essential to the operation of these programs is that public demand for these products is altogether insufficient to defray their costs. Presumably, the money to finance these ventures comes from somewhere in the organizational coffers. Consumers, employees, and others "contribute," as we previously noted, to the availability of these funds.

Who, however, is the primary beneficiary of these subsidized programs? For the most part, it seems fair to suggest that those who regularly attend ballets, operas, dance companies, live theatre, symphonies, and watch similar programming on public television are relatively more affluent. It would appear that real income is transferred from the poorer to the richer in this exercise of social responsibility.

Exceeding Province

One, if not the foremost, justification for government involvement in private affairs is market failure. When the market cannot provide, for whatever reasons, that which the public demands, then government is (or should be) enfranchised to supply or finance that product or service. National defense, health and safety, and welfare are a few of the services which the private sector is unable to supply. It may be that libraries, museums, parks and recreation, operas, symphonies, and support for other performing arts are in this category as well. The objection which is central here is that it is not the province of private organizations to decide which of these projects should be funded and to what extent. Such support should not be a function of the predilections of corporate officials; this is the charter of government.

The issue clearly goes beyond fighting over who is going to play with what toys. In theory, public officials are subject to review by the citizenry. If the public does not approve of the manner in which funds are being prioritized for social concerns, they may petition their various legislatures. Failing in this, they may not support the reelection of the appropriate public officials. The public, on the other hand, does not vote or in any other manner approve or endorse highly ranking officers of corporations. By what right should corporations decide what is "good" and what is "right." It may well be that a given corporate image of righteousness is somewhat different from your own.

The potential for corporate influence in this "public" area is enormous. Theodore Levitt, while (we hope) overstating the case somewhat, presents a clear view of the potential of business statesmanship:

"Proliferating employee welfare programs, its serpentine involvement in community, government, charitable, and educational affairs, its prodigious currying of political and public favor through hundreds of peripheral preoccupations, all these well-intended but insidious contrivances are greasing the rails for our collective descent into a social order that would be as repugnant to the corporations themselves as to their critics. The danger is that all things will turn the corporation into a twentieth-century equivalent of the medieval Church. The corporation would eventually invest itself with all-embracing duties, obligations, and finally powers--ministering to the whole man and molding him and society in the image of the corporation's narrow ambitions and its essentially unsocial needs."[4]

A grim scenario, to be sure. The fundamental point remains. Critics argue that any of these voluntary socially responsible behaviors simply exceed the province of the corporation.

Expense of Social Responsibility

A final objection to the general issue of social responsibility, whether mandated by regulation or voluntarily pursued by organizations, is that it is oppressively expensive. The necessity to comply with ever-stricter environmental standards, for example, has literally forced the closing of hundreds of industrial locations across the country. Furthermore, it has been argued that these regulations have seriously affected domestic industry's ability to compete in international markets.

No one would argue that expense alone is sufficient to discard programs of environmental protection, employee safety, consumer protection, or a host of other socially responsive concerns. However, it can be argued that these programs should be subjected to a cost/benefit analysis. Quite often, this is not done. An automobile, for example, could be manufactured so soundly that driver deaths in accidents could be practically eliminated on our highways. But at what cost? We do not intend to address the question of what a human life is worth. Obviously, its value is incalculable. The fact remains that we live in a finite world; resources are limited. When we choose to make expenditures in one area, we necessarily restrict or eliminate expenditures in another. At what point do safety programs become overly paternalistic? At some time, employees, for example, must bear a certain responsibility for their own safety. The same can be said for those who operate motor vehicles on public byways.

While this principle seems clear, it is often not considered. What expense is justifiable to renovate and refit public buildings to render them essentially fireproof? Or, if not fireproof, at least such that the loss of human life by fire is remote. The hard fact is that very few people die each year in fires in multi-storied buildings. Who is going to pay for such judicious safety? And for the benefit of how many?

The same approach can be pursued with respect to airliner safety. Fortunately, very few people lose their lives each year in commercial airplanes. There is no doubt that airplanes could be manufactured so that they would be even

293

safer in accidents. Again, at what cost? We do not wish to appear insensitive; the loss of a human life is a tragedy, especially if it could have been prevented. "Safety at any cost, however, is simply not viable in a society restricted by finite resources.

The objection regarding the expense of social responsibility is easily restated. Aside from its absolute expense, which can be formidable, critics argue that social responsibility is often not accompanied by sufficient benefits to justify its cost.

Once again, even while being both legal and responsible, an organization is likely to receive severe criticism.

We have suggested that every cell (Illegal/Irresponsible; Illegal/Responsible; Legal/Irresponsible; Legal/Responsible) is subject to criticism. Furthermore, the cell that your organization occupies may be determined by individuals outside of your firm--federal agencies or consumer groups, to name a few. It may be a classic expression of the aphorism, "You're damned if you do, you're damned if you don't." Inasmuch as all strategies are subject to criticism, where should the organization operate? Which is the optimum strategy?

We think there are three fundamental principles which should be considered by an organization with respect to choosing a strategy for social responsibility; *primum non nocere*, organizational accountability, and the double standard.

Primum Non Nocere

This notion was first explicated over 2,500 years ago in the Hippocratic oath. Freely translated, it means "Above all, knowingly do no harm." This would seem to be a sound principle for both legality and responsibility. Organizations should not engage in any behavior if they know that harm will be done as a result. This is not meant to be literally interpreted. Certainly, knowing that some individuals will injure themselves is insufficient to bar the manufacture and distribution of, for example, steak knives. This, like any principle, should be tempered with good sense.

Organizational Accountability

An organization should be responsible for its impacts, *to* or *for* society, whether they are intended or not. Ordinarily, in the course of providing a good or a service, costs are incurred. Presumably, the price of the product or service is, at least in part, a function of the costs of its manufacture or delivery. The difference between the cost and the price is profit--the *sine qua non* of private enterprise. This would be acceptable, except for one oversight--very often society underwrites portions of the cost. Historically, given that the production of energy through sulphurous coal leads to higher levels of air pollution, the costs of producing electricity have been artificially low. That pollution is a cost. Sooner or later, someone has to pay to clean it up. But who? The consumer did not have to pay a premium for the electricity to enter a "clean-up" fund. The power company made no such contribution.

Today, we could argue that cigarette manufacturing enterprises enjoy a certain cost reduction. The manufacturer and the smoker can be thought of as enjoying a subsidy. Arguably, the retail price of cigarettes does not approach that necessary to cover its total costs. Where, for instance, is the fund that will eventually be called upon to pay for the medical costs allegedly associated with smoking? The point is that someone should be accountable for these behaviors.

Double Standard

Traditionally, the concept of a "double standard" has had a negative connotation. In the area of social corporate responsible, we think it is reasonable, even commendable. As we have continuously noted, there are no rules that apply to organizations about what, where, when, how much, and how often they can engage in behaviors for society, but a certain power-responsibility equation has been suggested.[5] Essentially, this equation argues that the social responsibility expected of an organization should be commensurate with the size of the social power it exercises. Large companies--AT&T, General Motors, Exxon, IBM, General Electric, DuPont--whose operations can literally dominate entire regions of the country have a greater responsibility than smaller organizations with less influence.

The larger an organization becomes, the more actual and potential influence it commands over society. Society, necessarily, takes a greater interest in the affairs of such organizations. Society has correspondingly less expectation of social responsibility from smaller organizations.

This is the nature of the double standard to which we have referred. While any double standard is somewhat unfair, it highlights an observation made by Drucker. He argues that the quest for social responsibility is not a result of hostility towards the business community. Rather the demand for social responsibility is, in large measure, the price of success. Success and influence may well lead to a greater responsibility to society. A double standard, to be sure, but perhaps a reasonable one.

So Which Strategy?

We believe that organizations should adopt a strategy reflected in cell D-- legal and responsible. Remember, however, that the classification of cell "D" will be determined by the public (or government acting "for" the public). Organizations have to anticipate, and in some cases, influence the public reaction--be proactive. However, a proactive stance involves some risk. As we noted earlier, critics abound regardless of the cell in the table occupied by the organization. A certain risk, nevertheless, is necessary for any business to succeed. Drucker rightly states that to try to eliminate risk in business is futile. Risk is inherent in the commitment of present resources to future expectations. The attempt to eliminate risk may result in the greatest risk of all--rigidity.

We would argue that merely being a law-abiding corporate citizen is something less than social responsibility. It may be that large organizations must "do something." Affirmative action is a compelling analogy. It is not enough not to discriminate. Organizations must "do something" proactively to further the goals of equal employment opportunity. Perhaps this is true for other issues of corporate social responsibility as well. There may be an expectation that organizations must "do something" to further benefit society beyond following its formal laws.

Basically, some action is better than no action. Throughout the course of history, inaction has never advanced mankind. In our view, errors of commission are far better than those of omission. If our ancestors had heeded the critics who were opposed to doing something, we might all still be drawing on cave walls. This issue is not entirely philosophical; there are important pragmatic considerations as well, as evidenced in the remarks of DuPont chairperson, Irving S. Shapiro:

"I think we're a means to an end, and while producing goods and providing jobs is our primary function, we can't live successfully in a society if the hearts of its cities are decaying and its people can't make the whole system work. . . . It means that, just as you want libraries, and you want schools, and you want fire departments and police departments, you also want businesses to help do something about unsolved social problems."[6]

Occasionally, it is argued that true social responsibility does not exist. Organizations do not operate out of social responsibility--but good business. Many instances of activities which could be referred to as "responsible" are public relations strategies which are sound business; it pays to advertise. Truly philanthropic efforts occur without fanfare. Some argue that only when organizations anonymously contribute their executives and other resources to socially responsible programs do you have true responsiveness. Perhaps. But we choose not to define social responsibility as philanthropy. We have no objection to enlightened self-interest.

Assuming that society is not totally victimized by actions justified under the banner of social responsibility, then corporations, even pursuing their interests, present a win-win situation. If restoring land to its natural state after mining is *only* done because it is good business, fine. Society benefits. The same can be said for many, if not most, socially responsible behaviors by organizations. We are less concerned with *why* it is done than with the fact that it *is* done. We think it can be best done legally and responsibly.

Footnotes

[1] "Why Nobody Wants to Listen to OSHA," Business Week, June 14, 1976: 76, from Randall S. Schuler, Personnel and Human Resource Management (St. Paul: West Publishing Company, 1981).

[2] Grover Starling, The Changing Environment of Business (Boston: Kent Publishing Company, 1980).

[3] Discussion based largely on Dean Carson, "Companies as Heroes?" ... New York Times, 1977.

[4] Theodore Levitt, "The Dangers of Social Responsibility," Harvard Business Review, 1958: 44.

[5] Y.N. Chang and Filemon Campo-Flores, Business Policy and Strategy (Santa Monica, California: Goodyear Publishing Company, 1980).

[6] Irving S. Shapiro, "Today's Executive: Private Steward and Public Servant," Harvard Business Review, 1978: 101.

HAVE YOU GOT WHAT IT TAKES
TO RUN YOUR OWN BUSINESS?

Bobby C. Vaught
Frank Hoy

To paraphrase Mark Twain, reports of the death of small business have been greatly exaggerated. It has always been difficult to make a success of an independent enterprise. In the best of times, a firm has only a 50% chance of survival during its first 5 years. Governmental intervention in business processes is often blamed for retarding the growth of small firms and discouraging entry into certain fields. Examples frequently cited include the tax structure, costs of complying with government regulations (including paperwork), minimum-wage requirements, and so forth.

It may be, however, that we are entering a new era of small-business/government interactions that will result in new incentives for small-business owners. The debate taking place on the national level indicates that the small-business sector of the economy is a far more critical element than previously recognized. Small business is at last being seen as an avenue of economic growth and political and societal development. Particularly significant contributions by small business are occurring in the following areas:

1. *Innovation.* The history of the United States shows that innovation has been inseparable from entrepreneurship. The inventions and discoveries that have stimulated national economic development have traditionally come from small enterprises. In recognition of this, the National Science Foundation has funded innovation centers at universities for the purpose of encouraging new ventures that create, produce, and market new products.[1]

2. *Job creation.* A study of national employment from 1960 to 1976 found that, on the average, about 60% of all jobs in the United States are generated by firms with 20 or fewer employees. Only 15% of all new jobs have occurred in large companies (over 500 employees).[2] Forecasts for the 1980s indicate that small businesses will continue to be the prime source of new-job creation.

3. *Opportunities for women and minorities.* Currently, women represent less than 4% and minorities less than 5% of business ownership in the United States.[3] A doubling of those percentages would still mean significant underrepresentation and yet would be a phenomenal increase in opportunities for women and minorities. This could be done without sacrificing jobs for others. It would, in fact, create jobs.

A demonstration of the new interest in small business took place in Washington, D.C. in January 1980. The first White House Conference on Small Business was attended by over 2,000 delegates from throughout the United States. The participants arrived at a consensus on the needs and directions of small business for the next 10 years. The consensus has been embodied in a set of recommendations covering such topics as capital formation and retention, government regulations and paperwork, and economic policy and government programs.[4] The first concrete result of the conference occurred when President Carter signed into law "The Small Enterprise Regulatory Flexibility Act" in September 1980. This Act requires that the effects of regulations on small business be analyzed before the regulations are issued.[5]

A more important reason than government incentives underlies small-business survival, however: many people in this country simply cannot work for someone else. This may result from lack of choice--inability to obtain a position in another organization. More frequently, however, it is due to choice. The individualistic nature of entrepreneurs, their independent spirits, demand that they be their own bosses.

The individual considering self-employment should be aware that technical knowledge of a product or service may not be adequate to guarantee success. Prior to making such a decision, the prospective entrepreneur should be above to recognize the causes of business success and the personal characteristics frequently associated with small-business ownership.

Not Everyone Succeeds

Too, the failure record cannot be ignored. Small businesses are going under daily. A lot of information has been gathered about these failures over the years. In general, most of the causes can be traced to managerial incompetence and/or inadequate financing.[6]

Incompetent Management: First of all, it is important to recognize that an entrepreneur's attitude can influence business success. Many failures do not have the right attitude about hard work, and there is no substitute in the small firm for hard work.

One investor remodeled a vacant service station, filled it with cases of beer, hired a few part-time college students at minimum wage to collect the customers' money, and sat back waiting for the profits to roll in. They never did. The owner's absence and lack of control led to few sales, theft, general physical deterioration of the business, and ultimately to its closing.

Hard work alone is not enough, however. To succeed means working smart, using time effectively. Some managers who put in the most hours lose their businesses because their efforts were misdirected. A typical example is the inventor who spends all his time trying to sell a new product rather than hiring someone with marketing expertise who could free the inventor to spend his time back in the workshop doing what he does best.

Most incompetent managers fail to give adequate attention to the marketing function. They also ignore the need to deal with their employees as individual human beings. Another managerial pitfall is to discount experience. Too many people jump into ownership with little, if any, appropriate business experience. Incompetent managers fail to plan and do not prepare for expansion. They do not recognize that their role must change along with changes in their organization. As a company grows from a one-person enterprise to a team, to an organization with multiple levels of management, the entrepreneur must be flexible enough to change

298

managerial styles. The owner starts out as an operator, moves into the role of a manager, and gradually evolves into an executive. But each role requires different patterns of behavior.

Inadequate Financing: Poor and reckless money management can occur right from an organization's inception. There are many symptoms. Too much capital may have been put into fixed assets. The recordkeeping may be sloppy and haphazard. The owner may be taking too much money out. Cashflow problems may be caused by poor credit-granting practices or by inventory mismanagement. All these factors may mean the end for a business just as it is on the verge of success.

Few business owners anticipate all the expenses in the initial startup of an enterprise. If there is only the minimum cash necessary to meet normal daily requirements, the owner cannot make any major mistakes. One early, costly error can end an entrepreneurial career that might have been salvaged had the mistake occurred when the enterprise was more firmly established.

EXHIBIT 1
Characteristics of Entrepreneurs

DEMOGRAPHICS	ATTITUDES	BEHAVIORS
Male	Need for achievement	Technically competent
Oldest child in family	Desire for independence	Possesses relevant experience
First or second-generation American	Individualistic	Hard worker
	Fortitude	Lucky
Most influential family member: father	Self-confidence	Administrative skill
	Self-esteem	Willing to delegate
At least one other entrepreneur in family	Ambition	Willing to take responsibility
	Unconcerned with social self-image	Needs feedback
Married	Not motivated in large organizations	Effective leader
Has children	Future-oriented	Task-oriented
Spouse works	Money-oriented	Human-relations ability
Age: 30-40	High reward expectations	Self-starter
Education: increasing	Optimistic	Enthusiastic
	Objective	Communicates well
	Tolerance for ambiguity	Decisive
	Knowledge and acceptance of limitations and strengths	Methodical
		Reliable
		Adaptable
		Versatile
		Innovative
		Action-oriented
		Aggressive
		Moderate risk taker
		Self-sacrificing
		Active in church
		Active in participative sports
		Active in community

Who Are the Survivors?

There have been many studies of entrepreneurs conducted over the years.[7] Those who succeed have been found to share a variety of characteristics. In Exhibit 1, these characteristics have been classified as demographic, attitudinal, and behavioral. This exhibit identifies for a prospective small-business owner the potential barriers to successful entrepreneurship, due to a lack of specific attributes. The exhibit also identifies variables over which an individual may exert some control in order to increase the chances for success. Let us look at the various characteristics.

Demographics: This is the category of variables over which a prospective entrepreneur can exercise little, if any, control. In any instance, it is unlikely that anyone would choose to manipulate any of these variables strictly in anticipation of becoming a small-business owner. Certainly it is too late to do anything about being born a male and the first child in a family. Nevertheless, these demographic characteristics are overrepresented among entrepreneurs. This holds true as well for being an immigrant or the child of immigrants and having other entrepreneurs in the family. Studies of small-business owners have found that they are married, have children, and have working spouses. The entrepreneur's father was the predominant family-member influence. There are mixed findings regarding age and education. Most studies show that entrepreneurs start their businesses in their 30s, but average age at initiation appears to be going down. Early studies indicated that entrepreneurs had little formal education. More recently, average levels of education have been significantly higher, even to the master's degree level in some samples.

All these demographics are relatively uncontrollable by a prospective entrepreneur. It is highly unlikely that, having read this, anyone will decide to get married and have children simply to be able to open a business. It is important to be aware, however, that these characteristics are disproportionately distributed among small-business owners.

Attitudes: It is possible, though not easy, to change an attitude. Attitudes tend to be deeply ingrained and instilled over long periods of time. Some attitudes are clearly related to entrepreneurial success and may well be worth the effort to develop. Many feel that attitude changes follow behavioral changes; thus engaging in entrepreneurial behavior may lead to the development of desired attitudes.

Heading the list in Exhibit 1 is the need for achievement. David McClelland and others have conducted extensive research into three human needs: power, affiliation, and achievement. Their findings indicate that only perhaps 5% of the American population is characterized by a predominant need for achievement. Yet this need is consistently found among samples of entrepreneurs. Entrepreneurs direct their efforts toward goal accomplishment, and when they reach their objectives, they set higher goals. They measure their success in terms of their ability to achieve goals.

Entrepreneurs are individualists who seek to be independent of others. As a result, they generally are not motivated to perform well in large organizations. They have internal fortitude, are confident of their own abilities, and possess high levels of self-respect. Entrepreneurs are ambitious yet not concerned with their social images.

Entrepreneurs are future-oriented and money-oriented. They have high reward expectations and use rewards as measurements of their achievements. They are optimistic but still have reasonably objective perspectives of the world in which they work. They are tolerant of the ambiguities and ambivalences that they face in their environments on a daily basis.

Finally, entrepreneurs have attitudes of open-mindedness toward their own strengths and weaknesses. They are not so confident of their own abilities that they fail to recognize their limitations.

In short, entrepreneurs have a very positive self-image. They believe in themselves and their company's ability to be a success. And this type of perpetuating self-image tends to feed on itself. The attitude of "I can do it" can be seen in everything they do.

Behaviors: We all fall into patterns of behavior that become habitual after a while. These are easier to change than demographic and attitudinal characteristics. Habits, though, are difficult to break, and there will be some discomfort when taking on some of the behaviors associated with entrepreneurs.

First of all, as can be seen in Exhibit 1, small-business owners have developed a high level of technical competence. That is, they possess a certain amount of relevant experience in their business venture. For example, owners of successful automobile dealerships have acquired a significant amount of technical knowledge about selling and servicing automobiles. Entrepreneurs are also very hard workers, putting in many long hours inside and outside the business. But in many ways they have been lucky, i.e., in the right place at the right time.

Second, successful entrepreneurs are very good administrators. They have acquired the skills necessary to manage both the human and financial resources of their firm. They are willing to delegate the necessary authority to their subordinates in order to get the job completed. At the same time, they are willing to accept the responsibility for their decisions and actions. The need for constructive feedback is part of that administrative process.

Next, they are effective leaders. They are extremely task-oriented yet have learned how to mediate that with a certain amount of human-relations ability. They are self-starters and usually take the lead in enthusiastically supporting their subordinates and programs. A considerable amount of this leadership behavior is due to highly developed communications skills.

Small-business owners are very good at making critical decisions affecting their operations. They are decisive and methodical--as opposed to impulsive--in reaching their decisions. They think with their heads more than their hearts; decisions are right if they lead to accomplishment of the task.

Their self-images as successful entrepreneurs can be observed in the way they approach life as a whole. They are reliable, capable of adapting rapidly to change, and versatile in performing a variety of tasks in their organizations. In fact, many people become entrepreneurs because of innovative behavior; that is, they have a new product that they enthusiastically desire to market. They are action-oriented and aggressive, and their readiness to take moderate risks proves it. They are also self-sacrificing and willing to give up much for the sake of their business.

Finally, entrepreneurs have a sense of social responsibility that can be observed in their active participation in the church, sports, and the community.

Strategies for Success

Usually individuals go into business for themselves because they think they have the necessary qualifications for success. Indeed, when the business is just beginning, technical competence in the new venture is virtually all that is needed. But often as the business grows, entrepreneurs find themselves lacking in one or all of the important areas of marketing, finance, and administrative management. Technical know-how alone might get the business going, but it will not sustain it over the long run. If the entrepreneurs are astute enough to know they are lacking in managerial competence, they must then turn somewhere else for help for the floundering business.

What are some of the things entrepreneurs turned managers can do to strengthen themselves and, in turn, their firms? As Exhibit 2 shows, all the personal factors an individual brings to a new enterprise are important in the pursuit of goals. What kinds of strategies, therefore, are available to the average individual trying to make a go of the business? Opportunities appear endless. In fact, the present-day entrepreneur is probably aghast at the number and complexities of managerial strategies and tactics. As previously noted, little can be done about the demographic factors. The prospective entrepreneur is best off to recognize whatever limitations exist and proceed to build on strengths. Moreover, for behavioral and attitudinal strategies, he or she is not likely to have the time or inclination to weed through some set of complicated schemes usually designed for the large organization with its almost unlimited resources. What the entrepreneur wants is a simple, straightforward procedure that can be implemented in a short time with measurable results. Of course, we know that running an organization (even a small one) is not as simple as that. What we can do, however, is take a look at some distinguishable attitudes and behaviors over which each entrepreneur does have some control.

Administrative Skills: Most entrepreneurs just starting out like to do everything themselves. They feel an emotional attachment to the business and are thus very reluctant to let other members of the company do anything. As size increases, the entrepreneur by necessity must become more of an administrator than a doer. This point is critical!

The first step is to establish a simple goal structure. If the business is to be successful, everyone must be aware of its goals and the plans necessary to accomplish them. The young entrepreneur tends to forget that everyone in the organization is not as knowledgeable as the owner about the company's direction.

For example, one businessman had developed a complete 5-year operational plan regarding sales, expenses, and special programs to accomplish those goals. The problem was that he kept this well-guarded secret in the top left-hand drawer of his desk; no employee ever saw it. This small-business owner never really understood why the company was not very successful.

Next, the entrepreneur must attract competent individuals into the organization and learn to trust their expertise. Since the typical entrepreneur is such a high achiever, he or she finds it very difficult to delegate authority and responsibility to other members of the company. Nothing is so frustrating and dysfunctional from an employee's viewpoint as getting a job but having one's hands tied. Learning to trust other people's decisions is tough for the entrepreneur, but it is an important element in administration if the new business is to succeed.

302

Third, the entrepreneur must set up some simple control procedures. As Murphy's Law indicates, if anything can go wrong, it will. As the organization grows--sometimes exponentially in its early stages--this truism becomes even more noticeable. When size increases, there are simply more things that can go wrong. A few simple control procedures could help eliminate these types of worrisome problems. For example, standards of performance should be established that can be used for comparison purposes later. Members of the firm, including the owner, must be held accountable for any discrepancies in their performance. In this manner the entrepreneur concentrates only on the exceptions--not the entire operation. Questions must continually be asked: Does this activity contribute to the overall goals of the business? If it does, how much time does it warrant? Constant "fire fighting" can lead to disaster.

EXHIBIT 2
A Model of Entrepreneurial Success

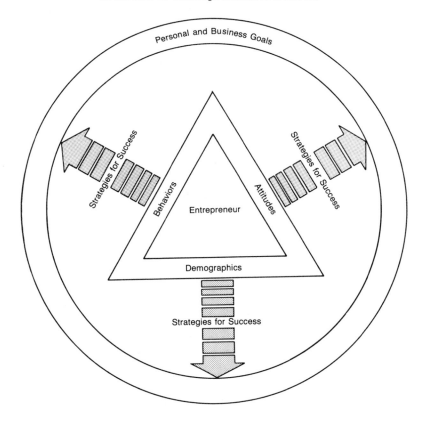

Leadership Skills: Most people have a natural inclination to use the traditional, autocratic style of leadership, and small-business owners are no exception. If entrepreneurs have put money and time on the line in a business venture, they expect others in the organization to follow their lead explicitly. The only problem is that this philosophy does not always work. Some changes are in order if the leader/owner is to be successful in supervising employees.

What many entrepreneurs must learn is that employees are just people. They have their own set of attitudes, feelings, and goals. The successful leader will learn to recognize this set of individual employee characteristics and use them to benefit the company. In short, he or she has to learn that people are not as predictable as machines. A different managerial style is clearly called for. The budding entrepreneur must learn to be a "people manager." And no matter how much we would like them to be, people are not perfect; they are going to make mistakes. How the owner/leader deals with these mistakes could be a deciding factor in the success of the business.

An example might help to underline these elements in successful leadership. It involves the managerial style of an owner/manager of a construction company. As an administrator he was excellent. He had established goals, timetables, and an equitable compensation program. He was successful in attracting very capable employees and managers. As a leader, however, he was ruthless. He expected perfection from his employees; there were no excuses for mistakes in his company. As he put it, "My people are being paid extremely well to perform their job; I expect results." His unwillingness to listen and incorporate his employees' values and perceptions into the company goal structure soon led to complacency and mediocrity.

More specifically, successful people managers have developed a keen set of interpersonal skills. They have that certain capability (largely learned) to understand and influence their employees' attitudes and behaviors. Although a task orientation is important for successful goal accomplishment, people orientation is just as important. An entrepreneur must learn to recognize employees' problems; many go by unnoticed until it is too late or too difficult to rectify the situation. The small-business owner has to learn to listen, empathize, and understand. But a good leader goes further than this. He or she has mastered the art of creative confrontation.

Creative confrontation is a combination of people orientation and task orientation. It means helping the employee recognize his or her own strengths and limitations in order to function more completely. Although the leader is available for help if needed, the employee must learn to solve his or her own problems. Most employees want to do things correctly if given the opportunity. The owner/leader must learn to recognize the critical situations and provide that opportunity.

Problem Solving: Much has been written about organizational problem solving-- usually from a specific operational viewpoint. But the average entrepreneur does not have the time or inclination to develop quantitative models to solve specific operational problems. He or she must learn to approach operations from the standpoint of an optimizer, not a maximizer; no organizational problem can be solved perfectly. And few problems can be solved in a way that prevents their recurrence sometime in the future.

Many problems encountered in day-to-day operations are of a behavioral nature. Employees or customers react to situations not as they actually exist but as seen from their own unique perspective. In other words, a problem may not exist at all; it may be only in the mind of the perceiver. This does not mean the employee or customer is making it up; it is very real to him or her.

For instance, the owner of a small parts manufacturer witnessed the constant recurrence of a scheduling problem between the production-control manager and the manufacturing superintendent. Several personnel meetings and procedural changes later, the "problem" still existed. Two in-depth interviews with the two men by an outside consultant exposed the essential problem: the older superintendent resented the younger production-control specialist telling him what and when to manufacture. Problems will not be solved if they are not accurately diagnosed.

If a problem does exist, try to pinpoint the exact cause(s) and standard(s) of performance. More often than not, a business owner looks at symptoms rather than causes. The proper questions asked at the right time can uncover a multitude of causality factors. And most importantly, find out what standard the performance is compared with. Many times a problem will cease to exist when the standard is carefully evaluated. Existing standards are not engraved in gold; they are subject to change through time. There is no substitute for a questioning, methodical approach to decision making.

Finally, learn from mistakes. The past does not have to be a predictor of the future. Much of the conflict that occurs within an organization can be used to advantage. Learn from disagreement; conflict can be constructive if handled properly. Indeed, a certain amount of conflict is necessary; it indicates that something or someone is amiss. Rather than point a finger of blame, try to pinpoint causes, eliminate barriers, and redefine roles within the organization. The leader is responsible for organizational peacemaking.

When solutions to problems are implemented, remember that people will be involved. Let them be a major part of the implementation, not just the development of another problem. Employees will be more likely to accept the solution if they are part of it.

One owner of a large wholesale operation spent over $50,000 to implement a computerized inventory-control system, only to discover that it would not work as designed. After several unsuccessful repair attempts by the same technical specialists who designed the system, the entire system was scrapped. Perhaps if the owner had explained the system's usefulness, and let them be part of the new process, the outcome might have been completely different.

Positive Self-Image: Much of what has already been said depends on the self-image of the entrepreneur. The owner's positive self-image, as defined by many interwoven attitudinal and behavioral factors, will do much to predict the future success of a new enterprise. If managers feel good about themselves and their organizations, this attitude tends to carry over to others in the business. On the other hand, a negative self-image tends to become a self-fulfilling prophecy: you do not think you have what it takes; therefore you fail. This is probably the most important factor in the entire mix of success characteristics!

A tremendous desire for achievement and independence is important. Learn to set moderate goals, personally and for the business. Goals that are too high or too low will not work. Low goals breed complacency; high goals not achieved breed frustration. A successful track record of goal accomplishment will do much to improve self-confidence and self-esteem. Another behavior important in enhancing your self-image as a successful entrepreneur is to practice being optimistic with employees and customers. Expect high performance. This will be personally reinforcing and will also provide a role model for others in the company. Most people want an optimistic and enthusiastic leader they can look up to; it is just part of human nature. On the other hand, learn to accept ambiguities in life and in the company. Not every goal can be accomplished.

Learn to be a proactor rather than a reactor. Start things moving. We know that successful business people are action-oriented and aggressive. At the same time, an entrepreneur must recognize his or her limitations. Make a list of personal strengths and weaknesses. Concentrate on strengths, but do not be frustrated by imperfection. Practicing these behaviors enhances self-confidence. All of these add to the self-image of a successful entrepreneur who know that success comes from taking two steps forward and one step backward.

We all know that hard work is important, and nothing important is accomplished without a great deal of perspiration. But hard work is not enough. Be constantly on the alert for ways to improve yourself and your business. In other words, be innovative and flexible. Increase productivity is one of the keys to a more profitable operation. Learning when to adapt to changing situations is the only constant element in the entrepreneur's world. One of the most successful businessmen we know has only two rules in running his business: (1) How can I accomplish this task with less effort than the last time? and (2) Since the situation is not likely to change to fit my needs, what can I do to adapt to the situation? The continued success of his company must be a testimony to his innovative, adaptable attitude.

The sad part of the story is that successful entrepreneurs are self-sacrificing. They recognize that nothing worth having is free. The piper must be paid. This means giving up that four-week vacation, that Saturday golf game, or that occasional trip to the mountains. Success comes with a high price tag.

Formulas for Success?

There are many opportunities for success--but no formulas. This article has looked only at some possible profiles and hints for successful entrepreneurship. What succeeds for one entrepreneur may not succeed for another. But we can learn from others' experience. We do know what successful entrepreneurs are doing to make a significant contribution to society as a whole, themselves, and their families. After all, entrepreneurs are the cornerstones of the free-enterprise system.

If your goal is to run your own business, the rewards are many. No one can guarantee success, but the opportunities are there. Both intrinsic and extrinsic rewards are available to the entrepreneur who has what it takes.

Footnotes

[1]   R. M. Burger, An Analysis of the National Science Foundation's Innovation Centers Experiment (Research Triangle Park, North Carolina: Research Triangle Institute, July 1977).
[2]   David L. Birch, The Job Generation Process (Cambridge, Massachusetts: Program on Neighborhood and Regional Change, Massachusetts Institute of Technology, 1979).

306

3   Task Force on Women Business Owners, <u>The Bottom Line: Unequal Enterprise in America</u> (Washington, D.C.: U.S. Government Printing Office, 1978); and U.S. Bureau of the Census, <u>1977 Survey of Minority Owned Business Enterprise</u> (Washington, D.C.: U.S. Government Printing Office, 1979).

4   U.S. Small Business Administration, Office of Advocacy, <u>Recommendations of the Conference</u>, White House Conference on Small Business, January 1980.

5   "Bonuses for Small Business," <u>Business Week</u>, November 3, 1980, pp. 100, 102.

6   Forrest H. Frantz, <u>Successful Small Business Management</u> (Englewood Cliffs, New Jersey: Prentice-Hall, 1978).

7   See Clifford M. Baumback and Kenneth Lawyer, <u>How to Organize and Operate a Small Business</u> (Englewood Cliffs, New Jersey: Prentice-Hall, 1979); H. N. Broom and Justin G. Longenecker, <u>Small Business Management</u> (Cincinnati: South-Western, 1975); J. Hornaday and J. Aboud, "Characteristics of Successful Entrepreneurs," <u>Personnel Psychology</u>, Summer 1971, pp. 141-153; Joseph R. Mancuso, <u>How to Start, Finance, and Manage Your Own Small Business</u> (Englewood Cliffs, New Jersey: Prentice-Hall, 1978); David C. McClelland, <u>The Achieving Society</u> (Princeton, New Jersey: Van Nostrand, 1961); and Kenneth R. Van Voorhis, <u>Entrepreneurship and Small Business Management</u> (Boston: Allyn and Bacon, 1980).

THE 1995 LABOR FORCE: A SECOND LOOK

Howard N. Fullerton, Jr.
John Tschetter

During 1982-95 period, the number of persons of prime working age (25-54) in the labor force is expected to grow considerably faster than the total labor force. Young workers will decline in absolute numbers as the rate of growth of the total labor force slows markedly. These growth trends reflect the aging of the baby-boom generation and a subsequent sharp decline in birth rates.

The Bureau of Labor Statistics has revised its labor force projections for the 1982-95 period.[1] For the middle scenario, which assumes that labor force participation of women will accelerate then taper off, the civilian labor force is projected to reach 131.4 million persons by 1995, 3.8 million more than projected earlier.[2] The labor force is expected to grow 1.6 percent per year over the 1982-90 period, slowing to 1.0 percent per year during 1990-95, thus continuing the slow growth which began in the late 1970's. Nearly two-thirds of the growth will be among women; nearly one-fourth will be among the black and other group.[3]

This article presents new projections for the 1995 labor force with alternative demographic and, for the first time, economic assumptions. The demographic alternatives illustrate the sensitivity of the size of the projected labor force to various assumptions regarding the behavior of age, sex, and racial groups.[4] The economic alternatives explore the sensitivity of labor force changes to assumptions about real earnings and the employment rate.

Methodology

Labor force projections require population projections. The latter have been prepared by the Bureau of the Census by age, sex, and race, based on trends in

Reprinted from <u>The Monthly Labor Review</u>, November 1983, pp. 3-10.

birth rates, death rates, and net migration.[5] Once the population projections are prepared, BLS can project labor force participation rates--the percent of each group in the population who will be working or seeking work--for 64 age, sex, and race groups.

To develop labor force participation rates for each group, rates of growth over the 1962-81 period (or subperiods) are analyzed using the most appropriate time period for each group. If past trends are deemed not likely to continue throughout the projection period, the rates are modified. The rate of change in labor force participation was modified for several groups: women ages 20-44 and 45 and over, and men ages 55 and over. The rates of change in participation for all groups are tapered so that the annual changes would be zero after the year 2004.

For women ages 20 to 44, it is assumed that the rate of change in participation will accelerate during the 1982-85 period to allow some partial recovery from the 1980-82 economic slowdown. These projections assume that some of the 1980-82 slowdown in female participation rates are permanent, particularly when compared with the trends of the early and mid-1970's.

For the older labor force, the participation rates have been declining over the 1962-81 period. It is assumed that these declines will moderate. If the historical trends for some older groups continue, the resulting participation rates would approach zero. These modifications for women and older workers were made to each age group within these broad groups. The historical rates of change in participation for all remaining labor force groups are assumed to continue.

The levels of anticipated labor force are calculated by applying projected participation rates to the Bureau of the Census' population projections.

Middle Growth Scenario

The overall growth in the labor force over the next 8 to 12 years will be influenced by the baby-boom generation, which will attain those ages at which both men and women have their highest participation; and by the continued, but slower, rise in participation among women ages 20 to 44. (See tables 1 and 2.) In contrast, the increases in the labor force during the 1970's were influenced by the initial entrance of the baby-boom generation, and by the very rapid increases in the labor force activity of women, particularly married women ages 20 to 44. As a consequence of these changing influences, labor force growth is expected to slow in the late 1980's and the 1990's.

The following tabulation shows labor force growth from 1950 to 1982 and projected growth from 1983 to 1995, by age group:

	1950-60	1960-70	1970-82	1982-90	1990-95
Age 16 and over	1.3	1.7	2.4	1.6	1.0
16 to 24	.0	4.5	2.7	-1.3	-.8
25 to 54	1.3	1.0	2.3	2.9	1.6
55 and over	1.6	1.4	.3	-.7	-?

308

The Uncertainty of Projections

Knowledge or insights concerning future employment trends is very valuable. . . . Such information is used to plan careers and training programs, and develop business expansion plans and public policy. However, information about future employment growth is clouded by uncertainty. . . . It is very important for users to understand the imprecise nature of projections so they can deal with the information properly.

Although virtually no data about changes in the economy over a 10-year period can be anticipated with absolute certainty, there are differing degrees of uncertainty. To illustrate, I would say with relative certitude that the younger labor force is going to decline in this decade. The population which will be 16 years older in 1990 is born and unless there are truly revolutionary changes in labor force participation rates for young people along with dramatic infusions through immigration of young people, the young labor force will decline. Perhaps, at the other end of the scale the uncertainty would be a projection of employment in the oil and gas well drilling industry. If I knew what the price of oil would be in 1990 or 1995, perhaps I could come close to projecting the level of employment in that industry. But the factors that will determine the price of oil in 1990 are themselves subject to great variances and uncertainty.

For much of the information on projections, the uncertainty lies between these two extremes. For example, the occupation "computer service technician" is projected to grow very rapidly. From 1982 to 1995, its projected growth is 97 percent. I am confident that employment in this occupation will grow rapidly, certainly much faster than the average growth of the economy over this period. However, I am not certain that the growth rate will be 97 percent or even fall within the 94-98 percent range shown in our alternatives. The growth rate could be significantly greater. Some occupations of this size, 55,000 in 1982, have grown much faster in the past. Still, a growth rate of only 50 percent is not beyond the realm of impossibility.

Concerns received from the public have led us to think and probe further in terms of asking questions about our projections. For example, in the last 6 months, the Department of Defense and some of the defense industries have said there is a critical shortage of engineers that should be reflected in our publications. During the same period, we have had three groups representing the engineering professions say that BLS has been painting such a rosy picture for engineers that we are causing a flood in the market and that their member engineers cannot find jobs.

Which of these groups is correct? We examined this dilemma and concluded that there probably are two distinct markets for engineers. One is new college graduates who are currently in short supply--in at least some engineering disciplines--and these are principally among the engineering categories used by defense contractors. But 45 year-old engineers who are working on a product or product line that has been cancelled are in a tough job market because they are not always able to compete with the young engineer. The important point here is that if this situation is true for engineers, it may also be true for accountants and auditors, lawyers, and many other occupations.

Economists and others involved in forecasting economic activity understand the uncertain nature of projections. However, others, including those who are primary users of the information, may not. Thus, the development of numerical projections is only the first task in presenting information on economic trends or employment growth. It is just as important to present the data in a meaningful way. Unfortunately, this task is neither simple nor straight forward. Despite BLS experience with and concern about the subject, we still are not sure our users understand the uncertainty attached to our projected data. The Bureau hopes that by indicating the factors underlying growth, preparing evaluation of previous projections, and discussing alternatives and assumptions, we will provide users with some idea of the uncertainties.

Ronald E. Kutscher
Associate Commissioner
Bureau of Labor Statistics
Remarks before a Labor Market Information
Conference in Atlanta, Ga., June 1983

The slowdown actually began in 1979. The peak labor force growth, 3.0 percent per year, occurred between 1976 and 1979. Over the 1979-82 period, growth was only 1.6 percent per year, reflecting the slowing of long-term growth, as well as the repercussions of 3 years of flat economic growth.

Over the 1982-95 period, there will be a pronounced shift in the age structure of the labor force. The 25- to 54-year-old labor force is expected to grow considerably faster than the total labor force, 1.3 percentage points per year faster during the 1982-90 period. At the same time, the number of 16- to 24-year-old participants is projected to decline in absolute numbers. During the 1960's and 1970's, the labor force growth of younger workers was by far the fastest of any age group, reflecting the baby-boom generation initially entering and then maturing in the labor force. As this young generation ages in the 1990's, the number of persons ages 25 to 34 will decline. A shift from a young to a prime working-age population in itself induces an increase in the overall participation rate, as prime-age persons are more likely to be in the labor force.

The population ages 55 and older will continue to increase. However, the participation rates for this group are projected to continue declining. For men, the increased population and declining participation have resulted in absolute declines in their number in the labor force. For women, this combination is expected to result in a relatively constant number in the labor force over the next decade. It is assumed that the new social security laws will not affect the trend of labor force participation for the population 55 and older between now and 1995.

Table 1. **Civilian labor force, by sex, age, and race, 1970-82, and middle growth projection to 1995**

Labor Group	Labor force (in thousands)					Participation rate				
	1970	1980	1982	1990	1995	1970	1980	1982	1990	1995
Total, age 16 and over	82,771	106,940	110,204	124,951	131,387	60.4	63.8	64.0	66.9	67.8
Men	51,228	61,453	62,450	67,701	69,970	79.7	77.4	76.6	76.5	76.1
16 to 24	9,725	13,606	13,074	11,274	10,573	69.4	74.4	72.6	74.7	74.5
16 to 19	4,008	4,999	4,470	4,123	4,043	56.1	60.5	56.7	62.3	62.9
20 to 24	5,717	8,607	8,604	7,151	6,530	83.3	85.9	84.9	84.4	84.1
25 to 54	32,213	38,712	40,357	48,180	51,358	95.8	94.2	94.0	93.8	93.4
25 to 34	11,327	16,971	17,793	19,569	18,105	96.4	95.2	94.7	93.7	93.1
35 to 44	10,469	11,836	12,781	17,469	19,446	96.9	95.5	95.3	95.6	95.3
45 to 54	10,417	9,905	9,784	11,142	13,807	94.3	91.2	91.2	91.3	91.1
55 and over	9,291	9,135	9,019	8,247	8,039	55.7	45.6	43.8	37.4	35.3
55 to 64	7,126	7,242	7,174	6,419	6,311	83.0	72.1	70.2	65.5	64.5
65 and over	2,165	1,893	1,845	1,828	1,728	26.8	19.0	17.8	14.9	13.3
Women	31,543	45,487	47,755	57,250	61,417	43.3	51.5	52.6	58.3	60.3
16 to 24	8,121	11,696	11,533	10,813	10,557	51.3	61.9	62.0	69.1	71.6
16 to 19	3,241	4,381	4,056	3,778	3,761	44.0	52.9	51.4	56.8	58.2
20 to 24	4,880	7,315	7,477	7,035	6,796	57.7	68.9	69.8	78.1	82.0
25 to 54	18,208	27,888	30,149	40,496	44,852	50.1	64.0	66.3	75.6	78.7
25 to 34	5,708	12,257	13,393	16,804	16,300	45.0	65.5	68.0	78.1	81.7
35 to 44	5,968	8,627	9,651	14,974	17,427	51.1	65.5	68.0	78.6	82.8
45 to 54	6,532	7,004	7,105	8,718	11,125	54.4	59.9	61.6	67.1	69.5
55 and over	5,213	5,904	6,073	5,941	6,008	25.3	22.8	22.7	20.5	19.9
55 to 64	4,157	4,742	4,888	4,612	4,671	43.0	41.3	41.8	41.5	42.5
65 and over	1,056	1,161	1,185	1,329	1,337	9.7	8.1	7.9	7.4	7.0
White	73,556	93,600	96,143	107,734	112,393	60.2	64.1	64.3	67.3	68.1
Men	46,035	54,473	55,133	59,201	60,757	80.0	78.2	77.4	77.4	77.0
16 to 24	8,540	11,902	11,371	9,854	9,271	70.2	76.7	74.9	78.5	79.1
25 to 54	29,000	34,224	35,565	41,864	44,232	96.3	95.0	94.9	94.8	94.5
55 and over	8,494	8,345	8,197	7,483	7,254	55.8	46.1	44.2	37.8	35.6
Women	27,521	39,127	41,010	48,533	51,636	42.6	51.2	52.4	58.1	60.0
16 to 24	7,141	10,179	10,013	9,285	9,025	52.1	64.4	64.7	72.5	75.4
25 to 54	15,690	23,723	25.619	34.081	37,433	43.9	63.4	66.1	75.6	78.7
55 and over	4,690	5,226	5,378	5,167	5,178	24.9	22.4	22.4	20.1	19.5
Black and other	9,218	13,340	14,062	17,217	18,994	61.8	61.7	61.6	64.8	65.7
Men	5,194	6,980	7,317	8,500	9,213	76.5	71.5	71.0	71.0	70.6
16 to 24	1,185	1,702	1,702	1,420	1,302	64.5	61.6	60.0	55.9	52.7
25 to 54	3,212	4,488	4,792	6,316	7,126	91.9	88.6	88.0	87.6	87.2
55 and over	796	790	822	764	785	54.7	40.8	40.5	34.3	32.6
Women	4,024	6,359	6,745	8,717	9,781	49.5	53.6	53.9	59.7	61.7
16 to 24	982	1,516	1,520	1,528	1,532	46.3	49.3	48.8	53.7	55.3
25 to 54	2,517	4,164	4,529	6,415	7,419	59.2	67.0	67.9	75.8	78.7
55 and over	524	678	695	774	830	30.0	26.4	25.5	23.5	22.8

These variations in growth rates by age groups mean that persons ages 25 to 54 will account for a much greater share of the 1995 labor force than the 1982 labor force. Prime working-age persons (25 to 54) are expected to account for about 73 percent of the 1995 labor force, up from 61 percent in 1970, and 64 percent in 1982. The growing proportion of prime-age participants could favorably affect productivity because of the greater continuity of participation by women and because of the higher educational attainment of all participants. This continuity and educational attainment imply that the future labor force will be more experienced and better trained, compared with the 1970's when younger workers (ages 16 to 24) accounted for a large share of labor force growth. The maturing of the labor force in the 1980's and 1990's means that employers may have difficulties finding young workers. The decline in the number of youths will be particularly important to the Armed Forces, the single largest employer of young men.

Table 2. **Black civilian labor force, by sex and age, 1972-82, and middle growth projection to 1995**

Labor Group	Labor force (in thousands)					Participation rate				
	1972	1980	1982	1990	1995	1972	1980	1982	1990	1995
Blacks, age 16 and over	8,707	10,865	11,331	13,600	14,833	59.9	61.0	61.0	64.5	65.4
Men	4,816	5,612	5,804	6,687	7,297	73.7	70.6	70.1	70.4	70.5
16 to 24	1,214	1,414	1,401	1,156	1,055	63.9	62.0	60.3	55.9	54.0
25 to 54	2,917	3,551	3,745	4,939	5,549	90.0	88.4	87.7	87.4	87.0
55 and over	687	647	660	592	583	49.1	39.3	39.0	33.2	31.3
Women	3,890	5,253	5,527	6,913	7,646	48.7	53.2	53.7	59.0	61.2
16 to 24	967	1,279	1,272	1,210	1,180	45.0	48.9	48.4	51.8	53.2
25 to 54	2,421	3,387	3,660	5,073	5,805	60.0	67.6	68.8	75.7	78.6
55 and over	503	588	595	630	661	27.8	26.1	25.3	23.6	22.9

Median Age. The median age of the labor force will rise slightly over the next 20 to 15 years. The median age was fairly constant between 1950 and 1970, but dropped sharply between 1970 and 1980 when the baby-boom generation entered the labor force. The following tabulation shows the median age of the labor force for 1950 to 1980 and the projected median age for 1990 and 1995, by sex and race:

	1950	1960	1970	1982	1990	1995
All participants	38.6	40.5	39.0	34.8	35.9	37.3
Men	39.3	40.5	39.4	35.3	36.4	37.8
Women	36.7	40.4	38.3	34.2	35.3	36.8
White	----	40.7	39.3	35.0	36.1	37.5
Black and other	----	38.2	36.6	32.8	34.8	36.3

The differences in median age between men and women and between whites and black and other minorities reflect the age mix of the respective labor forces. For example, in 1982, men ages 55 and over accounted for 14.4 percent of the male labor force; women ages 55 and over accounted for only 12.7 percent of the female labor force. These median age differences between the two groups are projected to continue.

Women and Minorities. during the 1982-95 period, the number of women and minorities in the labor force are projected to grow faster than the overall labor force. The following tabulation shows total labor force growth and growth for women, blacks, and black and other minorities for the 1950-82 period, and projected growth, 1982-95.

Women, both white and black, will account for about two-thirds of the labor force growth during the 1980's and 1990's, about the same proportion as in the 1950's. During the 1960's and 1970's, when men of the baby-boom generation entered the labor force, the proportion of growth attributed to women dropped despite rapid increases in their participation rates. With the young men of the baby-boom generation now in the labor force, the share of labor force growth attributed to women will be greater over the next decade.

	1950-60	1960-70	1970-82	1982-90	1990-95
Total	1.3	1.7	2.4	1.6	1.0
Women	2.4	3.1	3.5	2.3	1.4
Black and other	---	1.8	3.6	2.6	2.0
Blacks	---	---	---	2.3	1.8

The black and other group, should account for slightly more than 21 percent of the additions to the labor force during the 1982-90 period, increasing to nearly 28 percent in the 1990-95 period. Since 1960, this group's proportion of overall growth has been growing despite the continuing drop in participation by black men. The black labor force is projected to grow at almost twice the white rate, reflecting the younger age structure of the black population.

The two groups just discussed overlap. White women and black and other men and women together will account for 72.4 percent of the 1982-90 labor force growth, and 75.8 percent of the 1990-95 growth. These two groups accounted for only 66.8 percent of the 1970-82 labor force growth.

Economic dependency. Around 1986, more of the population should be in the labor force than not in the labor force. The economic dependency ratio, the number of persons not in the labor force divided by those in the labor force, was high in the 1960's, but declined sharply through the 1970's as the baby-boom generation and women entered the labor force in large numbers. During the 1980's and 1990's, the ratio should continue to decline, but at a considerably more moderate pace, reflecting only the continued increases in participation rates for women.

The numerator of the economic dependency ratio can be disaggregated into all persons who are (1) under age 16, (2) between ages 16 and 64, and (3) age 65 and over. The denominator of the ratio in each instance is the total labor force. The following tabulation shows the economic dependency ratio for 1960 to 1982 and projected for 1990 and 1995 for these age groups.

	1960	1970	1982	1990	1995
Total population	150.4	138.5	106.5	96.4	94.1
Under age 16	81.45	72.1	48.9	45.2	45.2
Age 16 to 64	50.2	46.8	36.0	28.4	26.0
Age 65 and over	18.7	19.6	21.6	22.5	22.9

The drop (from 50 to 36 persons per hundred workers) in the ratio attributed to the 16- to 64-year-olds reflects the steady entry of women into the work force.

313

The economic dependency ratio for persons under age 16 has declined over the 1960 to 1980 period, as the baby-boom generation and women entered the labor market. During the next decade, the ratio should be unchanged despite the "echo" of the baby boom, that is, the increase in the population attributed to the children of the baby-boom generation. The ratio for older workers is expected to rise slightly over the next decade, and should continue to rise into the middle of the next century; currently, their ratio is the lowest of the three groups.

These projected economic dependency ratios have several implications. There will be fewer children per labor force participant in the future, hence providing for primary and secondary education should be less of a burden. On the other hand, there will be more older persons not in the labor force per labor force participant, therefore, providing for retirement and the care of older workers should be slightly more of a burden.

Alternative Assumptions

The middle scenario just discussed reflects underlying assumptions and could be significantly affected by changes in these assumptions. BLS developed alternative projections to examine the range of outcomes attached to any projection. Two sets of alternative projections were developed for the current projection: demographic alternatives and economic alternatives. The following tabulations show the size of the civilian labor force during 1970, 1980, and 1982:

Civilian labor force (in millions)

	1970	1980	1982
Total	82.8	106.9	110.2

and the projected size under each scenario for 1990 and 1995:

	1990	1995
High demographic	131.3	141.0
High economic	125.3 to 125.4	131.9 to 132.8
Middle	125.0	131.4
Low economic	123.7 to 124.9	130.0 to 131.0
Low demographic	120.3	125.1

Demographic alternatives. One assumption in the middle scenario is that the growth in participation rates of women ages 20 to 44 will accelerate in the near term (that is, recover from the effects of the 1980 and 1981-82 recessions) before tapering off. If the rate of female labor force participation continues to accelerate through the late 1980's (rather than only through the mid-1980's) the 1995 participation rate and labor force for these women would be considerably higher than in the middle scenario, about 9.6 million *more* persons, or 7.3 percent. (See Table 3.)

On the other hand, it is possible that the participation rates for women ages 20 to 44 will not accelerate and instead will continue the modest upward trend

314

Table 3. Projections of the civilian labor force in 1995, by alternative demographic scenarios

Labor group	Labor force (in thousands)			Participation rate		
	High scenario	Middle scenario	Low scenario	High scenario	Middle scenario	Low scenario
Total, age 16 and over	140,973	131,387	125,058	72.7	67.8	64.5
Men	73,005	69,970	67,541	79.4	76.1	73.5
16 to 24	11,321	10,573	10,013	79.8	74.5	70.6
25 to 54	52,545	51,358	50,130	95.5	93.4	91.2
55 and over	9,139	8,039	7,398	40.1	35.3	32.5
Women	67,968	61,417	57,517	66.7	60.3	56.5
16 to 24	11,155	10,557	9,792	75.7	71.6	66.4
25 to 54	49,525	44,852	41,964	86.9	78.7	73.6
55 and over	7,288	6,008	5,761	24.2	19.9	19.1
White	119,560	112,393	107,170	72.5	68.1	65.0
Men	62,451	60,757	58,839	79.2	77.0	74.6
16 to 24	9,463	9,271	8,755	80.8	79.1	74.7
25 to 54	44,815	44,232	43,406	95.7	94.5	92.7
55 and over	8,173	7,254	6,678	40.2	35.6	32.8
Women	57,109	51,636	48,331	66.4	60.0	56.2
16 to 24	9,330	9,025	8,316	77.9	75.4	69.5
25 to 54	41,384	37,433	35,097	87.0	78.7	73.8
55 and over	6,395	5,178	4,918	24.1	19.5	18.6
Black and other	21,413	18,994	17,889	74.8	65.1	61.9
Men	10,554	9,213	8,709	80.0	70.2	66.7
16 to 24	1,858	1,302	1,253	75.9	52.7	50.9
25 to 54	7,730	7,126	6,725	94.6	87.1	82.3
55 and over	966	785	722	40.3	32.8	29.9
Women	10,859	9,781	9,182	68.7	61.2	58.0
16 to 24	1,825	1,532	1,471	65.7	55.4	53.2
25 to 54	8,141	7,419	6,863	86.8	78.7	72.9
55 and over	893	830	847	24.5	22.9	23.1
Black	16,517	14,833	13,984	72.5	65.6	61.7
Men	8,125	7,297	6,775	79.4	70.7	66.4
16 to 24	1,432	1,055	984	73.9	54.3	50.4
25 to 54	5,974	5,549	5,246	93.4	87.1	82.2
55 and over	719	583	549	38.2	31.0	29.1
Women	8,392	7,646	7,217	67.0	61.7	57.8
16 to 24	1,407	1,180	1,148	63.8	53.8	51.8
25 to 54	6,311	5,805	5,413	85.7	78.1	73.2
55 and over	674	661	650	23.6	22.3	22.7

shown during the 1979-82 period. If this occurs, there would be 6.3 million *fewer* persons (4.8 percent) in the 1995 labor force.

The two differences between the low, middle, and high assumptions concerning female participation rates, are substantial. The high scenario reflects female participation rates nearly converging to the higher male participation rates. The low scenario reflects a sharp deceleration from the trends of the 1970's. Over the 1979-82 period, the growth of female rates slowed, possibly in response to the 1980 and 1981-82 recessions. However, it might also reflect a change in the long-run trend. The low scenario, in essence, assumes that the recent trends reflect new secular trends for women.

The low-growth path assumes a more modest growth which is *not* a reversal of the upward growth in female participation rates or shifts in marital status. For example, regardless of which scenario is used, women should account for 65 to 66

315

percent of increases in the labor force. This stability occurs because increases in female participation will be the greatest source of labor force growth over the next decade.

A second demographic assumption in the middle scenario concerns the relative trends in black-white participation. Over the past two decades, the rates for black and white men have been diverging. (The rates for black and white women, on the other hand, appear to have converged, if not crossed.) The low and middle scenarios assume these respective trends will continue. The high scenario assumes that the rates for black and white men will converge to the higher white male rates. In the low scenario, black and other minorities account for 25.8 percent of the increase in the labor force over the 1982-95 period; in the high scenario, 23.9 percent; and in the middle scenario, 23.3 percent.

Economic alternatives. Labor force projections are only one segment of the BLS projections program. The program includes gross national product projections, in total and by major demand and income components; industry output and employment projections; and occupational requirements projections. To emphasize the uncertainty of these varied projections, BLS traditionally develops several scenarios which cover a number of alternative assumptions yielding a reasonably broad span of employment and gross national product level. The alternative projections of the economy as a whole use different assumptions for fiscal policy, productivity growth, the unemployment rate, and the price level.

At issue in these alternatives is the relationship between earnings and unemployment rates and labor force trends. Would alternative economic trends imply substantially or modestly different labor force trends? According to the models, modest changes in the unemployment rate for all workers and in real earnings of workers lead to relatively small changes in the total labor force. (See table 4.)

Alternative projections of labor force trends have been made with two econometric models. One, labeled the marital status model, focuses on the behavior of detailed labor force trends.[6] The second model, labeled the macro labor force model, focuses solely on total labor force trends in the context of a broader economic model.[7] The methodology for these economic scenarios is substantially different from that used in other BLS labor force projections. The assumptions here are based on econometric models, while the other alternatives were based on a demographic methodology.

The *marital status model* relates participation rates for 16 age, sex, and marital status groups to real earnings of full-time workers by sex, and the overall unemployment rate. The model was estimated with Standard Metropolitan Statistical Area data for 34 cities during the 1973-80 period. The data are constructed from the micro files of the Bureau of the Census' Current Population Survey. The following tabulation shows the unemployment rate and annual earnings data used in the model.

	1982	1990	1995
Unemployment rate:			
All workers			
High	9.7	5.4	5.2
Middle	9.7	6.3	6.0
Low	9.7	6.5	6.8

Real annual earnings
(1972 dollars):
Men

High	$7,497	$8,698	$9,074
Middle	7,497	8,905	9,804
Low	7,497	8,941	10,148

Women

High	4,441	5,152	5,375
Middle	4,441	5,275	5,807
Low	4,441	5,296	6,011

Developing the alternative scenarios with the marital status model required two steps. First, a middle scenario of labor force growth was developed for the 16 groups. This middle scenario for the 16 marital status groups was constrained to replicate the middle scenario described earlier. It was developed as in previous projections--extrapolating historical trends. Second, the differences in the two explanatory variables among scenarios were multiplied by the respective coefficients; then the products were added to obtain the differences from the middle scenario.

For the marital status model, the range between the high and low scenarios is only 900,000 persons in the total labor force and .4 percentage points in participation rates. (See table 4.) The groups most affected by the changes between the scenarios are married women ages 45 to 54, nonmarried women ages 35 to 44, married women ages 20 to 34, and nonmarried men ages 45 to 54 and ages 35 to 44. The finding that these groups are more sensitive than others to the changes in economic trends is consistent with the slower trends in participation rates during the 1979-82 period. The projected labor force participation rates for these five groups are all projected to change by between 1.0 and 1.7 percentage points between the high and low economic scenario.

The *macro labor force model* relates the labor force participation rate of all workers to the unemployment rate and real wages. As noted, the macro labor force model is part of a large-scale quarterly macroeconometric model that allows for interaction of labor force trends with employment, labor productivity, and other trends.

For the macro labor force model, the range between the high and low scenarios is 2.8 million persons and 1.4 percentage points in the total participation rates. The difference between the high and low scenarios for the macro labor force model, when compared to the marital status model, reflects, in part, the interaction of labor force trends with economic trends in the context of a macroeconometric model and, in part, the structural differences between the two labor force models.[8]

A comparison of the low and high economic scenarios with the middle scenario indicates that changes in economic assumptions do not result in substantial changes in labor force projections.

The most important finding across the four economic scenarios is that projections with two strikingly different labor force models yield *small* differences between the scenarios. By contrast, the difference between the high and low demographic scenarios is 15.9 million in 1995. Thus, the key factors in the size of the future labor force are demographic in nature.

Table 4. **Civilian labor force by alternative economic scenarios, 1982 and projected to 1995**

Labor group	Labor force (in thousands)				Participation rate			
	1982	High scenario	Middle scenario	Low scenario	1982	High scenario	Middle scenario	Low scenario
Marital status model:								
Total	110,204	131,887	131,387	130,977	64.0	68.0	67.8	67.6
Men	62,450	70,101	69,970	69,867	76.6	76.2	76.1	75.9
16 to 19	4,470	4,032	4,043	4,047	56.7	62.8	62.9	63.0
20 to 34	21,385	24,647	24,635	24,619	90.8	90.5	62.9	90.4
Married	14,212	11,071	11,071	11,062	97.1	95.6	90.4	95.6
Other	12,185	13,576	13,564	13,557	85.3	86.7	95.6	86.6
35 to 44	12,781	19,497	19,446	19,401	95.3	95.5	86.6	95.1
Married	10,321	14,971	14,956	14,937	96.8	97.0	95.3	96.8
Other	2,460	4,527	4,490	4,463	89.4	90.9	96.9	89.6
45 to 54	9,784	13,847	13,807	13,784	91.2	91.4	90.2	90.9
Married	8,320	11,553	11,531	11,523	93.4	93.8	91.1	93.5
Other	1,464	2,295	2,276	2,261	80.8	81.0	93.6	79.8
55 and over	9,019	8,076	8,039	8,017	43.8	35.5	80.3	35.2
							35.3	
Women	47,755	61,786	61,417	61,110	52.6	60.7	60.3	60.0
16 to 19	4,056	3,777	3,761	3,749	51.4	58.5	58.3	58.1
20 to 34	17,128	23,224	23,096	22,975	68.8	82.3	81.8	81.4
Married	10,592	11,160	11,087	11,021	61.6	80.8	80.3	79.8
Other	10,279	12,064	12,009	11,954	77.7	83.6	83.2	82.9
35 to 44	9,651	17,526	17,427	17,350	68.0	83.2	82.8	82.4
Married	6,723	11,968	11,932	11,902	64.1	81.8	81.5	81.3
Other	2,928	5,557	5,495	5,448	79.0	86.5	85.6	84.8
45 to 54	7,105	11,282	11,125	11,015	61.6	70.5	69.5	68.8
Married	4,993	7,927	7,798	7,708	57.9	68.4	67.3	66.5
Other	2,111	3,356	3,327	3,307	72.3	76.0	75.3	74.9
55 and over	6,073	5,976	6,008	8,017	22.7	19.9	20.0	20.0
Macro labor force model:								
Total	110,204	132,800	131,387	130,000	64.0	66.9	67.8	67.1

Revisions Reflect 1980 Census

Several factors necessitated updating the projections published in 1980: revisions in the historical labor force estimates, revisions in the projected population (which are used in determining the size of the future labor force), and availability of labor force participation rates for the 1979-82 period.[9] The historical labor force data were revised to incorporate the 1980 census. The revised population projections reflect incorporation of the 1980 population estimates and new, *higher* assumptions about life expectancy and net migration, and new, *lower* assumptions about fertility levels. These changes resulted in a larger projected population for 1995, with 8.8 million more persons over age 16. The new population projection alone would have raised the 1995 labor force by 5.3 million persons (after accounting for population shifts by age, sex, and race).

Offsetting the population growth is a lower projected change in labor force participation rates. This reflects the 1979-82 changes in participation which were lower than those of 1962-79. The 1979-82 changes reflect both cyclical factors and trend factors, such as an increased fertility after years of steady decline. If the previously projected participation rates were applied to the new population projections, the 1995 labor force would have been 132.4 million persons, 1 million more than the current projection. The most notable change in projected participation rates occurred for women ages 25 to 34, a group for which BLS has consistently underprojected participation. The rate for this group was lowered 2 percentage points in the current projection to 81.7 percent, compared with 83.7 percent in the previous projection. Still, participation for this group is expected to grow 13.7 percentage points over the 1982-95 period, the largest projected increase for any labor group. Projected participation rates for several groups have been revised upward, notably for men ages 35 to 54, and women 35 and older.

The following tabulation compares the previous and the revised projections of the 1995 labor force:

	1980 projection	1983 projection	Difference
Civilian labor force (in thousands)	127,542	131,387	3,845
Men	67,611	69,970	2,359
Women	59,931	61.417	1,486
White	109,292	112,393	3,101
Black and other	18,250	18,994	744

	1980 projection	1983 projection	Difference
Participation rate	68.6	67.8	-.8
Men	76.8	76.1	-.7
Women	61.2	60.3	-.9
White	68.8	68.1	-.7
Black and other	67.0	65.7	-1.3

Based on BLS' projections, several significant changes in labor force trends are expected during the next decade.

· The total labor force will grow more slowly during the next decade than during the past decade.
· Women will account for a greater proportion of labor force growth in the decade ahead (nearly two-thirds) than they did over the past decade.
· Blacks and other minority groups will account for a greater proportion of overall labor force growth, about one-quarter during the next decade.
· The younger members of the labor force, ages 16 to 24, will decline in absolute numbers.
· The number of prime-age members of the labor force, those ages 25 to 54, will grow faster than the total labor force, 1.0 percentage point per year faster.

These projections reflect the changing demographic structure of the U.S. population: the aging of the baby-boom generation and the growth of the black population. These general conclusions hold for several scenarios concerning future trends in labor force participation for detailed groups, although the specific projections differ.

319

Footnotes

[1] These projections replace those in Howard N. Fullerton, Jr., "The 1995 labor force: a first look," Monthly Labor Review, December 1980, pp. 11-21. For an evaluation of earlier projections, see Howard N. Fullerton, Jr., "How accurate were the 1980 labor force projections?" Monthly Labor Review, July 1982, pp. 15-21.

[2] The labor force (civilian labor force and resident Armed Forces) is projected to be 126,577,000 in 1990 and 133,018,000 in 1995. Of these, 57,415,000 will be women in 1980 and 61,582,000 will be women in 1995. Because there is no age or race detail in the resident Armed Forces measure of the labor force, this article is based on the civilian labor force.

[3] As with other current BLS presentations of data by race, this article presents data for blacks; however, for historical comparison, data are also presented for the black and other group, which also includes American Indians, Eskimos, and other minorities.

[4] For a short description of the BLS demographic labor force projection methodology, see BLS Handbook of Methods, Bulletin 2134-1 (Bureau of Labor Statistics, 1982). Chapter 18: for a complete description, see BLS Economic Growth Model System Used for Projections to 1990, Bulletin 2112 (Bureau of Labor Statistics, 1982), Chapter 2.

[5] Among the assumptions of the Census Bureau's projections of the population is that the total fertility rate will rise from 1.83 in 1980 to 1.96 in 2000, and then will decrease to 1.90 in 2050; and that life expectancy will rise from 78.3 in 1981 to 81.3 in 2005 for women, 70.7 to 73.3 for men. See Projections of the Population of the United States: 1982 to 2050. Current Population Reports, Series P-25, No. 922 (Bureau of the Census, 1982).

[6] For illustrations of other uses of the marital status model, see James E. Duggan, "Labor force participation of older workers" Industrial and Labor Relations Review, forthcoming; and James E. Duggan, "Relative price variability and the labor supply of married persons." Both papers are available from the Office of Economic Growth and Employment Projections, Bureau of Labor Statistics.

[7] The macro labor force model is the labor force equation in the Chase Econometric Model. For a description of the model, see Arthur J. Andreassen and others, "Economic outlook for the 1990's: three scenarios for economic growth," The Monthly Labor Review, November 1983, pp. 11-23.

[8] BLS' alternative scenarios of gross national product, industry output and employment trends and occupational requirements use the macro labor force model's projections of total labor force. This was done because of the small differences between the economic scenarios of labor force trends and because the macro labor force is part of the macroeconometric model of the economic projections.

[9] For a discussion of the revisions in labor force estimates, due to the 1980 Census of the Population, see Kenneth D. Buckley, Jennifer Marks, and Ronald J. Statt, "Revisions in the Current Population Survey Beginning in January 1982," Employment and Earnings, February 1982, pp. 7-15.

THE WORK ETHIC--AN IDEA WHOSE TIME HAS GONE?

Alan L. Porter

"The economic problem, the struggle for subsistence, always has been hitherto the primary, most pressing problem of the human race. If the economic problem is solved, mankind will be deprived of its traditional purpose.

"Will this be of a benefit? If one believes at all in the real values of life, the prospect at least opens up the possibility of benefit. Yet I think with dread of the readjustment of the habits and instincts of the ordinary man, bred into him for countless generations, which he may be

asked to discard within a few decades ... thus for the first time since his creation man will be faced with his real, his permanent problem--how to use his freedom from pressing economic cares, how to occupy his leisure, which science and compound interest will have won for him, to live wisely and agreeably and well."[1]

John Maynard Keynes

Work is something we take very seriously--as individuals and as a society. Just compare the warm, approving feeling we get from phrases like "a good worker," "a solid day's work," or "a steady job" with the negative, even frightening, associations of "out of work." Individuals who have lost jobs, particularly men, report a sense of failure, a loss of sexual identity, and a feeling of isolation in the absence of those 40 hours a week of contact with fellow workers. Retirement is a widely feared trauma: As one retiree put it, "I had no place to go, nothin' to do."[2] Lottery winners keep on working. Managers and employees, men and women, all share a virtually automatic approval for the notion of work. Our reactions on a societal level are analogous. We grow very concerned by stories of "hundreds idled in plant closing,"[3] "national productivity slipping," or "further movement toward the welfare state." There are automatic political points to be scored by decrying those evils and taking action to create jobs and produce more goods. Implicit in these concerns is a sense of moral duty associated with work--that is, the "work ethic."

For most of us, the work ethic is so obviously right that to question it seems foolish, if not downright sinful. Whether from religious belief, patriotic duty, or practical desire to better ourselves, is it not obvious that we must work? On scrutiny the evidence is not so clear. For instance, we have all heard enough (perhaps too much) about the "blue-collar blues," with hourly employees asking more from their jobs than their paychecks. We are now starting to see distinct signs of a similar discontent growing among middle managers.[4] Nationally, other troublesome instances arise. The last few years have forced us to take a second look at the costs of increasing production and consumption. Pressures on energy and material supplies lead to difficult foreign-policy squeezes; environmental damages loom serious; and the stability of our economy is challenged. As a society, as well as individually, are we striking a sound bargain in our single-minded emphasis on productive work?

This article proposes that the answer to the question just posed may, in fact, be "no!"--at least in some cases, for some people. I suggest that the complex set of values and beliefs comprising the work ethic is a rather recent and ephemeral phenomenon in our historical understanding of work. On closer examination, the concept of work is itself complex. It seems useful to distinguish work from basic individual and societal needs, which can then be used as yardsticks to assess the true worth of work. Simply put, people work for at least three different reasons-- extrinsic reward (a paycheck), intrinsic rewards (direct fulfillment of human needs through work itself), and societal good (much work that is not intrinsically very rewarding serves societal interests). The work ethic, however, adds a fourth factor--that one *ought* to work, regardless of how little one gets paid, how unpleasant the job is, or how little society is improved by the effort. It is this sense of "ought" that has passed its zenith and may become positively harmful as we move into post-industrial society. The work ethic is an idea whose time has come--and gone.

Historical Perspective

On first impulse, work might seem to be a basic attribute held in constant value by everyone, at all times. Not so! The work ethic as we know it is essentially a phenomenon of the last century or so and has primarily developed in America and Protestant Europe.

Prehistoric man's life consisted almost solely of the work necessary to meet basic needs for survival. "Man was born, he worked, and he died,"[5] Not until technological advance and the division of labor yielded a productive surplus did it generally make much sense to distinguish work from other human activities. Thereupon work became considered almost a curse, as by the ancient Hebrews and Greeks.[6] The Hebrews looked on work as painful drudgery and eyed the kingdom to come for blessed idleness.[7] Aristotle contrasted work to culture, finding little to applaud in physical labor.[8] The ancient world may not have regarded manual labor, per se, as degrading, but rather, the dependency created by working for others in return for payment.[9] The social subordination of the worker is epitomized in the form of slavery. The notion that work must in some way be irksome is a legacy from such roots. It is notable that "as late as 1789, Edmund Burke wrote that the occupation of a hairdresser or of a candlemaker could not be a matter of honor to any person--'to say nothing of a number of more servile employments.'"[10]

Then where did our high regard for the worker arise? Referring to the ethic of the worker, Simon succinctly summarizes:

"There can be no doubt that these notions and feelings represent one of the most interesting cultural trends in modern times. Their origin can be traced to the rising middle class which carried out the commercial and industrial revolutions between the sixteenth and nineteenth centuries, at which time these ideas and sentiments were eventually taken over in somewhat modified form by various labor movements. The belief that work is the highest value, the fullest and perhaps the only meaningful form of human activity appears to have been expressed most forcefully."[11]

The industrialization of society thus elevated work to a preeminent place. Adam Smith asserted that labor was the source of wealth, and Marx underlined that. Bourgeoisie and proletariat, capitalist and communist, all focused on work as the basis of personal worth.

What Is Work?

The following dimensions have been used by some scholars (some of the time) to characterize work:

Work-like	Non-work-like
Action on physical nature (manual labor)	Action on people (priests, politicians)
Externally oriented action	Contemplation
Yields social utility	Yields individual utility

Legal obligation	Free human development
Serious, even irksome	Enjoyable
Paid	Unpaid
Means	Ends

Kindred to the emerging work ethic was the "Protestant ethic," probably most pronounced in America. (The Protestants do not have a monopoly on the work ethic. The commercial success of the Iranian Baha'is, whose motto is "work is a prayer," may be attributed to their work ethic that has helped propel them into middle-class status.[12]) Without getting into which ethic--Protestant or work--led which, the emerging paradigm emphasized dedication to hard work with a strict repression of personal indulgence. This combination contains features that add up to a nasty paradox today.[13] For the Puritan, sloth was perhaps the deadliest of sins. (Passive contemplation, so highly regarded by the classicists such as Aristotle and by many Eastern philosophies of life, was rejected.) A compulsive thrust to be active toward industrious ends led to a boom in productivity. Productivity exerted pressure to consume the goods produced. Consumption, in turn, placed stress on the nonindulgent Protestant ethic that helped generate the productive surplus. Today one can observe a complex interplay between the promotion of consumption, the guilt associated with that consumption, and a fear that religious values are imperiled by a materialistic culture.

What are the implications of this historical progression? An important pattern can be inferred with respect to a society's stage of development and its attitudes toward work. In the most primitive situations, everyone must work nearly all of the time to eat, so work is a necessity. As agriculture and basic manufacturing emerge, society develops a bit of a surplus, so that some do not have to work continuously, and society places high esteem on that freedom from toil. As industrialization appears, there is a tremendous need for workers and a corresponding prestige for work. Post-industrial society requires fewer "productive" workers, allowing for a shift to service work--from making things for people to doing things for them.

As society's need for physical labor in the fields and factories decreases, the value placed on such work is apt to decline. Demands on the service sector depend on less concrete human needs and are liable to change (e.g., as self-reliance becomes a widely held social value). Furthermore, technological advances, such as computers and robotics, could reduce the requirements for human workers in the service sector. Where then would people work? What value would society place on work? The image of society with reduced work requirements is uncertain and frightening, but less so than that of a society clinging to a work ethic from an outmoded age of industrial development. As society grows beyond that industrial era, so must its norms with respect to work.

The Meaning(s) of Work

I should make clear that in questioning the work ethic, I am not trying to advocate some opposite notion, such as a "play ethic" or an "idleness ethic." The key to the critique of the work ethic is its implied moral obligation to engage in a certain form of activity for its own sake rather than for intended effects on the individual and/or society. The key to the concept is the meaning of "work."

Rather than offer a single definition, it seems more sensible to explore a number of dimensions in which people have tried to distinguish work from other human activities. The box above lists seven such dimensions.

Let's take a quick look at each of these dimensions. The prototype of the worker is someone who does physical labor. Simon recounts that academics reacted strongly to his definition of work, which excludes intellectual activity per se. Nonetheless, he holds that those who turn materials to human use perform a more fundamental work than those who are not direct producers (e.g., government employees, managers). External orientation and social utility are characteristics that distinguish work from inner-directed actions (e.g., contemplation, whittling). It should be emphasized that Simon places value (possibly of a higher order) on many human activities, such as meditation, that rise above the mere utility of work.[14] He also notes the distinction between legal obligation (required, necessary) and free development (of one's own volition). The obligatory characteristic of work is an important element in this critique of the work ethic, as is the notion that it is in some way irksome. The words for "work" in various European languages share a common association with pain (as in "labor," also often linked to the pangs of birth). Other associations tie to burden, poverty, and even torture (the French *travailler*).[15] While "work" can be our most general word for doing something, it is predominantly used to mean paid employment.[16] The tie between work and pay is growing stronger--in 1875 less than 50% of the employed people worked for wages or salaries; in 1971, some 88% of the nonagricultural work force in the United States fell in this category.[17] (Feminist efforts to have housework considered as work illustrate one dissatisfaction with that usage.)

The last of the seven dimensions follows Simon's sense that work is inherently a means to some other ends. C. Wright Mills states this position strongly: "Neither love nor hatred of work is inherent in man, or inherent in any given line of work. For work has no intrinsic meaning."[18] (I note that some would disagree. For example, Dorothy Sayers has said, "Work is not primarily a thing one does to live, but the thing one lives to do."[19] Also, the Task Force on Work in America concluded that satisfying work is a basic human need.[20]) The distinction between means and ends with respect to work has been most developed by psychologists. Herzberg, for one, distinguished between satisfaction, tending to arise from the content of the work, and dissatisfaction, tending to result from the ancillary features of a job.[21] There can be no doubt that many workers attain great personal reward (beyond any payments received) from their work. However, work does not seem to be the end in itself. As Best puts it, "Work is purposeful *human* activity directed toward the satisfaction of *human* needs and desires."[22]

To summarize, work connotes a host of meanings. For present purposes, a simple composite image is suitable. Thus the "work" in work ethic should be taken as serious, paid labor performed for others (as opposed, say, to self-motivated activities done for their own interest). It is vital to note that this definition allows for a wealth of rewarding activities besides "work." Again, the challenge to the work ethic is not a call for idleness.

Relationship to Human Needs

If work is not an end in itself, it is necessary to decide how it relates to individual and collective human ends. Maslow's framework will serve to consider individual need fulfillment; societal interests will be addressed in terms of certain critical issues.

The basic human needs identified and ordered by Maslow are *survival, security, belonging, esteem,* and *self-actualization.*[23] Both the intrinsic (psychological) and extrinsic (financial) rewards of work pertain. The financial returns translate into satisfying one's basic survival and security needs (e.g., through purchase of food and shelter), and, indirectly, the esteem needs (e.g., through prestige associated with the accouterments of income and consumption). Psychological returns may include job security, esteem, belongingness, and self-actualization. Thus work can play a prominent role in fulfilling the individual's needs.

What must be emphasized, however, is that there are other ways to achieve such fulfillment; work is not the only source. Indeed, phenomena such as American "leisure seizure" suggest that prevailing work arrangements are found wanting. Basic survival and security needs could be well-served by a guaranteed-income arrangement. Belonging and esteem needs might be better met by a system that allowed alternatives to paid work as a source of social status. Self-actualization would be more consistent with activities designed to provide direct fulfillment than through jobs designed for mass production or to make work. Schumacher shows that such an orientation is feasible in describing "Buddhist economics."[24] Release from the obligation to put in 40 hours at a paid job could open tremendous actualization potentials, were such freedom unaccompanied by social condemnation. If forecasts are right that this nation is moving toward greater emphasis on the higher needs, especially self-actualization, this may put further stress on traditional work patterns.[25] Alternative work schedules and part-time positions offer a first step to relieve such stress and enable individuals to better attain their personal ends.[26]

Determining social needs or national goals is even more daunting than consideration of individual needs. However, the following five national objectives provide a workable basis for consideration of work and the work ethic: Control *inflation*, improve social *equity*, enhance the *quality of life*, carefully manage energy and material *resources*, and preserve national *security*. (The attainment of full employment is also a national goal mandated by Congress since 1946.)[27]

Our national objectives are multiple in nature as we struggle with complex issues matched against pluralistic social values. A systems perspective warrants that we are unlikely to be successful in meeting multiple objectives if these are addressed one at a time. In particular, I am concerned by the trade-offs associated with the aim that everyone should have a job. Let me illustrate the point three ways.

One worry about our economy (with national-security overtones) is its inability to compete internationally, given its poor rate of productivity improvements. To encourage modernization we consider industrial-investment credits that often translate to reduced labor-intensiveness. Yet we cringe so at automation and layoffs that we guarantee featherbedding.

As a second instance, we try to control inflation by inflicting the miseries of unemployment on additional millions. Presumably this reduces consumption demand and puts pressure on the lower echelons of workers to moderate their wage demands because of the reserve army of unemployed eager for their jobs. Yet if the unemployed need be so for the economy to function better, shouldn't we

325

acknowledge their social value and our social equity objective by providing for them adequately? But if unemployment were freed from hardship and stigma, wouldn't that undermine its effectiveness as an inflation fighter?

A third instance consists of the effort to increase employment (make work) by prompting additional consumption. For example, income tax credits are urged in the hope that the money will be used to consume more, in turn boosting production and inducing jobs. In place of conspicuous consumption for consumption's sake, we push consumption to make work. But such an endless loop of ever-growing production and consumption fuels inflation, puts pressures on energy and material supplies (in turn increasing our dependence on foreign sources), and increases the waste-disposal burdens on our environment. Furthermore, the attendant increases in the standard of living have been challenged as lowering the quality of life.

In sum, attempts to maintain high employment can run counter to other societal interests. In particular, creation of artificial jobs fueled by unneeded consumption in a world of limited resources and environmental resilience would seriously endanger societal survival. Returning to the premise that work is not an end in itself, work should be considered as but one alternative means to achievement of our more basic aims.

Future Prospects

The preceding arguments add up to a call for a change in the work ethic. The patterns of historical progression and the emerging individual and societal needs suggest forces acting to bring about such change. However, these forces are confronted by a religious fervor ready to defend the work ethic at any cost. The outcome of this clash is hard to predict, confounded as it is with uncertainties in related factors such as the future state of the economy, war or peace, possible technological breakthroughs, and so on. To get a better feel for what the options may be, I sketch two alternative futures--one dominated by the work ethic and one that essentially abandons it.

"Jobs for All": The heading for this vignette on life in the United States in 2020 derives from a political campaign of the first decade of the 21st century. A succession of recessions and international crises coupled with continuing inflation had jolted the economic system. Unemployment levels rose and fell, but continuously drifted upward through each crest. What should be done to settle this economic situation became the dominant political issue. The Democrats responded by adopting a platform principle of provision for everyone's needs no matter whether they worked or not. Such a stance was far too "left" for the American voters, and they lined up behind the work-oriented, "jobs for all" position of the Republican majority.

The government still faces many difficulties. Resource constraints are severe. Energy shortages have strained transportation, electric-power generation, and industrial production in some sectors. Many types of materials (foods as well as minerals) are in increasingly short supply, inducing international tensions as these are power-brokered. Industrial production levels continue to rise, leading to a series of environmental crises related to healthful air and water supplies. New technologies have contributed greatly to keeping the world economy functional,

326

with great advances in energy production weaponry, information processing, and leisure products. Of course, these have raised fears for the environment, business competition, and protection of jobs.

Life is both similar to and different from that of 40 years ago. The basic human values held by most Americans are much like they were. Prominently emphasized in the values profile is the work ethic, held to be a keystone in America's efforts to meet international competition and to provide for its own. A key difference from the past is where people work. Fewer than 2% of the work force is employed in agriculture and only 7% in basic manufacturing (continuing long-standing trends).

The "service" and "knowledge" sectors dominate, with virtually half of the entire work force being government employees. Continual complaints are heard about the low productivity of the massive, and still growing, bureaucracies-- governmental and private. Employment is generally for life; it essentially takes court action (a growth sector in its own right) to fire someone. Jobs are precious and society functions to preserve them.

Consumption is pressed to fuel the economy, but the system is increasingly fragile as shortages of a critical mineral can shut down an industry, say automobiles, thus threatening the whole edifice. "Defense" is a recourse, just as when oil and aluminum supplies were cut off in the 20th century. Luckily, the resulting defense actions have not yet caused a general nuclear conflict.

Some observations on life-styles and general conditions convey what life is like in the early 21st century. Wages are high because of the pressure to maintain a high standard of living despite rising prices. This creates an inflationary spiral that encourages consumption. Surprisingly, some technological advances are actively opposed. For instance, the government now demands a "work-impact statement" in conjunction with research and development activities to demonstrate that further jobs will not be threatened.

The "post-industrial" society has less inherent need for human work, leading to tremendous emphasis on educational activities (often not work-related, as plumbers pick up doctorates in sociology) and increased leisure. The average work- week is now 28 hours (four 7-hour days), with average retirement at age 57. Tensions have arisen between older people pursuing their individual rights to keep working and the need for jobs for younger people.

Despite growth in the GNP, people report that things are likely to get worse before they get better. Concerns center on security--people fear the economic instabilities, crime is not under control, and war is a real threat. People cling strongly to the available anchors of security, especially work. As the party platform states--

. Every man has a right to employment by virtue of his nature, dignity, and need for personal growth.
. Every man has the obligation to work.
. Production, distribution, and consumption of goods are not ends in themselves, but creative activities to permit the development of working life.[28]

Nonetheless, support for the opposition's notion of "to each according to his need" seems to be growing.

"Justice for All": Many of the premises of the previous scenario hold true for life as it "really" is in the year 2020. The nation has progressed through a series of economic difficulties, and resources are severely constrained. However, international tensions are greatly reduced and technological developments have been focused on meeting the most pressing societal needs, especially energy and material conservation. Moreover, the outcome of the great political struggle actually went the other way--the Democrats with their platform of "justice for all" triumphed in the early days of the 21st century. The consequent national policy-- that all Americans merit financial support above the poverty level, regardless of whether or not they are working--has changed the face of the nation.

National policy and long-range planning focus on attainment of an equitable, secure, sustainable, resource-conserving economy. Equity and financial security have been gradually dissociated from employment. The negative income tax enacted over the past 15 years has removed the financial need to work to provide the basics of human survival, health care, and educational opportunity.

National security has been enhanced largely through reduced dependence on foreign materials. Although the concept of equity has not been significantly extended to sharing with other nations, our world image and relations are more positive than in the past. The sustainable, resource-conserving perspective has reduced our consumption of worldwide resources.

In lieu of the drive to maximize GNP, we now pursue the maximization of quality of life through balanced production of goods and provision of services, striving for environmental protection. Indeed, the GNP (no longer an accepted indicator) equates to under $1 trillion in 1980 terms. The levels of economic activity and consumption have decreased.

The value systems of many Americans have shifted rather drastically from those of 40 years ago. Material values have declined. For instance, conspicuous consumption is a social taboo, resulting in some interesting quirks as those who still hunger for the "good life" camouflage their activities (e.g., a black market in small electrical appliances and travel under assumed identities). Indeed, long-life product design is now mandated by several laws, in striking contrast to the planned obsolescence of days gone by. Not needing to pump up the economy to provide work has allowed for better balancing of the national objectives.

The most prominent change in values is the diminution of the work ethic. The old notion that an individual without a (paid) job had no basis for self-esteem has largely passed. Today, people are motivated by a more diverse set of aims. Of course, the overwhelming majority of American households (91%) still have at least one paid "worker" engaged over 1,500 hours per year. Over half (57%) of the households with two or more adults have two or more engaged in paid activities. What is striking is that many "work" part-time, on an ad hoc basis, on nonroutine work schedules, as volunteers, and/or on personal activities without serious prospect of monetary reward (such as painting).

In conjunction with the institution of the negative income tax came a demise of the regulations on working--the minimum-wage laws and hour limits--as well as the make-work programs. The "work" place has returned to a free-market arrangement over and above the guaranteed income floor. Nowadays, one negotiates on an individual basis to set an acceptable wage rate, work assignment, and pay rate for any job.

Besides the death of the unions, some interesting twists have resulted. For one, productivity has skyrocketed. Since people no longer feel compelled to stay at their jobs, they have a more positive orientation to them. Current average pay for less desirable jobs (not hard physical labor, which is much desired for health reasons) surpasses that for skilled work, for which supply outstrips demand (e.g., university professors, despite the boom in education).

Job security and its attendant inertia are gone--civil service and the need to show cause for firing an employee went out together when the Supreme Court ruled that there was no longer a basis for them, given the security of the national guaranteed-income system. One consequence was the dismemberment of many long-standing bureaucracies. Today, the "adhocracy" is alive and well.

Local, or even national computer files provide a prospective employer with information on available individuals. It is not uncommon for someone to take a project job for six months, to vacation for three months, then return to a new job for a period thereafter. This has caused psychological difficulties for some who long for the old format that guaranteed a routine lifetime on the job. The new freedom for personal development has resulted in expanded religious, social, and aesthetic activities--both conventional and radical. Very few people would willingly contemplate a return to the old "9-to-5" lifetime grind. Americans are more optimistic about the future than ever before.

Concluding Observations

The age-old premise "if one did not work, one did not eat" no longer fits the realities of our economy.[29] Simply put, the proportion of our potential work force required to produce food, shelter, and the other basics of human survival is small and shrinking. The continuing reduction in society's need for conventional, paid work is a force for change. One direction of change would be an increased commitment to the work ethic reflected in increasingly awkward struggles to make work. The opposite would be to recognize the evolving societal needs, to correspondingly reduce our emphasis on paid work, and to begin to take fuller advantage of the potentials for human development thereby opened. I advocate the latter.

Certainly, any attempt to lessen the role of work in our society deserves careful consideration. However, recalling our consideration of the term "work," a critical point was that it has no intrinsic meaning; it is not an end in itself. Work provides one way to meet our needs, but not the only way. As Keynes suggests in the quote at the beginning of this article, freedom from work can be a marvelous opportunity, albeit a staggering one. The work ethic is too deeply held to be quickly sloughed off. Thus in the near term any changes must be gradual.

Measures such as alternative work schedules, part-time work, and increased welfare and unemployment benefits can ease the constraints of the 40-hour work-week. Reduction in the average hours worked could both lower unemployment and increase leisure time. However, this would do nothing to reduce the dichotomy between work as drudgery and enjoyment obtained elsewhere. More ideal would be movement to integrate work and play so that one set of activities could better serve human needs, including self-actualization. At the national level, we should immediately reconsider whether attempting to make work for everyone impedes attainment of our objectives of a secure, equitable economic system. To the extent that this is the case, changes are due.

In the longer term, more drastic reconsideration of the place of conventional, paid work is required. The "Justice for All" scenario is just one of many possibilities, but it does suggest important points. First, the notion of a guaranteed-income plan is certainly feasible for a society that only requires 10% of its potential work force to provide for its necessities of life. Such a scheme could effectively satisfy the basic survival needs of people, but only if social approbation accompanied it. Second, the scenario implies drastic changes in the motivations and organizational structure associated with work. The implications of these need to be explored thoroughly. Moreover, the extent of the changes appears so great that they could come about only in conjunction with a broad consensus for value change with respect to the work ethic--a most difficult proposition.

Is such change in the work ethic of American society plausible? Based on a historical perspective, the answer seems to go beyond "yes" to "inevitable." The work ethic has evolved over time to meet changing societal needs as the industrial revolution progressed. It helped propel individuals, groups, and nations to the economic forefront. But it will grow increasingly out of place in a post-industrial society whose concerns lean to moderated consumption in a resource-constrained world. In such a setting, it is utter folly to stimulate consumption to make work, because that costs too much in terms of resource diminishment, ecological stresses, foreign dependence, and general reduction of the resilience of the economic system.

We must set aside our thoughtless allegiance to the work ethic. While the prospect of unemployment is personally frightening, it need not be. A combination of economic and social changes could help loosen us from this constraint. On a societal level, this is not to decry productivity. Rather, the suggested directions for change could enhance productivity by eliminating the unhappy psychosocial baggage that has accumulated with the notion of work. The moral obligation to work exerts a counterproductive force in many ways, such as prompting regulations that tend to ossify and bureaucratize both the public and private sectors. The work ethic is dangerous ideology that threatens our society's ability to develop a sustainable, post-industrial economic system. It demands harsh questioning. And that implies a difficult dialogue that ought to begin now.

Footnotes

[1] Quoted by Fred Best, ed., The Future of Work (Englewood Cliffs, New Jersey: Prentice-Hall, 1973), p. iii.

[2] Studs Terkel, Working (New York: Avon Books, 1975), p. 562.

[3] "Detroit: Hitting the Skids," Newsweek, April 28, 1980, p. 58.

[4] George A. Steiner, "Can Business Survive Its New Environment?" BUSINESS, January-February 1980, pp. 13-19.

[5] Melvin Kranzberg and Joseph Gies, By the Sweat of Thy Brow (New York: G. P. Putnam's Sons, 1975), p. 3.

[6] Lloyd H. Lofquist and Rene V. Davis, Adjustment to Work (New York: Appleton-Century-Crofts, 1969).

[7] C. Wright Mills, White Collar: The American Middle Class (New York: Oxford University Press, 1951), pp. 215-223.

[8] Yves R. Simon, Work, Society, and Culture (New York: Fordham University Press, 1971), p. 145. Simon notes that interpretation of Aristotle's views requires care; Aristotle's distinction between a craft and a profession may approach Simon's.

9   Kranzberg and Gies, <u>By the Sweat of Thy Brow</u>, p. 28.

10   Simon, <u>Work, Society, and Culture</u>, p. 3.

11   Ibid., pp. 40-41.

12   "The Minority That Iran Persecutes," <u>Newsweek</u>, March 24, 1980, p. 61.

13   George W. Albee, "The Protestant Ethic, Sex and Psychology," <u>American Psychologist</u>, February 1977, pp. 150-161.

14   Simon, <u>Work, Society, and Culture</u>, p. 110.

15   Ibid., p. 18.

16   Raymond Williams, <u>Keywords</u> (New York: Oxford University Press, 1976), p. 282.

17   Paul Dickson, <u>The Future of the Workplace</u> (New York: Weybright and Talley, 1975), p. 315.

18   Mills, <u>White Collar</u>, p. 215.

19   Quoted in Dennis Clark, <u>Work and the Human Spirit</u> (New York: Sheed and Ward, 1967), p. 110.

20   Cited by Dickson, <u>Future of the Workplace</u>, p. 22.

21   Frederick Herzberg, "The Motivation-Hygiene Concept and Problems of Manpower," <u>Personnel Administration</u>, January-February 1964, pp. 3-7.

22   Best, <u>The Future of Work</u>, p. 2.

23   See Abraham Maslow, <u>Motivation and Personality</u> (New York: Harper & Row, 1970).

24   E. F. Schumacher, <u>Small Is Beautiful: Economics as if People Mattered</u> (New York: Harper Torchbooks, 1973).

25   D. Elgin and A. Mitchell, "Voluntary Simplicity," <u>The Co-Evolution Quarterly</u>, Summer 1977, pp. 4-19.

26   John D. Owens, <u>Alternative Work Schedules: A Technology Assessment</u> (Washington, D.C., National Technical Information Service, 1977).

27   Dennis Clark, <u>Work and the Human Spirit</u> (New York: Sheed and Ward, 1967), p. 80.

28   Clark, ibid., proposes these as some principles of a new work ethic.

29   Best, <u>The Future of Work</u>, p. 126.

PRODUCTIVITY IN AMERICA:
WHERE IT WENT AND HOW TO GET IT BACK

Charles H. Kepner

There is probably no one in the United States who is not aware that our nation has a productivity problem. We hear about it from all sides. American auto manufacturers are in serious trouble as buyers choose foreign cars over domestic, citing both price and quality as the basis for their decisions. Japanese television, optical, and electronic products dominate the market. The names Toyota, Sony, and Nikon are as common to us as Ford, General Electric, and Kodak. The balance of trade continues to flow outward from the United States. Only a few years ago we considered ourselves world leaders in business and manufacture, yet by almost every present indicator we are forced to acknowledge that we barely compete.

Productivity is a general term, an expression of the ratio between resources input to production and the value of goods produced. The greater the disparity between input and output, the greater the productivity of the unit. A favorable balance between input and output is healthy but not enough; the advantage must grow through time if the unit is to remain competitive. This year the input required should be less than it was last year, and the output greater, or we are standing still. We should be smarter this year in our use of resources so that we get more value from them. We should have learned how to make our product better and at less cost than we did last year. We should show a percentage increase in our productivity, this year compared to last, and next year should show an even further gain.

Stagnation

But this is not what has been happening. The percentage increase of productivity for the United States has been declining steadily for years, while the Japanese show a seven to nine percent increase from one year to the next. West Germany holds at a yearly increase of about five percent. Even Great Britain, with all its problems, shows a yearly increase of from two to three percent. But in the United States the trend goes steadily downward toward the vanishing point. Productivity is stagnant, not increasing. Our competitors improve while we do not.

There has been intense speculation concerning the cause of this decline. The oil shortage, government regulations, the unions, unfair marketing on the part of foreign competitors, overage plant and equipment, and many other possible causes have been suggested. But none is sufficient. There are, in fact, many causes, for productivity is a multifaceted thing. Nor can there be one single action to restore it. The problem is complex, as are its causes and potential cures.

In order to understand the productivity problem and what we might be able to do about it, we have drawn on the available literature, our experience working with more than 1,500 client organizations around the world, and interviews with persons knowledgeable in the field. Most especially, we have drawn on our clients in Japan--Honda Motors, Mitsubishi, Nissan Motors, Seiko Watch, Kobe Steel, and Sony, among others--and their counterparts in the United States, where we work with 60 of the 100 largest corporations.

Our method has been that of comparison. We have studied high productivity enterprises and contrasted them against low. We have compared Japanese companies against American. We have examined the winners against the losers, attempting to isolate the characteristics that make some successful and others less so. From this we have identified five factors which we believe go far in explaining the decline in productivity in the United States.

Five Causal Factors

The first factor comes from a comparison of American culture and ways of working against other cultures, particularly that of the Japanese. Over the last 30 years, there has grown an extreme emphasis on individualism and specialization in the United States. The expectation is that everyone will make it on his or her own merits, independent of anyone else. Take care of Number One. Don't get lost in group or cooperative efforts if at all possible. Be the expert in your chosen field, for knowledge is power, but don't share with others everything you know. Stand aloof and self-reliant, for you are in competition with everyone else for a place in the sun. This ethic has mediated against teamwork and cooperation in dealing with problems and has made the American organization a confederation of little kingdoms, segmented and fractioned.

In Japan the ruling ethic is exactly the opposite. People work together for the good of the group out of loyalty and pride. They have a strong sense of obligation toward their organization, their subordinates, and peers. They pool effort and information to solve the organization's problems. They are proud of the work they do and are particularly concerned with maintaining a high level of quality. They seldom move from one organization to another, but progress steadily upward through their chosen company during their entire career. They subordinate self to the collectivity of which they are a part.

The second factor has to do with the organization of work. In the United States the precepts of Frederick W. Taylor are widely practiced. "Scientific management" says that jobs and organizations may be engineered, with human and machine functions relegated to boxes in a production flow diagram. Job descriptions, procedures, time and motion studies, and definitive manuals that state every last function and its relation to every other function have become essential tools of management. Taylor summed his approach up with these words: "In the past, man has been first; in the future, the system must be first." Practice of these precepts has dehumanized work, alienated workers and driven them into the arms of organized labor, and created an adversarial relationship between the manager and the people upon whom he or she depends.

The third factor relates to the emergence of return on investment as the main criterion of management. Over the last 30- years, maximization of profit in the short term has become the index by which organizations are judged. Decisions are taken that will make the ROI look good at the end of the next quarter instead of being concerned with the long-term growth of the organization, its products, and its people. Quality improvement is sacrificed in order to meet the current production quota. Management by the financial numbers obscures other variables that may be more important over the long haul. The pursuit of immediate results allows for little compassion, and the judgment that people are expendable has come to pervade much of American management thinking. Careers are made and forfeited on the strength of profit center performance against ROI.

The fourth factor was the advent of the business computer. Overnight it was possible to obtain more numbers than had ever been available before. Preoccupation with managing against ROI was abetted by ready access to unlimited financial data. From the mid-1950s on, misuse of the computer complicated an already complex situation. Everything was converted to numbers and printout reigned supreme. Managers spent more time with numerical reports than they did with the substance of the situation they were managing. People became digits and personal contact tended to be lost. Financial experts and lawyers became chief executive officers of major organizations, and intimate knowledge of production was downgraded as no longer essential. The American corporation became a money-machine, with more concern for immediate return on investment than for maintaining or improving the quality of the product.

The fifth factor is the accident of history that put all of these conditions together, the unprecedented economic good times that followed World War II. The world was hungry for new products and services; almost anything could be sold. In the prosperity that followed, management practices that otherwise might have been questioned were adopted. Everything worked, apparently. The long slide into reduced productivity had begun, but managers preoccupied with numbers didn't see it. They made shorter and shorter term decisions and kept the profits high. It is difficult to be self-critical concerning management philosophy and techniques when you are making money.

C. Jackson Grayson said it well: "American management coasted off the great R&D gains made during World War II," and the prosperity that followed. Adjustments were made to periodic recessions; people were laid off during hard times and extra dividends were paid during good. Innovation was sacrificed to expediency, and things important to the growth of the organization were sacrificed to its profitability. "Responsibility for this (reduction in productivity) belongs not just to a set of external conditions but also to the attitudes, preoccupations, and practices of American managers. By their preference for servicing existing markets rather than creating new ones and by their devotion to short-term returns and 'management by the numbers,' many of them have effectively forsworn long-term technological superiority as a competitive weapon," according to Robert Hayes and William Abernathy, writing in the *Harvard Business Review*.

We Did It Ourselves

In other words, our long-term decline in productivity is something we ourselves have created. It is the result of poor management practices selected and installed over the last three decades, under the luxury of good times. But what has been put on can be taken off. A reversal of management attitudes and correction of management practices can put us back where we ought to be, equal to anyone in productivity. A study carried out by McKinsey indicates that fully 85 percent of the variables affecting productivity are internal to the organization and lie within the control of management, while only 15 percent are external and beyond management control. Our own studies suggest that four-fifths of these internal variables can be changed by executive and managerial actions, while one-fifth must be effected at the worker level. From top to bottom the organization can do something positive about productivity. Our 30 years' decline in productivity can be turned around and eradicated through five years of concerted effort.

In order to understand how to do this, we must first understand what conditions bring about an increase in productivity or quality of performance. Year by year improvement of productivity comes about through the progressive reduction of the input necessary to accomplish a given result, through better management of available resources. Year by year, operational problems in the use of resources are solved so that barriers to their most effective use are removed. Year by year, optimal productive efficiency is approached more closely. The solving of operational problems through time is what makes possible a year to year percentage improvement in productivity. To understand this more clearly, let us examine two cases.

Low Quality and Low Productivity

Hewlett-Packard had a requirement for a certain semiconductor product, the 16-K bit random-access-memory (RAM) component, obtainable from a number of manufacturers. Concerned with quality, H-P asked for large samples from each of a number of potential vendors and subjected these to intense reliability testing. RAMs from the best Japanese supplier tested out with three-tenths of one percent unreliability. The second-best Japanese supplier produced at .45 of one percent failure. The best American supplier tested out at 1.8 percent unreliability, and the second-best vendor in the United States produced a three percent rate of failure. This is a factor of ten times between the best Japanese and the second-best American supplier.

What makes this case instructive is the fact that the 16K RAM was developed in the United States, the technology was developed here, and the machines upon which it was produced were designed and developed in America. The 16K RAM, from start to finish, was an American innovation, yet the Japanese were able to produce it with one-tenth the failure rate experienced by a reputable U.S. manufacturing firm that considered itself competitive in the semiconductor market.

What happened? The 16K RAM was initially produced in the United States at an even higher failure rate. One company was able to bring the unreliability figure down to three percent but then stopped, did not improve the component further. The best U.S. manufacturer reduced failures to 1.8 percent and considered that good enough. But the Japanese went further in perfecting the RAM, and the process and equipment by which it was made. They improved the component so that it became significantly different and better. They improved the equipment and process so that these became a different generation of technology. They did this by solving problems and removing barriers that stood in the way of efficient production. The American companies could have done the same thing but didn't. According to the printout, the profits were acceptable at the 1.8 percent and 3 percent failure rates, so why invest more time and money? Concern for quality, and willingness to deal with production problems in a search for perfection, put the Japanese companies far ahead of the American. Hewlett-Packard buys from the Japanese, as does most of the rest of the world, because the American companies had allowed solvable operational problems to persist to the detriment of their product and so render them noncompetitive. In the last few months, that condition has changed somewhat. David Earle, H-P manager of quality and reliability, says that a lot more testing by American companies and "close work with the end user to identify and resolve problems" has led to significant quality improvement. Which could have been done in the beginning, he might have added.

The second case is closer to home and does not involve differences in national culture. The Comptroller General of the United States, Elmer B. Staats, commissioned a study of productivity in 20 coal mines in one corner of the State of Wyoming. All were mining coal from the same geological structures, with comparable equipment, drawing manpower from the same highly unionized labor pool, and subject to the same governmental regulations. Productivity was measured in tons of coal produced per man per shift. The lowest productivity mine brought out 58 tons per man, the highest 242, a factor of four times between the extremes of the distribution. The other 18 mines were scattered in between.

The conclusion reached by the study was as follows: "The main difference was how company management worked with its employees. The most productive firm provided its employees with the greatest amount of individual responsibility and involvement in problem solving." One can imagine conditions in the low productivity mine without much trouble. It is dirty, run down, with numerous safety hazards. Equipment downtime is high and maintenance is poor. When something breaks down, there is no backup, spare parts are not readily available and no one seems to care whether it gets fixed or not. There is a lot of confusion as to who should be doing what. Scheduling is poor and management is conspicuous by its absence below ground. The mine is not managed very well and nothing works the way it should. There are a great many grievances filed with the union.

In the other mine, things are different. It is cleaner, safer, and equipment downtime is less. When something breaks down, parts are available and equipment is soon put back into operation or backup is provided. Schedules are better, there is less confusion, and it is apparent that people are concerned and aware of what is going on. Management is not solely preoccupied with the numbers but is actively engaged in dealing with operational problems that occur underground. Disputes between management and labor tend to be settled on the spot and seldom move into the formal grievance stage. The productive mine is managed better, from top to bottom.

The Critical Difference

What distinguishes the Japanese semiconductor companies from the American? What is strikingly different between the high productivity mine and the low? Above all else, it is the number of people who are involved and feel responsibility for solving problems. In the more productive units, more people at different levels in the organization are asked and expected to contribute to the solving of operational problems. When something goes wrong, they do something about it. If they can't handle the problem themselves, they see that someone gets on the problem who can. It's as simple as that: More horsepower is brought to bear against the organization's problems.

On the average, a Japanese firm will have nearly six times as many people involved in solving operational problems as its American counterpart. In the United States, where the precepts of "scientific management" still prevail, concern is with span of control. American executives continually ask how many persons a given manager can supervise. With the dubious criterion of efficiency in mind, they employ the smallest number of managers they can. In Japan, on the other hand, concern is with the number of managers needed to achieve optimum supervision for quality production. As a result, they employ more than twice as many people in middle management and levels of supervision than we do.

On the plant floor, operators and assemblers are also involved. Between 30 and 50 percent will be members of some kind of problem solving group, dealing with the operational problems that plague them every day. Many of these seem trivial at first glance, such as oil dripping from milling machines. But this is not a trivial problem if it impedes quality or production. Often the resolution of a "trivial" problem has effects of major importance that were not recognized at the outset. In the Japanese view, all operational problems should be solved. No problem which has a deleterious effect on production is trivial. They organize their people to deal with *all* operational problems, wherever and whenever they may arise.

In a typical American plant, between 10 and 12 percent of the people will be doing the thinking and problem solving for all the rest, who are expected to do as directed. In a composite of four Japanese plants, we found the comparable figure to be slightly more than 61 percent. Nearly two-thirds of the people in the plant were solving problems and working to make things better, compared to one-fifth as many in the American case. More people can solve more problems, everything else being equal, simply by the weight of effort expended. Even discounting the importance of problems solved at lower levels of the organization, more of the barriers to full productivity are resolved by this extra effort.

But all things are not equal. In addition, most Japanese are better trained to deal with problems than their American counterparts. The average Japanese coming into an organization receives 500 days of training in the first ten years. That is 50 days per year, or one day per working week. Much of this is on-the-job training, supplemented by formal classroom study. Problem solving techniques are taught at the plant floor level and more sophisticated techniques at higher levels. So six times as many *prepared* people are trying to solve problems in the Japanese firm as in ours. Six-to-one odds do not augur well for the future.

Problems Solved Where Problems Are

But there is another aspect that may be of even greater importance. Note where the problems are being solved within the organizational structure. Top and middle management tend to solve those problems which are seen from the top and whose priorities are felt at the top. Operational problems which occur further down in the organization receive scant attention. Middle managers tend to ignore them in favor of helping top management solve the problems important to them. Top management will probably never even know about many of the operational problems that are impeding productivity at the lower levels. We suspect this may have been the case with the low productivity coal mine. Top management doesn't know and perhaps doesn't care that spare parts are not always available at the point of need when equipment breaks down. That is someone else's problem. So a great many operational problems are allowed to slide along without every being solved, becoming chronic and ever-present barriers to productivity, industrial cancers as it were.

With the Japanese more participative approach, there is a different outcome. At all levels of the organization, there are people who are concerned with quality. Few problems can occur without someone becoming personally aware of them and personally challenged to correct them. Problems tend to be solved at the level at which they occur, by the people who know most about them and have the most pressing reasons for wishing them resolved. All kinds of problems, large and small, are dealt with. Few are likely to develop into chronic barriers to productivity.

Another effect follows directly. As more problems are solved, fewer barriers to productivity remain. The organization is able to realize increasingly more from the resources it commits and output goes up relative to input. As problems are solved, the quality of production increases. Fewer defective units are turned out that require rework with its attendant extra costs. Wasted time and effort is reduced to a minimum.

A third effect is obvious. People feel commitment to an organization when they are allowed to make a substantive contribution to its success. They feel more important, more needed, more a part of the organization. They develop a loyalty and concern for the organization and its products they would never feel otherwise.

337

The organization's problems become their problems, the organization's goals become theirs as well, so they solve those problems and are personally challenged to achieve those goals. They become more productive contributors for the future as well as more effective workers in the present.

How Well Does This Work?

Very well indeed. Toyota Motors supports problem solving at all levels. In one year, a total of 859,039 suggestions for improvement, based upon operational problems analyzed and solved, were received from their 48,757 people. This works out to a rate of 17.62 positive suggestions per person. Of course, not all of these were worthy of implementation in the eyes of top management; six percent had to be dropped upon the recommendation of upper-level screening committees. Ninety-four percent were put into effect, or 807,497 practical proposals for the improvement of productivity and quality. Toyota's auditors computed the dollar savings from these suggestions in excess of $30 million. Far more important was the improvement of corporate capability that more than three-quarters of a million worthwhile solutions for existing operational problems represent. Toyota's competitive strength had been increased immeasurably, and the process continues unabated. Other Japanese companies report similar results. An American company of that size would expect perhaps a thousand workable ideas in a year. Toyota implemented 3,365 suggestions every working day!

There is nothing magic about the Japanese success. They simply use their human resources more intelligently. They enlist all of their managers, supervisors and foremen, and many of their operators in the task of solving operational problems and improving quality. They give them problem solving skills and the opportunity to make the product better. They mobilize their people in a way that most American organizations do not, and the barriers to productivity are pushed aside. Nationwide, between 25 and 30 million people in Japanese industry are involved in productivity and quality improvement. The sheer weight of effort put against the task of producing quality products is their secret. They have discovered that technology alone does not assure success. Technology plus people using it and supporting it fully give an organization the competitive edge.

What To Do About It

Any organization anywhere can change from a few people trying to solve all the problems themselves to a large number of people feeling responsible for solving operational problems, if it wants to. Having a lot of people concerned about quality and willing to do something to improve it is not a Japanese invention. A number of American companies do this very well: Kodak, IBM, and Hewlett-Packard are three that come to mind. They suffer no productivity problem. They are competitive with anything the world has to offer as a challenge. They do this by effectively mobilizing their human problem solving resources against the operational barriers that stand between them and full productivity.

How can an organization move from an elitist structure to something more akin to the Japanese model? We have worked with hundreds of organizations around the world that are making this transition and have identified six conditions

338

necessary for success. We have never seen an organization where these six conditions were in effect that did not have high productivity and a high quality output. The reverse is true as well. We have never seen an organization where the six conditions were *not* present that had a satisfactory, problem-free, productive, high quality operation.

The Six Conditions for Success

The first condition is an unshakeable, totally sincere commitment by the organization to improve quality. It accepts the fact that current methods of managing have not been working well enough, are not good enough to keep the organization competitive, and must be improved. The organization states that it will seek better ways of operating and that it will change from its present methods as valid new ways are discovered. It avers that this commitment is intended for all future time and is not just a temporary expedient to be relaxed as soon as things get a little better. The organization commits to spend the necessary time, effort and money to bring about improvement throughout its structure. Above all, the organization pledges that in all decisions to be made from this time forward, *quality* is to be the first criterion. Quality is the most important concern of management; it will not be compromised. If the organization is willing to make this fundamental commitment to quality, it can transform itself. If it does not really mean to change its quality standards, nothing much will happen.

The second condition is that the organization provides new problem solving skills to everyone, from top to bottom. A commitment to improve quality, without the means to actually bring improvement about, is of little value to anyone. Quality improvement and the increase of productivity requires action, and action implies that something different will be done from what has been done in the past. If people are to solve problems, they must have the skills to do so. The organization has the obligation to provide these, appropriate to the tasks people must deal with at their individual levels, so they can begin to handle problems differently. These new techniques must be taught by qualified teachers, and practice in their use must also be provided. Finally, the people receiving new problem solving skills must understand that they have the authority and responsibility to use them, that they are now expected to resolve operational problems when they encounter them.

The third condition is that the organization provides opportunity for problems to be solved. Use of new problem solving techniques is not left up to chance; time and place for their application is scheduled and arranged by the organization. And use is not individual but group in nature. An organization is a collection of people brought together to deal with issues that individuals cannot deal with alone. It makes no sense for a new organizational skill to be deprived of opportunity for use in an organizational, group setting. Coaching and guidance in applying the new techniques to company problems must also be provided by the organization if it is to get the most out of its investment. Finally, expectation that the new skills are to be used must be made clear to everyone.

The fourth condition is that the organization provides leadership in the use of problem solving techniques. The supervisor or manager works with his or her people, using the techniques together against common organizational problems. The leader provides the necessary support for people using the new problem solving methods, counsels, coaches and teaches them how to use these more effectively for the good of the organization. The leader also listens to those who are solving company problems learning what they are finding out, becoming aware of what can be done to make their efforts even more rewarding. Above all, the leader uses these people as an extension of his or her managing capability. If others can now deal with problems in the same manner as the manager, they can act on behalf of the manager and extend that person's effectiveness substantially.

Providing organizational reward for successful problem solving is the fifth condition. The most important reward is an audience to seriously consider solutions and recommendations that have been developed. This provides important recognition and assures that there will be some follow-through, that something will be done with the suggestion made. Those recommendations which make sense are implemented by the organization, a substantial reward in itself. The organization also records the progress made in solving operational problems, the effects of peoples' efforts, and the money saved. It is only by gathering such information that the organization and its people can know the value of their contributions.

The last condition is that the organization assures the long-term continuation of its program of quality and productivity improvement. This requires that there be continuing leadership and support, that the gains made so far will not be lost through inattention in the future. It also underlines the need for supplying additional problem solving techniques as these are needed. The organization also provides new assignments, challenges and stimulation to keep quality always in the forefront of everyone's consciousness.

All six conditions are necessary if there is to be a real transformation of an organization: commitment to quality, problem solving techniques to achieve it, opportunity to use them, leadership, reward, and continuation of the effort through time. Given these, an organization can turn around surprisingly quickly, increasing its productivity and improving quality. This turnaround can move rapidly because a majority of the people in any organization have a desperate need to be involved. Recent studies have shown that most people, at all levels of management, feel strongly that there should be more participation than there currently is in the important activities of the company. They know that they can make a contribution to its improvement because they are aware of the operational problems that stand in the way of higher quality. They know that they can help solve these problems, if only they have the opportunity. When they are given a chance to take part, they respond positively and productively.

How the Japanese Did It

The six conditions described above constitute the basis for Japanese success. After World War II, the Japanese realized that they needed to improve the quality of their products if they were to compete, so they invited some consultants from the United States to tell them how. In 1950, Dr. J. Edward Deming gave a series of addresses to top management on the subject of Quality Control. These were extremely well received, and Japanese executives became convinced that quality improvement must be given top national priority. This accomplished the first condition of full management commitment.

In 1954 Dr. J.M. Juran, another consultant from the United States, introduced practical quality control techniques at the plant level. These were the problem solving skills needed to carry out the quality commitment made earlier.

Over the next six years, these and other techniques pervaded Japanese industry. First managers, then section leaders, then working foremen began to use these techniques on the job with their people. Problems were solved and productivity began to increase. Thus the second, third, and fourth conditions were realized; problem solving techniques were introduced, opportunity for their practice was provided, and leadership was given in their use.

By 1962 working foremen had invented Quality Circles, voluntary task groups dedicated to solving operational problems at the plant floor level, within the foreman's and workers' own job environment. Recommendations from these circles were made to top management in formal presentations, recognition was given for successful efforts at problem solving in company and national competition, and a reward structure was instituted compatible with the Japanese culture. This satisfied the fifth condition.

The sixth condition was provided by virtue of the growth and continuation of the quality movement within Japan. As success in the world marketplace came to Japanese products and organizations, the entire quality movement was reinforced and encouraged. It has now become the organizational way of life within Japan and will probably go on forever. Thus all the conditions necessary for productivity and quality improvement were spontaneously developed as a product of history in Japan, supported and nurtured by the Japanese culture.

How We Must Do It

Here in the United States we have not been so fortunate. Recent history has not handed us to the conditions of high productivity on a silver tray. Over the past 30 years, we have internalized a great number of management practices and beliefs that now have to be corrected, for they have proven counterproductive in the markets of the world. We must reorient our way of doing business so that more of our people can share the responsibility for quality improvement and the satisfactions that come from seeing a job well done. We must recover the values we have lost or mislaid. This is not as hard to do as it might seem, for most of our people recall those better values of concern for quality and want to return to them. Few of our people like being second best or doing a second-rate job. As many of our clients have demonstrated, marked quality and productivity improvement can take place in a matter of one or two years.

The key is to get more people in the organization actively involved in solving the operational problems that stand as barriers to productivity. This is accomplished by providing them with problem solving skills in a setting that supports and encourages them to use those skills on the job. As they solve operational problems, quality improves and productivity increases.

The first step in implementing a program of improvement like this is to gain the full commitment of top management that the necessary changes will in fact be made. Objectives for the program must be spelled out in detail: what is to be accomplished, in what degree or amount, and how it is to be measured. These objectives become the criteria around which the program is designed.

Next, a working plan is drawn up. This specifies the population to receive new problem solving skills, what particular skills will be appropriate for whom, the timing and sequence in which these will be delivered, and how the people can be expected to use them on the job. A steering committee is drawn up, composed of those line managers who will most directly benefit from quality improvement, to direct the program from start to finish. A full-time coordinator is appointed, to act as the supervisory link between the steering committee and those who will actually carry the program out. All of these people, working together, are needed to bring about the changes that will improve quality and productivity.

Other line managers are selected to teach problem solving skills within the organization. These should be the best people obtainable, who know the organization inside out, who know its problems, and who have line responsibility for its products. Teaching is a temporary assignment, for no more than six months, and is understood as a step in career development for the managers involved. For the time that these people are in this role, they function as problem solving experts for the organization, adding immensely to their personal skills and value as managers.

Teaching consists of both classroom work and on-the-job application. Problem solving techniques are presented, discussed and given practice on relevant cases, then are immediately taken out to the shop floor and put to work dealing with real problems. The most valuable part of the teaching is the guidance the instructor gives to participants as they grapple with actual barriers to productivity. The instructor acts as a problem solving task force leader and the participants are correcting faults they have seen ignored and passed over, sometimes for years. By the end of the training period, participants *know* they can make their new problem solving techniques work on the job, *know* that the organization supports them in solving problems, and *know* that quality can be improved. By the end of the training period, a dozen or so problems have been solved, and the savings have paid for the program several times over.

The steering committee is kept aware of progress by the coordinator, almost on a daily basis. Results are documented as they are achieved through application of the techniques. Company auditors compute costs and savings for management so that informed decisions can be made as to the further direction of the program. Recommendations are reviewed, good suggestions are implemented, and rewards and recognition are given out as warranted.

Continuation of the program is assured by the efforts of top management. Quality and productivity improvement is a moneymaking proposition, and as savings become evident, management has abundant motivation to keep the process going. It need never stop. High quality becomes a way of life, a way of thinking.

It Works

Does it work? Most emphatically *yes*. Dayton Power and Light, a large utility in the Midwest, started their program of quality and productivity improvement five years ago. Now their generators operate 82 percent of the time, compared to an industry average of 72 percent, because of problems solved and downtime prevented. The value of this has been stated by management to be $15 million per year. More than half of their people have been given problem solving skills and are using them every day. Big problems and little are solved as they arise, where they occur. And productivity increases every year.

In the late 1970s the United States Air Force introduced a problem solving program at Tinker Air Force Base, at Oklahoma City. Within two years a complex index of productivity, measuring turnaround time on aircraft serviced at the base and a number of other technical events, had increased by 26 percent. Morale had improved, the base was cleaner, people had more pride in the work they were doing, and decisions tended to be made further down in the organization.

"The Kepner-Tregoe problem solving program has given us a solid tool to allow our plant people to make significant safety improvements, contributing directly to productivity," is the way one works manager put it. "This program has helped us crack problems we had accepted as unsolvable," said another. A sugar mill reduced downtime by 45 percent in the first year of such a program, while a paper mill saved $912,000 in its first year. The examples go on and on.

This approach cannot help but work. If more people are solving operational problems for their organization, there cannot help but be fewer barriers to full productivity. If the quality of product or service is higher, there cannot help but be less effort required to rework or redo what should have been done right the first time. If the product or service is better, it cannot help but be more attractive on the competitive market. If people know they are doing a good job, they cannot help but feel more pride and loyalty toward their organization and their workmates. When people work together, they cannot help but produce more and get more out of doing it.

The Japanese have no monopoly on quality and productivity. Working together is an American tradition. Some of our organizations have never lost the art and can give foreign competition a run for their money. Others have let cooperation and participation fall into relative neglect, tending to think that only a few people are equipped to solve problems, and underusing their most valuable resource as a consequence. When they take conscious steps to correct their oversight, rapid improvement follows.

There is no question but that many factors influence productivity. All must receive some attention in order to achieve maximum improvement. But increasing the number of people within an organization who can and will solve operational problems is the easiest, cheapest, and most readily accessible point at which to start. Any organization that wants to can begin tomorrow.